W9-CLG-143

QUALITATIVE RESEARCH METHODS

About the website

This text has a comprehensive companion website which features resources for instructors and students alike.

Instructors

- Powerpoint slides to accompany each chapter
- Sample syllabi for both undergraduate and graduate courses
- A testbank, containing problems for each chapter, including answers
- Lesson plan outlines for each chapter
- 23 additional activities created by guest contributors

Students

- Master list of key terms and definitions
- Worksheets for each chapter
- Exam guides, containing key terms and concepts for each chapter
- List of helpful websites, videos, movies, and blogs

Please visit www.wiley.com/go/tracy to access these materials.

SARAH J. TRACY

QUALITATIVE RESEARCH METHODS

COLLECTING EVIDENCE, CRAFTING ANALYSIS, COMMUNICATING IMPACT

WILEY-BLACKWELL

A John Wiley & Sons, Ltd., Publication

This edition first published 2013
© 2013 Sarah J. Tracy

Blackwell Publishing was acquired by John Wiley & Sons in February 2007.
Blackwell's publishing program has been merged with Wiley's global Scientific,
Technical, and Medical business to form Wiley-Blackwell.

Registered Office
John Wiley & Sons, Ltd, The Atrium, Southern Gate, Chichester, West Sussex,
PO19 8SQ, UK

Editorial Offices
350 Main Street, Malden, MA 02148-5020, USA
9600 Garsington Road, Oxford, OX4 2DQ, UK
The Atrium, Southern Gate, Chichester, West Sussex, PO19 8SQ, UK

For details of our global editorial offices, for customer services, and for information
about how to apply for permission to reuse the copyright material in this book please
see our website at www.wiley.com/wiley-blackwell.

The right of Sarah J. Tracy to be identified as the author of this work has been
asserted in accordance with the UK Copyright, Designs and Patents Act 1988.

All rights reserved. No part of this publication may be reproduced, stored in
a retrieval system, or transmitted, in any form or by any means, electronic,
mechanical, photocopying, recording or otherwise, except as permitted by the UK
Copyright, Designs and Patents Act 1988, without the prior permission of the
publisher.

Wiley also publishes its books in a variety of electronic formats. Some content that
appears in print may not be available in electronic books.

Designations used by companies to distinguish their products are often claimed as
trademarks. All brand names and product names used in this book are trade names,
service marks, trademarks or registered trademarks of their respective owners. The
publisher is not associated with any product or vendor mentioned in this book. This
publication is designed to provide accurate and authoritative information in regard
to the subject matter covered. It is sold on the understanding that the publisher is not
engaged in rendering professional services. If professional advice or other expert
assistance is required, the services of a competent professional should be sought.

Library of Congress Cataloging-in-Publication data is available for this book.

978-1-4051-9203-3 (hardback)
978-1-4051-9202-6 (paperback)

A catalogue record for this book is available from the British Library.

Cover image © Stockbyte / Getty Images
Cover design by Simon Levy

Set in 10/12pt Minion by SPi Publisher Services, Pondicherry, India
Printed in Malaysia by Ho Printing (M) Sdn Bhd

2   2013

I dedicate this book to all my past students, research participants, mentors, and colleagues who have taught me that anything worth doing well is worth doing badly in the beginning.

Contents

Detailed Contents

Preface
Is this book for me?

As I've developed this book on qualitative methodology, I've consistently kept in mind Bud Goodall's (2000) suggestion in *Writing the New Ethnography* that good writing engages the reader as a participative audience. A good read is dialogic and creates space for a conversation. The reader of this book will ultimately be its judge. But, before we begin, I want to share several ways this book and my experience may be of value in your own qualitative journey.

This book takes a "praxis"-centered approach. Stanley Deetz, my advisor at the University of Colorado-Boulder, first turned me on to the idea of problem-centered analyses as a method for doing research that matters (consider Deetz, 2009). Since then, I have written about problem-focused research, and colleagues at Arizona State University have further motivated me to value public scholarship that can improve or transform life for everyday people. Similarly, and as informed by the recent move toward positive scholarship, another poignant starting place comes through examining how positive issues like passion, energy, compassion, or resilience may be constructed and maintained.

This approach has laid the groundwork for my researching a variety of contexts and writing in a range of styles. My home field of speech communication, like many disciplines, is marked by paradigmatic arguments about whether the best and most valid research comes from counting or narrating. Even those who live squarely in the qualitative camp find other issues to debate – definitions of terminology, whether telling stories about ourselves is a valid way to do research, how we should best write or perform our research, and so on.

Some students may not know or care to know about these controversies. However, others view their choice of research method as a decision laden with political ramifications. The book covers paradigmatic debates. However, in what may be of greater interest and value, my advice comes from the standpoint of someone who has practiced a variety of approaches. I will spend more time focusing on what methods will impact the issue at hand than discussing whether one methodological brand is inherently better than another. Indeed, I think researchers can successfully practice a variety of approaches to qualitative methods. My research includes journal articles in traditional deductive form, but also creative nonfictions and performance scripts for the stage. I have fruitfully worked with colleagues who specialize in autoethnographic performance texts as well as with those who use qualitative methods as a complement to their grant-funded quantitative research.

Good qualitative scholarship is rigorous, interesting, practical, aesthetic, and ethical. Of course, sometimes not all the aims can be equally achieved in the same piece. The aspects of research that should be most highlighted may largely depend on the audience – whether that is a group of scholars, of employees, or of artists. Here I provide a big-tent approach to evaluating qualitative quality, one that can help students strive for high-quality qualitative methods despite their paradigmatic approach. Further, I provide a detailed step-by-step explanation of qualitative data gathering, writing, and analysis.

Indeed, another aim of the book is to fill a gap in terms of data analysis. This book provides a step-by-step explanation of analysis in commonsense terms, understandable both to newcomers and to those well versed in the practice. My focus on data analysis has developed through discussions I have had with a variety of qualitative methods experts over the years – people including Bud Goodall, Robin Clair, Amira DeLaGarza, Carolyn Ellis, Larry Frey, Patricia Geist Martin, Bob Krizek, Bryan Taylor, and Nick Trujillo. We have discussed a number of joys and challenges associated with teaching qualitative research in the communication discipline. We have also agreed that our students have a wealth of available pedagogical resources on how best to *design* qualitative research, *gather* qualitative data through interviews, focus groups, and fieldnotes, and *write up* the research report. However, as a community, qualitative researchers could better communicate and teach the qualitative data *analysis* process. Indeed students often complain that they need more instruction on what happens *in between* the time they collect the data and the time they write it into a polished research report. In other words, little explicit instruction exists that clearly delineates a variety of systematic data analysis practices.

The book is designed to be accessible to advanced undergraduate students, yet provide enough methodological detail to be helpful to graduate students and advanced scholars. I try to convey methodological information in an easy to understand and engaging manner. People are more attracted to reading something that has a plot line, and they best retain information in the form of narratives. Hence, in the course of discussing the building blocks of qualitative research methods, I share my own joys and frustrations. By sharing these stories – marked as they are by twists and turns, celebrations and disappointments – I aim to make the research process poignant, interesting, real, and occasionally humorous.

This book is appropriate for a variety of disciplines and classes. My examples rely heavily on interdisciplinary communication scholarship, but the qualitative methods described here also apply to students and scholars in numerous other fields, such as management, sociology, psychology, education, social work, justice studies, and ethnic and gender studies. The book is appropriate for college courses that appear under course names such as research methods, qualitative research methods, ethnography, ethnographic methods, critical research methods, interpretive research, grounded approaches to research, naturalistic inquiry, autoethnography, performance studies, narrative research methods, and field methods. And, although this book is designed primarily for an academic audience, practitioners wishing to engage in qualitative research to solve organizational and societal dilemmas may also find good advice within these pages.

I should note that, although this book presents unique aspects, its format is similar to that of some of the most popular qualitative books on the market. Therefore it should be fairly easy to adopt and transition into. The book is an all-inclusive treatment that leads readers through a qualitative research project from beginning to end. It can be adapted both to one-semester/quarter and to two-semester/quarter classes. Furthermore, although the book includes a story of myself as researcher (and therefore it differs from a "manual"), it need not be read from cover to cover in order to be useful. A summary of the chapters is as follows:

- Chapter 1 introduces qualitative methods, discussing the importance of self-reflexivity and context, introducing the notion of phronetic research, and providing tips for choosing a topic and devising research.
- Chapter 2 overviews qualitative terminology, discusses how qualitative research focuses on action and structure, examines significant historical issues, and concludes with current controversies that situate qualitative methods today.
- Chapter 3 discusses four primary research paradigms and how qualitative research is situated in each – in a way that makes theoretically dense material easy to understand even for those who are new to research methods. The chapter also reviews seven theoretical approaches that commonly use qualitative data and methodology, namely Geertz's interpretivism, symbolic interactionism, ethnography of communication, sensemaking, participatory action research, feminism, and structuration theory.
- Chapter 4 introduces the concept of field "play" and examines methods for navigating access in order to conduct qualitative research. These include tactics like keeping a contact log, creating

an access proposal, organizing a participant table, or considering early investigative methods.

- Chapter 5 provides an explanation of human subjects review, tips for navigating institutional review boards, and a step-by-step guide to writing a research proposal.
- Chapter 6 gives insight on different participant–observer roles, on how to write fieldnotes, on methods for focusing on data collection, and on how to manage various ethical dilemmas in the field.
- Chapter 7 offers the nuts and bolts of planning and designing good interviews, including how to choose the best samples and how to write, structure, and order interview questions and dialogue.
- Chapter 8 focuses on conducting an actual interview or focus group session. It discusses recruitment, developing rapport, ethical engagement, logistics, transcription, and considering advantages and disadvantages of various interview formats – face-to-face, mediated, one-on-one, or group.
- Chapters 9 and 10 detail how researchers can best analyze their interviews, fieldnotes and documents. I provide step-by-step best practices for transforming a heap of data into meaning endowed with theoretical and practical significance. In doing so, I reference tried-and-true grounded analysis methods, but I also introduce new approaches such as discourse tracing. Furthermore, I cover the role of computer-aided data analysis software. Along the way, I present vignettes and methodology text examples from my own and others' projects to illustrate.
- Chapter 11 offers an overview of qualitative quality – something that is often missing or implicit in other methodology books. In doing so, it reviews traditional measures of research quality and then lays out a multi-paradigmatic approach for ensuring that qualitative research is rigorous, ethical, and credible.
- Chapters 12 and 13 provide detailed information on how to write the qualitative research report. There I talk about various types of qualitative tales, about writing nuts and bolts, about overcoming common errors, and about how to write a lot!
- Chapter 14 comes full circle, overviewing logistical issues for leaving the scene and showing how researchers can frame and deliver their qualitative work so that it impacts the world.

Along the way, I include recurring text boxes. These highlight activities and assignments labeled "Exercise," examples and narratives stored under "Consider this," practical "Tips and tools," and data excerpts or experiences called "Researcher's notepad." Some of these boxes are written in the words of other scholars and students – words in which they talk about their particular experiences. The text boxes provide a break and encourage reader engagement and activity along the way.

Furthermore, I intermittently include sections called "Following, Forgetting, and Improvising." Practicing any interpretive art requires learning the "rules" first, and only then playing with them and improvising. I suggest ways in which researchers might fruitfully improvise with qualitative best practices, or in some cases forget them altogether. Like in all dialectics, the paradox of "following, then forgetting" qualitative best practices is not something that can be solved or resolved. But, by discussing the tension, we can manage it rather than being trapped by it. There's no easy way out; but there are better ways of navigating than others. I hope this book can serve as a guide.

Finally, an accompanying website with teaching manual materials is available with the book. Materials include:

- sample syllabi for both undergraduate and graduate classes;
- lesson plan outlines of each chapter;
- a list of helpful website links, such as videos, blogs, tutorials, and methodology programs;
- test bank and exam review materials;
- auxiliary exercises and worksheets, some by guest contributors;
- power point slide masters.

These materials will help those who are new to teaching qualitative research methods: they'll be up and running in no time. For experienced instructors, they may serve as a supplement and launching pad for new pedagogical options.

Acknowledgments

Let me close by offering some acknowledgments. I am blessed to have worked with a host of good mentors and colleagues. You'll see me repeat some of their advice verbatim; and, where I do not, remnants and iterations of their wisdom are indelibly stamped upon the guidance offered here. I am indebted to Bryan Taylor, my ethnography instructor at University of Colorado-Boulder and co-author of *Qualitative Communication Research Methods* – his coauthored book on qualitative methods, now in its third edition (Lindlof & Taylor, 2011). Hopefully, the book in your hand can serve as a complement and extension to the pearls of wisdom I first read years ago and have since used in my teaching so many times.

I also am thankful to other mentors at University of Colorado-Boulder. Stanley Deetz offered me invaluable insight on examining the larger structures that liberate and constrain everyday practices and talk. Karen Tracy trained me in close discourse analysis and helped me forge an entrée to my first field project with 911 call-takers. Margaret Eisenhart, in the School of Education, provided a cross-disciplinary examination of ethnography and introduced me to the multiple ways in which cultures can be envisaged, approached, and studied. Bob Craig introduced me to grounded practical theory, and this informs my phronetic problem-based approach to qualitative methodology (Tracy, 2002a). Furthermore, Brenda Allen, George Cheney, Sally Planalp, and Phil Tompkins have served as wonderful friends and life-long mentors.

Colleagues in the Hugh Downs School of Human Communication and throughout Arizona State University have also contributed to the development of this book. Jennifer Scarduzio and Elizabeth Eger have been instrumental in editing, developing teacher manual materials, creating the glossary of terms, and reference checking. Additionally, Shawna Malvini Redden, Kendra Rivera, Lisi Willner, Scott Parr, Desiree Rowe, Karen Stewart, Timothy Huffman, Deborah Way, Amy Pearson, Ragan Fox, Kurt Lindemann, Miriam Sobre-Denton, Amy Way, and Emily Cripe – among many former COM 609 students – have provided excellent input.

I feel thankful to Patricia Geist-Martin and her students, who "test ran" the book. Bud Goodall provided extensive internal reviews, Kory Floyd book-writing advice, Larry Frey an invaluable qualitative reference list, and Angela Trethewey buoyed the project. Furthermore, local colleagues Amira De La Garza, Johnny Saldaña, and Michael Shafer have provided support along the way.

Additionally, I feel indebted to Wiley-Blackwell acquisitions editor Elizabeth Swayze. Over coffee at multiple scholarly conventions, and numerous emails, Elizabeth persuaded me that this would be a good project. Along the way, she and her Wiley-Blackwell team – and especially Amanda Banner, Ginny Graham, Simon Eckley, Julia Kirk, and Deirdre Ilkson – have provided support, patience, and promotion. I am also so appreciative of Kitty Bocking at Pixlink who found the perfect photos and Manuela Tecusan (and Hazel Harris, the project manager) for providing such timely, supportive, and expert copy-editing of the project. This book is a team effort and I am eternally grateful for your help with it.

Finally, I feel appreciative of my friends, colleagues, and family who provided encouragement, advice, and feedback. A special thanks to my family – Boyd, Malinda, Judi, Merl, Van, Julia, Zander and Lydia. My "mastermind sisters" Isa and Amy listened and helped me make sense of my misgivings and triumphs. Other friends – Belle, Dan, Alec, Catherine, Karen, Lori, Jess, and my entire Facebook family – encouraged me throughout the long journey. Most especially, thank you to Brad for being my patient cheerleader, for believing in me, and for providing much laughter, even as I spent way too many weekends writing in the casita. All of these people made the whole book-writing process not nearly as lonely as it would have been otherwise – which is important for a qualitative researcher who likes to spend time in the field playing with others, and not just behind the computer. May their joy and hope infuse these pages and motivate others as much as they motivated me.

CHAPTER 1

Developing contextual research that matters

Contents

Qualitative Research Methods: Collecting Evidence, Crafting Analysis, Communicating Impact, First Edition. Sarah J. Tracy.
© 2013 Sarah J. Tracy. Published 2013 by Blackwell Publishing Ltd.

What is the first thing that comes to mind when you hear the words, "research methods?"

Many people never think explicitly about this question, and if they do, they think that research methods are difficult to learn and painstaking to conduct. However, you might be surprised to discover that you engage in research every day – and these methods not only provide important resources for understanding the world, but are actually a common and enjoyable way to spend our time.

We ask questions, listen to stories, watch others, participate in meetings, check our text messages, gossip, and engage in dialogue. In doing so, we gather qualitative data about social phenomena. Through talking to others we learn about their quirks, interests, pet peeves, and sense of humor. We learn about their culture. We think about these experiences, make patterns of meanings, and absorb the scene.

Simultaneously, share our own understandings in conversations, blog entries, and emails. In telling these stories we call out the most important players and evaluate their behavior. We do this to pass the time, interact, and have fun. But we also do it to understand the world and our place within it. We make sense through our talk, and our meaning making helps us know what to expect at future events. So, at a basic level, we all engage in research everyday. The focused study of research methods takes these everyday actions one step further: to a systematic analysis that may lead to better understandings – not only for us, but for others.

Overview and introduction

This book guides readers step by step through the qualitative methods process – research design, data collection, analysis, and creating a representation that can be shared with others, be that a class paper, a publication, a performance, a service portfolio, a website entry, or a letter to the editor. I will impart aspects of qualitative research I have found most methodologically sound, helpful, beautiful, fun, and interesting. I will also pause to discuss concepts that I have not practiced myself, but that are common in the field. This book offers guidance no matter whether you are a graduate student learning the basics of qualitative methods, an undergraduate completing a service project, a critical performance artist wishing to interrogate power relations, a rhetorician interested in complementing textual analysis, or a quantitative researcher hoping to augment statistical findings through qualitative insights.

Chapter 1 opens by introducing three central concepts that can jumpstart a qualitative project: self-reflexivity, context, and thick description. Next, I overview the unique, praxis-based, contextual approach of the book and how qualitative research is well poised for researching a number of disciplinary areas. Finally, I discuss the first steps in conducting a research project, including choosing a context and developing research questions.

Three core qualitative concepts: self-reflexivity, context, and thick description

Self-reflexivity

Self-reflexivity refers to the careful consideration of the ways in which researchers' past experiences, points of view, and roles impact these same researchers' interactions with, and interpretations of, the research scene. Let's examine this definition in more detail.

Every researcher has a point a view, an opinion, or a way of seeing the world. Some people call this "baggage"; others call it wisdom. Rather than deny our way of seeing and being in the world, qualitative researchers acknowledge, and even celebrate it. A person's demographic information provides the basic ingredients of a researcher's perspective. For example, I am female, white, heterosexual, forty-something, partnered, and an aunt. My work roles have included professor, public relations coordinator, and cruise ship activities director. I raced an "Ironman" triathlon, and I drive a Mini Cooper Clubman. I believe that success rewards virtuous action and that good research provides opportunities for transformation.

This background shapes my approach toward various topics and research in general. Likewise, your own background, values, and beliefs fundamentally shape the way you approach and conduct research. The mind and body of a qualitative researcher literally serve as research instruments – absorbing, sifting through, and interpreting the world through observation, participation, and interviewing. These are the analytical resources of our own "subjectivity." Of course, our bodies and minds also live in a context.

Context

Qualitative research is about immersing oneself in a scene and trying to make sense of it – whether at a company meeting, in a community festival, or during an interview. Qualitative researchers purposefully examine and make note of small cues in order to decide how to behave, as well as to make sense of the context and build larger knowledge claims about the culture.

Clifford Geertz, sometimes referred to as the father of interpretive anthropology, focused specifically on context, preferring to examine the field's rich specificity. As Geertz (1973) famously put it: "Man is an animal suspended in webs of significance he himself has spun, I take culture to be those webs, and the analysis of it to be therefore not an experimental science in search of law but an interpretive one in search of meaning" (p. 5). Ethnographers construct meaning through immersion in a context comparable to that of scientific research – say, an experimental laboratory study – that isolates variables and controls circumstances, so that findings can be replicated.

Indeed qualitative researchers believe that the empirical and theoretical resources needed to comprehend a particular idea, or to predict its future trajectory, are themselves interwoven with, and throughout, the context. Social theories are based in the ever-changing, biased, and contextualized social conditions of their production. So, for example, we can read detailed analyses of inner-city poverty and glean emergent theories of social justice from these rich evocations.

Thick description

Directly related to context is the idea of **thick description**, according to which researchers immerse themselves in a culture, investigate the particular circumstances present in that scene, and only then move toward grander statements and theories. Meaning cannot be divorced from this thick contextual description. For instance, without a context, a person's winking could mean any number of things, including that the person is flirting, is trying to communicate secretly, has an uncontrollable facial twitch, or is imitating someone else's twitch (Geertz, 1973). The meaning of the wink comes precisely from the complex specificity and the circumstances that inform interpretations of intention; "The aim is to draw large conclusions from small, but very densely textured facts; to support broad assertions about the role of culture in the construction of collective life by engaging them exactly with complex specifics" (p. 28).

By describing the background and context of action, researchers can decipher a twitch and tell it apart from a wink and from a parody of a wink – and they may interpret the meaning(s) of all these gestures and help predict whether we are likely to see the behavior again. This process of interpretation is dependent upon the scene's particulars. This being the case, context provides a central role for qualitative research, while *a priori* theory takes a back seat. Given the focus on context, the driving force of much qualitative research is practical in nature.

A phronetic approach: doing qualitative research that matters

I take a praxis-based or "phronetic" approach to research (Tracy, 2007). This approach suggests that qualitative data can be systematically gathered, organized, interpreted, analyzed, and communicated so as to address real world concerns. I suggest that researchers begin their research process by identifying a particular issue, problem, or dilemma in the world and then proceed to systematically interpret the data in order to provide an analysis that sheds light on the issue and/or opens a path for possible social transformation. Doing "use-inspired" (Stokes, 1997) contextual research is especially well suited for service learning, socially embedded research, public intellectualism, funded projects, and community partnerships.

What is **phronetic research?** The ancient Greek noun *phronēsis* is generally translated as 'prudence' or 'practical wisdom' (Aristotle, 2004). *Phronēsis* is concerned with contextual knowledge that is interactively constructed, action oriented and imbued with certain values (Cairns & Śliwa, 2008). Research conducted under its guidance serves "to clarify and deliberate about the problems and risks we face and to outline how things may be done differently, in full knowledge that we cannot find ultimate answers to these questions or even a single version of what the questions are" (Flyvbjerg, 2001, p. 140). This approach assumes that perception comes from a specific (self-reflexive) subject position and that the social and historical roots of an issue precede individual motivations and actions. It also assumes that communication produces identity for the researchers as well as for those researched, and that it generates knowledge that benefits some more than others. Qualitative methods are especially suited for examining phronetic questions about morality and values. Social action is always changing; therefore contextual explanations and situated meanings are integral to ongoing sensemaking.

Strengths of qualitative research

Through a phronetic approach that focuses on self-reflexivity, context, and thick description, qualitative research has a number of advantages as a research method. First, many researchers – especially young scholars who do not have the luxury of comfy offices or high-tech laboratories – are all too happy to escape their shared apartments and cramped graduate school offices and venture into the field. This may be why so many excellent ethnographies are conducted by people under the age of 30. As Goffman (1989) said about naturalistic field research: "You're going to be an ass… And that's one reason why you have to be young to do fieldwork. It's harder to be an ass when you are old" (p. 128).

Second, qualitative research is excellent for studying contexts you are personally curious about but have never before had a "valid" reason for entering. Third, in addition to personal interest or disciplined voyeurism, qualitative data provide insight into cultural activities that might otherwise be missed in structured surveys or experiments.

Fourth, qualitative research can uncover salient issues that can later be studied using more structured methods. Indeed field research may lead to close and trusting relationships that encourage a level of disclosure unparalleled in self-reports or snapshot examinations of a scene. Such work has the potential to provide insight about marginalized, stereotyped, or unknown populations – a peek into regularly guarded worlds, and an opportunity to tell a story that few know about. Such was the case with Lindemann's (2007) work with homeless street vendors who sell newspapers in San Francisco to survive.

Fifth, qualitative research is especially well suited for accessing tacit, taken-for-granted, intuitive understandings of a culture. Rather than merely *asking about* what people *say* they do, researching in context provides an opportunity to see and hear what people *actually* do. Rather than relying on participants' espoused values, we come to understand participants' values-in-use (Schein, 2004) and how they live out these values on a daily basis. The more researchers become immersed in the scene, the more they can make **second-order interpretations** – meaning that researchers construct explanations for the participants' explanations.

Sixth, and perhaps most importantly, good qualitative research helps people to understand the world, their society, and its institutions. Qualitative methodology can provide knowledge that targets societal issues, questions, or problems and therefore serves humankind. In summary, qualitative research:

- is rich and holistic;
- offers more than a snapshot – provides understanding of a sustained process;
- focuses on lived experience, placed in its context;
- honors participants' local meanings;
- can help explain, illuminate, or reinterpret quantitative data;
- interprets participant viewpoints and stories;
- preserves the chronological flow, documenting what events lead to what consequences, and explaining *why* this chronology may have occurred;
- celebrates how research representations (reports, articles, performances) constitute reality and affect the questions we can ask and what we can know;
- illustrates how a multitude of interpretations are possible, but how some are more theoretically compelling, morally significant, or practically important than others.

In short, qualitative methods are appropriate and helpful for achieving a variety of research goals – either on their own or in a complementary relationship with other research methods.

Foci of qualitative research

Qualitative research can be found in a range of disciplines and topic areas. The annual Congress for Qualitative Inquiry held at the University of Illinois regularly boasts representation from over 40 disciplines and 55 nations. This involvement serves as a testament to the global reach and cross-disciplinary popularity of qualitative methods.

Understanding the self

Critical self-examination offers one important context for qualitative research. **Autoethnography** is an autobiographical genre of writing that connects the analysis of one's own identity, culture, feelings, and values to larger societal issues. Jago (2002), for instance, undertakes a powerful examination of mental illness and academic life in critically examining her own "academic depression." Goodall (2006) takes readers along on his own journey of understanding the secrets of his family life and of his father's cloaked career in the Central Intelligence Agency. Ellis (2008) chronicles personal life loss and trauma by constructing "narrative snapshots" and compiling them together, in a manner akin to that of a video or text in motion.

Qualitative researchers frequently consider their own personal stories or experiences as spaces for further exploration, examination, and representation. A particular joy, tragedy, or experience is especially fruitful for study if it is rare or understudied, if it connects up with larger social narratives, or if current research on the topic is lacking in personal standpoint. Focusing on the micro-events of one's own life can also provide important lessons about larger societal structures and problems. Through a vivid focus on power and justice, autoethnography can improve social conditions and unpack the personal implications of difficult issues – such as abortion (Minge, 2006) or eating disorders (Tillmann-Healy, 1996).

Understanding relationships

Qualitative research can also provide important insight into interpersonal relationships. Through interviews and participant observation, researchers examine romantic partnerships, friendships, customer-service encounters, superior–subordinate and doctor–patient relationships (Real, Bramson, & Poole, 2009), learning why people engage in such relationships, the way their interactions emerge and change, and how they evidence their feelings for each other. For example, Vande Berg and Trujillo (2008) bravely told their final love story in *Cancer and death: A love story in two voices*. Erbert and Alemán (2008) interviewed grandparents about the tensions of surrogate parenting. Qualitative studies can also illuminate the "dark side" of relationships, including conflict, emotional abuse, and deviance (Olson, Daggs, Ellevold, & Rogers, 2007).

Much qualitative research is itself relational, in that data are gathered by using one-to-one interactions between researcher and participants. For example, Ellis (2010) interviewed holocaust survivors and their children and in doing so explored what happens when the interviewer and the interviewee jointly construct the meaning of an historical event. Such methods provide an opportunity for learning "what it feels like" to be in one of these relationships.

Understanding groups and organizations

Families, work groups, sports teams, clubs, support circles, or volunteers are often the topics of qualitative research. For example, Adelman and Frey (1997) volunteered at the Bonaventure House facility for people living with AIDS and studied how communication practices mediate the tension between individual clients' needs and the groups' need for a community. Other qualitative research on groups covers topics such as the shared ideology espoused in Alcoholics Anonymous meetings (Right, 1997), the communication dialectics in a community theater troupe (Kramer, 2004) and coping processes in post-divorce families (Afifi, Hutchinson, & Krouse, 2006).

Organizational studies are replete with qualitative accounts of a wide variety of topics: gender, power, leadership, followership, socialization – and more. These come in the form of the famous Harvard Business School Case Studies – detailed narratives of business situations describing typical management dilemmas and no obvious right answers – as well as in a myriad of other examinations of organizational culture (Tracy & Geist-Martin, in press).

Some qualitative researchers become full participants in the organization – as employees, interns, or volunteers (Murphy, 1998). Other researchers gain enough access to attend meetings and generally to hang out (Ashcraft, 2001). Meanwhile, others conduct qualitative research that speaks to hot-button issues like sexual harassment – and they do it by interviewing stakeholders (Scarduzio & Geist-Martin, 2008) or by textually examining emails, training materials, or news articles (Lyon & Mirivel, 2011).

Contexts of organizational qualitative study may include profit-making organizations (Nike, Disneyland), governmental institutions (prisons, institutions in a military context), nonprofit organizations (Habitat for Humanity, the Red Cross), educational contexts, hospitals, or churches. Qualitative studies provide an insider's view on organizing – through examining meetings, power lunches, water-cooler chat, and after-hours parties.

Understanding cultures

Qualitative research is useful for understanding a range of societal issues that arise from particular cultural contexts (Drew, 2001; Covarrubias, 2002; LaFever, 2007). For example, in order to better understand tourist (mis)behavior, Schneider-Bean (2008) coupled the qualitative analysis of promotional material related to tourism with the on-site study of exotic vacation spots.

The qualitative analysis of today's stories and yesterday's historical documents is integral to understanding significant societal events such as social movements (Pompper, Lee, & Lerner, 2009). For instance, Haskins (2007) examined how people across the globe catalogued and wrote their own views of the 9/11 World Trade Center attacks, and by the same move uncovered how cultural members narrate their own history.

Furthermore, issues such as ethnicity, race, gender, and sexual orientation can be understood, critiqued, and transformed through contextual studies that examine how demographic categories are ever-changing and communicatively constituted (Trethewey, 2001). For instance, Lindemann and Cherney (2008) coupled a field study of quadriplegic rugby players with an analysis of the movie "Murderball," providing a fascinating examination of masculinity and disability.

Understanding mediated and virtual contexts

Finally, qualitative research is increasingly being used to study virtual and mediated contexts. Romantic relationships and the "hook-up" culture can be analyzed through websites such as Match.Com, E-Harmony, Facebook, and MySpace. Forums and chat-rooms open a window into marginalized cultures – such as those of drugs, or those of extreme thinness (Murguía, Tackett-Gibson, & Lessem, 2007). The best way to gather data from students and to learn about their communication tactics may be through text-messaging. Personalized blogs and podcasts can give insight into a number of contemporary issues, for instance teenager self-presentation (Bortree, 2005). Online data may also provide access to illegal, blasphemous, or stigmatized activities that may otherwise be unavailable.

In short, although qualitative analysis is linked to some disciplinary areas more than to others, it is a research method that is increasingly being used by a variety of researchers across topical areas. As reviewed above, qualitative research is salient for the understanding of personal, relational, group, organizational, cultural, and virtual contexts in a range of different ways.

Moving from ideas to sites, settings, and participants

Some researchers choose a particular research site that fascinates them without knowing what to expect. For instance, researchers interested in medicine may hang out in a hospital's waiting room, unsure of what exactly they will end up studying. Potential foci may include the flow of patients in the waiting room, or the frequency of buzzers, beeps, or announcements broadcast across the loudspeakers. This open-ended approach is particularly worthwhile for brand new researchers who are perfectly content studying "whatever happens." Other researchers begin by studying a specific phenomenon, defined in advance by some grant priority or by the desire to advance a particular line of research. In such cases, first they determine what they want to focus on, and only then do they find a scene.

A middle option is an **iterative approach** (Miles & Huberman, 1994), in which the researcher alternates between considering existing theories and research interests on the one hand, emergent qualitative data on the other (see Figure 1.1). In this scenario the researcher may first determine a general idea, then come up with several potential sites, and then gradually become more specific about the phenomena to be studied. For example, when my co-author Debbie Way studied a hospice, at first she was interested in burnout, then she learned that the theoretical lens of compassion suited the data more clearly (Way & Tracy, in press).

In determining a potential research site, it is important to remember that the phenomenon under study is not the same as the field of study. The **phenomenon** – or locus of study – is the issue or theme brought to bear by research questions (e.g. burnout, code switching behavior, socialization, terrorist activity, greeting behaviors). The **field** of study, in contrast, is the collection of spaces and places in which the phenomenon may be found and explored. So, for instance, a person interested in the phenomenon of "hazing" might be particularly attracted to studying groups that put new members through rigorous rites of passage. Potential fields of study could then include army boot camp, fraternity/sorority pledge periods, or the training of investment bankers.

Within the field there are **sites**, or specific geographical or architectural areas (e.g. a fraternity house), and within the site there are even more specific **settings**, which refer to

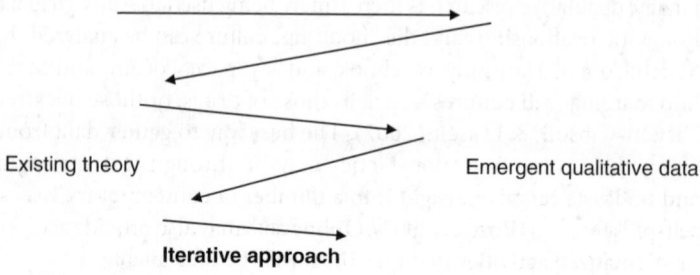

Figure 1.1 An iterative approach alternates between considering existing theories and research interests on the one hand, and emergent qualitative data on the other.

Existing theory   Emergent qualitative data

Iterative approach

EXERCISE 1.1

Field/site brainstorm

The table below provides an example of systematically comparing and contrasting potential field sites and their advantages and disadvantages. In this table it becomes clear that there is no one perfect site but, instead, each one holds specific advantages and disadvantages. Creating your own table can help you brainstorm several potential sites and consider advantages and disadvantages to each.

Table 1.1 The "field" for this brainstorm consists of all the spaces and places where employees regularly show a negative or controlling emotion toward their clients/customers as a paid part of their job, and where doing so repeatedly may challenge their emotional well-being.

Potential Site	Prison	Bar or Club	Bill Collection
Potential Participants	Correctional officers	Bouncers	Collection agents
Potential Settings	Inmate booking area, prison lobby, inmate cafeteria, inmate pods	Front door	Call room floor; shadowing collector on street
Advantages	Emotions running high for those just arrested; complex scene; long-term employee–client relationship; current research suggests high burnout; very little research exists	Easy, immediate access; researcher could be a full participant by getting a job or pretending to act like a patron	Multiply-focused and intense sessions; wide range of emotions; interaction with client may be audio recorded
Disadvantages	One needs official permission and security check to enter scene; participants wary of researcher; really busy; no clear place to sit and watch; research may be intrusive	Routine, short-term interaction with customers; research exists (e.g. Scheibel, 1992); complex interaction more sporadic	Somewhat scripted; research already exists (e.g. Sutton, 1991)

To do Determine a field of study – a context or group that revolves around a certain issue, dilemma, or topic of interest. If you're stuck, examples might include: (1) reunions/goodbye interactions; (2) rites of passage; (3) food purchasing and eating; or (4) sibling rivalry.

Then create your own table, where you fill in the potential site, participants, settings, advantages, and disadvantages.

the specific parameters of the space (e.g. the basement). Also, within each site there are different sets of **participants** – the focal people of the study (e.g. the alumni, the officers, the pledgers). A field consists of many potential sites, settings, and participants. However, some sites or participants will be more valuable than others for studying certain phenomena. I use the term **scene** to refer generally to the field, sites, settings, and groups of participants.

Sources of research ideas

Just as in learning to ride a bicycle or learning to paint a picture, the best way to learn qualitative research is by actually *practicing* it. Where should you begin? The first step is devising potential research ideas and considering the suitability of various contexts.

Some of the best ideas for qualitative research come from your personal life. Ask yourself: what has happened to me, or around me, that is particularly interesting or puzzling? Perhaps your life has been touched by certain religious practices, political beliefs, or health issues that encourage deeper reflection. Experiences such as travel, education, work, family, sports, or volunteering can also suggest venues for research. The best ethnographers read a lot about the world around them and live interesting, rich, and multi-faceted lives. They dip into these knowledge reservoirs for research inspiration.

Another good source for research ideas are societal problems or organizational dilemmas. For example, I first became interested in 911 emergency communications because of a number of highly publicized cases in which emergency help had not been dispatched in a timely manner. My colleague Karen Tracy and I entered the research with the goal to learn more about the behind-the-scenes interactions of citizen calls to the police and about how calls could go awry (S. J. Tracy & K. Tracy, 1998).

A third resource for research ideas is current events. Good ethnographers keep apprised of societal trends, policy debates, politics, and issues in which target populations are struggling or succeeding. They consistently read newspapers, magazines, websites, and blogs associated with their key interests.

A fourth resource for ideas are scholarly research texts. For example, "state of the discipline" research articles synthesize current theoretical concerns and provide suggestions for future work. These pieces offer guidance, a wealth of background literature, key theoretical advancements, and a ready-made study rationale. Good launching points for research inspiration can emerge from inconsistent findings, gaps in current theories, topics or concepts that have only been studied through certain methodologies, or the study of established theoretical concepts in new contexts. I encourage you to read widely from a variety of interdisciplinary sources in order to find ways to bridge and transform arguments in novel ways. What is "old news" to one group of scholars can be the hottest new way of approaching an issue in another discipline. The *lack* of research in a certain context or on a specific topic may also point to a promising area for study. However, scholars should be cautious about adopting a study simply because "no one's ever studied this before." Such a rationale invites counterargument. Furthermore, there may be a *very good reason* why something has not been studied in the past (maybe the topic or angle of research is not feasible, or not very significant).

Additional sources of ideas are the field contexts and the participants themselves. Participatory action research (Kemmis & McTaggart, 2005) is based on the notion that researchers should work together with research participants to help them address, make sense of, or improve upon local issues or dilemmas. In this way qualitative research is

CONSIDER THIS 1.1

Sources of research ideas

1   What are my ongoing interests and activities? What interests, confuses, or puzzles me?
2   What past personal or work experiences are appropriate for additional study?
3   What opportunities present themselves right now?
4   What organizational, societal, political, or community predicaments/dilemmas are ripe for investigation?
5   What are the hot topics being discussed in magazines, in blogs, and on websites associated with my research interests?
6   When I read about my favorite theories or scholarly topic areas, what are the inconsistencies? What is missing? What types of research are other scholars calling for?
7   How could a qualitative methodology provide new insight into an issue or concept that has historically been studied quantitatively?
8   What topics of research are primed to receive grant money from federal agencies or private foundations? What topics might I get paid to provide consulting on?

well positioned to address contextual priorities pinpointed by consulting, grant, and contract work (Cheek, 2005). At the same time, keep in mind that focusing on organizational research priorities – especially when the research is funded – increases the ethical and political complexities of the project. For instance, it is difficult to know what might happen if the organization suggests a certain research question, but in analyzing this question it turns out that low-power employees are required to provide information that negatively impacts their job security. Those new to qualitative research, in particular, are certainly encouraged to listen to contextual priorities for research inspiration, but they would be wise to avoid promising too much to research participants about their specific research foci.

Finally, when considering various topics or issues for study, it can be helpful to consider, design, and develop a list of advantages and disadvantages of several different research approaches. As human beings, we tend to **satisifice** – meaning that it is common to come up with a single decision that is merely adequate rather than with one that is optimal (Simon, 1997). By considering several potential research ideas, we are more likely to come up with a better, more creative, and smarter array of research options.

Compatibility, suitability, yield, and feasibility

Compatibility, yield, suitability, and feasibility are key considerations to entertain before diving into a qualitative research project (Lindlof & Taylor, 2011). Given that the researcher *is* the qualitative research instrument, it is important to consider your personality, demographic background, traits, and preferences. Important questions to consider are: How will I fit into the scene? How will I be accepted or regarded? How will I navigate, make sense of, or bracket my preconceived notions? Will my being different or similar to the participants be helpful or problematic? What are the potential advantages and disadvantages of my subjectivity?

Good qualitative researchers think carefully about how they, personally, will experience research in a certain context, both *despite of* and *because of* who they are. For instance, a current employee who wants to study the organization where she is employed will have the advantages of already being "in" the scene and of understanding a wealth of background information. However, this same background limits fresh insight, and the researcher will have to navigate the power and personality issues that come with her position (e.g. interview responses will be affected by the fact that she is also an employee).

Some researchers prefer to study people who have similar subject positions (e.g. a triathlete studying a triathlon club). However, researching an unfamiliar group of people can provide a unique standpoint – offering insights that an insider would not have (e.g. an outsider might be able to better pinpoint the unique race day rituals that triathletes come to see as normal – such as wearing baggies on their feet as they slither into wetsuits). No matter the site, self-reflexive researchers carefully consider how their culture, age, gender, sexuality, and physical appearance will be interpreted by others. A white male Brit might find it more difficult to study a group of Middle Eastern women than would someone who has more similarities to the participants (Whitaker, 2006). At the same time, it's important to weigh "fit" with other factors. When researchers only study people like themselves, this exacerbates the fact that huge portions of the population are remarkably underrepresented in academic scholarship.

In terms of identity, researchers should also critically consider their own ego and the extent to which they are willing to adapt in order for participants to accept them. Conquergood (1992b), for instance, moved into the "Big Red," a Chicago slum neighborhood, and was treated as an outsider and impostor for a long time before he was able to finally gain the trust of the community and to conduct his intended research project with gang members. Researchers must thoughtfully consider whether they have the personal sustenance and resilience for the countless phone calls, follow-up emails, and "courtship rituals" required in order to get access to their chosen scene of study.

Another issue to consider is your level of passion and drive for the project. Qualitative research includes a wide range of emotions and challenges. As Lindlof and Taylor (2011) note, researchers face "stretches of confusing, disagreeable, or apparently pointless activity" in the field (p. 86). Your interest in the project must rise above and propel you through these moments of frustration, difficulty, and tedium. You are most likely to enjoy a project that is complex enough to keep your attention, but simple enough that you do not get overwhelmed and frustrated.

A good research project must also provide appropriate **yield** in terms of research results. Researchers should ask themselves a very practical question: *Will this study deliver my desired outcome?* Outcomes could include a class paper, a job experience, a thesis or dissertation project, research that will build a tenure-worthy research program, a project that attends to the priorities of a funded research grant, or a publication. Although pursuing qualitative research also has intrinsic joy, most of us must produce specific outcomes. Hence considering the potential yield of a study is crucial from the beginning.

The research project also needs to be **suitable**, in that it should encompass most, if not all of the theoretical issues and characteristics of interest in terms of the research topic or problem. When I was choosing directions for my dissertation research, I learned several key issues: (1) there was still much to understand about a concept called "emotional labor" (expressing emotion for organizational pay) and, although many studies had focused on cheery customer-service settings, few had analyzed employees who got angry or had to remain stoic; (2) I wanted to study a significant social or organizational problem (e.g. burnout and turnover); and (3) I held an enduring interest in the notion of "total institutions" (24-hour organizations in which certain members never go home) (Tracy, 2000). On the basis of these considerations, a *suitable* group of participants would need to have the following characteristics: (1) perform emotional labor – preferably of a type that varied from traditional customer-service type settings; (2) experience challenges with burnout; and (3) work in a total institution. I chose to pursue research in prisons and jails – contexts that satisfy these criteria, and therefore were suitable.

Researchers must additionally ask whether a certain project is **feasible** or practical. Finding a site that is perfectly suited to your identity and to your research problem is unlikely if access to the site – or to the key informants – is impossible within the research timeframe. Researchers need to ask themselves tough questions about how quickly they might gain access and, more importantly, how long they need to be in the field before developing the relationships necessary to understand participants' cultural practices, rules, and ways of being – especially when the context is very different from the researcher's familiar territory. Qualitative research can take you to places far away, as it did for Sundae Bean, who studied tourist–host encounters in Belize (Schneider-Bean, 2008). However, Sundae pursued this study only after a year's worth of planning and conducting a pilot study closer to home.

Gaining access to secretive organizations – such as the FBI, the border patrol, or backstage at Disneyland – can be interesting, but challenging. Gheeta Khurana (2010) studied Marriages of Convenience (MOCs) – arrangements in which homosexual South Asian Indians heterosexually marry another South Asian, yet secretly agree to carry on relationships with their actual homosexual partners. The MOCs are "convenient" because they allow participants to simultaneously please their family, yet maintain their romance with their "true" love – a person whom they fear would be rejected by their family. For obvious reasons, this population is largely hidden from view. In Researcher's Notepad 1.1, Gheeta discusses how she negotiated access.

Despite the allure of hidden populations, when a researcher is new to qualitative research, focusing on issues or sites that are close to home can be easier. Many excellent research projects have emerged from public places like airports, amusement parks, college campuses, virtual worlds, rock concerts, and restaurants (see Bryant, 2010 for a study of community and technology usage on the city's metro shuttle bus). Researchers can also fruitfully conduct research in a place that is local, yet not personally familiar; such was the case with Trujillo's (1992) study of baseball and ballparks as American cultural institutions.

Finally, when thinking about a topic and context, I recommend that you seek advice. Other students may have leads. Professors or colleagues can provide a fresh viewpoint on a project's advantages and disadvantages. Internet list-serves and forums provide quick input from specialists across the world. Given the role of peer review in many journal articles, it simply makes sense to get the opinion of others *before* spending hours, semesters, or years pursuing access to a context, collecting field observations, conducting interviews, and interpreting the data.

As you make decisions about your data and about the context of qualitative examination, I encourage you to consider the factors of compatibility, suitability, yield, and feasibility, as well as factors that ease or complicate research in the field (see Tips and Tools 1.1). These tips are especially relevant for those who are new to qualitative research, or have a specified time period within which to observe and cogently make sense of a data set.

RESEARCHER'S NOTEPAD 1.1

Feasibility challenges with hidden populations

By Gheeta Khurana, in her own words

I wanted to study Marriages of Convenience (MOCs) for my qualitative class project. Ideally, direct observation would have been my preferred method; however, queer South Asians engaged in MOCs aren't exactly running rampant, because that would defeat the purpose of the secretive arrangement. So, could this be feasible?

My first step was to locate the actual population, so I referred to a foundational article by Akram (2006) that discussed websites devoted to queer South Asians seeking mates for MOCs. I turned to Google, typed in several variations of the phrase *South Asian marriages of convenience* adding the terms *website*, *discussion forum*, and *post*. I came across a few relevant websites and began researching.

I chose preferred websites using criteria such as the number of postings, the recency of posts, and the site's aesthetic appeal. I then read the postings of individuals seeking MOCs that provided information regarding qualities the individuals were looking for in their spouses, in addition to the reasons why they needed MOCs. However, I also wanted to ask probing questions to better understand this population.

I waited for a few weeks before making my presence known, because I was worried they would feel as though I was violating their privacy or judging their choices. Then I created an information letter introducing myself as a researcher who had studied South Asian families and now wanted to gain insight into MOCs. Luckily, I received five responses from participants who agreed to complete an emailed open-ended questionnaire. One person even agreed to a phone interview. I was thrilled to receive responses, but at the same time I wanted more data.

After voicing my concerns to my instructor and cursing myself for not choosing a more feasible research project, I knew that I needed to find an alternative route. After a few sleepless nights, I realized that I could usefully augment my research by learning more about queer South Asians in general. Through doing some background research, I learned that queer South Asians feel as though their orientation is still taboo, and therefore they feel a lack of support from their community.

I again did some googling and I quickly found an organization dedicated to lesbian, gay, bisexual, and transgender South Asians. I sent an email to the organization's board members, introducing myself as a researcher and indicating that I had conducted interviews with queer South Asians engaged in MOCs but was eager for more insight.

As a result, I interviewed the president of the organization. This led to an interview with a South Asian civil rights coordinator, a therapist who caters to queer South Asians, and another board member. I was able to access first-hand accounts of being queer by listening to their tales of why they considered MOCs in addition to their stories of individuals who were in MOCs. Thus I gained a more holistic understanding by interviewing those pursuing MOCs, as well as others, who were just familiar with them.

In retrospect, I am grateful that I hit a dead-end after only getting five responses from the first MOC website. I'd be lying if I said there weren't instances when I wished I had chosen a more feasible project. However, those moments forced me to expand my research focus by finding new ways to get access to better understand MOCs. Granted, researching this hidden population took creative effort, but in the end I was able to piece the multiple perspectives together, which allowed my research to be more illustrative of the complexity of MOCs within the South Asian population.

TIPS AND TOOLS 1.1

Factoring the ease of fieldwork

A number of factors (Spradley, 1980) affect the relative ease of fieldwork. Here I provide examples of research contexts that are easier or trickier in relation to these factors. I encourage you to consider your own topic and how certain field sites might be easier or trickier.

Factor	Easier	Trickier
Simplicity	Single bus	Entire village
Accessibility	Street corner	Family dinner
Unobtrusiveness	Coffee shop	Prison
Permission requirements	Beach	Street gang or AA meeting
Frequently recurring activity	Flirting	Public drunkenness
Opportunity for participation	Open mike night	Courtroom

Moving toward a research question

Research questions are the core feature of beginning a qualitative research project. Qualitative researchers begin with the basic question: "What is going on here?" (Lindlof & Taylor, 2011). Of course, "here" may refer to various practices, contexts, cultures, groups of people, documents, or electronic sources. A phronetic approach would suggest that good initial questions include: (1) Where are we going? (2) Who gains, and who loses? (3) Is it desirable? and (4) What should be done? (Flyvbjerg, 2001). Along the way, researchers devise more specific research questions, such as:

- What are people saying? What are they doing? Are participants' opinions and actions complementary or contradictory? What does this say about the scene?
- How is the scene changing over time?
- What rules or norms are research participants following? Resisting? Shaping?
- How does this population create and interpret messages? Consume media and construct news?

Many researchers hesitate to devise research questions before they enter the field. However, creating several questions can help you navigate an unfamiliar research context. These early questions provide orientation and a launching pad for action even if they do not replicate the scene's exact territory. Once you begin to collect data and cue into the context, you'll be able to better craft questions that guide interpretation and explanation. To illustrate the importance of research questions, I share a classic war story, created by Albert Szent-Györgyi, constructed as a poem by Holub (1977) and amplified into the following story by Karl Weick:

> [A]young lieutenant of a small Hungarian detachment in the Alps sent a reconnaissance unit into the icy wilderness. It began to snow immediately, snowed for 2 days, and the unit

did not return. The lieutenant suffered, fearing that he had dispatched his own people to death. But on the third day the unit came back. Where had they been? How had they made their way? Yes, they said, we considered ourselves lost and waited for the end. And then one of us found a map in his pocket. That calmed us down. We pitched camp, lasted out the snowstorm, and then with the map we discovered our bearings. And here we are. The lieutenant borrowed this remarkable map and had a good look at it. He discovered to his astonishment that it was not a map of the Alps, but a map of the Pyrenees. This incident raises the intriguing possibility that when you are lost, any old map will do. (Weick, 1995, p. 55)

Indeed, you should not worry too much – especially in the beginning – about whether your research questions are "right." Your general research interests and the context are enough to construct one or two guiding questions. In contrast to quantitative research, in which hypotheses are determined before data is collected, qualitative research questions can and should be influenced by the field and are usually modified over time. With preliminary research questions in hand, you can enter the scene with a sense of purpose, keep moving, notice new cues and update research questions along the way.

RESEARCHER'S NOTEPAD 1.2

Published examples of research questions

Although research questions that make it into published articles usually have changed multiple times before they are "in print," the published questions nevertheless can provide inspiration.

In his study with wheelchair rugby players, Lindemann (2008) posed the following three research questions:

> How are the tensions between inclusiveness and competitiveness embodied by players? How does the display of the disabled body in sport communicatively construct disability? How do the communicatively constructed meanings of disability inform quad rugby participation? (2008, p. 103)

Lutgen-Sandvik (2006) asked the following questions in order to obtain guidance for her study of the ways employees resist workplace bullying:

> What resistance [techniques] do bullying-affected workers use to counter abusive treatment? What is the processual nature of resistance? How are case outcomes related to resistance? How does the dialectic tension between control and resistance produce contradictory meanings? (2006, p. 409)

And in their research into the ways firefighters are socialized into emotion labor expectations and norms, Scott and Myers (2005) asked questions that included:

> What emotion management challenges do emergency response workers face? (p. 70); How are newcomers socialized to conform to emotion management rules? (p. 70); How do members of an emergency response organization actively participate in their own socialization to emotion rules? (2005, p. 71).

These research questions highlight the primary foci of the study and the ways the data are collected and analyzed may extend and illustrate previous understandings and findings.

Several tips can help you devise research questions. First, research questions can relate to issues that the participants find salient, problematic, or especially significant. This grounds the research question within the context. Examples of research questions tied to context include: "How do research participants communicate about the risks and rewards of their job,?" "What situations spur family members to argue?," or "Why do participants turn to this support group in their time of need?"

Second, research questions can also relate to certain theoretical or research areas: "How do participants resist the norms of appropriate behavior and what does this tell us about counterpublics theory?," or "In what ways do the stories of stay-at-home fathers extend and contrast with existing theories of work–life balance?"

Third, I recommend limiting the number of research questions posed, at least in the beginning of the project. Many people wonder *how many* research questions are appropriate. There is no magic number, but I suggest having one to two overall research questions and several more specific ones. For instance, in researching 911 call-takers, my original guiding research question was: "How do emergency 911 call-takers manage emotion through communication?" Inherent in this overall question were smaller, embedded questions about the call-takers' use of metaphor, jargon, and joking.

These tips are helpful to get you started, but qualitative research also demands that you play with the rules and perhaps, at some point, even forget them.

FOLLOWING, FORGETTING, AND IMPROVISING

As you embark on your research journey, I provide a number of rules of thumb and best practices. Clear guidelines about how to practice qualitative methodology are helpful for several reasons. First, given that many research areas are governed by positivist approaches, those who are conversant with their own methodological guidelines can enter a conversation of more traditional rules-based paradigms. Being fluent in an established language of systematic practices makes it easier to enter into dialogue with a variety of people. By speaking the language of rules and best practices, qualitative researchers can frame their research so that it may be more likely to be read and appreciated by audiences that might otherwise regard qualitative research merely as "a good story."

Second, an explicit focus on best practices is crucial for effectively teaching qualitative research. According to research on learning (Dreyfus, Athanasiou, & Dreyfus, 1986), people rely heavily on rule-based structures in order to learn. Learning a clear structure opens a path to follow, which is especially important for those who have little qualitative research experience.

Third, following rules and best practices is a common way to become expert in many interpretive arts. Musicians learn scales and chords as methods that prime them for improvising or jamming with others. Cooks follow tried-and-true recipes as preparation for experimenting with new flavor and texture combinations. In short, when people are new to a certain field, following clear guidelines can help them improve and gain credibility even before they are considered experts themselves.

So there are good reasons for learning best practices. However, I also believe that strict guidelines can be constraining and problematic. Rules can inhibit playing and having fun – and it is important to have fun in the attempt to learn an art or skill. This is especially true when the new craft is difficult, as in the case of qualitative research methods. Without some aspect of pleasure, fun, or playfulness being involved, most people will not keep practicing long enough to become expert.

Throughout this book I endeavor to clarify and illustrate guidelines for engaging in qualitative methods. At the same time, there is much of qualitative research that cannot be explicated in rules, best practices, or even in a textbook filled with anecdotes and stories. To become "good," you have to get out in the field, work with other experienced qualitative researchers, and sometimes forget and/or play with the rules. To provide some insight into situations primed for play, I revisit this notion of "following, forgetting, and improvising" throughout the book.

In summary

This chapter has introduced qualitative methods, discussed the importance of self-reflexivity, context, and thick description, introduced the notion of phronetic research, and provided tips for choosing a topic and for devising research questions. Furthermore, it has offered some guidance on following, then forgetting the rules. Chapters 2 and 3 give additional theoretical grounding. Chapters 4 through to 14 make up the phronetic heart of the book, providing an in-depth understanding of how to navigate qualitative methodology in ways that help ensure that our research matters.

EXERCISE 1.2

Three potential field sites

We humans often "satisfice," going with the first workable decision we stumble upon, rather than searching for the "best" possible decision. In the effort to determine a "better" qualitative project, describe three potential field sites and/or group of participants for your study. For inspiration, consider your personal interests and experiences, questions in the literature, hot topics, or issues that confuse and/or energize you. For each item, discuss:

1   the site or the people you want to work with and the general research issue(s) you want to explore;
2   how the site or the people of interest are complementary with your theoretical, practical, or professional interests;
3   how your background and your experience affect the ability to gain access to these contexts or people;
4   what logistical steps you must take to access this context or group.

KEY TERMS

autoethnography the systematic study, analysis, and narrative description of one's own experiences, interactions, culture, and identity

feasible the research project should be practical, given the time and resources available

field all the types of spaces where one could observe a phenomenon of interest; it consists of many potential sites, settings, and participants

iterative approach the researcher alternates between considering existing theories and paying heed to emergent field site data

participants the focal people of the study (e.g. the alumni, the officers, the pledgers)

phenomenon the locus or topic of study

phronetic research research that is concerned with practical contextual knowledge and is carried out with an aim toward social commentary, action, and transformation

satisifice the common practice of coming up with a decision that is merely adequate rather than optimal (Simon, 1997)

scene a catch-all term that refers to the field, sites, settings, and groups of participants

second-order interpretations researchers' interpretations or explanations of participants' interpretations or explanations

self-reflexivity the practice of carefully considering the ways in which the researcher's background, points of view, and role impact the researcher's interactions within and interpretations of the research scene

setting the specific parameters of the space of study within a field and a site (e.g. the basement)

site a geographical or architectural area within a field (e.g. a fraternity house)

suitable the research project should encompass most, if not all of the theoretical issues and characteristics that are of interest in terms of the research topic or problem

thick description a concept coined by Clifford Geertz (1973), which captures the fact that researchers immerse themselves in, and report on, particulars before moving toward grander statements and theories

yield the specific desired research project outcomes (e.g. a class paper, a dissertation project, a publication)

CHAPTER 2

Entering the conversation of qualitative research

Contents

Qualitative Research Methods: Collecting Evidence, Crafting Analysis, Communicating Impact, First Edition. Sarah J. Tracy.
© 2013 Sarah J. Tracy. Published 2013 by Blackwell Publishing Ltd.

How is qualitative research best understood or described? How is it different from other kinds of research? There is no single answer, but the following tale illustrates the unique nature of qualitative methods and how my approach is distinct from other types of empirical research.

> I peer through a fractured window. Pad and pencil in hand, I squint through the cracked glass. When I step to the side or even slightly move my head, I see something different – a smirk here, a wink of an eye there. At the same time, the glass provides a reflection of me trying to observe what is beyond. I note my sometimes curious, sometimes bewildered reactions.
>
> I see a door and run inside and throughout the scene; I am a character, almost. I trip. I get up. I ask others what they're doing, what's going on. Some look at me quizzically. Others smile. I may be too naïve to understand it by myself. They quietly accommodate me. Every once in a while, I ask the participants about their actions or point out something that seems confusing. Some are irritated. Others explain.
>
> Effusive with thanks, I leave the scene. I can only hope they will allow my work with them to continue. I dash home to write up fieldnotes. Despite my best efforts, the text glosses the complexity and richness of the scene. I'll never be able to write *the* story of what is going on. The best I can do is open up the story through one telling of my own.

This tale makes clear several key notions of qualitative inquiry. For instance, it exemplifies how every scene is not clearly recordable, but is fractured and impossible to fully capture. Depending on where researchers stand (literally or figuratively), they will see something different. Further, ethnographers themselves participate in the context, but they rarely do so inconspicuously. They ask questions and watch. Some participants may appreciate their presence, while others do not. Through these processes – some of which are fun, others challenging – qualitative researchers do their best to create a significant representation of the scene.

The purpose of this chapter is to introduce the key characteristics of qualitative inquiry. In doing so it overviews qualitative terminology, discusses how qualitative research focuses on action and structure, examines significant historical issues, and concludes with current controversies that situate qualitative methods today.

The nature of qualitative research

As discussed in Chapter 1, qualitative research focuses on the thick description of context and often emerges from situated problems in the field. One of the best ways to understand qualitative research is by becoming aware of how it differs from other types of research. Here I compare inductive and deductive reasoning, qualitative and quantitative research, and action and structure.

Inductive/emic vs. deductive/etic approaches

In logic, reasoning is often categorized as either inductive (a bottom-up, "little-to-big" approach) or deductive (a top-down, "big-to-little" approach). In qualitative methods, we often speak of **emic** understandings of the scene, which means that behavior is described from the actor's point of view and is context-specific. This is contrasted with **etic** understandings, in which researchers describe behavior in terms of external criteria that are already derived and not specific to a given culture. A good way to remember the difference between these approaches is that inductive and EMic research refers to meanings that EMerge from the field. In contrast, a deductive and ETic research begins with External Theories (presuppositions or criteria) to determine and frame meanings.

Researchers using an inductive emic approach (a) begin with observing specific interactions; (b) conceptualize general patterns from these observations; (c) make tentative claims (that are then re-examined in the field); and (d) draw conclusions that build theory. What does an emic and inductive approach look like in action? Suppose you were studying romantic relationships amongst college students. Research could begin with gathering specific interactions or conversations, or with asking couples to describe their most common disagreements. Then the researcher would analyze these data to find and make claims about patterns. Only after this data immersion would the researcher provide a conclusion that could add to theory. For instance, after analyzing multiple conversations the researcher might conclude that today's college students frame their relationships in terms of "hooking up" more frequently than they did 15 years ago, when "dating" was a more common way to frame courtship.

This approach contrasts with deductive reasoning, in which researchers (a) begin with a broad or general theory; (b) make an educated guess or a hypothesis about the social world on the basis of this theory; (c) conduct research that tests the hypothesis; and (d) use the evidence gathered from that research to confirm or disconfirm the original theory. A researcher using the deductive and etic approach would use predetermined models or explanations and would make sense of the contextual behavior through these lenses. For example, a romantic relationship researcher could start from Baxter's (1990) dialectical theory and hypothesize that all couples, regardless of their satisfaction level, must manage relational dialectics such as autonomy vs. connectedness. Then the researcher could examine how the couple's most common disagreements aligned with, contrasted with, or extended relational dialectic theory.

Most social science research involves both inductive and deductive reasoning. Furthermore, qualitative research *can* work with both approaches. However, qualitative approaches tend to be contextual and generally they use inductive, emic approaches to understand local meanings and rules for behavior. At the same time, many researchers will turn to established theoretical models after they have examined their data, to see how emergent findings extend or complicate existing theories. They may also "hold on loosely" to developed models as they enter the analysis of qualitative data, where these models sensitize them to potential meanings.

Action and structure

When studying a context, qualitative researchers examine people's actions (local performances) and the structures (informal guidelines and formal rules) that encourage, shape, and constrain such actions. Different researchers discuss this action–structure duality using a variety of terms. Lindlof and Taylor (2011) talk about contextual "performances" and structuring "practices." Discourse scholars use the term "*discourses*" with a small "d" to refer to everyday talk and text and "*Discourses*" with a big "D" to refer to larger systems of thought (Fairhurst & Putnam, 2004). An example of a performance or small-d discourse is the action of facing the door when standing in an elevator. A structuring practice or big-D discourse is the socialized norm or unwritten rule that facing the door (rather than facing the sides, the back wall, or other people) is the appropriate, polite, and normal way to stand in an elevator.

Despite the different terminologies, for our purposes I use the term **action** to refer to contextual talk, texts, and interactions (e.g. documents, emails, verbal routines, text messages, and comments) and **structure** to refer to enduring schools of knowledge, societal norms, and myths. Action and structure continuously construct and reflect upon each

CONSIDER THIS 2.1

Why am I standing in line?

Action and structure can be illustrated through the simple example of standing in line. In most Western nations, people learn to stand in line (for buses, ticket booths, or financial aid offices) through authoritative messages, informal admonitions, official documents, and printed signs. Most of us, at some time in our lives, have heard: "Don't cut in line!" or "Get to the back of the line!" Because of continual rules, reminders, and practices of line-standing, people often form lines even when the formal authority is absent (e.g. waiting overnight for concert tickets). In this way the line-standing structure is reinforced.

People begin to act and interpret the world – as well as judge others – via structures that normalize certain behaviors as being more moral and natural than others. People who stand in line are evaluated as polite and good, and those who do not are judged as rude and poorly behaved. In this process, "standing in line" creates a grand narrative that is helpful in some ways, but makes it difficult to imagine alternative possibilities.

When I worked on a cruise ship for eight months, I observed line behavior numerous times each week. In many situations, standing in line was appropriate (e.g. when passengers had to wait for a tender boat to get to shore). However, I also noticed inappropriate line-standing. Some passengers joined a long line for the evening's show at one entrance when an adjacent entrance had no line at all. Lines formed at the end of food buffet tables when, because of the repetition of the same dishes several times along a table, it would have been more appropriate to approach the table in groups scattered at different angles.

Passengers would occasionally go to the back of a line without even knowing what the line was for. This was the case especially in complex or new situations, such as when passengers first embarked. Some would join other passengers, who stood in line at the main reception desk, even though they already had everything they needed to go straight to their room. They followed the structure they had been accustomed to for their entire life (moreover, they had repeatedly followed it in the preceding hours) and assumed that "getting to the back of the line" was an acceptable and moral behavior – even when it was unnecessary.

This example shows how action and structure are cyclical and co-constitutive. The repeated *actions* of getting into line create a *structure* of line-standing regarded as appropriate. This, in turn, encourages more line-forming *action*, and so on. The actions and the structures are helpful in some ways, but when they become mindless and habitual they can lead to bizarre, inappropriate, and sometimes problematic responses to a situation.

other. Language and actions cannot be separated from the way knowledge is institutionalized and produced (Du Gay, 2007), and this is illustrated in Consider This 2.1.

Action and structure relate to qualitative methods in several ways. First, qualitative researchers investigate action through close examinations of everyday mundane practices, talk, and interaction – such as line-standing behavior. They take as a guiding premise that one cannot *not* perform or communicate. At the same time, qualitative researchers examine structures as **grand narratives** – systems of stories driven by our formal expectations for things to unfold in a particular way. The continued domination of certain ways of being over time creates normalcy, powerful ideologies, assumptions about the truth, and larger

EXERCISE 2.1

Action vs. structure

1 What are some of the common *structures* (rules, expectations, and grand narratives) for the typical college classroom?
2 What are the actions and performances that support these structures? Which ones are obvious? Which ones are hidden or less obvious?
3 How do these actions and structures create a helpful classroom culture or climate?
4 How are the actions and structures constraining, or potentially problematic?

discourses of power (Eisenberg, 2007). It's much easier to note action than to notice the larger structures – as structures become taken for granted and second nature. However, a key part of qualitative research is highlighting the existence of these structures and theorizing the purposes served by their acceptance as normal.

For example, a researcher may note how historical norms about appropriate "first-date" behavior suggest that people should avoid using their hand-held electronic devices during that date. However, the researcher may also note that people resist and reshape these expectations, and in fact regularly use their hand-held devices during first dates, without any intended or perceived offense. Qualitative researchers would take note of these everyday actions and would also examine how they maintain, transform, and are shaped by larger structures and norms. By examining these dualities, researchers may open up windows for transformation and change.

Comparing qualitative and quantitative methods

One of the most common ways in which qualitative research is understood is through comparison with key features of **quantitative methods**. Quantitative research transforms data – including conversations, actions, media stories, facial twitches, or any other social or physical activity – into numbers. Quantitative methodologies employ measurement and statistics to develop mathematical models and predictions.

A quantitative researcher, for instance, may aggregate survey answers to measure how often respondents engage in a certain activity, or how much they prefer a certain product. Interaction may be observed in the laboratory, or it may be collected physiologically and examined in terms of how many times participants engage in various activities, or how much of a hormone is detected in their saliva (Floyd, Pauley, & Hesse, 2010). Quantitative researchers may also use field data – for example by studying the drinking patterns of patrons in bars or coffee shops. However, in contrast to a qualitative thick description of the scene, quantitative research is usually driven by questions of scale of the type "How much?" and "How often?" For qualitative researchers, counting and transforming data into numbers are much less frequent activities.

Another key difference between qualitative and quantitative methods is the role each one gives to the researcher. In quantitative research, the research instrument and the researcher controlling the instrument are two separate and distinctly different entities. For instance, the nurse is separate from the research instrument of the thermometer, the biologist watches but is separate from a chemical catalyst, and a social scientist is separate from a survey that measures participant attitudes. As noted in Chapter 1, in qualitative methods the researcher *is* the instrument. Observations are registered *through* the researcher's mind and body. In such circumstances, self-reflexivity about one's goals, interests, proclivities, and biases is especially important.

Finally – and this is something we will cover in greater detail in Chapters 12 and 13 – the representation of the methodology, findings, and discussions of qualitative research differs from that of quantitative research. Articles that report statistical studies usually separate out the description of the research instrument (say, a survey) from a report on the findings (often represented in charts and graphs). In contrast, in qualitative research reports, the description of the research methods often flows into the stories, observations, and interactions collected. Qualitative researchers do not reserve the writing for the end of the project, using it as a way to reflect on their already discovered results. Rather they write in the process of collecting the data, analyzing, reflecting, and inquiring.

Some researchers choose one method over the other. However, it is not absolutely necessary to confine oneself to either qualitative or quantitative research. Some of the strongest research programs are built upon multiple methods of data collection (Abbott, 2004). For instance, to understand the concept of workplace bullying (Lutgen-Sandvik, Namie, & Namie, 2009), researchers have used a quantitative survey to document its prevalence and its most common characteristics, and qualitative interviews to understand the feelings associated with bullying and the ways targets try to make sense of abuse and combat it.

The key questions to consider when choosing a research methodology and approach are: "What types of methods are best suited for the goals of my research project?" and "Which methodologies am I most equipped to use, or most attracted to?" Methodology is a tool. Just like a hammer is a better tool than a screwdriver for banging a nail into a wall, qualitative methodology is better than quantitative methodology for richly describing a scene, or for understanding the stories people use to narrate their lives. But sometimes two tools can do a job well. For instance, an artist could use chalk, markers, paint, or clay. The choice depends in part on the goal of the piece and in part on the artist's preferred medium. Likewise, choosing which methodology to use depends on the research goals as well as on your personal proclivities, preferences, and talents.

Key characteristics of the qualitative research process

What does qualitative research actually look like, and how does it proceed? In this section I briefly discuss several key characteristics of the qualitative research process, including gestalt, bricolage, research as a funnel, and the use of sensitizing concepts. These are not methods in and of themselves, but central characteristics that mark many of the theories and approaches used in qualitative research.

Gestalt

Qualitative researchers approach cultures holistically, or as **gestalt** – a German word meaning "essence of form or shape," but whose philosophical and psychological underpinnings (what is widely known as "gestaltism") make it untranslatable; hence it has

Figure 2.1 This image represents an example of a person's predisposition to organize pieces of information into more than just a collection of its separate parts. Do you see two faces, a vase, or both?

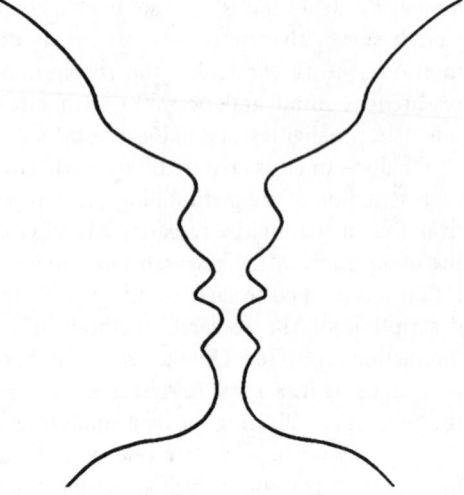

been appropriated as such in English and many other European languages. Roughly speaking, it captures people's tendency to piece together various parts into an integrated system or culture. The meaning of these systems comes through their interdependence and integration: the perceived whole is more than a sum of its parts (see Figure 2.1).

A gestalt approach suggests that examining a culture's elements as integrated together is preferable to parsing them out as separate variables. In other words, one aspect of a culture is best understood *in relation to* others. Participant observation is an excellent method for understanding gestalt meanings, but ethnographers may also use statistics and quantitative approaches to complement their qualitative study of a culture. For instance, Geertz (1973) counted and statistically analyzed the different types of bets made by Bali men during cockfights, and this analysis played a key role in his interpretation.

Bricolage

Second, qualitative methods establish the researcher as a "bricoleur." **Bricolage** is "a pieced-together set of representations that is fitted to the specifics of a complex situation" (Denzin & Lincoln, 2005, p. 4; see also Derrida, 1978). In other words, qualitative researchers are like quilters, borrowing and interweaving viewpoints and multiple perspectives. They make do with a variety of data – all of which are partial and mismatched – in order to construct a meaningful, aesthetically pleasing, and useful research synthesis (see Figure 2.2). This means that qualitative researchers are flexible, creative, and make the most of the information available, whether that includes interviews, observations, documents, websites, or archival material.

A qualitative researcher using the concept of bricolage makes use of various data in order to create an interesting whole. For instance, as she begins with the examination of advertisements for products that help women look younger, Trethewey (2001) asks what happens when we accept as normal the grand narrative that suggests that "getting older" equals "decline." She answers the question through interviews with women in mid-life and by showing how their views of aging both resist and reinforce the notion that aging and showing one's true age is problematic. As illustrated through Trethewey's use of multiple types of data (advertisements, interviews, observations), the qualitative researcher attempts to create meaning out of a variety of practices and performances available to her.

Figure 2.2 This image from the Garbage Museum pictures the "Trashosaurus." This piece of art is an example of bricolage in that it borrows and uses multiple items – items that have been "trash" on their own – to create a delightful and moving piece of art. Reproduced by permission of the Connecticut Resources Recovery Authority.

Finally, another way to consider bricolage is in terms of cooking. Imagine searching inside the refrigerator and finding the remainders of a rotisserie chicken, a heel of cheddar cheese, a half-eaten can of black beans, and some salsa. Most people might only see here leftovers and exclaim, "We've got to go the store, there's nothing to eat!" But a chef who is a bricoleur will see something else. By piecing together these bits, along with a can of chicken broth, a handful of corn chips, and some packets of garlic salt and hot pepper flakes from last week's pizza delivery, the bricoleur chef creates a wonderful chicken tortilla soup. Similarly, the qualitative researcher creates something beautiful and significant from the ingredients that show up in the "fridge" – the data – and therefore she is a bricoleur.

The funnel metaphor

Another metaphor helpful for illustrating the process of qualitative inquiry is that of the funnel. Like a funnel, qualitative inquiry usually begins with a broad and wide-open research question – such as "What is going on here?" By starting broad, researchers examine from the start a wide range of behavior, attuning themselves to a variety of interesting issues and circumstances that come from the field. Then, as they further scout the scene and collect more data, they slowly but surely circle through the funnel, narrowing their focus. Through ongoing analysis, interpretation, and collection of data, the purpose of the study becomes more distinct.

Given that the initial focus of a research study is quite broad, investigators must be flexible to contingencies in the scene. Every research project is different, and the practices that worked well in one scene may not work in another. For instance, some scenes may allow the researcher to act as him-/herself (e.g. hanging out at a concert), while a scene more difficult to access (e.g. a presidential press conference) may require him/her to dress or act in a different way from the usual.

When I conducted research with correctional officers, I purposely wore nondescript, baggy, and loose clothing, I tied my hair back in a ponytail, and I avoided any type of glitzy makeup. I did this so that I may blend in with inmates and officers and hopefully avoid any attention related to gender, age, or sex. This was much different from the persona I displayed when working and conducting research on a commercial cruise ship – where lots of makeup and formal dresses were exactly what I needed in order to fit in. Another difference among the two contexts was that in prisons and jails I carried a yellow notepad most of the time.

The notepad marked me as an official person and was easy to handle when I was hanging out in the correctional officer's observation booths. On the cruise ship it was not feasible to carry around a notebook and take notes, so I was taking notes on scraps of paper and recorded observations in a journal, back in my cabin.

None of the preceding actions about my appearance and note-taking are things I could have predicted before experiencing the research scene. As a qualitative researcher, it is important to be comfortable with a certain amount of lack of control and to have some tolerance for ambiguity. Ethnographers take on the role of "learner." They listen, watch, and absorb meaning from the field and from the research participants.

Sensitizing concepts

Even though most qualitative researchers start broad, they also frequently begin with several concepts in mind about potential issues or theories that may become salient. Indeed, it is perfectly acceptable and quite helpful for qualitative researchers to read literature and to gather sensitizing concepts along the way. **Sensitizing concepts** are theories or interpretive devices that serve as jumping-off points or lenses for qualitative study (Charmaz, 2003; Glaser & Strauss, 1967). These concepts – gleaned from past experience or research, or mentioned in former scholarship – serve as background ideas that offer frameworks through which researchers see, organize, and experience the research problem. Most researchers begin with an inventory of favorite concepts, theories, and personal interests to draw attention to certain features in the scene.

For instance, in a study of children on a playground, researchers may begin with concepts such as *bonding*, *conflict*, and *shyness*. By acknowledging these sensitizing concepts, they are more likely to be self-reflexive about the interests they bring to the project. A researcher may have a long-standing interest in how children bond as friends because he personally has vivid memories about his best friend in kindergarten. A different researcher may instead focus on shy children because of her theoretical expertise in social anxiety. Meanwhile, another researcher may be interested in conflict because he is working on a grant that is funding research on this topic.

Simply put, sensitizing concepts are issues to which the researcher is most attuned. They effectively help narrow and focus perception in research scenes that are complex, chaotic, and overflowing with multiple issues. Just like research questions, sensitizing concepts provide a guide on where to start, deepening perception and analysis along the way (Bowen, 2006). As time is spent in the scene, researchers can go back to the literature, learn more about certain theoretical concepts, and examine how they are playing out in the data.

Key definitions and territories of qualitative research

In order to enter *any* conversation – whether it's about sports, theater, food, or fashion – it is important to understand key categories, typologies, and classifications. The same is true in qualitative research. Definitions are different depending on whom you talk to, and some terms are fraught with political ramifications of who "owns" specific parts of academic territory. The following definitions are some of the most commonly used in qualitative research.

The phrase **qualitative methods** is an umbrella concept that covers interviews (group or one-on-one), participant observation (in person or online), and document analysis (paper or electronic). Such methods can include research in the field, a focus-group room, an office, or a classroom. Qualitative methods by definition need not include long-term immersion into a culture or require a holistic examination of *all* social practices. Indeed, some qualitative studies cover the course of a single day (e.g. Trujillo, 1993) and others come in the form of open-ended qualitative survey approaches (Howard & Prividera, 2008). Furthermore, researchers can engage in qualitative methods over a long time period or for an extremely short duration. The definition of qualitative methods is purposefully broad and encompasses several more specific types of inquiry.

Naturalistic inquiry refers to the process of analyzing social action in uncontrived field settings in which the inquirer does not impose predetermined theories or manipulate the setting (Lincoln & Guba, 1985). Naturalistic research is described as value-laden and, by definition, *always* takes place in the field, which may be an organization, a park, an airport, or a far-away culture – but it cannot be a focus-group room or laboratory (unless the topic of study is naturally occurring lab behavior). Some might argue that every setting is contrived and changed inasmuch as the researcher's presence influences it. However, the general notion of naturalistic inquiry is that the researcher travels to a regularly occurring context and examines participants as they regularly act.

Long-term immersion into a culture is a hallmark of **ethnography**, another key type of qualitative research. Ethnography combines two ancient Greek words: *ethnos*, which meant "tribe, nation, people," and *graphein*, "to write." As they write and describe people and cultures, ethnographers tend to live intimately beside and among other cultural members. Ethnographers focus on a wide range of cultural aspects, including language use, rituals, ceremonies, relationships, and artifacts. Some researchers frame their work slightly differently, by adopting the label **ethnographic methods** or approaches to specific contextual research needs (e.g. Ashcraft, 2007). Researchers who use ethnographic methods tend to engage in participant observation and field interviewing. In addition, they may augment field observation through archival research and interviews from a variety of different contexts. Further, they are more likely to focus their analyses on one or two particular concepts connected to their research questions rather than analyze an entire range of cultural issues. The phrase "ethnographic methods" provides a helpful way to describe one's methodological approach and to sidestep potential criticism from scholars who want to reserve the term *ethnography* for long-term, side-by-side, immersed, and holistic studies of a culture.

Another territory of qualitative research is **narrative inquiry**. Narrative researchers view stories – whether gathered through fieldnotes, interviews, oral tales, blogs, letters, or autobiographies – as fundamental to human experience (Clandinin, 2007). People reveal the ways they interpret their identities and experiences through their stories. Lawler notes:

> We all tell stories about our lives, both to ourselves and to others; and it is through such stories that we make sense of the world, of our relationship to that world, and of the relationship between ourselves and other selves. Further, it is through such stories that we produce identities. (Lawler, 2002, p. 239)

From this point of view, stories are not just after-the-fact representations or mirrors of reality. Rather, they serve to construct and shape experience. Even when people lie, exaggerate, and forget (Riessman, 1993), narrative provides a window for understanding how others interpret a certain situation and create a reality that they, in turn, act upon.

Stories are also common in another territory of qualitative research, called autoethnography. As noted in Chapter 1, **autoethnography** refers to the systematic study, analysis, and narrative description of one's own experiences, interactions, culture, and identity. Many autoethnographic texts are marked by vulnerability, emotion, and making the personal political (Holman Jones, 2005). Autoethnographers' methodology includes systematic introspection and emotional recall (Ellis & Bochner, 2000), often about painful or tragic experiences, and writing as a form of inquiry (Richardson, 2000b). These practices can lead to evocative tales that encourage dialogue, change, and social justice. Fox (2007), for instance, suggests how his story of being a thin gay man (whom other people read as HIV positive) functions as a "narrative blueprint" for living – a "personal tale made public with the intent of inspiring identification among audience members seeking a narrative model to help guide future attitudes and behaviors" (p. 9). In other words, our auto-ethnographic stories – even when intensely personal – can provide sensemaking guides for others in similar spaces.

There is some controversy as to whether autoethnography should be conceptually divided into "analytical" and "evocative." Anderson (2006) explains that analytic autoethnography is characterized by complete membership, reflexivity, and narrative visibility of the self. However, he differentiates it as theoretically more committed and not requiring the considerable expressive representational skills of the more well-known "evocative" autoethnography. Despite any distinctions within autoethnography, most scholars agree that autoethnographic work is not and should not be about narcissistic naval gazing or personal catharsis (Krizek, 2003). Certainly, autoethnography honors a rigorous self-reflexivity and may end up being therapeutic both for the writer and for the reader. However, autoethnography also engages dialogue with others, connects to theoretical and scholarly concerns, and expresses stories about the self in ways that provide alternative ways to live and see the world.

Autoethnography also serves as a common venue for another territory of qualitative sensibilities, which may collectively be called **impressionist tales** (Van Maanen, 1988); these have variously been termed performance and messy texts (Denzin, 1997), creative analytic practice ethnography (Richardson, 2000b) and the new ethnography (Goodall, 2000). Qualitative research can be performative, messy, creative, and "new" whether authors analyze their own stories or the stories of others. Impressionist tales present ethnographic knowledge in the form of poems, scripts, short stories, layered accounts, and dramas. These texts are creative, personal, shaped from personal experience, and addressed to both academic and public audiences. They are often "messy" because they exist in an in-between, liminal space where rhetoric, performance, ethnography and cultural studies converge (Conquergood, 1992a). We will talk more about writing and representation in Chapters 12 and 13. However, it is important to be familiar with these types of qualitative practices from the beginning, as they are not only methods of representing or writing; they also provide valuable ways of approaching, inquiring, and knowing.

Finally another common phrase used to class a certain territory of qualitative research is grounded theory. **Grounded theory**, developed by Glaser and Strauss (1967) and extended by Strauss and Corbin (1990, 1998) and Charmaz (2006), refers to a systematic inductive analysis of data that is made from the ground up. Rather than approaching the data with pre-existing theories and concepts and applying these theories to the data (an etic approach), the researcher begins instead by collecting data, engaging in open line-by-line analysis, creating larger themes from these data, and linking them together in a larger story. This emic approach, in turn, produces grounded theory. We will turn to a more detailed discussion of grounded theory and grounded data analysis techniques in Chapter 9.

Historical matters

A quick historical tour about ethnography and research methods can shed light on the ongoing theoretical and methodological issues related to qualitative research. Furthermore, understanding our past can help shape our future, as we consider preferences for and biases against qualitative research, ethical concerns, and various political issues that continue to shape qualitative research today.

The early days

Clair (2003) provides an excellent history of ethnography and its checkered past. Ethnography draws its origins from investigations into foreign cultures. Although perhaps this was not the intention of some researchers, many early ethnographic investigations constituted a type of **colonialism** – the control and exploitation of a weaker or racially different culture by a stronger group.

Western Europeans such as Christopher Columbus went in search of new lands in the fifteenth century – not only to describe them, but also to make them their own. Conquerors viewed the native people as primitive and in need of their help in order to become civilized. Indeed colonialism is closely connected to **ethnocentrism**, the belief that one's own racial and ethnic values and ways of being are superior to those of other groups. Dark-skinned natives were oftentimes killed, abused, and enslaved. Colonialist annihilation was so complete in some cultures that a new wave of ethnography began in the 1800s as a means of saving cultures from extinction and of documenting exotic cultural legends, myths, history, language, and medicines. An ongoing ethical concern of ethnography is the extent to which one can fairly use another society's culture, stories, artifacts, and histories for the purpose of one's own entertainment, education, or advancement.

In the early 1900s, researchers such as W. E. B. DuBois – an African American scholar who studied Black culture in Philadelphia – began questioning colonization and linking it to racial prejudice. Ethnographers also found themselves in unique situations that were not of their planning. Such was the case with Austrian-born Bronislaw Malinowski, who traveled to Australia with a British contingent just as World War II began. Considered an enemy by Australian forces, Malinowski was exiled to the Trobiand Islands. He was allowed to conduct fieldwork in New Guinea during his incarceration, and he eventually decided to participate in Trobiand society. Malinowski, considered one of the most significant anthropologists of the twentieth century, did some of his most important work during this period, producing foundational theories about participant observation (Clair, 2003).

The two world wars of the 1900s encouraged researchers to examine cultures closer to home. George Orwell examined his own poverty, W. F. Whyte studied war's impact on organizations, and Antonio Gramsci wrote from his prison cell about power and politics. Scholars at the Chicago School of Sociology became known for applying ethnography to social problems such as drug abuse, poverty, crime and disease in urban settings (Abbott, 1999). In short, naturalistic research into, and the in-depth cultural examination of, local concerns became just as important as studying exotic people in distant lands.

Ethically problematic research and the creation of the IRB

World War II brought with it the **Nuremberg Code**, which uncovered and judged the atrocious and inhumane experimentation conducted by Nazi physicians on prisoners of war. The code included principles that are now required ethical guidelines for research, for instance

Figure 2.3 Stanford Prison Experiment. Chuck Painter/Stanford News Service.

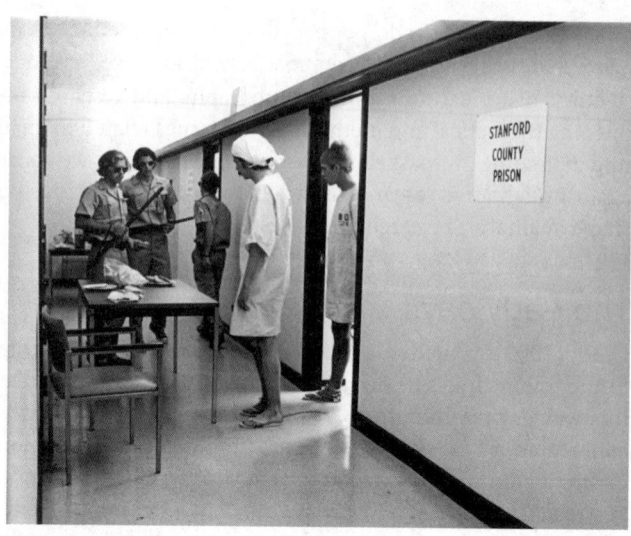

voluntary and informed consent, freedom from coercion, comprehension of the potential risks and benefits of the research, and a scientifically valid research design, which could produce results for the good of society. Similar recommendations were made by the World Medical Association in its *Declaration of Helsinki: Recommendations Guiding Medical Doctors in Biomedical Research Involving Human Subjects* (World Medical Association, 1975). Despite these codes, ethically problematic social science research continued. Two famous social science studies were the Milgram experiment and the Stanford Prison experiment.

In the early 1960s, Stanley Milgram examined the willingness of ordinary people to deliver what they believed to be painful electric shocks to someone whom they thought to be another innocent participant (in reality they were giving fake shocks to an actor). The experiment was devised as a response to the Nazi war crimes and inquired into the likelihood that well-intentioned people could be coerced into hurting others (Milgram, 1974). When gently encouraged by the experimenter in a white lab coat, a surprisingly high percentage of everyday people were willing to proceed with administering what they thought to be increasingly higher voltage shocks. Although the shocks were not real, the experiment nonetheless created extreme stress in the participants and would not be allowed by today's research guidelines.

Another famous and ethically questionable study was the Stanford Prison experiment, conducted in 1971 and led by psychologist Philip Zimbardo (Zimbardo, Maslach, & Stanford University California Department of Psychology, 1973). In this experiment, 24 male undergraduates were paid the equivalent of $80 a day to "play" as guards and prisoners in the basement of a Stanford classroom building. The students quickly adapted to their roles and this rapidly led to a surprisingly abusive, sadistic, and dangerous environment, in which the prisoners were emotionally traumatized (see Figure 2.3). Two "prisoners" showed signs of a nervous breakdown and were released within a couple of days. Because of the unpredictable effects of the experiment and resulting ethical concerns, Zimbardo terminated the planned two-week experiment after only six days.

Ethnography's colonialist history, coupled with the atrocities of the Nazis and with questionable research practices such as those typified in the Milgram and Stanford Prison experiments, paved the road toward the creation of **human subject protections**. These measures, required by institutional review boards, are designed to protect people ("human subjects") from unethical research – a topic to be detailed in Chapter 5. Although most qualitative researchers do not encounter the same ethical trappings of experimental studies, researchers using a variety of approaches are now faced with increasing institutional reviews of their work.

Recent history

As World War II came to a close, increasing numbers of ethnographers began studying places close to home. These included descriptions of labor–management relations (Roy, 1959) and descriptive accounts of daily work (Argyris, 1953). However, ethnographers were also sent far away, to study "third worlds." Such was the case of Geertz (1973), who was funded by the Ford Foundation in the 1970s to conduct research that would improve the economic growth of depressed cultures. Social science research began to take an "interpretive turn," with increasing focus on interaction and linguistics. Furthermore, a "crisis of ethnographic authority" (Erickson, 2011, p. 48) in which people began to question the credibility of reigning ethnographic texts led to more participatory, autoethnographic, and self-reflexive reports.

At about this time, a range of social science scholars began to take seriously qualitative methods and the cultural approach. Communication historian and theorist James Carey (1975) encouraged researchers to make "large claims from small matters" by studying "particular rituals in poems, plays, conversations, songs, dances, stories, and myths" (p. 190). Interpretive and critical points of view stood in stark contrast to a more dominant tradition of factually based realist ethnography. While realist researchers studied poems, plays, conversations, songs, dances, stories, and myths, they did so being informed by the notion of a scientific separation of the researcher from the data, whereas the new ethnographers increasingly denied that such a separation can, or should, exist.

In the 1980s and in conjunction with the rise of postmodern viewpoints, researchers began to seriously question the notion of one true reality and the very concept of representation. Anthropologists Clifford and Marcus (1986) claimed that ethnographic truths are "inherently *partial*" (p. 7). Organizational ethnographer Van Maanen (1988) suggested in his famous *Tales of the Field* that the most commonly accepted "realist tale," characterized by an all-knowing author, is just one out of several different ways to represent culture. He also described autoethnographic "confessional" tales, dramatic and creatively written "impressionistic" tales, literary tales, jointly told tales, and critical tales (all presented in more detail in Chapter 12).

Pacanowsky and O'Donnell-Trujillo (1982, 1983), pioneers in the study of organizations as cultures, drew from Geertz's interpretivism – studying organizations *not* as machines, but rather as tribes, and viewing familiar phenomena as strange, exotic, and full of special-ized meanings. The 1981 Alta Organizational Communication Conference encouraged researchers to move beyond the transmission model of communication and to examine instead how communication serves to construct or constitute relationships, cultures, and organizations (Kuhn, 2005). This "linguistic turn" not only signified a methodological shift away from studying communication as a measurable outcome, but also indicated a fundamental transformation in researchers' ways of building knowledge and of knowing the world (Deetz, 2003).

Current controversies

Today's period in qualitative inquiry celebrates more transparent displays of various research processes, reflexivity, and subjectivity. The increasing interest in qualitative research across many disciplines – together with the recognition that qualitative research is rigorous and important – is evidenced by the exploding attendance rates at academic conferences such as the Congress for Qualitative Inquiry (http://www.icqi.org/) and the Qualitative Research in Management and Organizations (http://www.hull.ac.uk/hubs/qrm/), and at established ethnographic divisions in long-standing professional associations, such as the National Communication Association (http://natcom.org). Examples of qualitative work are increasingly common in top journals from a variety of social scientific disciplines: communication, education, sociology, management, health, gender, ethnic studies – and more. In short, increasing research engages interpretive issues of language, power, and discourse for the purpose of providing grounded, contextual insight.

Although qualitative research practices have been well disseminated and accepted within a number of academic disciplines, much of the scholarly community is still unfamiliar with methodologies that don't align with quantitative methods (Cannella & Lincoln, 2004). Some of the best known qualitative researchers believe that a methodological conservatism has crept upon social science since the early 2000s, as evidenced in an increasing preference for research that is experimental and quantitative (Denzin & Giardina, 2008).

Governmental policies such as the federal No Child Left Behind Act of 2001 and the 2002 National Research Council (NRC) report have had the consequence of suggesting that the only rigorous type of social science research is replicable and generalizable across settings (de Marrais, 2004). This has challenged qualitative researchers to communicate better about, and to earn greater respect for, our work in a new research landscape, which is marked by an attendant "politics of evidence" (Lather, 2004; Lincoln & Cannella, 2004). Such a landscape provides fewer rewards or incentives for conducting in-depth inquiry or for practicing methods associated with ethnographic, critical, postmodern, and feminist approaches.

For research diversity to survive in this environment, qualitative researchers must claim a space that avoids consenting to realist or quantitative research norms, yet recognizes the constraints of collisions among institutional review boards, an audit culture, and the politics of evidence (Cheek, 2007). Hence qualitative researchers must not only learn the practical tools of making sense of their data, but also be able to discuss their approach with power holders who decide what types of research count as significant and important.

In summary

This chapter has introduced and explained qualitative research principles at a basic level, comparing them with the principles of quantitative research, discussing the difference between inductive/emic and deductive/etic approaches, and highlighting the importance of studying both action and structure. Qualitative research can be understood through the metaphor of the funnel, considering research as gestalt and viewing the researcher as bricoleur. We have also discussed several main territories of qualitative research, including ethnography, naturalistic inquiry, narrative approaches, autoethnography, messy texts, and grounded theory.

I offered a brief history of ethnography and research to help provide the background needed to understand enduring ethical concerns and human subjects' controversies. This discussion also previews some of the paradigmatic tensions that still frame today's research and theoretical approaches. In the following chapter we delve in greater detail into research paradigms and the theoretical frameworks most common to qualitative research.

EXERCISE 2.2

Research problems and questions

Describe an issue that sparks your curiosity and that you plan to explore in your research site. This could be a social and/or a theoretical problem, or just an issue that confuses or fascinates you.

1   Phrase your approach in the form of one or more research questions (see Chapter 1 to refresh your memory on how to write these).
2   Describe why an emic qualitative study of this phenomenon is especially warranted and valuable given the research questions/problems.
3   Explain several sensitizing concepts from past experience or research that align with your research interests. How will these concepts help focus your research?
4   As a bricoleur, what different types of data could you piece together in order to answer your research questions?

KEY TERMS

→ **action**   contextual talk, texts, and interactions (e.g. documents, emails, verbal routines, text messages, and comments)

→ **autoethnography**   the systematic study, analysis, and narrative description of one's own experiences, interactions, culture, and identity

→ **bricolage**   the practice of making creative and resourceful use of a variety of pieces of data that happen to be available

→ **colonialism**   refers to the control and exploitation of a weaker or racially different culture by a stronger (usually Western European) culture

→ **deductive reasoning**   a "top-down" type of reasoning that begins with broad generalizations and theories and then moves to the observation of particular circumstances in order to confirm or falsify the theory

→ **emic**   a perspective in which behavior is described from the actor's point of view and is context-specific

→ **ethnocentrism**   the belief that one's own racial and ethnic values and way of being are more important than, or superior to, those of other groups

→ **ethnographic methods**   the use of participant observation and field interviews, but not necessarily accompanied by immersion in the field or by a holistic cultural analysis

→ **ethnography**   research marked by long-term immersion into a culture and by the thick description of a variety of cultural aspects including language use, rituals, ceremonies, relationships, and artifacts

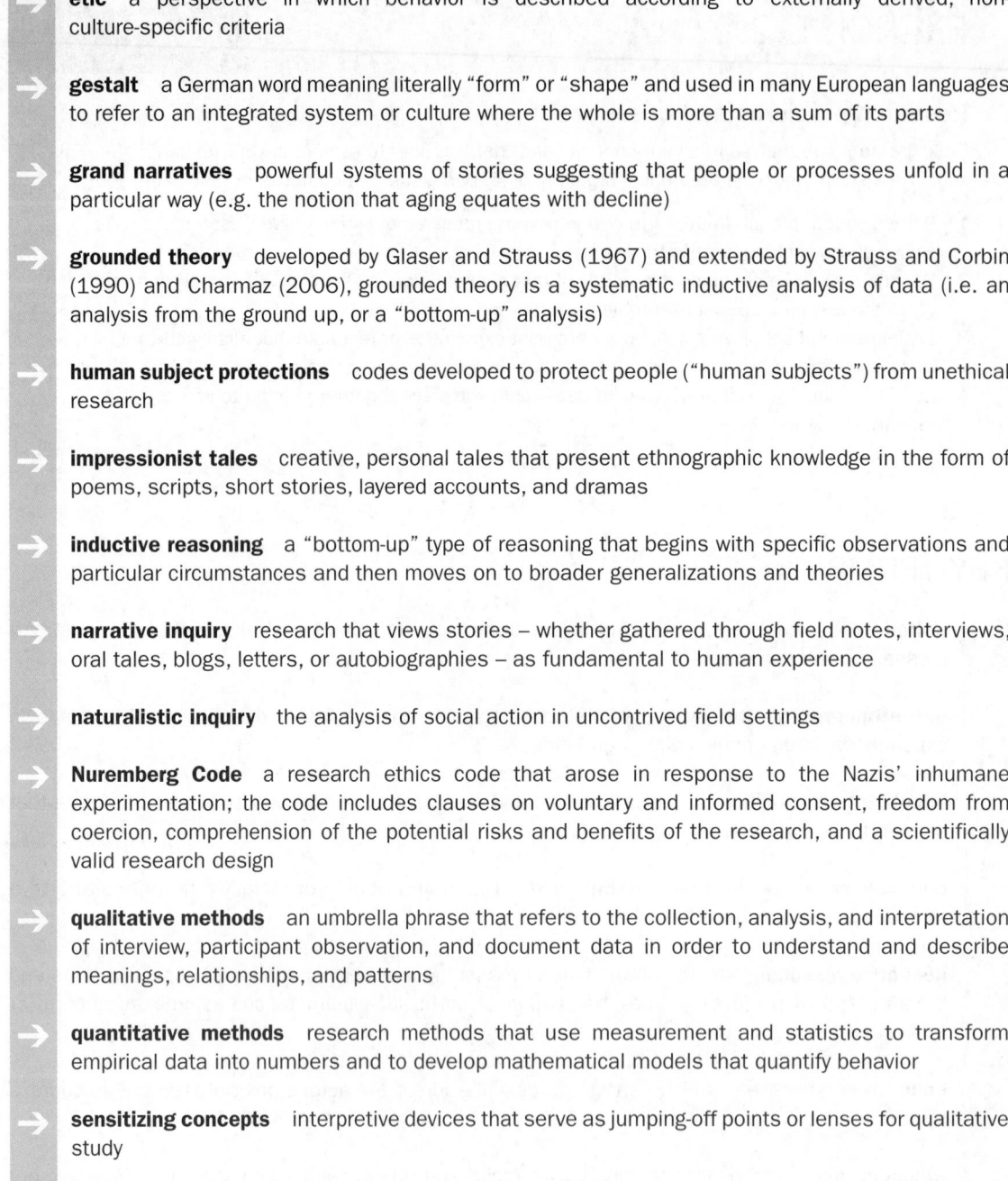

etic   a perspective in which behavior is described according to externally derived, non-culture-specific criteria

gestalt   a German word meaning literally "form" or "shape" and used in many European languages to refer to an integrated system or culture where the whole is more than a sum of its parts

grand narratives   powerful systems of stories suggesting that people or processes unfold in a particular way (e.g. the notion that aging equates with decline)

grounded theory   developed by Glaser and Strauss (1967) and extended by Strauss and Corbin (1990) and Charmaz (2006), grounded theory is a systematic inductive analysis of data (i.e. an analysis from the ground up, or a "bottom-up" analysis)

human subject protections   codes developed to protect people ("human subjects") from unethical research

impressionist tales   creative, personal tales that present ethnographic knowledge in the form of poems, scripts, short stories, layered accounts, and dramas

inductive reasoning   a "bottom-up" type of reasoning that begins with specific observations and particular circumstances and then moves on to broader generalizations and theories

narrative inquiry   research that views stories – whether gathered through field notes, interviews, oral tales, blogs, letters, or autobiographies – as fundamental to human experience

naturalistic inquiry   the analysis of social action in uncontrived field settings

Nuremberg Code   a research ethics code that arose in response to the Nazis' inhumane experimentation; the code includes clauses on voluntary and informed consent, freedom from coercion, comprehension of the potential risks and benefits of the research, and a scientifically valid research design

qualitative methods   an umbrella phrase that refers to the collection, analysis, and interpretation of interview, participant observation, and document data in order to understand and describe meanings, relationships, and patterns

quantitative methods   research methods that use measurement and statistics to transform empirical data into numbers and to develop mathematical models that quantify behavior

sensitizing concepts   interpretive devices that serve as jumping-off points or lenses for qualitative study

structure   enduring schools of knowledge, societal norms, and myths that shape and delimit action

CHAPTER 3

Paradigmatic reflections and theoretical foundations

Contents

Qualitative Research Methods: Collecting Evidence, Crafting Analysis, Communicating Impact, First Edition. Sarah J. Tracy.
© 2013 Sarah J. Tracy. Published 2013 by Blackwell Publishing Ltd.

The type of glasses you wear affects the world you see. It makes sense to learn about different kinds of glasses, to ensure that you choose the pair that best suits you, and hence that you understand how different people, wearing different glasses, see the world in such different ways. This chapter introduces different ways of viewing knowledge and reality and reviews several theoretical approaches commonly used in qualitative methods. The information contained in this chapter is denser than in the rest of the book, and it may be best to read it in "chunks" along the way during one's journey through a qualitative project. Despite the theoretical nature of this chapter, it provides language that will help in situating your beliefs and approach, and tools that will help in investigating and making meaning of qualitative data.

Paradigms are preferred ways of understanding reality, building knowledge, and gathering information about the world. A researcher's paradigm can differ on the basis of **ontology** (the nature of reality), **epistemology** (the nature of knowledge), **axiology** (the values associated with areas of research and theorizing), or **methodology** (strategies for gathering, collecting, and analyzing data). Because people take different stances on these issues, it is important to understand the primary arguments and points of view that make up the paradigms. Before getting into the nitty-gritty of paradigms, Consider This 3.1 shares a story that sheds light on the role of paradigmatic approaches in research.

CONSIDER THIS 3.1

A paradigm parable

I, like most doctoral students in their comprehensive exams, was asked by my supervisory committee to overview various paradigms, and also to defend my own. In my answer, I referenced concepts from several different paradigms and described how I pulled together different concepts depending on the needs of the specific research project. I made the argument that paradigms are toolboxes full of theories, practices, and ways of thinking and that *all* tools can be useful and destructive in their own way. They all can be used to solve problems, empirically demonstrate issues, provide artistic pleasure, or prove someone else wrong.

When I arrived at my postcomprehensive exam meeting, I learned that my written answer had caused some disagreement among the five faculty members in my committee. I watched as the faculty debated whether I really could mix and match concepts from different paradigms on the basis of the particular project – or whether I needed to be more definitive about my chosen paradigm. One committee member said that there was a difference between *using* different paradigms as tools and *confusing* them. Although he did not come out and say it, I think he put me in the "confused" category. However, another committee member, Phil Tompkins, jumped to my defense. Phil was my beloved master's thesis advisor, and he was about to retire. Pretty much no one said anything else, and that is where I *thought* the conversation ended.

Later that day, Phil saw me in the hallway and surreptitiously motioned me into his office. He darted his eyes down the hall and, after seeing no one, closed the office door. The air was electric with secrecy. And then, in the hushed tone that was his signature, he said: "Sarah, I probably shouldn't be telling you this, but some people *really don't think you should be using multiple paradigms*." These "people" remained nameless, but the intensity in Phil's eyes communicated the significance of his message. Could it be that other committee members were out to quell my hope of using my own signature combination of theories? I never actually found out any details – and Phil's story was never corroborated. Regardless, it was during that closed-door conversation that I viscerally learned that, at least to some people, paradigms are *serious business* – and I should treat them as such. My choice to mix and match them could affront those who spent their scholarly lives building, defending, and arguing for the pre-eminence of some ways of seeing and knowing the world over others.

Just as I was feeling then – and as I communicated it in my comprehensive exams – I still wonder, even today, whether all the time we spend defining, differentiating, and fighting about paradigms really matters that much. And, since that time, increasingly researchers have made explicit arguments about blurring their boundaries (Ellingson, 2011). Nonetheless, paradigms still are used as ways of categorizing and classifying research. In order to enter the conversation of qualitative methods, it is important to understand their basics.

Paradigms

Different disciplines use different terms and categorization schemes for paradigms – so readers are encouraged to seek out specific articles in their field to "talk the talk" of their discipline (for good overviews, see Deetz, 2001; Lincoln, Lynham, & Guba, 2011). Below I discuss four commonly referenced and differentiated paradigms – positivist/post-positivist, interpretive, critical, and postmodern/poststructural – and how each can make use of qualitative methodology. At the close of the discussion, Table 3.1 summarizes the major characteristics of each paradigm.

Positivist and post-positivist paradigm

Researchers from a **positivist paradigm** – which is sometimes also referred to as a *realist* or *functional* paradigm – assume that a single true reality already exists "out there" in the world and is waiting to be discovered. Positivists conduct research in order to observe, measure, and predict empirical phenomena and build tangible, material knowledge. They strive for research to mirror reality – to represent clearly what is being examined. Consider that famous puzzle: "If a tree falls in the woods and there is no one there to hear it, did it really make a sound?" Positivists would likely respond with a resounding "Yes, if we can prove it" and would go on to measure the vibrations made when the tree falls. They might conclude that, given the right tools and research methods, the vibrations suggest there was a "sound," whether or not anyone was there to hear it.

A **post-positivist** paradigm is similar to a positivist one in terms of aiming toward knowing a single material reality and searching for causal explanations of patterned phenomena. However, in contrast to positivists, post-positivists believe that humans' understanding of reality is inherently partial. Post-positivists believe with certainty that reality exists and that there is good reason to try to know it. However, they also submit that human researchers and their methods have inherent weaknesses and biases. Given all this, capturing reality – in all its blooming, buzzing confusion – is improbable.

Data collectors coming from (post-)positivism believe that researcher biases and backgrounds are liabilities – and, as such, they should be corrected or minimized. Humans are flawed, while science is considered objective and self-correcting. From this perspective it follows that, if there is a single truth to be known, the personal background and biases of the researcher should not affect that truth. In consequence, (post-)positivist researchers rarely discuss their own background, hopes, dreams, fears, or the ways they may be biased or have a stake in the study. Talk about the self is viewed as unnecessary, indulgent, and a mark of low credibility. If anything, talk about the researcher is reserved for discussions about measures taken to be objective and guard against researcher influence.

From a positivist or post-positivist point of view, qualitative methods aim toward garnering representative samples that provide a clear answer to the question, "What is happening here?" In the quest for an answer to this question, researchers from these approaches are likely to **triangulate** – to use multiple types and sources of data, diverse methods of collection, various theoretical frames, and multiple researchers (Denzin, 1978) in order to settle upon what is "really" happening. Methodological triangulation is considered worthwhile because a key concern for good research in this paradigm is its reliability and formal generalizability (characteristics of research quality that I'll return to in Chapter 11).

An example of well-known qualitative researchers who have worked from this paradigm are Matthew B. Miles and A. Michael Huberman (1994), who developed one of the most thorough and popularly used sourcebooks available on qualitative data analysis. They describe themselves as post-positivist "realists," meaning that they "think that social phenomena exist not only in the mind but also in the objective world – and that some lawful and reasonably stable relationships are to be found among them" (p. 4). Methodology, from this point of view, appears as a *strategy* and not as a value-filled moral concern. Researchers such as Miles and Huberman have used qualitative methods in order to capture realist and causal descriptions of empirical events, for instance to examine why some educational innovations work better than others, or as to how some interventions are more likely than others to help a society, a group, or an organization cope with change.

An example of my own research that comes from a (post-)positivist paradigmatic lens is a study that examines the prevalence and costs of workplace bullying. In order to convince power holders (such as granting agencies and business executives) that workplace bullying is actually a problem, I have worked with colleagues to document its frequency and negative effects (Lutgen-Sandvik, Tracy, & Alberts, 2007). In this research project we made use of quantitative surveys supplemented with qualitative survey responses, interviews, and focus groups, in order to demonstrate that bullying is a common and costly problem in the United States. Our goal was to come up with scientific "proof" that workplace bullying exists as a material reality. This study served as a foundation for our second and more interpretive research project, which was focused on the feelings of workplace bullying.

Interpretive paradigm

From an interpretive point of view – which is also termed *constructivist* or *constructionist* – reality is *not* something "out there," which a researcher can clearly explain, describe, or translate into a research report. Rather, both reality and knowledge are constructed and reproduced through communication, interaction, and practice. Knowledge about reality is therefore always mediated through the researcher.

If you asked an interpretive scholar, "If a tree falls in the woods and there is no one there to hear it, did it really make a sound?" answers would be less clear-cut and more involved than the positivist answer. Interpretive scholars might say that the issue depends on the meaning of the word "sound." Given that sound requires a listener, perhaps the tree did not have sound if no one was listening; or maybe it had a different sound, depending on who or what was present at the scene (a baby, a chipmunk, a researcher, a digital tape-recorder, or a journalist). Also, interpretive researchers might argue that what is classified as having a sound differs from person to person. Does the air conditioner in the background create "sound"? What about the sound of your own breath or heart beat? Perhaps you are getting bored or hungry or agitated; do any of these states have sounds? Interpretivists would ask and gain insight from multiple points of view, from multiple participants, and from themselves, to answer the question.

Indeed, the interpretive paradigm suggests that it is absolutely necessary to analyze social action from the actors' standpoint – a concept often referred to by using the German word *verstehen* ("to understand"). The German philosopher Wilhelm Dilthey introduced this concept to the study of humanities to refer to the participatory approach of gaining empathic insight into others' viewpoints, beliefs, and attitudes. **Verstehen** describes the first-person perspective that participants have on their personal experience as well as on their society, culture, and history. Max Weber brought the concept to the study of the social sciences, where it refers to an interpretive study of groups on their own terms and from their own point of view. Although interpretivists do not believe it is ever truly possible to see the world from their participants' eyes, *verstehen* refers to the practice of striving toward empathic understanding.

In addition to attempting to see the world from participants' eyes, interpretive researchers view their choice of qualitative methodology as a moral and value decision, fraught with ethical and political repercussions. Indeed, interpretivists view knowledge as **socially constructed** through language and interaction, and reality as connected and known through society's cultural and ideological categories. Human activity is not regarded as a tangible material reality to be discovered and measured; rather it is considered to be a "text" that can be read, interpreted, deconstructed, and analyzed.

EXERCISE 3.1

Verstehen/understanding

The interpretive paradigm emphasizes the importance of examining the world from participants' points of view – a *verstehen* approach illustrated in the following activity.

1   Choose a scene that you regularly watch from afar but do not usually engage in yourself. This may be people waiting at a bus stop, your roommate playing video games, your relatives making holiday dinner, or children playing in a park. Take several notes that answer the question, "What is going on here?"

2   Now, place yourself in that scene. Wait at the bus stop, play the video game, make holiday dinner, or play in the park. As you do so, talk to the people who are there and try to understand their point of view, their goals, their hopes, their ways of being. Take notes, and again answer the question, "What is going on here?"

3   Finally, compare your notes from 1 and 2. What are the differences? How does an attempt at *verstehen* (understanding) enhance or complicate the interpretation of what is happening in the scene?

In this way interpretivism draws from **hermeneutics**, which aims at a holistic understanding. Researchers using a hermeneutical method examine talk or text by empathically imagining the experience, motivations, and context of the speaker/author, and then by engaging in a circular analysis that alternates between the data text and the situated scene (Schwandt, 2000). This practice suggests that, to understand any text, one must also simultaneously consider its cultural and historical context. For instance, to understand hermeneutically the Torah, the Bible, or any other religious text, the researcher also considers the context in which it was written and how people of that age would understand its teachings. Likewise, to understand their own ethnographic texts, researchers must consider their own subjectivity and life worlds (Berry, 2011).

Much of my own research – as well as much of the research covered in this book – stems from an interpretive framework. For instance, my colleague and I asked the question, "How do 911 call-takers manage emotion?" (S. Tracy & Tracy, 1998). This research attempted to understand the 911 experience through the eyes of the call-takers and, as such, we hung out with our participants, listened to hundreds of calls, and asked call-takers why they responded the way they did. From our immersion in the scene, we were able to understand why call-takers sometimes became exasperated and how their story-telling helped them deal with the job's frustrations and tragedies.

Critical paradigm

Critical research is based on the idea that thought is fundamentally mediated by power relations and that data cannot be separated from **ideology** – a set of doctrines, myths, and beliefs that guide and have power over individuals, groups, and societies (Kinchloe & McLaren, 2000). An example of just one ideology is patriarchy, which suggests that males should be at the center and head of social organization. Critical researchers view cultural life as a constant tension between control and resistance, and they frame language as a type of power. Thus ideas and knowledge can both control and liberate. Knowledge is constructed through communication and historical power relations. Hierarchical power differences (for example, that men are more powerful than women) unfold through everyday interaction (e.g. Dad always sitting at the head of the table or driving the car). Over time, these power differences come to be seen as normal and natural. At the very least, critical research brings power relations to conscious awareness and, by doing so, provides space for questioning and transformation.

Critical research can fall either into the modern (positivist) or into the postmodern camp, depending on its emphasis. For instance, a critical approach focusing on power and change may be more positivist in nature – assuming a stable reality to be captured and providing guidance on how to transform, change, and improve that reality. This realist critical approach characterizes scholarship coming from the Frankfurt School or from Marxist or Neo-Marxist backgrounds. Such scholarship blames capitalism for many of today's social ills and argues that society should create structures and spaces in which all people can have equal access, voice, and opportunity (Habermas, 1979). Alternatively, a theorist may be critical from a postmodern framework (which will be discussed in detail in the next section). Critical postmodernists are more concerned with the shifting, fluid, and constructed nature of power relations.

Whether from a modern or postmodern point of view, what holds together critical approaches is the idea that research has an ethical obligation, such as helping to emancipate or liberate those who find themselves in situations that are immoral, unfair, unethical, violent, or generally "not nice." Many critical ethnographers choose topics based upon a passion to investigate injustice. Research from a critical paradigm asks not only "what is?" but "what could be?" (Thomas, 1993, p. 4). By talking and arguing about "what is better," we engage in the process of knowledge production, and the study of culture goes beyond *describing* a scene to *changing* it. In extension to the interpretive goal of *verstehen*, critical researchers believe that commonsense face-value assumptions must be questioned. Things aren't always what they seem, and research may challenge or subvert taken-for-granted assumptions ("Why does Dad always sit at the head of the table? What would happen if the youngest child sat there instead?")

Let us return to the question, "If a tree falls in the woods and there is no one there to hear it, did it really make a sound?" Critical researchers might argue that the answer to this question depends on who has the power to claim the truth at that particular time in history. Given a landscape of research that generally values positivist quantitative research more than interpretive qualitative research, critical researchers might argue that the answer to the sound question lies with the most powerful positivist researchers – not necessarily because they are right, but because they have a stronghold on grant dollars and on publication in prestigious journals, and therefore they get to determine the "truth." Another "critical" response to the question might come in the form of asking additional questions, such as, "Well, why did the tree have to fall in the first place? Who cut it down? How might we shed light on the problem of deforestation?"

An additional hallmark of the critical paradigm is the idea that oppression is most forceful when subordinates do not consciously understand their domination. In other words, power differences are potentially most destructive when people view their own powerlessness as natural, necessary, or inevitable. Italian philosopher and political theorist Antonio Gramsci introduced the concept of **hegemony** to refer to situations in which people accept, consent to, internalize, and are complicit in reproducing values and norms that are not in their own best interests (Laclau & Mouffe, 1985). People often see hierarchical relationships (e.g. adults over children, men over women, Caucasians over other races, teachers over students) as normal and unchangeable rather than socially constructed.

For instance, hegemony is illustrated when a young female preschool teacher says, "Well, I think it's fine that I have a lower salary than a man, because teaching just pays less than most male jobs. I love kids, so making less money is okay." Such a comment shows hegemony in action: the teacher's comment glosses the arbitrary and socially constructed nature of occupational pay. Caring for children is not *inherently* less valuable than, say, fixing a pipe or driving a truck. Rather this hierarchical relationship – that jobs held by men generally pay more than those held by women – has been normalized through interaction and power relations. Hegemony is at work when people accept, consent, and reproduce practices that are not in their own interest.

Qualitative research emerging from a critical point of view can be found in a number of disciplines, but it is more common in sociology, justice studies, communication, and education than in disciplines such as psychology or management. Thomas (2003) has made his career as a critical ethnographer in criminology, conducting studies of race, self-injury, prisoner rights, and faith-based intervention systems in prisons and jails. His qualitative research is ethically motivated by his desire to improve America's correctional systems and problematize the treatment of those behind bars.

I have used critical viewpoints in my analysis of the ways employees actively consent and subordinate themselves to organizational regulations that can result in their own harassment from customers. In a study of cruise ship staff (Tracy, 2000), I explored how emotional labor expectations (that employees smile and defer to passengers) are not absolutely necessary, neutral, or objective. Rather, these expectations emerged in the process of cruise ships changing from *transportation* to *destination*. The organization's emotional rules are therefore connected to historically produced power relations – a process by which some individuals (cruise ship management and customers) profit more than others (employees). By pointing out the arbitrary nature of such rules, we see how normalized practices might be disrupted, altered, improved, or changed.

In summary, critical approaches are oriented toward investigating exploitation, unfairness, and false communication – and how cultural participants reaffirm, challenge, self-subordinate to, or accommodate existing asymmetrical power relations (Alvesson & Deetz, 1996).

Postmodern/poststructuralist paradigm

A postmodern/poststructuralist paradigm is similar to the critical paradigm in tying knowledge to power relations (Foucault, 1980). In contrast to modern critical scholars, though, postmodern scholars approach knowledge and power as something dispersed, unstable, and plural. As such, the paradigm not only highlights occasions of domination and self-subordination, but also accentuates avenues for resistance and change.

Poststructuralists assume that all people have space for agency (the ability to act in a scene) and free will (the ability to choose among alternatives). Even people in weak circumstances have some power to challenge and reshape the constraints they face. Hence transformation and change are possible, even if they come slowly, through individual micro-practices rather than grand gestures or revolts (Mumby, 1997; Trethewey, 1997). For example, micro-practices of resistance can be seen in children who talk back to their parents, in students who refuse to take notes in class, or in employees who yawn when they are supposed to be smiling (Tracy, 2000).

Postmodernists question totalizing truths and certainty, reject grand theories and master narratives that tidily explain a phenomenon, and resist the idea that, with just more research, we can better control the world. Postmodern researchers view reality and knowledge as fragmented, multiple, situated, and multi-faceted. On these premises, reality is thought to be nearly impossible to know or represent. Data collection may just as likely get us further away from the truth, not closer to its understanding. For example, postmodernists would argue that the conspiracy theories, movies, books, and media reports developed to explain the death of Michael Jackson may just have confused the situation further.

If radical postmodern scholars were to answer the puzzle about a tree falling in the woods, they may provide a variety of answers that were partial yet had some merit. Postmodernists would also point out that, in focusing on the tree question, the researcher left out other (potentially more) important questions. Like critical scholars, postmodernists believe that things are not what they first seem, and they dig below surface interpretations for many layers of meaning.

Finally, poststructural scholars would argue that examination of power relations is necessary for understanding why some problems are so **sedimented** (solid and difficult to remedy), and how some ideas are held with more merit than others. When knowledge, education, and credentialing are only available to dominant and wealthy people, the knowledge of subordinate members – which may be crucial for understanding a research problem – is often hidden, ignored, or undermined (Foucault, 1980). Indeed reality is

CONSIDER THIS 3.2

Whose stylistic rules?

Both the critical and the postmodern paradigms highlight the importance of power, knowledge, and hegemony (the consent and normalization of hierarchical relations). To apply these concepts, consider some rules of grammar. For instance, among other admonitions, most guides on style and gurus agree that "ain't" is not a word and should not be used. To interrogate this assumption using concepts from the critical and postmodern paradigm, you might consider the following questions:

1   Who are the authors of stylistic guides? Who gets to make the rules?
2   What are the effects of having rules of style? In what ways do some people, because of their environment and social class, more easily succeed at being "stylistically correct" than other people?
3   Is the collection of letters that spell "ain't" inherently better or worse than the collection of letters that spell "is not?" How is this stylistic rule arbitrary?
4   How does a focus on grammar in typical American grade schools preclude a focus on other issues?
5   In avoiding the word "ain't" and critiquing those who use it, how do people consent to and reaffirm existing stylistic rules?

"fixed" in particular ways, which tend to favor powerful interests over others. Therefore alternative ways of seeing the world are often ignored.

In addition to focusing on power and hegemonic processes, postmodern scholars are also interested in layers of reality. Indeed, a key part of the postmodern paradigm is the **crisis of representation** – which refers to the idea that all representations of meaning depend on their relations with other signs and representations. The crisis of representation suggests that meaning is **rhizomatic**, or root-like (Deleuze & Guattari, 1987). Just as roots are interconnected and interweaving, so, too, is meaning. As pictured in Figure 3.1, the meaning of words and images is constantly shifting and growing, and it is interdependent with the meaning of other words and images. For instance, an understanding of the word "cold" requires knowing the word "hot." To understand the meaning of the slang word "Crackberry," one must know about the mobile phone "Blackberry," and also to understand the addictive nature of "crack" cocaine. In short, the meaning of "Crackberry" is dependent on the ever shifting meanings of other concepts.

From this point of view, all explanations and descriptions are unstable and interrelational. Photos have borders, stories have points of view, music is bound by chord structures, and journal articles can only be so long. In stark contrast to positivists, who view good research as mirroring reality, postmodernists would note that mirrors are warped, fractured, and reflect back onto the scene (and therefore affect it). The best a postmodern researcher can do, then, is to choose a shard of a shattered mirror and realize that it only reflects one sliver of the world. As a result, research necessarily *leaves out* data – and therefore researchers can never represent anything unproblematically.

Figure 3.1 Postmodernists view reality as rhizomatic or root-like, with meaning constantly shifting, growing, and being interdependent with other meanings.
© Mike Kiev/iStockphoto.com

Several key terms emerge from the postmodern/poststructural paradigm. These include the concept of **pastiche**, or the endless appropriation and recycling of older cultural forms to make new but familiar forms. For instance, researchers examining fashion might note that today's trendy clothes are reformulations of past fads – such as 1960s Jackie O-style sunglasses, 1970s bell-bottoms, or 1980s moon boots.

Another key postmodern concept is that of **hyperreality**, or the idea that many representations or signifiers (such as media stories, action figures, theme parks) are constructed and consumed but lack a specific "real" referent. Postmodern scholar Jean Baudrillard (2001) suggests that reality is merely a copy or enhancement of a previous representation, and that the mind is unable to distinguish between reality and representation. For example, a man addicted to pornography begins to assume that sex is like the virtual world he views on his computer screen. However, the computerized representation in the fantasy lacks a clear connection to any type of sexuality that "really" exists. The pornographic movie becomes "reality by proxy."

Relatedly, the concept of **simulacrum** refers to a representation that is a copy of something that never actually existed. For instance, Disneyland's "Main Street" copies a "typical" main street, yet this main street never really existed (Boje, 1995). "The Bachelor" reality TV show provides a representation of dating and courtship, and this representation is consumed, reproduced, and in many ways more real than "real" courtship. Las Vegas features a number of hotel casinos that replicate famous sites from around the world. They are copies of the buildings, and in some ways the copies are "better" (cleaner, nicer, newer, and easier to capture in a photo) than the originals.

Finally, postmodernists often use Derrida's (1982) concepts of **deconstructionism** and **différance** as methods of data analysis in order to dismantle a text and accentuate foundational word oppositions (e.g. the researcher may replace the word "high" in the text with "low," or "woman" with "man," and see what happens to the text's meaning). A key theoretical principle of this method is to draw attention to words and meanings that are *absent*. For example, Martin (1990) employs deconstructionism to analyze and reconstruct a story told by a corporate chief executive officer (CEO) about the ways he "helps" women balance work and life. In so doing, she shows the complex absurdity of the CEO's notion of good work–life balance – in which the CEO applauds a female employee for planning her cesarean delivery so that it may not interrupt the company's introduction of a new product.

In sum, from a postmodern or poststructuralist point of view, qualitative methods aim toward examining discourses of power, multi-faceted ways of being, and the dialectical nature of hegemony. Postmodernists are extremely attuned to schisms and potentially antagonistic ideas within the scene.

Paradigmatic complexities and intersections

In this chapter, so far, I have described four of the most common and easily differentiated paradigms. Just as tools may be used (or abused) in various ways to achieve different ends, a researcher can also use the methods of participant observation, interviewing, focus groups, and document analysis for different goals. Qualitative methods can stem from any one of the paradigmatic frameworks, but it may be inappropriate to choose bits of them all at once. Choosing one of the paradigms can preclude the choice of another – an issue subsumed under **incommensurability** (Corman & Poole, 2000). For instance, a positivist believes that the world is knowable and strives to show the one true world. This comes into direct conflict, and is therefore incommensurable, with the postmodern goal of analyzing multiple and antagonistic meanings of the scene in which each meaning is partial and significant in its own way, but never holds the whole truth. Critical theorists and interpretive researchers also have a historical conflict, because critical scholars sometimes view interpretive work as naïve when it derives meaning only from the situated data. Critical scholars argue that interpretive researchers ignore the political complexity of the scene and should question the face-value meaning of participants' words. Meanwhile, some interpretive ethnographers frame critical scholarship as elitist and negative on the grounds that it presupposes the importance of power and ideology even when the participants themselves do not bring up these issues.

Despite these controversies, many people, myself included, use concepts and tools from various paradigmatic approaches depending on the specific goal of a research project. Indeed it seems to be more common among contemporary scholars, trained as they are in multiple methods, to blur the paradigmatic edges; scholars operating from older traditions, who plant themselves firmly in one paradigm, are, by comparison, rarer to find. Further, moving beyond your comfort zone paradigmatically can expand your repertoire of tools and techniques to "enrich your understanding of some aspects of your self, participants, data, and/or research process" (Ellingson, 2008, p. 77). By moving among different paradigms, researchers may better appreciate a new topic, have a renewed sense of humility, dialogue with a variety of people, and continually remind themselves of the multiple ways a problem or issue may be fruitfully addressed.

Table 3.1 lists the overall characteristics of the central paradigms.

Table 3.1 Assumptions of Four Primary Paradigmatic Approaches: (Post-)Positivist, Interpretive, Critical, Postmodern/Poststructural.

	(Post-)Positivist	Interpretive	Critical	Postmodern/ Poststructural
Ontology (nature of reality)	Single, true, apprehensible	Socially constructed	Constructed through power relations and shaped over history	Multiple, fragmented, layered, fluid, and multi-faceted
Epistemology (nature of knowledge)	Discovered; a priori, true, objective	Produced; dependent and value-laden; subjective, co-created	Mediated, hidden, distorted, and produced through power relations	Relative, skeptical, "truth" is a myth; knowledge is as much fantasy as it is reality
Goal of research	To measure, predict, control; to be formally generalizable, reliable, and a mirroring representation	To understand why and how; to be useful and interesting; to provide opportunities for participant voice	To ask "what should be?" to improve and transform; to disrupt power relations	To highlight chaos, show multiple points of view, and examine absence and the relativism of meaning
A good researcher...	Expertly uses research and measurement devices; brackets out background and biases so they do not taint research findings	Is a self-reflexive research instrument, aware of biases and subjectivities; background is imperative for understanding the research	Considers social class and powerful structures such as "isms" (sexism, homophobia, racism, ageism); asks how the scene is affected by, and constructs, power relations	Acknowledges the crisis of representation, writes stories that open up multiple themes, examines the reappropriation and layering of reality
Method (strategies for gathering, collecting and analyzing data)	Viewed as value-free; multiple methods (often quantitative and experimental) triangulated to ensure accuracy and validity	A value choice with ethical and political ramifications; multiple methods show the contexts' layered and partial nature; hermeneutical; seeks *verstehen*	Qualitative methods often coupled with historical considerations of power and class	Qualitative methods often coupled with considerations of various and overlapping mediated representations of the scene
Focus	Building knowledge through analysis of objective behavior (behavior that can be measured, counted, or coded)	"Making sense" of scene from the participants' point of view – examining not only behaviors but intentions and emotions	Pointing out domination; aiming toward emancipation and transformation	Highlighting absence, pastiche, hyper-reality, simulacra and rhizomatic meaning

Table 3.1 *(cont'd)*

	(Post-)Positivist	Interpretive	Critical	Postmodern/ Poststructural
Theory creation	Deductive and incremental; researchers systematically propose and test scientific explanations on the basis of existing knowledge	Inductive, expansionistic and iterative. Researchers hold on loosely to tentative explanations, compare them with emergent data, revise their claims, go back to the data and repeat. As a result, the study may solve a problem, attend to a given controversy, critique an existing school of thought, strengthen a fledgling theory, or construct a new one		

EXERCISE 3.2

Paradigmatic approaches

Our epistemological, ontological, and methodological premises represent a framework or set of beliefs that guide our understanding of the world and shape our approach to conducting research.

1   What paradigm or paradigms most closely accord with your own research beliefs and philosophies?
2   Why? What appeals to you? What are the limitations of other approaches?
3   In what ways has this framework shaped your approach to research in the past, and how might it shape it in the future?

Theoretical approaches that commonly use qualitative methods

The following section reviews theoretical frameworks that are commonly paired with qualitative research. I call them "theoretical frameworks" because these approaches are not narrow edicts that can be proven true or false, but open-ended clusters of concepts that help make sense of meaning. Some readers may be interested in reviewing all of the following before they begin fieldwork. Others may choose to overview the theories that are most pertinent to their topic. Readers who are mainly interested in the "how-to" of qualitative methods may decide to skip this theory section altogether. That said, most researchers will profit from circling back to these theoretical frameworks various times throughout their research journey.

To many students, the word "theory" sounds scary. However, **theories** are simply bundled systems of principles that strive to explain or make sense of certain phenomena. For instance, Darwin's theory of evolution and the religious theory of creationism are dueling theories, each striving to explain the development of human life. These theories are famous and attached to lots of science, debate, and expertise. However, people make lay theories all the time. For instance, if a student walks in late for a class, theories adduced to explain this fact might be "slept late," "had a doctor's appointment," "couldn't find parking," or something else. These theories may never be fully proven true or false. Rather, researchers continue to gather data, and these data transform, refute, or bolster their theory. Furthermore, new theories (explanations) emerge from new data. Qualitative researchers can benefit from being familiar with theories, because theories serve as sensitizing concepts that help direct attention to meaningful data – helping determine what to observe, take notes on, or ask questions about. Although theories should not be viewed as strict recipes, they provide guidance and potential organizational frameworks.

Keep in mind that the following descriptions of theoretical frameworks are necessarily brief and partial. These descriptions encompass Geertz's interpretivism, symbolic interactionism, ethnography of communication, feminism, participatory action research, sensemaking, and structuration theory. Indeed, many volumes have been written on each one of these theoretical approaches – and I could have included any number of other theories. Hence advanced readers interested in a certain approach are encouraged to seek out further resources and examples.

Geertz's interpretivism and thick description

Although contemporary scholars may critique Geertz's work on the grounds that it speaks in an omniscient voice, or that it overlooks issues of gender, power, and race, few can dispute that he is a foundational figure in developing interpretivism. Geertz views researchers as "cultural interpreters" who provide vivid descriptions that unpack values, beliefs, and action in a group, society, or organization. As noted in Chapter 1, ethnographers make use of their own interpretation of interpretations of other members of their culture, their goal being to construct a **thick description**. As illustrated through Geertz's famous research on the Balinese, a cockfight may appear to be a grotesque and barbaric ritual, in which onlookers find entertainment watching roosters hack each other to bits. A "thin" description may present cockfighting in these simple terms. But, as Geertz learned through long-term immersion and painstaking fieldwork, the cockfight is more than a game, and betting on cockfights is more than a way to earn material rewards. Rather, he found that the Balinese interpret cockfights as being about esteem, honor, dignity, respect, and, most importantly, status.

But Geertz did not stop here. Another step to thick description is for the researcher to make interpretations of the participants' interpretations. Geertz realized that, although cockfighting might be *about* status, through the fights, no one's status really changes. So what is the purpose of this ritual? Geertz concluded that cockfights function to display, structure, maintain, and reconstruct the themes of death, masculinity, rage, and pride: "It is a Balinese reading of Balinese experience, a story they tell themselves about themselves" (Geertz, 1973, p. 447). This is Geertz's interpretation of participants' interpretations, and it helps the outsider make sense of a ritual that, on its face, is violent and incomprehensible.

A vital part of interpretivism is analyzing how culture is symbolically constructed and reconstructed. As Geertz implies when he compares a culture to a spider web, a cultural web not only exists, it is spun. Ethnographers in this tradition pay attention to how and why people talk and act their culture – their "webs" – into being.

Another example of the interpretivist framework is found in Goodall's (2004) study of Ferrari owners who participate annually in a "Poker Rally." What Goodall discovers is that, while the risk of damage to expensive cars is a part of status that doesn't change with the game, expressions of masculinity, symbolic exchanges of low-status but highly valued "prizes" (e.g. Ferrari baseball caps), and shared stories of individual "performances" sum up the event's meaning to the participants and explain how an elite group defines "fun." Examples of Geertz's approach are also evident in the organizational culture approach (e.g. Pacanowsky & O'Donnell-Trujillo, 1982, 1983), in which researchers examine *how* and *why* specific practices, rituals, or stories come to be significant and important in a particular culture or group.

Potential research questions from Geertz's interpretivist point of view include:

- How do participants view their world?
- What does a ritual or a practice mean within *this* context or culture and at *this* particular moment in time?
- How do certain stories come to be significant in a given culture?
- What do small rituals or practices say about the culture's larger values or priorities?

Symbolic interaction

Symbolic interaction (SI) is a theory developed by Herbert Blumer (1969), a student of George Herbert Mead, the famous Chicago School sociologist. More recently, Athens, who was Blumer's last doctoral student and is now a legendary criminologist, has summarized the approach, saying that symbolic interaction rests on the assumption that "people's actions result from their interpretations of the situations that confront them in their everyday lives" (Athens, 2010, p. 92). So, what does this mean? Researchers using symbolic interactionism investigate how meaning and identity are co-created through interaction. A central tenet of the theory is that people act and make meaning in the world on the basis of how they define and interpret the situation and people around them.

Symbolic interactionism focuses on the *symbolic* dimensions of human communication. Animals only communicate through **signs**, which are natural symptoms or indicators of an immediate (here and now) stimulus in the environment. Humans, on the other hand, use **symbols**, which are words, numbers, or gestures that "stand for" something else. For instance, imagine someone shaking a can of pet treats. To a pet, the shaking sound serves as a **sign** that a treat is about to be dispensed. In contrast, if someone said to another person, "Please give the dog a treat after dinner," the word "treat" is a **symbol**, which stands for an abstract concept. The word "treat" could refer to a biscuit or a bone, just as "after dinner" could imply dispensing the treat here and now or some time in the future. There is nothing in the physical presence of a shaking can of pet treats that is inherently connected to the (sequentially ordered) symbols T, R, E, A, and T. This word (TREAT) is a symbol that English speakers have assigned to a treat arbitrarily: history and etymology do play a role in the process, but this does not change the essentially arbitrary nature of the relation between signifier and signified. Signs, on the other hand, have a meaning that is naturally connected to the things they signify.

Symbolic interactionism suggests that participants' reactions to situations are mediated through symbols (such as language) and signs (such as the sound of pet treats rattling around in a can). The use of symbols makes conceptual thought possible. Unlike other animals, humans can discuss and imagine things that are not immediately present. In this way, through language, we construct opinions about the past, engage in small talk about the present, and philosophize about the future.

Given the importance of language, symbolic interactionists claim that the capacity of *knowing* is directly connected to the capacity of *naming*. A bigger vocabulary represents a more expansionistic and nuanced bank of knowledge. An example of this principle may be found in the **Sapir–Whorf hypothesis**, which suggests that we do not see or understand issues or concepts for which we do not have words. For instance, before the 1970s we did not have the phrase "sexual harassment." Before the 2000s we did not use the term "blogging." Only with the introduction of these expressions did people begin to thoughtfully contemplate, understand, or know the corresponding realities (what the concepts in question refer to). Through language we understand the world, as well as ourselves.

A foundational aspect of symbolic interaction is its explanation of how people come to know their own identity and have a concept of their own self. Symbolic interaction suggests that we know ourselves largely by taking the point of view of significant others in our life. In this way we create a **looking-glass self** – a self that is created by the others' reactions to us. In other words, we know ourselves by imagining how we look to others. For instance, if your friends and family laugh when you are around them, and if you hear others describe you as silly and good-natured, you might then describe yourself as "fun." The significant others in our lives – friends, family members, teachers, coaches, employers, colleagues, and lovers – play an integral role in creating our identity. However, symbolic interactionists also suggest that the self is a process, created through our own agency as well as through other people's opinions.

This process of identity is made up of the "I" and the "me." The "I" is the novel, unpredictable, unsocialized self that serves as agent and creative force. The "me" is the self as an object, which is constructed through the looking glass of interaction. For instance, consider a person ("Sarah") who is faced with a choice to (1) get to work on time or (2) sleep late. Sarah's "I" thinks about this choice. Although she may want to hit the snooze button, Sarah considers that other people view her as responsible and dedicated (Sarah's "me"). In the end Sarah's "I" drags her out of bed, thinking that sleeping late is just not like "me" – the stable self-concept, which is based on past experience and others' viewpoints.

Qualitative researchers using the symbolic interaction lens view identity, action, and environment as mutually co-constituted. Participants know themselves through their social performances and through others' reactions to them. People learn to perform various selves

---

CONSIDER THIS 3.3

How do I know myself?

Symbolic interactionism suggests that our identity is largely created through interaction and the way other people see us. Consider the following questions:

1   Which few words describe your personality?
2   How is it that you know this about yourself?
3   How did you come to know yourself this way?
4   What evidence do you have that you are this way?
5   In what ways do other people's comments about you or reactions to you help to maintain these notions about your personality?

in different environments or at different stages (Goffman, 1959), and by considering other's actions. In this capacity, language can serve as a **self-fulfilling prophecy**. This means that people tend to shape themselves after others' expectations. An example of a self-fulfilling prophecy is the way in which confident people, who expect to be treated with respect and privacy, indeed attract this treatment from others. In contrast, those who are consistently bullied and treated as idiots are, conversely, more likely to begin seeing themselves as incompetent and worthy of abuse. The self-fulfilling prophecy idea has important practical implications in child rearing, employee socialization, and self-esteem.

Key research foci for symbolic interactionists include identity management, socialization into roles, self-fulfilling prophecies, and the performance of multiple selves in different contexts (such as frontstage and backstage). Ethnographers using this approach believe that participant observation is ideal for studying human interaction, and therefore they pay attention to cultural or organizational myths, rituals, and stages.

A classic qualitative piece using symbolic interaction concepts is "Becoming the Easter Bunny" (Hickey, Thompson, & Foster, 1988). The authors examined the identity development of a mall Easter Bunny over 11 days, through interaction with customers and the environment. The bunny actor reported being initially self-conscious and uncomfortable in the role. However, in the process of interacting with children who shrieked with joy upon seeing him, the bunny began to transform. He no longer felt like a man trapped in a bunny suit but had "become" the Easter Bunny. Work in symbolic interactionism also includes research on the creation of cyber selves through online interaction (Robinson, 2007); on the way sorority coeds negotiate meaning with male gatekeeper bouncers (Scheibel, 1992); and on the way spiritual entities and "divine others" play key roles in the construction of identity (Chatham-Carpenter, 2006).

Potential research questions emanating from this approach include:

- What are the expectations for behavior?
- How do participants define and make sense of themselves in light of others' expectations?
- How do different stages or scenes encourage different types of identity performances? When do participants know to play different roles?
- How do people define themselves? How does this differ from the ways they are described by others?
- How are employees, students, and family or group members socialized into their roles? Are there differences based on gender, sexuality, age or race?
- How do students learn what it means to be successful? Popular?
- What types of family communication affect the self-esteem of children?

Ethnography of communication

The **ethnography of communication (EOC)**, formerly known as the ethnography of speaking, was developed by Dell Hymes (1962) and draws from many different intellectual traditions – including anthropology, folklore, and socio-linguistics. Hymes called for an anthropological approach that focused on speaking as a culturally distinctive activity. EOC, examining local language in use, is both a theoretical perspective and a method in studying the cultural patterns of communication. Hymes and subsequent EOC researchers (e.g. Carbaugh, 2005; Fitch, 1991; Katriel, 1986; Philipsen, 1975) have primarily analyzed oral, spoken, and nonverbal norms of interaction.

Key units of analysis for EOC researchers are the communication event (e.g. a talk show), the communication act (e.g. a specific sentence or a nonverbal signal such as a person who raises the palm and says, "Talk to the hand"), the communication situation (a specific scene or setting of communication, such as backstage), and the speech community (a group that shares expectations for how communication practice should proceed, such as a talk-show audience). EOC researchers study patterns of communication and what those patterns tell us about the people or group studied.

Hymes (1962) developed the mnemonic device SPEAKING to highlight various parts of the EOC approach:

- *S* stands for *setting* or *scene* – suggesting that researchers explore the physical context of the communication.
- *P* refers to the *participants* in the communicative event.
- *E* asks what the *ends*, goals, or outcomes of a particular communicative practice are. These include the intentions of the speaker as well as the consequences of the communication – and the understanding that the two may not be complementary.
- *A* stands for *act sequence*, which refers to the fact that the communication is part of a larger sequence of patterned social interaction.
- *K* asks how the communicative event is *keyed*. This means that researchers should examine the spirit or tone of communication. For example, a joke could be light-hearted or mean-spirited.
- *I* stands for the *instrument* used for communication, whether that be oral voice, embodied gesture, or mediated message.
- *N* refers to the *norms*, rules, or habits of the communicative situation. For example, is it normal to clap, judge, or watch silently in this scene?
- *G* is the *genre* or category of which this event is a type. For example, is the message a type of joking, story-telling, insulting, reminiscing, or something else?

The SPEAKING mnemonic device serves as a helpful way to organize and explore different aspects of data about communication and culture.

EOC is concerned with three central issues (Carbaugh, 2007). First, theorists in this tradition *examine the linguistic rules and resources used by participants*. For example, in some cultures, a woman who holds eye contact with a man for more than a moment is considered flirtatious. Second, EOC researchers examine and *compare messages across different communication media*. For instance, the researcher may examine how rules about flirting are different in face-to-face interactions and in electronic text messages. Third, EOC draws attention to the way *communication reveals rules and norms of identity, relationships, or culture*. Through watching flirtatious communication, for instance, we may better understand a culture's norms about gender, age, status, and power.

EOC studies tend to highlight distinct cultural codes and rules for when and how to speak, as well as the functions and patterns of communication in a particular cultural context – such as a school, an organization, a nation, or an ethnic culture. Every group has its own distinct preferences about communication competence and privileged speech, and these preferences and rules vary across cultures. A classic example of EOC is Philipsen's (1975) research on "speaking like a man" in a town he called "Teamsterville." Using field records of speech behavior, informants' statements, participant observation fieldnotes, and tape-recorded verbal interaction, Philipsen documented the rules for male speech in this working-class community. In particular, by focusing on cultural members' reactions to "out-of-role" behavior, he was able to understand rule expectations and their violations.

The data bolstered the argument that mere talk was an unacceptable means of expression for Teamsterville men, who wanted to assert power or influence. In contrast to physical aggression, speech was seen as ineffective and unmanly, especially in interaction with lower status women and children.

Most EOC research has continued to focus on spoken words in various cultural contexts. However, research has also examined the way people discuss and evaluate mediated communication, such as in television shows and computer use (Katriel, 2004). No matter what the context or topic may be, EOC researchers examine the patterned rules, codes, and expectations for culturally distinctive speech communities. Potential research questions emanating from this theoretical approach include:

- What are the patterns or habits of speech in this group?
- What are the functions of this speech?
- What are the cultural rules for speaking in this group? How do they differ among different demographic groups?
- What counts as being a competent speaker in this group?

Feminism

Feminism is a theoretical approach that begins with several key assumptions, including the following: (a) that patriarchy (or male dominance) exists; (b) that it unfairly reduces the role and value of women; and (c) that change – usually defined as equity – is preferable to the status quo. Feminism is not the same as being feminine or being a female. Indeed, men can and do conduct feminist research. As in many theories connected to the critical paradigm, a common focus in feminism is emancipation or liberation. Feminists aim to free a marginalized group from oppressive situations in society, organizations, families, or relationships.

There are various types of feminism, which I will only briefly describe here (but see Butler, 1999; Lindlof & Taylor, 2011). *Liberal feminism* suggests that women should be included in the same structures and should have the same rights as men; *Marxist feminism* links the oppression of women to capitalism; and *radical feminism* argues that women are foundationally dissimilar to men and should work toward overthrowing patriarchy. *Standpoint feminism* asserts that, because women hold a marginalized place, they are able to have a unique and significant view of the world, which is not available to dominant groups. In consequence, their voices are integral to processes of transformation. *Transnational/postcolonial feminists* examine how discourses of gender, race, and citizenship justify and reproduce relationships of dominance within and between nation-states. Finally, *poststructuralist* or *postmodern feminists* examine how gender identities are continually reconstructed through societal and organizational discourses of power and hegemony.

An example of qualitative research using feminist theory is Trethewey's (1997) study of low-income single mothers. Trethewey explored the ways participants resisted their social service organization by breaking rules, not showing up for appointments, and refusing to divulge their life situation in the researcher's presence. Feminists have examined the intersections of sex, race, and class (Allen, 1998; Ashcraft, 2011), and in this way they continue to grapple with the politics of various types of difference and marginalization. They have also studied sexual harassment and abuse (Scarduzio & Geist-Martin, 2008), work–life balance concerns (Buzzanell & Liu, 2005), and issues of masculinity (Ashcraft, 2005; Mumby, 1998).

Feminists are often interested in better understanding how gender influences researcher authority or autonomy in the field, or how it plays a role in the type of responses received in an interview. Indeed feminist research is characterized by its method and form as much as by its topic and theoretical approach (Wheatley, 1994). Feminists believe that researchers have a *moral* responsibility to be aware of their own power, the potential for its abuse, and issues of reciprocity. They adopt an *ethic of care*, treating the people they study as collaborative research partners. Another hallmark of feminist research is *polyvocality*, or the "possibility for allowing for many voices, rather than simply that of the researcher" (Sanger, 2003, p. 37). Given this feature, feminists are more likely to relinquish control in interviews and approach them as friendly free-flowing discussions rather than structured question–answer sessions.

Research questions emanating from feminist theory might include:

- How do these data evidence issues of patriarchy? Gender differences? Femininity? Masculinity? Sexuality?
- How are people of different genders, sexes, and sexual orientations differently socialized, treated, or awarded power in this context?
- What is missing in these data that speaks to issues of gender?
- How can the methods of the study best embody a feminist ethic of care?

Participatory action research

Participatory action research (PAR) (Kemmis & McTaggart, 2000, 2005) is based upon the notion that researchers should work together with research participants to help them address, understand, or improve local issues or dilemmas. PAR – and similar approaches such as critical action research, classroom action research, action learning, and industrial action research – explores the contextual dynamics of the field by viewing participants as co-researchers. So PAR is collaborative and dictates that the researcher work *with* participants rather than conduct research *on* them (Reason, 1994).

Given its focus on action, PAR is especially well suited for understanding and promoting transformation. In the PAR framework, researchers engage in a cyclical process in which they collectively address and solve problems through a spiral of (1) planning a change; (2) acting on that change; (3) observing and reflecting on the process and consequences of that change; (4) and then repeating (Kemmis & McTaggart, 2005). The goal of PAR is to combine the researcher's theoretical knowledge and experience with the participants' practical knowledge in ways that make the two parties inform and challenge each other. In acting toward this goal, PAR research is marked by shared ownership of research projects, community-based analysis of social problems, and an orientation toward community action.

PAR and other action approaches are especially well suited for those who take a *phronetic* (or problem-based) contextual approach to research. Because participants are engaged from the beginning in helping solve a problem, by their design, PAR projects have a built-in practical rationale. However, PAR researchers must also feel comfortable with sacrificing some level of ownership and control – and, in some cases, with giving up strict methodological and technical rigor – so that participants can truly serve as co-researchers. Furthermore, PAR researchers tread a fine line between guiding the participants and imposing their own opinion or methodology.

Using participatory approaches, qualitative researchers have examined myriad topics – for instance, as pictured in Figure 3.2, access to healthy foods (LeGreco, 2012), classroom learning (Mills, 2000), community engagement (Sarri & Sarri, 1992), and organizational transformation. In a study of an emergency room, Eisenberg, Baglia, and Pynes (2006) paired with hospital administrators to improve the flow and speed of patient care. The research team analyzed hospital documents, signs, and emergency room layout. They also engaged in participant observation of the emergency room and conducted interviews with various stakeholders. The result? Using PAR, the research team created a narrative that described the challenges of the emergency room and offered potential remedies. The narrative was circulated among employees and revised on the basis of employee feedback. This combination or coupling of employee insider knowledge with the research team's qualitative analysis served to produce a final narrative in commonsense terms. The report helped the hospital's advisory board to understand challenges with the emergency room's current practices and encouraged its members to implement procedural and practical changes. In the process, the perspectives of typically marginalized employees were heard by hospital officials, and the study extended theoretical notions related to backstage communication and the localization of illness.

Researchers can embrace some participatory goals while still maintaining a more traditional research approach (Tracy, 2007). For example, researchers can (a) ask participants about current dilemmas and shape research to help shed light on these issues; (b) incorporate participant voices; and (c) present their research findings back to practitioners. Through dialogue, participants can help produce knowledge that is directly useful. As Giddens (1979) points out, research participants are not "cultural dopes" (p. 71) – rather "they can give cogent reasons for their intentions and actions, and generally demonstrate a sophisticated (although not necessarily social scientific) understanding of the situations they inhabit" (Kemmis & McTaggart, 2000, p. 573).

Figure 3.2 Students from the University of North Carolina at Greensboro interview a farmer in a participatory action research class project. The farmer's market is part of the Warnersville Community Food effort, which addresses food deserts and access to healthy foods in low-income communities. Pictured from left: Larry Smith, Matthew Wallace, Cynthia Cukiernik, and Kelsey Griffith. Photo taken by supervising researcher on the project, Marianne LeGreco (LeGreco, 2012).

Research questions emerging from participatory action research may include:

- What do participants articulate as dilemmas or key issues in the scene?
- What do participants have to say about the reasons why these issues are problematic?
- How and in what ways would participants like to transform their culture/classroom/organization/community/family?
- How do participants make sense of, and reflect upon, the issues that are evident in participant observation, interviews, and other data collected?

Sensemaking

Karl Weick's (1979) theory of **sensemaking** emphasizes meaning making, ambiguity, and identity. As such, it is well suited for qualitative and interpretive data analyses. According to Weick, people make sense of their environments retrospectively, by taking into account their behaviors, talk, and action. Sensemaking theory is often summed up in the question, "How can I know what I think until I see what I say?" (Weick, 2001, p. 189). This approach contrasts with cognitive approaches, which suggest that thinking *precedes* external talk and action. Sensemaking theory encourages researchers to examine participants' (inter) actions as a method for understanding what they are thinking and believing. It's an "outside-in" approach.

Sensemaking is made manifest in collective and chaotic situations – and its study has been especially fruitful for examining the ways groups act in ambiguous emergency crises such as wildfires, airline crashes, and other disasters. These studies show how people lose and regain sense – as well as their sense of self – through talk and action. An actual, implied, or imagined presence of others is imperative for sensemaking to occur. In consequence, methods that include actors and audiences – such as participant observation and interviewing – are ideal for exploring how participants make sense of a scene.

Sensemaking is made up of three interrelated phases: *enactment, selection,* and *retention.* To understand these phases, it's important to reflect back on the core question of the theory: "How do I know what I think until I see what I say?" *Enactment* refers to the "what I say" part of the theory, which is best taken to be the chaotic raw data and mundane interaction that make up our lives. Through enactment, participants single out certain issues for acting and commenting upon. Our environment is complex and open to numerous conflicting interpretations. Through enactment, participants limit the potential interpretations of a situation – drawing attention to some issues more than to others.

For example, imagine two roommates – Derrick and Pete – hanging out, checking email, and surfing their social networking websites. The duo begins to talk about (the "what I say" part of sensemaking) some recently uploaded photos of his cousin bungee jumping off a cliff in New Zealand. By chatting about these photos and messages (instead of talking about all the other messages from, or aspects of, his cousin or New Zealand), Derrick and Pete begin to *enact* a response that frames and begins to organize the situation.

The second phase of sensemaking is *selection* ("until I see"). Here, participants begin to notice and select possible interpretations of the situation. Through selection, they attend to the question of "what is *a* story here" (Weick, 2001, p. 461) – one that is significant, relevant, interesting, or preferred. Relating again to social networking messages, after the discussion about Derrick's cousin bungee jumping in the selection phase, the roommates may joke about how New Zealanders are "endorphin addicts." In doing so, the duo constructs an interpretation according to which New Zealanders are crazy, quirky, and cool.

Finally, in the third phase of sensemaking, the selected interpretation ("what I think") is *retained* for future situations. For instance, the roommates will remember the above script – that Kiwis are endorphin junkies. When thrilling opportunities arise in the future (e.g. sky-diving, hiking, shark swimming), the duo may call upon this retained interpretation. For instance, they may automatically assume that a co-worker from New Zealand would love to go parasailing. In many ways, the process of *retention* can be considered the outcome of sensemaking. However, the three-phase process is circular in nature. Information amassed in the retention phase is acted out in future enacted activity.

The three-phase sensemaking process serves to sensitize researchers to the ways meaning is chosen, interpreted, and retained by participants. My colleagues and I have used this theory in examining the challenges faced by firefighters in making sense of their identities and of unpredictable organizational environments (Tracy, Myers, & Scott, 2006). Firefighters work in an environment that is – alternately – dangerous, boring, and disgusting, and they are expected to be tough, yet nurturing. Sensemaking theory helped us to see how firefighters' derogatory jokes about clients serve as a shorthand that simplifies the complex expectations in their job. Although the use of humor helps employees make sense of identity-threatening and chaotic situations, jokes can simultaneously over-simplify the environment or stereotype clients. In this way sensemaking is both liberating and constraining.

Researchers interested in using a sensemaking theoretical framework might consider the following research questions:

- What parts of the scene are marked by paradox, ambiguity, and identity threat?
- What do participants say and how do they act in such situations?
- How do participants define themselves in the face of their actions and environment?
- How do participants make sense of the scene through enactment, selection, and retention?
- How do participants construct the environment in terms of how they have defined themselves?
- What are the multiple interpretations available for a certain scene? What interpretations are chosen by the actors, and what does this suggest about their sensemaking?
- How are these interpretations retained and called upon for future sensemaking?

Structuration

As noted in Chapter 2, a theory that is particularly helpful for examining action and structure is Giddens' (1979; 1984) **structuration theory**. This theory directs the researcher's attention to the relationship between individuals and institutions. In particular, it focuses on the ways in which cultures, organizations, and social systems are constituted or created through the micro-practices of individual people. A key part of structuration theory is the **duality of structure**. This refers to the idea that rules, policies, and structures are only made "valid" when individuals follow them and make decisions based upon them. Oftentimes, people turn to societal or institutional rules as helpful resources; but, as I explain below, people reproduce these rules in doing so.

For instance, a student might refer to a syllabus that states that every student can get two absences without penalty, thus claiming his right to these "freebie" absences. By calling upon and reproducing the policy, the student strengthens and further engrains it. Future students will likely get two freebie absences, even if in the future it may be more appropriate for them to receive more or less. In short, structures limit a person's resources, and individual action simultaneously strengthens the structure. The duality of structure helps to explain why institutional rules are so difficult to change. In fact, ironically, resistance can strengthen the constraints people face. For instance, by complaining about people who cut in in a line, people reaffirm that, if one is going to wait, lines are the proper form in which to do it (rather than, for instance, waiting in a big loose crowd, or taking a number and then lounging in the adjacent bar).

Structuration theory, through Giddens' concept of the *dialectic of control*, also helps to explain transformation and change. The dialectic of control – which is similar to that of hegemony – suggests that the power of dominant groups is not just top-down; rather it depends on the action of less powerful people. The power of politicians, teachers, and bosses is only maintained when their subordinates agree to give up a part of their freedom in order to receive benefits in return – for example in the form of safety from criminals, a college degree, or a paycheck. However, the less powerful groups never give up all their autonomy; therefore they can transform even the strongest rules or institutions. Employees can steal office supplies; students can cheat; and citizens can break the law.

Qualitative researchers coming from a structuration perspective examine how individual micro-practices serve to uphold and disrupt larger structures of power in work, play, and relationships. Indeed, by examining talk, we can see how individuals begin to rely on recipes and scripts to receive guidance in their social action (Golden, Kirby, & Jorgenson, 2006). Such scripts may serve to reproduce or disrupt societal structures of gender, race, and class (Tracy & Rivera, 2010), organizational values, norms, or policies (Kirby & Krone, 2002), or patterns of behavior among roommates and lovers – such as who takes out the trash (Alberts & Trethewey, 2007). Structuration researchers carefully analyze these scripts and how they interrelate with societal and institutional structures.

Research questions that emerge from a structuration approach may include:

- What are the primary rules and structures that are governing action in this scene?
- How are everyday practices or actions serving to resist, reproduce, or legitimize these structures?
- How does mundane communication and interaction serve to transform or weaken these structures?

In summary

This chapter has reviewed four primary research paradigms and the ways in which qualitative research is situated within them. Having a basic understanding of these paradigms is essential for entering the conversation of research and ensuring that your methodological practices are consistent with your way of understanding knowledge and reality. Furthermore, the paradigms help delineate how and why people view research, methodology, and knowledge in different ways and hold different goals and criteria for what counts as "good" research. For instance, an interpretive scholar strives for empathic understanding, a critical scholar for transformation, a postmodernist for messy alternative representations, and a positivist scholar for generalization – issues that we will return to in Chapter 11.

We also looked at seven theoretical approaches that commonly use qualitative data and methodology: Geertz's interpretivism, symbolic interactionism, the ethnography of communication, feminism, participatory action research, sensemaking, and structuration theory. As theoretical frameworks, all these approaches attempt to explain phenomena – issues like identity, power, structures, change, and habits of speech. Many of these approaches overlap in topic or conceptual focus, and researchers often choose tools and ideas from various theories and paradigmatic lenses to explain phenomena or contexts.

In the early stages of research, these theories can usefully serve as lenses that guide methodological practices and the choice of points of focus. Revisiting this chapter, as well as exploring other applicable conceptual frameworks, will be helpful as you travel through the qualitative research project. Different theories and concepts will feel more applicable and more important at various times, and circling back to them will provide fresh insight for bringing meaning to your data.

KEY TERMS

→ **axiology**   a discipline dealing with the values associated with an area of research and theorizing (e.g. the values of social justice are emphasized by the critical paradigm)

→ **crisis of representation**   a common postmodern notion according to which all representations of meaning depend on their relationships with other signs, and therefore it is impossible to identify one single true representation of reality

→ **critical paradigm**   a way of viewing the world that is based on the idea that thought is fundamentally mediated by power relations and that data cannot be separated from ideology (see *ideology*)

→ **deconstructionism**   a postmodern method of analysis introduced by Derrida in which researchers dismantle a text, accentuate foundational word opposition, and show the complexity and instability of the text

→ **différance**   a primary theoretical basis of deconstructionism, this is a method in which researchers point out the non-presence of certain words or meanings in a text

→ **duality of structure**   a key part of structuration theory, this concept refers to the idea that structure is created from the top down *and* from the the bottom up; structures are only made "valid" when individuals follow them and make decisions that are based upon them

→ **epistemology**   a traditional branch of philosophy that is concerned with the nature of knowledge

→ **ethnography of communication (EOC)**   a theoretical framework developed by Dell Hymes, which is concerned with linguistic rules and how communication reveals norms of identity, relationships, or culture

→ **feminism**   a theoretical approach that seeks to transform patriarchy; often marked by research on topics related to women, an ethical method of care, self-reflexivity, and attention to multiple voices in the field

→ **hegemony**   occurs when people see hierarchical relationships as normal, natural, and unchangeable and therefore accept, consent, internalize, and are complicit in reproducing norms that are not in their own best interests

hermeneutics   the discipline of interpreting texts by empathically imagining the experience, motivations, and context of the speaker/author, and then by engaging in a circular analysis that alternates between the data text and the situated scene

hyperreality   the postmodern idea that many representations or signifiers are constructed and consumed, but lack a specific or materially authentic referent

ideology   a set of doctrines, myths, or beliefs, which guide or have power over individuals, groups, or societies

incommensurability   a situation where choosing one paradigm or way of seeing the world necessarily precludes another paradigm or way of seeing the world (e.g. the positivist notion of a single true reality is incommensurable with the postmodern view that reality is multiple)

interpretive paradigm   a way of seeing both reality and knowledge as constructed and reproduced through communication, interaction, and practice

looking-glass self   a concept borrowed from symbolic interactionism, which suggests that identity is largely created through the reactions of others (i.e. we see what others tell us they see)

methodology   strategies for gathering, collecting, and analyzing data

ontology   a traditional branch of philosophy, which is concerned with the nature of reality

paradigms   preferred ways of understanding reality, building knowledge, and gathering information about the world

participatory action research (PAR)   a form of research based upon the notion that researchers should work together with research participants to help them address, understand, or improve local issues or dilemmas

pastiche   a postmodern term that refers to the endless imitation, appropriation, and recycling of older cultural forms with a view to making new but familiar forms (e.g. much of what is fashionable today layers trends from the past)

positivist paradigm   perhaps the most common paradigm among traditional scientists, it suggests that there is one true reality "out there" in the world – one that already exists and is waiting to be discovered

postmodern/poststructural paradigm   a paradigm that approaches knowledge and power as dispersed, unstable, and plural, highlighting occasions of domination and self-subordination, but also avenues for resistance and change

post-positivism   like positivism, this paradigm assumes a single true reality, but it suggests that humans' understanding of reality is inherently partial and that it is impossible to fully capture reality

rhizomatic   a term derived from the ancient Greek noun *rhizoma* ("root"), this qualifier emerges in the postmodern paradigm, where it refers to the idea that meaning is root-like and therefore interconnected, interdependent, and complex

Sapir–Whorf hypothesis   a hypothesis connected to symbolic interactionism; it suggests that we do not see or understand issues or concepts for which we do not have words

sedimented   solid and difficult to remedy; the term is used by poststructural scholars, who argue that the examination of power relations is necessary in order to understand why some problems and ideas are held with more merit than others

self-fulfilling prophecy   the idea that people tend to shape themselves according to the expectations of others

sensemaking   a theory developed by Karl Weick and typified by the three-part process of enactment, selection, and retention; it emphasizes meaning making, ambiguity, and identity

signs   natural symptoms or indicators of an immediate (here and now) stimulus in the environment (e.g. thunder is a *sign* of storm)

simulacrum   in postmodern theory, this term refers to a representation that is a copy of something that never actually existed (e.g. Disneyland's "Main Street")

social construction   the interpretive idea that reality and knowledge are constructed and reproduced by people through communication, interaction, and practice

structuration theory   this theory directs the researcher's attention to the relationship between individuals and institutions; it focuses on the ways cultures, organizations, and social systems are constituted or created through the micro-practices of individual people

symbol   a word or gesture that arbitrarily stands for an abstract concept; the linear sequence of letters S-T-O-R-M serves as an English-language symbol for a storm, with which it has no inherent connection

symbolic interactionism   researchers using this theoretical approach (which was developed by Herbert Blumer) investigate how meaning and identity are co-created through interaction

theory   a bundled system of principles that serve to explain certain phenomena

thick description   a concept coined by Clifford Geertz, "thick description" refers to the practice of going beyond surface understandings, to explore the contextual meanings of behaviors

triangulate   a practice in which researchers use multiple types and sources of data, variant methods of collection, as well as various theoretical frames and multiple researchers

verstehen   a German verb (meaning "to understand"), used in English as a noun describing participants' first-person perspective on their personal experience as well as on their society, culture, and history.

CHAPTER 4

Fieldwork and fieldplay
Negotiating access and exploring the scene

Qualitative Research Methods: Collecting Evidence, Crafting Analysis, Communicating Impact, First Edition. Sarah J. Tracy.
© 2013 Sarah J. Tracy. Published 2013 by Blackwell Publishing Ltd.

Fieldwork – or what often feels to me like "fieldplay" – is among the most engaging and interesting parts of conducting qualitative research. In this chapter we will discuss what it means to be a fieldworker and, specifically, how to prepare yourself for participant observation, negotiate access, and begin exploring the scene. Along the way, this chapter investigates various tools of fieldwork that will prepare you for its joys and challenges. Some of these tools are personal, such as how to best prepare your body and soul for field uncertainties. Others are logistical, for instance creating contact logs and participant demographic breakdown grids. Finally, I introduce several exploratory methods: briefing interviews, participant diaries, documents, artifacts, maps, and narrative tours.

Please note: some readers may want to skip ahead to Chapter 5 and read about research proposals and institutional review board (IRB) approval before this one. That said, I place this chapter on negotiating access first because, in my experience, until researchers know which sites and participants are willing to be studied, it's virtually impossible to write up a focused research proposal and get human subjects' approval. Furthermore, the process of negotiating access allows important insight into the phenomena and research questions that the project will most fruitfully examine. Suffice it to say that negotiating access and writing research proposals are an iterative dance, and proof of site support may be necessary before an IRB application is approved.

A participant observation primer

Participant observation, also known as **fieldwork**, is a method through which researchers generate understanding and knowledge by watching, interacting, asking questions, collecting documents, making audio or video recordings, and reflecting after the fact (Lofland & Lofland, 1995). Delamont (2004) explains that fieldwork refers to "the data-collection phase, when the investigators leave their desks and go out 'into the field.' The 'field' is metaphorical: it is not a real field, but a setting or a population" (p. 218). I add the term **fieldplay** because my experiences suggest that adventure, curiosity and playfulness are big parts of the participant observation experience. *Fieldplayers* are filled with good humor, improvise, and do not take themselves too seriously. Although I primarily use the expression "fieldwork" in this book, field research includes lots of play as well.

The good news is that, even before reading about participant observation, you can feel assured that you already have some experience of doing it. However, there is a huge difference between the casual type of hanging-out participant observation we might do at a coffee shop or fitness center, and the focused systematic participant observation that is a hallmark of field research. Fieldworkers systematically plan their research, are mindful of their surroundings, and take note of a wide spectrum of information – even the mundane and trivial. Along the way, they reflect on their own biases and engage all their senses. Participant observation includes not only *studying people*, but also *learning from* (and *with*) *people* – particularly through analyzing three fundamental aspects of human experience: (a) what people do (*cultural behavior*); (b) what people know (*cultural knowledge*); and (c) what things people make and use (*cultural artifacts*) (Spradley, 1980).

In learning about these issues, fieldworkers may collect a range of pertinent data such as activities, stories, conversations, maps, photos, brochures, or electronic and mediated messages. In addition to narrating the scene through words, field researchers may also count things (e.g. residents, the size of classes, or the number of women or men in a certain profession), conduct a survey, or take a census – but these data are collected within the naturalistic context. To collect such data, participant observation is sustained over time, explicitly notes the goals of observation, attends alertly to various issues in the scene, and includes the interpretation and the words of participants in their naturally occurring context (Weick, 1985). Of course, to succeed in any of these endeavors, first you need to get access to the scene.

Knock, knock, knocking on participants' doors: negotiating access

As discussed in Chapter 1, the most basic question for qualitative researchers is "What is going on here?" A key part of this question is the word "here." And before you can even begin to answer such a question, you need to find people and places that will let you "in" to study their lives, viewpoints, and routines. Despite the popularity of reality television and websites like YouTube, many people do not purposefully seek out publicity for their every move and word. A key part of qualitative research design is finding people who want to participate in research. This is one reason why qualitative researchers call the people involved "**participants**" rather than "subjects."

Participants have agency and free will. They can be agreeable, helpful, cantankerous, secretive, cautious, or a combination of these. Qualitative researchers study *with* participants, rather than conduct research *on* them. Unfortunately, the back stories of negotiating access and seeking out participants are usually hidden and missing from published reports. Below are several narratives that illustrate the complexities and significant amount of time necessary for getting "in."

Confessional tales of getting in

Qualitative researchers have to be comfortable with not being in charge. As a field researcher, your status or acceptance is not likely to be determined by your title, degree, or level of education. Instead, particular participants in that scene will determine what deserves access. Do you fit in? Are you likeable? Can you offer something to participants in return for their cooperation? There is no one right way of negotiating access, and each situation will be unique, even for the most seasoned researcher. Here are several confessional tales of how I negotiated access for qualitative research.

Riding my mentor's coattails: Citywest 911 emergency call-takers

One of my first qualitative research projects took place at an emergency call center, Citywest 911 (this is a pseudonym). At the time, I was a 22-year-old MA student interested in what I called the "routinization of crisis." I wanted to study interactions in which one of the participants viewed the communicative sequence as routine, whereas the other participant viewed it as an emergency or crisis. Earlier that year I had tried, unsuccessfully, to get access to study HIV counselors and their patients. Then a professor and mentor, Dr. Karen Tracy (no relation), asked whether I might be interested in working with her on a research project with 911 call-takers. I was delighted and readily agreed. The site and participants fit my theoretical interests. Additionally, I was excited to learn from Karen and felt lucky that her credibility as a credentialed and well-networked expert may rub off on me.

We began the research project by first reviewing news articles about 911 in order to learn about recent challenges from the emergency communication systems throughout the nation, and how problems during 911 calls could lead to tragedy. We also asked our friends and family whether anyone knew a 911 call-taker we could interview. Using our personal networks, we found two operators who provided an overview of their job, its challenges, and the contact information for their supervisors. With this background in hand, Karen drafted a letter and made a phone call to the "captain" of a nearby city's 911 center. We met with him, and Karen did most of the talking. She convinced him that we would not be a bother and that our research might instead provide insight into 911 communication breakdowns. About two months after conceptualizing the project, Karen and I were regularly spending time observing the inner workings of a 911 dispatch center.

Given Karen's interest in the conversational specifics of calls, she focused her data-gathering on archived recorded calls. Meanwhile, I got my own headset and hung out with the call-takers on the call-room floor. Over the course of six months, my research interest moved from the "routinization of crisis" to emotional labor – considered to be the work employees do to shape their emotional performances in line with organizational norms and expectations. I had read some articles about how some workers must create an emotional façade in their work, and I realized that this concept could be really helpful for my own study. My focal research question was: *How do call-takers manage emotion through communication?*

Becoming a full participant: Radiant Sun *cruise ship*

One year later, my grandmother treated the family to a holiday cruise. I was approaching the end of my MA studies, and I thought: "Heck, this is a perfect emotional labor job." From my vantage point as a cruise passenger, such a job seemed glamorous and virtually unattainable. I wondered what it might be like to actually work there. I proceeded to contact several companies based in the US and compiled an application. I had performed as a singer, dancer, and actress in high school, and that, coupled with my teaching background, seemed to fit the "cruise staff" requirements. I was called back by one of the companies, and during the on-site interview I was that told the company was "seeking enthusiastic young people willing to work with old people." I was offered an eight-month gig as a "junior assistant cruise director," and notions of actually conducting focused research were fleeting and fuzzy.

After accepting the job, I decided it would indeed be worthwhile to conduct some research while working on the ship. I discussed the possibility with my direct supervisor, the cruise director, who viewed my request as harmless. I wrote up a description of the research, and he granted permission. I dug up all my old 911 informed consent forms (more on informed consent and institutional review in Chapter 5) and modified them for the cruise ship. I began to take fieldnotes, keep a personal journal, and record interviews with the staff. My guiding research question was: *How do cruise ship activities coordinators play a part in their own emotional subordination?*

Two years later, my first single-authored article, which was based on these data, was "in press" – when I received a phone call from the journal's editor. She wanted to ensure that my research had passed Human Subjects and Institutional Review.

Uh oh.

I explained that I had not been a university employee or a student at the time of the research, and, given that I was out at sea (without phone or Internet access in the 1990s), I had no idea how to get such approvals. The editor asked if I had received signed approval from the cruise ship's parent company, and again I said no. I explained that, as an employee, I was directed to never contact headquarters, but to direct all inquiries to my direct supervisor instead. The journal requested evidence of all those informed consent forms. I also was asked to omit a few identifying and potentially damaging details from the essay.

I complied. After several anxious weeks, the editor was convinced of my due diligence, and the journal's lawyers felt as though there was nothing in the piece that would prompt a lawsuit. They went forward with the article. I sighed with relief, and pledged that I would never again forgo formal institutional review.

Accessing a closed organization: women's minimum and Nouveau jail

For my doctoral dissertation I wanted to turn my eyes to a profession that experienced high levels of burnout. I had read about America's skyrocketing incarceration rate, prison overcrowding, and correctional officers' (aka guards') abysmally low life expectancy – 59 years (Tracy, 2005). These contextual problems, coupled with my interest in what Goffman (1961a) calls **total institutions** – organizations like cruise ships, prisons, and hospitals, where some inhabitants of the institution never go home and therefore are controlled in a more total manner than in typical organizations – spurred me to study correctional officers.

Unfortunately, I had absolutely no background in the criminal justice literature and no relationships with people associated with jails or prisons. I also learned that very few qualitative studies had ever been done behind bars, due to correctional institutions' concerns with security and secrecy. Nonetheless, I felt determined to find a way in. Through a preliminary literature review, I found several researchers at nearby universities who had conducted qualitative research on prisons and jails. I called, emailed, and met with them, explained my research interests, and they generously offered advice about their contacts at various facilities. I also attended several volunteer sessions for prison ministry groups. These interactions armed me not only with an interesting viewpoint on prison work, but with contact information for local correctional employees.

I constructed a database of names, phone numbers, my relationship with the contact, and its relevance to my research. I eventually phoned the volunteer coordinators at five facilities and referenced the key personnel and the researchers I had met with so far. I explained my qualitative experience and my desire to "hang out" with correctional officers and tell their story from their point of view. I offered my volunteer services (whether they wanted me to sweep the lobby or teach public speaking). I also offered to share feedback based on my research.

Through a series of discussions, I narrowed down my choices to two different facilities: Nouveau Jail and Women's Minimum Prison (both are pseudonyms). I then sent the volunteer coordinators at each of these facilities a packet of information that included my academic résumé, a copy of one of my earlier published 911 articles, and a cover letter that overviewed my research interests. A week later, I set up a face-to-face meeting with the volunteer coordinator, jail captain, and prison warden. During the meeting I distributed and discussed a one-page proposal that overviewed the study's rationale, the proposed method, my past experience, and a statement about confidentiality (this proposal will be detailed later in this chapter). At the end of the meeting – about three months after I began pursuing the project – the gatekeepers agreed to my research.

I immediately set up a schedule for my ongoing participant observation. I also carefully filled out my institutional review board forms and ensured that I had official permission on letterhead from my correctional contacts. Over the course of 11 months I shadowed officers, attended training sessions, and conducted interviews. The research was guided by the question: *How is emotion discursively constructed through employee interactions and organizational norms?*

When I was about three quarters through with my data collection, I received a sinister phone message from the director of research at the Department of Corrections (DOC) – someone whom I had never spoken or been referred to. His message was something like this:

Hi Sarah. This is the director of research for the Department of Corrections. I understand that you have been conducting research at one of our facilities, and you have *not* gone through the official permission process. *You must immediately cease all research activities and contact our office at once.*

Oh no. Not again. Needless to say, I was confounded. I thought I had gone through all the right permissions. What had gone wrong?

After calling the DOC research office, I learned that, because I had negotiated access through the prison *volunteer* office rather than through the *research* office, the institution had not given proper permission. After a series of tense conversations with various members of the organization, I filled out the proper permission forms, and the DOC research office accorded me retroactive permission. I was able to resume research and, more importantly, use the 171 hours of data I had previously collected. Whew!

Several months later I presented my findings to the organization. The director of research who had left the sinister message showed interest – especially about a typology of contradictions I constructed, which explained how correctional officers navigate their jobs and how these tensions play a key role in their burnout. I told the director that this finding was actually a surprise to me. Before engaging in data collection and analysis, I would never have been able to predict the role of contradiction in officers' burnout, nor was that finding documented previously in the research literature.

As the director turned to leave, I stopped him and said, "Sir, when I was first negotiating access, I had no idea what I would find. I just wanted to tell correctional officers' stories from their points of view." He nodded, and I continued, "I'm curious. Would you have given me – a doctoral student with no background in criminal justice – permission to 'hang out' in your facility if I would have actually gone through the official path of seeking permission from your office?"

Without a beat, he answered, "Absolutely not." I let the irony of this sink in.

My "mistake" of seeking access to the organization as a volunteer was a key part of my success in navigating research into this closed and total organization. If I had gone about negotiating access the "right" way, I likely would have never gotten in. Mind you, I'm not encouraging you to make that mistake. I'm just sayin'.

Do some homework before approaching the scene

These three vignettes personify the unique circumstances of negotiating access. My confessional tales illustrate the twists and turns of "getting in" and how access is a continual and time-consuming process. The approach is different depending on the context, the participants, the season, and – perhaps – who picks up the phone on a certain day. However, there are several tips that can hopefully ease the way.

First, many researchers begin their qualitative projects in spaces in which they are already a member. This may include your own family, place of work, church, school group, or classroom. Being a member gives you instant access; however, just the fact that you're in the scene does not mean that the scene comes with a magical set of research questions or a built-in research design.

It also makes sense to make use of family and friends' networks. Do you want to study a high-tech company? A softball teammate may work at one. How about the courtroom? Perhaps one of your parents knows someone who is a judge or bailiff. Send out emails or post inquiries on your social networking websites. Knowing someone, even if it's a friend of a friend, can greatly ease the way.

Another option is to work with someone who has credibility in that scene. You could enter as an intern, apprentice, or volunteer and get to know a boss before seeking research access. Or you may partner with a more senior researcher, as I did in my 911 project. Senior researchers have more experience and maturity. At the same time, a fancy title or expert credentials can also be a liability. Gatekeepers may be more willing to open their doors to a young student who pleads "I have to do a class assignment" than to a high-level expert who makes them feel nervous about official research.

Finally, negotiating access usually requires a fair amount of homework and legwork. As noted in my confessional tales, I met with various people – researchers, volunteers, and employees – before I ever tried to contact the actual organizational gatekeepers. Doing so provided an understanding of the context and a handy list of contacts. Although I do not advise name-dropping, researchers who subtly communicate a familiarity with the scene and its primary actors are more likely to be viewed by gatekeepers as friendly and potentially trustworthy.

Given the need for keeping track of contacts, I recommend creating a **contact information log** from the beginning of your research project and adding to it throughout your work. This shorthand log (which is separate from thick descriptions in fieldnotes) should include contact information at the very least. Furthermore, noting some personal details can be useful later, sometimes long after the project is complete, when your memories are less immediate. Researcher's Notepad 4.1 provides an excerpt from a contact log I used in my prison and jail dissertation research.

RESEARCHER'S NOTEPAD 4.1

Contact information log

Jail/Prison Contact Sheet	Last Revised: [Date]
Name and Contact Information	**Comments**
Joe Smith (assistant, Sally) Volunteer Coordinator Women's Minimum [Contact information]	Main contact at Women's Minimum. Met with him and took tour of facility 4/12/99. Set to meet with him again to finalize my work. Note to self: down the line, bring his assistant donuts for the office.
Michael Todd Education Coordinator [Contact information]	Spoke with him 4/17/99 on phone. He seems friendly and liked my past work. Asked if I would speak at an inmate graduation. Remember to mention him in future chats with prison warden.
Dr. Samuel Johns Professor, Metro State [Contact information]	Referred to me by a criminal justice professor. Met with him at Charlie's coffee shop 4/16/99. He gave me several articles – is past jail captain for Nouveau Jail – was instrumental in new jail design.
Scott Sams, Program Director Information Center/Library National Institute of Corrections [Address and directions to center]	Samuel Johns gave me Scott's name. Samuel said that he could connect me with a trainer at the Academy of Corrections and with a scholar who has researched female correctional officers dealing with stress.

Note: For the purpose of this example, the names above are pseudonyms.

Please don't reject me! Seeking research permission

An important step in contacting the scene is determining the **gatekeeper**, or the "decider," who actually has the power to grant access. This is usually easier said than done. The person at the front desk or the name listed as "contact" on the website may only field initial inquiries, while holding very little authority. Or perhaps your initial contact is a personal friend – say, a long-lost uncle who is a member of the group – and while this is convenient, you do not know whether your uncle is well liked and respected by the people you want to work with. You can make use of advocates, but try to avoid having your research idea contaminated by unpopular people in the scene. No matter who the initial contact person is, generally the researcher must talk to a series of gatekeepers.

Depending on your communication strengths and the nature of the gatekeeper, you need to recognize if you are likely to make a better impression via email, letter, appearing in person, or interacting on the phone. Whatever communication medium you select, given the high stakes of initial discussions with gatekeepers, it makes sense to carefully practice how you will frame your research and experience. Written correspondence needs to be professional and phone messages articulate. It makes sense to hone the pitch for your study. As they say, "there is only one chance to make a first impression." In early interactions, I recommend that researchers provide a *broad overview* of their interests and qualifications – rather than a detailed description of a specific research interest. You might explain that you simply want to learn about the culture of a group, or want to understand the participants' story from their point of view. Your initial spiel with gatekeepers is not the time to use technical, academic, or theoretical language.

Researchers should also consider their visual and physical presentation. A rule of thumb is to present yourself similarly to participants, just like when interviewing for a new job (Goodall, Goodall, & Schiefelbein, 2010). If members dress casually, avoid showing up in a tailored suit. If gatekeepers congregate at the local coffee shop, ask to meet them there and treat them to their favorite coffee.

In all meetings, it's important to be up front and honest about the research focus, but also to take care with the project's *framing*. For instance, imagine a researcher who studies the interactional patterns among extended family members. Gatekeepers may be more friendly to a project framed as "friendship and kinship" than to one framed as "rivalry and jealousy." Of course, familial interaction patterns necessarily include *both* these positive and negative valences, but initial conversations will likely go more smoothly if you avoid raising red flags. So, how do critical researchers frame their research in a way that is ethically truthful, but will not preclude access? A critical researcher may say, "I am exploring a wide spectrum of beliefs about these phenomena," or "I'm investigating a multitude of solutions – both those that are held by group leaders and those that are held by more marginal groups." Language is key. I have learned through trial and error that I am much more successful at getting access if I initially frame my research as a desire to study "the emotional highs and lows of employees" than by saying that I want to study "employee stress and burnout." Indeed, early on in my research tenure, one organizational gatekeeper said he would not allow access, because he was sure my research would "plant the idea of burnout in employees' heads." Argh!

In early conversations with gatekeepers, a primary goal should be to learn who will make the final decision about research access. Near the end of the conversation you might ask directly: "Do you have the authority to grant research permission?" If the answer is yes, the participant may grant it on the spot or commit to responding by a certain date. If not, you can ask who has the authority to make a decision and how you might best talk with that person. Try to avoid a situation in which a participant who does not have the authority promises to "take your request" to the final decision-maker. As in the childhood game of "telephone," the description of one's research project can morph as it gets relayed across various players. Researchers have a better chance of gaining access when they can talk – in real time – with the actual gatekeeper. In doing so, they can adjust their pitch to the opportunities available and immediately attend to any questions or concerns.

It also makes sense to examine the group's missions and needs and to tailor conversations to those needs. Examine the group's website. Talk with people who are familiar with the context. Part of your research may help to diagnose contextual priorities or problems. At the same time, it is important to consider your own research needs and timeline. Researchers should avoid making commitments about their study's focus or deliverables unless they are sure they want to follow through.

In many cases, an **access proposal** – a document that efficiently describes the research project to gatekeepers – can ease access. Good access proposals include:

- a descriptive and non-threatening title;
- a rationale that rings true with the gatekeepers;
- a description of the proposed research;
- a statement of experience (to show credibility);
- contact information.

The tone of the access proposal should be confident yet modest, friendly but not obsequious, explicit but not too rigid. In some contexts, a formal proposal – especially if presented too soon – may scare off gatekeepers. When my former student Kendra Rivera presented a proposal similar to the one below, her gatekeeper at the US Border Patrol took out his pen and scrawled an X over the entire sheet, saying: "Never show that to a Border Patrol agent." Kendra was advised to do more background research and to come in as "a blank slate." However, in many contexts, the proposal offered in Researcher's Notepad 4.2 can professionalize the project. I recommend that you take an access proposal with you to gatekeeper meetings and pull it out when the time feels right.

One last note about contacting gatekeepers at the scene: in some organizations, no one ever identifies him-/herself as having the authority to provide access. This can be extremely frustrating, because, although no one ever says "no," no one ever says "yes" either. This situation is especially widespread in self-help and support franchises such as Alcoholics Anonymous, Weight Watchers, and other groups. If you discover this to be the case, the universe might be gently suggesting that you seek access elsewhere. However, if you are determined to get into such a context, a route to access may lie in your becoming a member yourself and convincing people in the scene, over time, that your research is worthy and ethical. Another tactic is to pass university institutional review board (IRB) approval first (this is discussed in Chapter 5) and then to display this approval as a badge toward gaining access. You might also pass along articles that document past research in similar contexts, and, in some cases, volunteer gentle assurance that certain people in the scene do indeed have the authority to grant permission. Of course, in some research settings, you never come face to face with participants – a topic to which we turn next.

RESEARCHER'S NOTEPAD 4.2

Sample access proposal
Emotion, culture and organizational communication

Submitted by Sarah J. Tracy to Nouveau Jail

Study rationale

I am a doctoral student in organizational communication at the University of Colorado-Boulder studying organizational culture, emotion, and communication issues in "non-traditional" organizations. This document serves as a proposal to conduct an in-depth study of these issues with the Nouveau Jail. This study will serve a dual purpose: It will provide information that will add to our academic understanding of emotional and cultural issues within organizations, and it will offer these organizations volunteer expertise from someone versed in organizational communication issues. Throughout my research, I would be able to give feedback to jail personnel and, if desired, make suggestions regarding the organization's communication efforts.

Proposal

I am flexible about the way in which this study unfolds, and I assume it will change throughout discussions with administrators at the jail. My initial idea is to focus upon jail staff through participant observation and interviews – especially correctional officers and other personnel who are in contact with inmates. My aim is to be as unobtrusive and helpful as possible. As a participant observer, I would observe staff members in their daily activities, and occasionally take notes. Through this depth of involvement I am better able to garner the trust of the staff and better poised to understand how employees are experiencing their work positions.

My hope is to do in-depth research/volunteering for up to 20 hours per week, beginning in June. I have a very flexible schedule and will work with the Jail Captain or another contact person in developing a schedule. I hope to spend a considerable amount of my summer with the jail – and I would continue into the fall as needed. Upon completion of the study, I would be happy to share the results of my analysis with employees.

Experience

I have studied organizational culture issues in the context of a metropolitan city's 911 emergency communications center, on a commercial cruise ship, and in multiple Rocky Mountain area public relations firms. I have presented research reports at national and international conferences, have published articles in major journals, and am currently co-authoring a book on organizational change. In short, I am trained in conducting organizational research, have expert knowledge in the area I propose studying, and my past work has been valuable and well accepted.

Confidentiality and organizational protection

The organization's name and identifying details will remain completely confidential. Further, the identities of those who grant me interviews will be kept confidential, and the data will be collapsed in such a way so that the identities of employees and inmates will be hidden. Before giving interviews or making observations, participants will be informed as to the general purpose and nature of the study. Employees will be asked to sign "informed consent" forms that detail their rights, including their right to not participate in the study. All the data are kept in a secure location, and information that could identify the organization or individual employees will be destroyed. Written reports resulting from the data gathered are used for academic and scholarly purposes.

I look forward to working with the jail. For additional information about my experience or expertise, feel free to contact my doctoral dissertation advisor, [name] at [phone number].

Sarah J. Tracy, MA   [my address]
Department of Communication   [my email]
University of Colorado-Boulder   [my phone number]

Negotiating access to a virtual site

Increasing numbers of researchers are turning to virtual, computer-mediated, and new media contexts to understand a variety of phenomena such as social networking, support groups, work teams, and otherwise hidden relationships or activities. These researchers include scholars who combine rhetorical textual methods with qualitative thematic analysis, as in the case of Brouwer and Hess's (2007) analysis of military blog responses to hate speech. Many of the same issues of gaining access with embodied participants also come to bear in virtual environments.

First, as is the case of face-to-face research encounters, some online communities are public, whereas others are private. Just as a researcher need not seek official permission to watch people at a coffee shop or airport, researchers may not feel they are ethically required to announce their research agenda in a public discussion forum, such as a webpage devoted to comments on newspaper articles. People commenting on a public forum, just like people playing in the city park, should understand the public nature of their behavior. This is not the case, however, for online communities that require a specific password, credential, or application in order to become a member and view their activity. Just as researchers need permission to observe a group's private meetings, they should seek permission before researching and recording groups' private online activity.

In many situations, the ability to distinguish between public and private online communities can be difficult. For instance, former student Charee Mooney analyzed a virtual community of parents who had lost their children through miscarriage or infant sicknesses. She chose to focus her study on a blogger who called herself "Mrs. Dub." Charee "entered" the community through her aunt's sister, who had blogged about child loss. Through hyper-linking to comments left on her aunt's blog, Charee discovered an extended network of women writing online about their lost children. These data served to open a rich avenue for understanding infant death and compassionate communication. Mrs. Dub was aware that Charee was a reader, and, because the blog was public, Charee was not required to receive official consent from the bloggers. It is important to note that the goals of this particular research project did not include critique but rather were limited to an interpretive description of the stories used to cope with child loss. If Charee had planned critique, the ethics regarding consent would have become more pronounced.

In many online forums that are technically "public," it is nonetheless ethically important to seek more structured consent from participants. Indeed, even if institutional review boards do not require signed informed consent, remaining unseen and unheard as an online "lurker" is usually inadvisable. Researchers may choose from a variety of strategies of visibility. Gheeta, who studied the online "marriage of convenience" (MOC) forums discussed in Chapter 1, announced her presence and research interests many times over chat forums. By doing so she created space and opportunity for participants to respond (and potentially to invite, affirm, or reject) her research interests. The legality of certain recording practices may not necessarily equate with what participants feel are ethical methodological tactics. Researchers should ask themselves to what extent participants in online communities have a reasonable expectation for privacy and then proceed accordingly. Additionally, they should check the frequently asked questions (FAQ) sections of websites, as some of them have specific policies regarding research activities.

Some researchers maintain unobtrusively low profiles in their virtual fieldwork and only seek informed consent if they plan to use a direct quotation from someone in a publication. However, because searching for direct quotations through Internet search engines is so simple, researchers need to take care with the practice of **textual harvesting** (Sharf, 1999) – a phrase used derogatorily, to describe the practice of gathering and using the words of others without permission. The availability of archives, coupled with far-reaching online search browsers, can result in less anonymity for an online identity than for an offline one. For instance, even if researchers change a participant's screen name to a pseudonym, a word-for-word excerpt from an active blog can be searched for and found quite easily. Certainly, informed consent can be difficult to obtain online. Researchers should periodically provide updates about their presence and research goals and should invite participants to respond. Another option is to create and post a link to one's own webpage that describes the study, the author(s), the intended outcomes, and the participants' rights.

Abandoning the ego, engaging embodiment, embracing liminality

In addition to considering the logistical hurdles of negotiating access, a key part of preparing for the scene is readying one's own identity and body. So, does this mean that you must become expert before commencing fieldwork? No. Some may find it ironic, but a mindful stance of *ignorance* is absolutely crucial for becoming an *expert* qualitative researcher. Fieldworkers must be comfortable letting go of preconceived notions or assumptions about a culture, people, or activity. They must leave their ego, credentials, and jargon-laden academic talk at the door. Goffman (1989) goes so far as to say that researchers must be willing to act like "a horse's ass," to participate in "silly" rituals, and to ask "simple questions." Fieldplayers have a child-like curiosity, are not preoccupied with impressing others, and focus their energies on listening and learning.

The best participant observers are complex and multi-faceted – people who read a lot and seek out contradictory, unfamiliar, divergent, and multi-faceted crystallized life experiences (Tracy & Trethewey, 2005). Indeed, a researcher who "knows many theories, metaphors, images, and beliefs and who has had varied experiences" (Weick, 1985, p. 581) is much more adept at examining and making sense of the world's complexity. I encourage qualitative researchers to consistently learn, travel, and seek out opinions contrary to (or simply divergent from) their own. In today's era of niche media, gated communities, and walled freeways, people can easily surround themselves with others who share the same viewpoints, interpretations, and experiences. This narrow view of the world, in turn, can lend itself to a flattened, one-dimensional way of interpreting it. If the field seems boring, this may be just a mirror of the researcher. The research instrument needs to be intricate and fresh in order to capture the vitality of the field.

Keeping yourself vibrant as researcher can be a challenge. Field research is physically, emotionally, and mentally exhausting. Some contexts – such as rape crisis centers, funeral homes, or emergency rooms – are by their nature contexts of stress, violence, and sadness. Even in more comfortable contexts, field research is marked by long periods of tedium, and you will sometimes feel bored and wonder whether you are wasting your time. In such situations, your participants may also be bored or distracted, and therefore your own feelings can serve as insightful evidence about the context at hand. Very few jobs or contexts are always exciting. Indeed, participant observation is valuable *precisely because* it reveals the multi-faceted nature of the scene.

Your body also serves as an important participant observation tool. Conquergood calls ethnography an embodied practice, "an intensely sensuous way of knowing" (1991, p. 180), and suggests that researchers not only acknowledge but also embrace a return of the body into research. Good fieldworkers not only look and listen; they also smell, taste, touch, and feel. They engage the scene with their whole person, taking notes on the details of activities as well as on their own emotional insights and gut reactions. This includes paying attention to feeling nervous, excited, repulsed, or spiritually engaged. Good researchers consider how they dress, groom, and show emotion. Amira De La Garza's "four seasons" approach to ethnography provides an excellent template for the embodied research path (González, 2000). In the early, "spring" stage that is typical to negotiating access, researchers should be introspective, assess their biases and motivations, and ask whether they are personally ready to study a certain site at the chosen time. Perhaps your identity or body is not yet capable of studying a certain issue – because of emotional sensitivity, maturity, or vulnerability. A recovering methamphetamine addict is not well poised to study the drug scene; a parent devastated by a terminated pregnancy may not be ready to study the maternity ward. Considering and acknowledging early on the stumbling blocks of personal identity will ease the later seasons of research, filled as they are with exhilaration, disappointment, frustration, breakthroughs, and isolation.

Some researchers go so far as to costume or position themselves to see the world in the same ways as their participants. For researchers studying children, this may entail getting on their hands and knees and seeing the world at toddler level. For someone studying the homeless, this may mean panhandling or living on the street. For Hickey and colleagues (1988), who studied the Easter Bunny character, this meant actually donning the Easter Bunny costume at a local mall. At the very least, fieldworkers need to respect the knowledge that comes through their body and equip themselves to use all their senses. Further, because our bodies and identities make a difference to the type of access and to the data we collect, researchers need to be reflexive about how their embodied identities ease or limit their research. Among other things, I encourage fieldworkers to take stock of their demographic markers, social attributes, and personality characteristics and to consider the values that others may ascribe to them (see Exercise 4.1 for a self-identity audit).

Even if you are reflexive about your body in relation to the scene, initial fieldwork visits can feel awkward. Victor Turner's concept of **liminality** aptly characterizes ethnographic positions in the field: "liminal entities [people] are neither here nor there; they are betwixt and between the positions assigned and arrayed by law, custom, convention, and ceremony" (Turner, 1969, p. 95). Participant observers must be close enough to others in the scene to gain an understanding, yet simultaneously far enough to create distance and see what is occurring from an outsider's standpoint. Although the liminal space can feel ambiguous, "it is those very aspects of the experience that we prefer to ignore – the emotional, the intuitive, the liminal aspects – that enable that understanding of both self and other" (Eastland, 1993, p. 136). So, if you feel a little unbalanced or a little left out when doing fieldwork, try to embrace it as normal.

EXERCISE 4.1

Self-identity audit

Before entering a scene, fieldworkers should be reflexive about their own identities. Describe the following aspects of yourself (and consider seeking input from a trusted friend or colleague).

1   What are my demographic markers (e.g. age, sex, ethnicity, sexual orientation)?
2   What are my social attributes (e.g. religion, social class, education level, fitness level, appearance)?
3   How do others describe my personality characteristics (e.g. shy, boisterous, flirtatious, awkward, charming, self-deprecating, obsequious, nervous, bored, gracious)?
4   What value labels do people ascribe to me and my body (e.g. attractive, disciplined, snobbish, naïve, chubby, elitist, judgmental, intimidating, jovial, friendly)?
5   Ask yourself how these identity attributes may affect your involvement and reception in a specific research context.
    a   How might these characteristics affect participants' reaction to me?
    b   How might they enable or constrain the data I have access to?
6   Write a self-reflexive account of your musings in relation to your fieldwork scene.

Thankfully, there is no one perfect type of identity or embodiment for fieldwork. Appearing young, naïve, and shy may help your participants feel more comfortable about sharing their vulnerabilities, but these same attributes could make them refrain from inviting you to happy hour. Being big, boisterous, and jovial may enable participants to feel comfortable to include you in their humorous pranks, but it may discourage them from sharing their deepest confidences. Fieldworkers' identities are "read" and evaluated by participants just as much as participants' identities are read and evaluated by fieldworkers. Our bodies and identities can both help and hurt as we study various groups, and the best we can do is to try to put ourselves in our participants' shoes and reflect critically on our identity's strengths and constraints vis-à-vis any particular scene.

Navigating those first few visits

Accompanying the process of reflecting critically on your own body and its place in the scene is the exhilaration that comes with doing fieldwork and meeting participants for the first time. This is usually a time fraught with both anxiety and anticipation. The first few visits to any scene can be uncomfortable and bewildering. In fact, discomfort experienced early on makes for ripe fieldnotes and interesting data. Much classic work begins with ethnographers telling the story of how they arrived in a research scene that made no sense, where the locals ignored them or treated them with scorn, and where the problem they thought they came to study no longer seemed relevant or interesting (Geertz, 1973; Goodall, 1989; Malinowski, 1922). But these scenes of early conflict and awkwardness – as well as the researcher feeling conflicted – help produce a unique and interesting account. You can feel assured that, even if you feel unsettled during these first visits, you will eventually feel more natural. Indeed, over time, you might begin to perceive yourself as being so "normal" in the scene that you feel like you could remain there, comfortably, forever. Some even argue that it is exactly when researchers become comfortable in a culture that once seemed foreign or exotic that they should abandon the scene and seek out another project (Agar, 1994). If everything feels natural, nothing will seem new.

As you enter the field, remember the funnel metaphor of qualitative research. During these first visits, keep your focus wide and take notes on everything – even events or meetings that seem "unsuccessful" on their face. For instance, perhaps you planned on meeting a key informant and the meeting was cancelled. Noting the reasons given and the process in which you were informed of the cancellation might be just as revealing as actually conducting the scheduled interview. As you enter the field and continue your research, make the most of every single data collection opportunity. There is never a guarantee that you will interact with a certain person or see the same scene again.

Even in initial meetings, you may gently inquire for additional information or access. For instance, immediately upon entering the prison and jail scene, I began asking about correctional officer training seminars. Asking early was of the essence, because attending training took several layers of permission and had to be planned well in advance. At the same time, good qualitative researchers are tactful and use good judgment, asking for information in stages. It was only after I had visited the prison many times and created a modicum of trust that I dared ask the head trainer whether I could *take home* several training videos and manuals, to analyze them. I am quite sure the trainer would have refused my request if I had asked immediately.

Participants' initial reactions to you can serve as helpful data. Are they welcoming? Friendly? Cautious? Indifferent? Suspicious? If people in the scene judge you or your research project negatively, it may be that they simply do not want to be micro-analyzed. They may have something to hide, or they may believe that your presence and questions would take time away from what they are supposed to be doing. There are any number of reasons why some people will not appreciate your need to know them up close and personal. Their reactions to your presence reveal attitudes, values, and assumptions they may never directly articulate to you in other ways. Indeed, I learned much about the wariness and suspicion of correctional officers through their reactions – as illustrated in Researcher's Notepad 4.3 as narrative for reflection.

Participants' opinions and reactions (whether good or bad) say as much (if not more) about them as they do about you or your project. Indeed the old adage goes that, when someone points a finger, they have three fingers pointing back at them. So, if you feel yourself being judged or evaluated, reflect on your own behaviors and feelings (the one finger pointing at you), but also consider the participants' behaviors, potential motivations, and reactions to you in the scene (the three fingers pointing back at them). Make friends with the idea you may feel vulnerable, frustrated, marginalized, or humbled. These feelings are evidence of moving out of a comfort zone and into a space of conscious learning and growth.

Encouraging participant cooperation

Negotiating access to a site is an ongoing process. Even after you receive permission from official gatekeepers, there is no guarantee that this consent has been communicated to others in the group. Furthermore, even if administrators provide official consent, this does not guarantee that other members will want to be studied. As Goffman (1989) notes, in

RESEARCHER'S NOTEPAD 4.3

Initial reactions speak volumes

Nouveau Jail: Fieldnotes

Visit 1

It is an early Tuesday morning in June 1999. With IRB and organizational approval in hand, I am eager for my first day of research. At the age of 29, with several research projects under my belt, I feel confident, experienced, and ready. I arrive outside the jail's reception area several minutes before the shift start at 7:30 a.m., but the front door is locked. I knock loudly on the glass door, and the woman at the front desk glances at me dismissively. I can just barely hear her words as she says in my general direction, "You'll have to wait." I respond with a nervous smile and try to sound professional as I yell through the door, "I have a meeting with Lt. Turner." She responds without looking up, "Lt. Turner won't be here until 9 a.m."

I reply fervently, "I'm scheduled to give a talk during the 7:30 a.m. roll call." Without comment, she disappears out of sight. Meanwhile, two other people have joined me at the front entrance. From eavesdropping on their conversation I learn that they are here to visit their friend, who got arrested last night. Finally, after what seems like forever, two sergeants come to the door and crack it open. They look at me skeptically and say they have no idea who I am.

What? How could this be? I had met several times earlier and confirmed this morning's presentation. I eagerly explain, and they reluctantly allow me through. I glimpse back at the two others, still huddled by the door. They scowl at me.

Visit 5

This is my fifth observation at Nouveau Jail and my second observation in the booking area. I had hoped that the officers would trust and like me by this time. Not tonight. Even though I am supposedly given "full access," and I am surrounded by staff and inmates, I feel lonely and left out. No one even looks at me. I am scheduled to observe from 11:30 p.m. to 3:30 a.m. Early in the evening, I asked an officer about a form he was filling out. Without meeting my eyes, he jerked his head around to another officer and said, "Is she allowed to see this?" The other officer replied coolly, "I doubt it."

Feeling the heat of anger and embarrassment crawl up my neck, I said apologetically, "Hey, it's no big deal," and retreated to my perch on the booking-room counter. I try to console myself that this interaction is actually a helpful learning experience, because it allows me to see what "really happens" in the booking room of Nouveau Jail. However, I feel dismissed and disrespected. I am learning how the officers treat outsiders by being an outsider myself.

field research "You can't move down a social system" (p. 130). By this he means that, if you want to study people from various status or class levels in a scene, you should start with those who are most marginalized and then move up the hierarchy. This principle of field research is due to trust and fear. If a researcher associates too closely with high-powered administrators from the beginning, other participants may remain convinced that the researcher is a "fink."

How do you obtain permission from power holders, yet assuage fears that you are not too closely associated with them? One way I attempted to navigate this tension in the correctional setting (obviously with mixed success) was by insisting that I introduce myself to officers at their roll call – rather than being introduced by a power holder. In my opening spiel, I explicitly said: "I am not a management spy or a journalist trying to get a story. I am a PhD student hoping to tell the correctional officer story from your point of view." I explained that inmates' stories dominated existing prison research and that I wanted to share the important viewpoints of correctional officers. Although some participants continued to be distrustful, most were cooperative, even supportive.

I recommend that, in the scene, researchers are truthful and transparent about their topics of interest. Goffman (1989) suggests that researchers should, at the very least, provide a "story such that if they find out what you are doing, the story you presented could not be an absolute lie" (p. 127). Members' agreeableness to research has less to do with scientific interests or specific academic topics than it does with how much they like the researcher.

Although every scene is different, I recommend you befriend key informants, gatekeepers, sponsors, and mentors – people who are well regarded both by official gatekeepers and by those populations you hope to study. Sometimes these informants have an official title; but more likely they are informal yet popular leaders. Good qualitative researchers keep these people happy and well informed, flexing to their needs and schedules, paying them favors, and listening to what they have to say. It also makes sense to treat participants as "whole people" who have a variety of facets, needs, interests, and desires (which may include, for instance, really appreciating an unprompted delivery of their favorite afternoon snack). Being friendly, polite, gracious, generous, and fun will go a long way toward ongoing access and ease of research. Acting like this is also just a good way to live.

Seeking informed consent in the scene

Once you have received official permission from gatekeepers, the path toward research consent in the field is still not exhausted. Researchers must continually negotiate informal approval to observe and formal approval to conduct audio-recorded interviews and focus groups. Informing participants about the study can happen in a variety of different ways. In public contexts – such as buses, parks, restaurants, and theatres – formal consent for observation is not compulsory. In private group settings – such as a church, an organization, a support group or a club – I recommend a brief overview of the project that includes its goals, scope, and time for questions and comments. Other briefing options could be one-page flyers or emails, bulletins posted in the break-room, web-based descriptions of the project, and so on.

Once you begin observing, I recommend that you use informed consent forms (to be described in Chapter 5) as a useful way of discussing the project one on one. When I have chosen to "shadow" employees, I have supplied them with an informed consent form and asked: "Is it okay if I hang out with you today?" Usually this has led to introductions and a friendly conversation. On the other hand, some participants may have questions, and having the form gives a reason to talk through any concerns. Finally, sometimes participants may give indifferent or unclear reactions to researcher presence. In these cases, it may make sense to move along and observe a different participant. That said, what may appear as initial negativity to researcher presence may really just be indifference. In Tips and Tools 4.1 I provide an overview of tips that summarize the preceding discussion on fieldwork, fieldplay, and negotiating access.

TIPS AND TOOLS 4.1

Participant observation tips

- Leave your ego at the door – fieldwork is not the space to seek recognition or affirmation of your identity or scholarship.
- Be a good person.
- Listen to the context and to your participants.
- Immerse yourself in the scene – yet be patient about exclusion.
- Investigate artifacts and collect relevant documents.
- Realize that any scene can have a number of meanings and be open to myriad interpretations.
- Go beyond recording just the words people say – to capture the tastes, smells, tempers, touches, colors, lights, and shapes.
- Observation can be physically, emotionally, and spiritually draining. Prepare for and embrace the challenge. Properly give yourself time to recover and renew.

Exploratory methods

In many ways, fieldwork negotiators are like explorers on an adventure. Explorers travel in one direction, then in another; they linger and watch the sunset, take note of impressive landmarks, note the places worth a return visit. Explorers do not know what they will find. They circle around and back. Their paths are not linear. They do not know exactly what they are looking for, but they maintain curiosity. At the same time, explorers use certain tools to guide their way. They bring supplies, draw maps, and consider tactics that will structure their exploration.

As you negotiate access, this is a good time to begin considering several exploratory methods that can acquaint you with the scene. In what follows I describe several such methods: briefing interviews, participant tables, member diaries, public documents, artifacts, maps, and narrative tours. These serve as helpful tools for transitioning into the field when you have gained access and are getting to know research participants.

Briefing interviews and participant information table

A **briefing interview** records information gathered as you informally meet with a series of gatekeepers and other participants, invite questions, and ask advice as you move forward. Briefing interviews may occur over the phone, in early meetings, in the hallway, or in the break room. So that you can best keep tabs on demographic information and pseudonyms, I recommend creating a **participant information table** – perhaps just adding on to the initial contact log described and pictured in Researcher's Notepad 4.1. This table can usefully list information such as:

1 the real name of the participant (if you have permission to record real names);
2 the pseudonym (that is, the fake name chosen by the participant or researcher);
3 the name of the subgroup a participant is associated with (if you are studying, for instance, multiple groups or organizations);

RESEARCHER'S NOTEPAD 4.4

Participant information table

I designed the following version (abbreviated) of a participant information table in Microsoft Excel. By marking the columns with numbers (1), I was quickly able to add up the participants in different categories (e.g. administrator vs. officer; male vs. female).

Name	Pseudonym	Administrator?	Officer?	Observation?	Interview?	Male?	Female?	Caucasian?	Hispanic?	Black?	Asian?	Other?	Nouveau?	Women's Min?	Thank you note?
Sgt. Sarah	Sgt. Sandy	1		1			1	1					1		1
Ofc. Jake	Ofc. Tom		1	1	1	1				1				1	
Lt. Jones	Lt. Smith	1		1		1		1					1		1
Total		2	1	3	1	2	1	2		1			2	1	2

4 position in the group (parent, manager, custodian);
5 key demographic characteristics (age, gender, ethnicity, education level, or any other significant identity markers);
6 whether the participant was observed;
7 whether the participant was interviewed;
8 whether the participant was involved in other types of data collection;
9 participant contact phone number, address, and/or email;
10 whether the participant has been involved with follow-up such as member reflections, thank you notes, and so on.

Such a document is a complement to, not a substitute for, rich description. It illustrates, at a glance, the demographic picture of participants – something that will be invaluable down the line, when analyzing the data and writing the methods section. The list also allows you to match up pseudonyms with real names, and this may be necessary if you want to follow up with certain participants or to align multiple data sources. Researcher's Notepad 4.4 offers an example of a *participant information table*.

Member diaries

Member diaries are another helpful exploratory method – especially when an actual geographical scene is difficult to access, or simply it doesn't exist. For instance, researchers interested in household television viewing habits would likely have a hard time negotiating access to observe multiple households. The researcher could ask participants instead to record certain behaviors in a diary, intermittently – such as when and what they watched on television, for how long, whether they were in a group or alone, and how much control they had over the remote control (Lindlof, 1987). Or consider a researcher interested in how the household chores were divided up. Jess Alberts and her colleagues (Alberts, Tracy, & Trethewey, 2011), for instance, investigated domestic labor by asking college students to record the length of time spent by family members on various chores.

Member diaries can provide a nice overview of current behavior – data that can helpfully set the stage for later participant observation and/or interviews. Member diaries can also be used throughout the data collection process and are occasionally used in field interventions. Participants, for example, may record their behavior in diaries, then take part in an experimental intervention (say, a training session on how to better divide household chores), and then again journal about their behavior. The researcher can examine the difference in the data recorded in the diaries before and after the intervention.

Public documents and artifacts

A third exploratory approach is analyzing **public documents** – such as websites, brochures, pamphlets, or advertisements – and **artifacts** – which are man-made objects such as technological equipment, toys, furniture, or artwork – in the context. Fieldwork provides the opportunity to know how artifacts are used, abused, cherished, or neglected on a daily basis. Documents furnish background on the group's history, information about rules, policies, or requirements for members, and the group's basic facts and figures. Learning this background via public documents creates familiarity with the existing hierarchies or coalitions and can help you to avoid squandering the participants' time with questions that are easily answered elsewhere.

Furthermore, documents and websites communicate the group's publicly espoused values and image. As you begin to gather data, it may become interesting to compare and contrast the culture's publicly espoused values with the practices actually in use (Deetz, Tracy, & Simpson, 2000). Whereas journalists and rhetoricians may build an entire case from documents, fieldworkers couple data from the documents' content with an understanding of how the documents *are used by* participants. For instance, you might examine a group's training materials but also conduct enough fieldwork to see how various training mandates are taken up, ignored, or resisted in everyday practice.

Maps and narrative tours

One of my favorite exploratory approaches comes in the form of the tour. A tour offers you an opportunity to attune to the surroundings, understand the people who inhabit different spaces, discover the group's history, and learn how you might best embody your participant observation role. Furthermore, many people like to display their space – whether that is a synagogue, an apartment, a backyard, or a corporate campus. Tours work especially well when you may otherwise feel anxious and uncertain. During a tour, conversations emerge naturally and long pauses are no need for concern. So, if you are prone to communication anxiety, a tour may be an especially worthwhile exploratory method. Ask your tour guide if you may bring along a notebook, a small audio recorder, or – for public spaces – a camera. Try to record impressions of the sights, smells, sounds, and feelings evoked by various parts of the space. Furthermore, asking different people to give tours covering the same space can be extremely valuable – as the variant issues focused upon by multiple actors reveal the context's layered meanings.

Another significant exercise during a tour is to draw a **visual map** of the scene. Doing so helps move researchers from left-brain and logical explanations to right-brain, creative, visual understandings of the scene. Creating a map does not require advanced drafting or artistic skills. Stick figures and approximations of certain artifacts and objects are sufficient. The primary goal is to create a working picture of the temporal, ritual, and routine features of the people and issues in the scene (Denzin, 1976). Maps quickly communicate the context's social networks, culture, values, and priorities. Recording notes on how closely people sit together – and whether they face each other or sit side by side – gives clues about coalitions in the scene. For example, mapping the living room and the dining room of a home can quickly communicate mealtime routines. Is the dining room stacked with old magazines and scattered with fancy dishes covered in dust? Is a half-eaten microwave dinner still on the kitchen counter? These data may suggest that the occupants do not regularly have large, family-style dinners together but rather eat separately, on the go. I recommend that maps include people, objects, and artifacts. Don't forget the people and how they are interacting with each other and the scene!

Lastly, in a written-up **narrative tour**, researchers hypothesize about the meanings and interpretations of the map. In narrating the scene, they should go beyond visual placement and also take note of feelings, smells, and temperatures.

- Does the space reek of stale cigarette smoke, or of the smell of disinfectant, or of both?
- Does the context feel stuffy and claustrophobic? Is this because of the lighting, the humidity, the barred windows, the number of people stuffed inside, or the low ceiling?
- How might these sensory issues affect the interaction inside the space? What are the scene's regular sounds?
- Does the sound of the context – its silence, hum of activity, or intermittent outbursts of screaming – imply anything about the stress level or camaraderie of participants?

By noting such contextual specifics, researchers use the data collected in the map and narrative tour as evidence for potential claims or meanings in the scene. Exercise 4.2 provides a map and a narrative tour exercise.

EXERCISE 4.2

Map and narrative tour

Complete a detailed map and narrative tour of your site (or of a key part of your site)

1   Note key people (or types of people), artifacts, and objects and their relation to each other.
2   Accompany the map with a narrative tour – a mini interpretation of the scene – that explains what the map says about the research participants' values, rules, priorities, ways of being, status, power, and so on.
  a   Ask the question: What does this tell me conceptually about this place? (Try to see things as "evidence" of certain arguments.)
  b   Include as many "senses" (sight, sound, smell, taste, feel, mood) as possible.
3   Provide an updated version of your guiding research question(s) at the top of the map and narrative tour.

In summary

In this chapter I have discussed methods for navigating access for qualitative research. As my confessional tales reveal, there is no one best recipe for how to negotiate one's entrée, and researchers must be flexible and attentive to the opportunities provided to them. Tactics like keeping a contact log and creating an access proposal can ease the way. Finally, I provided several different tactics for exploring the scene. These included briefing interviews, participant tables, member diaries, public documents, artifacts, maps, and narrative tours.

One final note: if you get rejected, try not to take it personally. It takes practice to learn how to negotiate access, and failure is part of this learning process. One of my favorite adages is this: "Anything worth doing well is worth doing badly in the beginning" (Canfield, 2005, p. 137, citing business consultant Marshall Thurber). Rejection is part of the game, and good qualitative researchers need to have ingenuity, courage, and resilience to negotiate access. If you have obstacles in negotiating access, get up, dust yourself off, tweak your pitch, and try again – using a different route or a different research destination.

KEY TERMS

→ **access proposal**   a proposal for scene gatekeepers that efficiently describes the research project (it has title, practical rationale, description of the proposed research, statement of experience, and contact information)

→ **artifacts**   man-made objects in the research context

→ **briefing interview**   an interview that creates the opportunity to informally meet with a series of participants, invite questions, and ask participants for advice as one moves forward in negotiating access

→ **contact information log**   a database document that tracks key contacts met in the process of negotiating access and doing research; it contains names, phone numbers, the researcher's relationship with the contact, and relevance to the research

→ **fieldplay**   the adventure, curiosity and playfulness that occur during participant observation experiences.

→ **fieldwork (**also see **participant observation)**   a method through which researchers generate understanding and knowledge by watching, interacting, asking questions, collecting documents, and making audio or video recordings

→ **gatekeeper(s)**   the person(s) who hold the figurative (or at times literal) keys to research site access

→ **liminality**   a term originally defined by Victor Turner, which describes the sense of being betwixt and between two locations

→ **member diaries**   journals in which participants are asked to enter personal information related to research

→ **narrative tour**   a written document, usually accompanying a visual map, that explores a scene's physical layout, feelings, smells, sounds, tastes, and temperatures, also providing rich descriptions and tentative interpretations

→ **participants**   the individuals whom qualitative researchers study are not known as "subjects," but as participants, because they create, and participate in, the research process *together with* researchers

→ **participant information table**   a table used to organize information about participants; it may include a variety of demographic and methodological data

→ **participant observation** (also see **fieldwork**)   a method through which researchers generate understanding and knowledge by watching, interacting, asking questions, collecting documents, and making audio or video recordings

→ **public documents**   websites, brochures, pamphlets, or advertisements that provide information about a research site

→ **textual harvesting**   the practice of using information (usually gathered from the Internet) without permission from the participant or regard for ethically questionable repercussions

→ **total institutions**   a term developed by Goffman to refer to organizations like cruise ships, prisons, and hospitals, where some inhabitants of the institution never go home and therefore are controlled in a more total manner than in typical organizations

→ **visual map**   a visual representation of a research site, roughly drawn or professionally developed, that details the physical scene and key positions of the participants

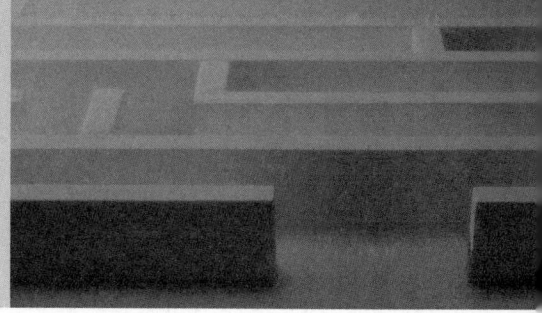

CHAPTER 5

Proposal writing
Explaining your research to institutional review boards, instructors, supervisory committees, and funding agencies

Qualitative Research Methods: Collecting Evidence, Crafting Analysis, Communicating Impact, First Edition. Sarah J. Tracy.
© 2013 Sarah J. Tracy. Published 2013 by Blackwell Publishing Ltd.

At some point in the qualitative process, most researchers will write one or more research proposals. A **research proposal** is a detailed plan that lays out the purpose, path, and procedures of the project. It serves as a wonderful tool for organizing and mapping the project and for communicating its worth to key audiences – people like teachers, advisors, funding agencies, and institutional review boards (IRBs). Research proposals offer an opportunity for these key audiences to give feedback that can enrich the project and ensure that it aligns with ethical, legal, and other institutional guidelines.

This chapter presents a review of United States institutional review boards, an explanation of different "levels" of human subjects' review, and tips for how to navigate the IRB approval process. Some qualitative researchers have an ambivalent or hostile attitude toward IRB. I will review controversial issues related to IRB and provide suggestions about how you can best incorporate human subject protections in your own research.

The chapter also supplies a step-by-step guide to writing a research proposal – a course assignment that often serves as a centerpiece project in methodology courses. A proposal in the form of a prospectus is usually required for graduate students pursuing master's theses or doctoral dissertations. Furthermore, granting agencies and scholarship boards usually ask for their own specialized research proposal. Whether or not you are required to write a research proposal, doing so generates focus for forthcoming projects.

Getting started with institutional review

As discussed in Chapter 2, the creation of **human subject protections** was prompted by ethically questionable research practices. Furthermore, after the atrocities committed by Nazi doctors in World War II, member countries of the United Nations adopted the Nuremberg Code, which requires voluntary informed consent. Most review boards are governed by the **Belmont Report** – a statement of basic human subject principles issued by the National Commission for the Protection of Human Subjects, which includes a number of ethical edicts discussed below. Review boards are typically made up of administrators, researchers, and scholars. They generally require a scientifically valid research design, which protects research participants' safety, privacy, health, and welfare. Furthermore, they try to ensure that the study's benefits outweigh its risks and have the potential to improve society.

To begin the IRB process, researchers should access their own university's procedures and protocol. A good place to start is the review board's website. This is usually found by Internet search phrases such as "institutional review board" or "human subjects" on the university's homepage. These websites usually provide information on workshops and downloads of proposal worksheets. The website will also list answers to frequently asked questions (FAQs), provide examples of consent/assent forms and verbal scripts, and gives you the university's IRB contact information. Researchers may also be required to complete a web-based training program – such as the one hosted by the American National Institute of Health – and offer proof of certification when they submit research protocols to the IRB.

You can get good IRB advice by talking to other students or teachers who have gone through the review process and are willing to share past proposals. Also, keep in mind that IRB staff are well versed on how to navigate the review process. Although you should not waste their time with questions easily answered online, IRB employees may provide individual, group, or classroom consultations as you design your project, determine the level of review necessary, and fill out forms.

The IRB proposal: rationale, instruments, informed consent, and confidentiality

A primary part of most IRB proposals is explaining the study's rationale. This part consists of a brief description, purpose, and design of the project. It may include:

- the guiding research questions;
- the project's duration and scope;
- the participant recruitment procedures;
- the methods of data collection, for example interviews, participant observation, website analysis.

The presentation of the rationale should avoid technical terms, theoretical jargon, and overuse of citations. The document must be understandable to personnel from a variety of disciplinary backgrounds. It should also explain clearly why the research is significant (see Chapter 11 for more on significance).

Another key part of the IRB proposal is describing the **research instruments**, considered to be the tools used to carry out the research. For laboratory or survey studies, research instrumentation may be quite involved. However, in qualitative studies, *the researcher is the instrument*. In view of this, most qualitative researchers need only provide a list of interview questions, and perhaps discuss their focus group and observation procedures. In providing interview questions for IRBs, I recommend that researchers be as all-inclusive and broad as possible. This will help ensure that the questions are still applicable even if the exact foci of the study morph over time. If the study's goals are relatively undetermined – or if they change dramatically – the researcher should provide an addendum to the original IRB application when s/he determines the specific direction of interviews or focus groups. This is a common practice for qualitative researchers, as we rarely know what our interview questions should be until we spend some time in the field.

The IRB also requires that researchers demonstrate the ways participants (or participants' representatives) will provide voluntary and **informed consent**. This means that participants are free from coercion and comprehend the potential risks and benefits of the study. Participants must understand that they can withdraw from the research at any time and will not lose any benefit or entitlement by refusing to participate. For example, researchers are not allowed to withhold health care to inmates who do not sign up for the study, or to withhold a grade because students do not participate. Indeed, if research participation provides students with extra credit, students should also be offered alternative opportunities for extra credit.

Like other parts of the IRB proposal, consent forms should be written so as to be understandable to the study population. They should include simple explanations of the purposes, procedures, and planned outcomes of research. Potential risks and benefits should be brief and to the point. In a study investigating a family history of conflict, the researcher might note that interview questions could present the risk of bringing up emotionally troubling memories. However, the benefit of the study may be that participants are able to talk through potential future conflicts.

Researcher's Notepad 5.1 provides an example of a consent letter used by former student Jennifer Scarduzio in her study of wellness and the judicial system. Because many institutions require their own special format (and in some cases they may only require an informational letter rather than signed informed consent), researchers should check their institution's guidelines when creating consent letters and other required materials.

RESEARCHER'S NOTEPAD 5.1

Participant consent letter

WELLNESS IN THE JUDICIAL SYSTEM: INFORMED CONSENT FORM

Please read the following explanation of this study. Signing this form will indicate you have been informed about the study and that you consent to participate. I want to ensure you understand what you are being asked to do and what risks and benefits – if any – are associated with the study. This should help you decide whether you want to participate.

You are being asked to take part in a research project conducted by Jennifer Scarduzio, MA, a doctoral student under the direction of Sarah J. Tracy, PhD – both at [name of department, university and address].

Project description   This study is about judges' emotions as they communicate to the public, along with wellness issues in their occupations. Your participation in this study is entirely voluntary. You may decline to participate at any time.

Procedures   If you agree to take part in the study, I will observe you in your daily work. Furthermore, here are examples of questions I may ask you during an interview:

- What are the ways in which you try to remain neutral when communicating decisions?
- Can you provide a specific example of a situation in which a defendant frustrated you?
- Can you provide a specific example of a situation in which a defendant made you laugh?
- What are some of the ways in which you try to balance your work and your outside life?
- What are your favorite and your least favorite parts of your job?

Approximately 15 participants over the age of 18 will be invited to participate in this study. The interviews will occur at a time and place that is most convenient for you. Interviews will be audio-recorded and recordings will only be used for research purposes.

Risks and discomforts   Risks for participating in this study are minimal. You will be participating in an interview that may elicit emotions about your job. The only risk of the study is the possibility of experiencing some stress from discussing aspects of the job. If you feel uncomfortable at any time, you may choose to skip questions, or you may ask to be withdrawn.

Benefits   There are no direct benefits for participating in this study other than the possibility of gaining greater understanding of wellness issues related to your job.

Study withdrawal   You have the right to withdraw your consent or stop participating at any time, for any reason. You have the right to refuse to answer any question(s).

Confidentiality   Every effort will be made to maintain the privacy of your data. To protect confidentiality, no personally identifying information will be used. The results may be used in reports, presentations, or publications, but your name will not be used.

   To reduce concerns about confidentiality, you will choose or be assigned a pseudonym, and none of your information will be kept under your real name. All electronic files of observation notes, interview transcripts, and audio files will be kept in physically secured locations by using password-protected files and locked drawers.

Invitation for questions   If you have questions about this study, you should ask a researcher before you sign this consent form. If you have any questions following this study, please feel free to contact Jennifer Scarduzio at [contact email].

If you have any questions regarding your rights as a participant, any concerns regarding this project, or any dissatisfaction with any aspect of this study, you may report them – confidentially, if you wish – to the Chair of Human Subjects Institutional Review Board, at [contact phone number].

Authorization   I have read this paper about the study, or it was read to me. I know the possible risks and benefits. I know that being in this study is voluntary. I choose to be in this study. I know that I can withdraw at any time. I have received, on the date of the signature, a copy of this document. I realize I will be audio-recorded.

Name of Participant (printed) _____

Signature of Participant _____ Date _____

For some research projects, forms of *assent* rather than of *consent* are most appropriate. **Assent** is used with participants who are particularly vulnerable on account of their age (minors under the age of 18 in the United States) or have diminished capacities due to mental impairment, sickness, or educational disadvantage. Research with members of these groups requires *consent* from a guardian, parent, or trustee; additionally it should also (if possible) garner *assent* from the participant. The form of assent varies from population to population, but in most cases the researcher verbally describes the project in a way that can be easily understood, discusses the voluntary nature of the study, explains that a guardian has provided consent, and notes the participants' right to withdraw at any time.

If you are examining a private group, club, or organization, IRB may request a letter of permission from an official gatekeeper. Given the usual time constraints, I recommend drafting such a letter yourself and then allowing organizational members to modify it, print it out on the group's letterhead, sign it, and return it. The letter should indicate the title of the project and the researcher's name and make a statement to the effect that gatekeepers understand the duration and type of the proposed research. Researcher's Notepad 5.2 provides an example of a letter I drafted for Nouveau Jail, whose gatekeepers ended up copying it on their stationery, under their official letterhead, pretty much word for word.

In addition to consent and permissions, another principal component of the IRB proposal is explaining how private information about participants will be protected. Tactics to do so include keeping data under lock and key, in password-protected computers, and assigning pseudonyms to participants who desire confidentiality.

Additionally, in order to ensure confidentiality and avoid the **deductive disclosure** of a research participant (Sales & Folkman, 2000), researchers may need to modify slightly, or even to omit some data – especially in publications. *Deductive disclosure* is the indirect identification of respondents through the use and piecing together of known data. For example, Elizabeth Eger (formerly Rush) chose to collapse data when one of her police

RESEARCHER'S NOTEPAD 5.2

Gatekeeper permission letter

[Date]

[IRB Contact Information]

This letter serves as official permission for Sarah J. Tracy to conduct a research study, entitled *Communication and Correctional Employees*, at the Nouveau County Jail.

We have met with Sarah and understand that this research study will include several different aspects. She will observe jail employees in their daily work, shadowing them and taking notes. She will also conduct in-depth interviews with employees so that she can learn more about correctional officers' emotion labor and burnout issues.

We understand that the on-site research may last for a period of six months, and that Sarah might be present for up to 20 hours per week. We will work with her on developing a schedule.

Sarah has made it clear that all employees will be given a choice as to whether they would like to participate in the study. We understand she will offer employees informed consent forms to sign before they are observed or interviewed and audio-recorded.

In sum, we are fully informed about and give Sarah J. Tracy official approval to conduct her research at [context]. If you have any questions, feel free to call me at [phone].

Sincerely,

[Gatekeeper and Contact Information]

officer participants recounted experiences that were tied to both his job position and his race (Rush, 2012). Because he was the only officer with these unique indentifying markers, she modified these specific details in published reports in order to avoid deductive disclosure.

Different levels of IRB review

Some types of research projects require more careful review than others. In the following section, I explain the different types of review and the types of project that fit into them. From reading over human subjects' requirements, researchers make an educated guess about the correct level of review, but the IRB makes the final decision.

Exempt review

The quickest and least involved type of review, the **exempt review**, is generally used for qualitative studies of public behavior. For the study to be exempt, information must be recorded in such a manner that participants cannot be identified. Furthermore, the data cannot reasonably place participants at risk of criminal or civil liability or damage their financial standing, employability, or reputation. An examination of greeting behavior in an airport – especially if the researcher does not record specific names or identifying details – is an example of an exempt study. Exempt review requires an abbreviated IRB form and a copy of interview questions. Furthermore, exempt researchers supply a cover letter informing participants of their rights, rather than asking them to sign a letter of consent (which could be traced back to the participant). The researcher supplies this letter to participants before conducting "on-the-spot" interviews – and s/he may not even need such a letter if s/he is just observing people from afar.

Expedited review

The most common type of review for qualitative projects is the **expedited review**. This type of review includes the standard IRB application, and the permission turnaround period is typically several weeks longer than for exempt reviews. Expedited review is necessary when the researcher keeps a record of participants' names or identifying details – such as a contact log, or a name attached to the interview transcript. In short, if data are connected to identifying details of a participant – for example their name or phone number (even if this information is kept in a password-protected file) – an expedited review is usually necessary. Furthermore, if the participants' data may potentially harm them criminally, financially, or occupationally, the research must go through an expedited rather than an exempt review. Signed consent or assent forms – rather than just informational letters – are also required for projects in this category.

Kendra Rivera, a past student and co-author, went through expedited review for her research on border patrol agents (Rivera & Tracy, 2012). Negotiating access and tracking progress in the field necessitated writing down research participants' names and contact information. Furthermore, studies of law enforcement always hold increased risks of viewing criminal activity. Because the study opened this possibility, and because it included potentially sensitive questions about border patrol agents' jobs, the project fit the parameters of expedited research review.

Full-board review

Finally, research projects with especially sensitive topics or vulnerable populations must go through the most rigorous full-board review. **Full-board review** is required for studies with participants who have a diminished capability (or none at all) to give their consent – such as children, people who are mentally, physically, and educationally impaired, and non-native-language speakers. Research on economically disadvantaged persons is also closely scrutinized, so as to ensure that financial remuneration for the research is not unduly coercive. Given the ethical missteps of past research, it is no surprise that Native peoples, prisoners, and detainees also receive extra levels of human subjects' protection.

Full-board review can take more than three months. Studying protected populations requires that researchers plan ahead and budget their time accordingly. Amy Way was required to go through full-board review when she researched a young girls' running team (2012) and a youth outreach club (in press). Even though it took Amy longer than other students to receive permission for her project, the extra time paid off. Amy's research goals were to collect personal accounts of gender, wellness, and work socialization from the youths' point of view, and without her actually talking to them this research would have been impossible.

Indeed, just because some groups have special protections, it does not follow that they cannot or should not be studied. Some of the ethically and socially most important research – of gang members, homeless people, drug addicts, sick people, children, pregnant teenagers – may require full-board review. Such was the case, for instance, with Adelman and Frey's (1997) study of communication and community among people living with AIDS. It is just as unethical and problematic to purposefully leave out certain populations from research as it is to focus upon them. However, research that includes these groups requires a stronger rationale about the potential good emanating from the research, and very clear information about how the participants will be protected.

The quirks of IRB

As discussed in Chapter 2, the IRB emerged in response to ethically problematic medical and psychological experiments rather than in response to qualitative field research. However, review boards are increasing their overview (some would say surveillance) of a range of qualitative projects emanating from the humanities and social sciences (Nelson, 2004). IRB review boards face criticism on the grounds that they lack familiarity with qualitative methods, use formulaic approaches that are at odds with interpretive research, and are staffed by personnel whose members are most familiar with value-free empirical methods, which assume neutrality and objectivity (Christians, 2005; Hamilton, 2005). Unfortunately, many of IRB's current procedures, practices, forms, and rules still assume a paradigmatic approach that may not pertain to qualitative inquiry (Tracy, 2007).

For instance, as evidenced by the National Research Council report (Shavelson & Towne, 2002), many governmental leaders in the United States believe that, for something to "count" as research, it must be scientific, objective (value-free), and generalizable (that is, it must pertain to contexts or participants beyond the ones in the particular study). These assumptions trickle into human subjects' definitions and practices. Here is a case in point: the United States Department of Health and Human Service's Office of Human Research Protections (2009) uses the following definition of research:

> Research means a systematic investigation, including research development, testing and evaluation, designed to develop or contribute to *generalizable* knowledge. (Italics added)

Most IRBs indicate that, if researchers are not engaged in a systematic investigation specifically designed to develop generalizable knowledge, then they need not seek IRB approval. This would suggest that autoethnographic, creative nonfiction, or oral history projects – in which researchers examine their own life experiences or record personal narratives, making no claim to formal generalizability – may be able to skip IRB review. On the other hand, this rule ostensibly serves as a loophole by encouraging some ethnographers to forgo IRB approval altogether (and indeed, some highly esteemed qualitative scholars do not submit their research for IRB review).

Despite the lure of opting out of review, a research project that has not been reviewed carries potential disadvantages – including the possibility that universities may not back the researcher if the project goes awry. Furthermore, there are horror stories of ethnographers being asked by department heads or institutional review boards to quash ethnographic publications in the eleventh hour (for a compelling account of this, see Rambo, 2007). Also, research projects that are not reviewed by IRB may be judged as being less rigorous, significant, and "real" than reviewed research (Krizek, 2008). Finally, for legal and ethical reasons, some publications will refuse to publish research that has not been reviewed.

So, is IRB approval absolutely essential? IRB review may be unnecessary for qualitative exercises designed solely for pedagogical purposes (e.g. students doing a fieldnote assignment in their undergraduate methods class). In such cases the course instructor should check with his/her IRB office and ensure that the methods are carried out in line with the ethical principles of voluntary consent. However, if the qualitative exercise may eventually result in presentation or publication outside of the classroom, then review is advisable.

Review is advisable in most cases, even if the approval process is filled with challenges. Fitch discusses typical qualitative IRB troubles, which may include:

> working in a community where obtaining written consent is at odds with cultural norms or associated with repressive governmental authority, conducting focus group discussions where the primary threat to confidentiality comes from the other group members themselves, beginning with a loosely structured set of questions to explore rather than hypotheses to test, and being personally involved with the community to be studied. (Fitch, 2005, p. 270)

Despite these potential issues, Fitch explains that researchers can successfully navigate IRB skirmishes by asking questions and by actively responding to IRB personnel – in person when necessary. She urges researchers to be accountable and reasonable, remember that their research procedures may indeed involve some risk, and realize that human subjects' protection is a complex issue, where no one person has a monopoly on the truth.

Additionally, every university's rules are slightly different regarding what types of projects need review and what level of review is necessary – and human subjects' guidelines vary widely across international requirements. To be on the safe side, researchers are encouraged to seek out the procedures of their institution earlier rather than later. Review boards certainly hold some principles in common (e.g. informed consent); however, many IRB decisions are a matter of interpretation. Some IRBs allow graduate students to serve as "principal investigators," while others require full-time faculty members to act as their sponsors. Some require informed consent for participant observation and informal interviews, while others require consent forms only for audio-taped formal interviews. Some IRBs ask for a clear timeline of when the data will be destroyed, while others are more concerned about where the data is stored. Some view narrative, autoethnographic, and oral history projects as scientific research in need of being reviewed, while others do not.

If time is an issue, researchers have the easiest route toward approval when they align their research plan and proposal with familiar IRB practices. Deviation from typical procedures requires that researchers make a case for their approach. For instance, a researcher might be called on to explain that a printed consent form is inappropriate for her study because participants in that culture view print as paternalistic, individualistic, intrusive, and therefore unnecessary (Fitch, 2005). In its place, the researcher should describe alternative avenues of informed consent that are culturally more appropriate.

In summary, creating an application for IRB is an integral step for most qualitative research projects that will result in public presentations or publications. Despite concerns that review boards are still more familiar with and friendly toward quantitative scientific projects, my experience with IRB has largely been positive. The application process helps to clarify the project and serves as an ethics check. Furthermore, IRB staff and boards tend to be quite friendly toward problem-based contextual research that provides opportunities for improvement and transformation.

Creating the scholarly research proposal

As noted in the introduction to this chapter, research proposals are a requirement not only for review boards, but also for other scholarly audiences. Such proposals tend to be rule-governed documents. Their success is often determined by the ability of the writer to closely adhere to the standards and guidelines of the professor(s), the institution, or the agency requiring it. For example, if a grant-giving organization asks for a four-page proposal with 12-point font and one-inch margins, this is exactly what applicants should submit. Many great projects are eliminated from grant and scholarship competitions solely because they do not follow format directions.

In the following section you will find information on how to create your own research proposal. Regardless of individual idiosyncrasies, most research proposals consist of the parts outlined in Tips and Tools 5.1: title, abstract, and key words; rationale; research purposes and goals; review of existing knowledge and/or literature related to the project; delineation of guiding research questions or problems to address; plans for data collection and analysis procedures; and, in some cases, timeline, budget, and projected outcomes.

For those researchers taking a top-down, deductive, or *etic* approach – or for those who are required to write up a proposal earlier rather than later, for a class, grant, or scholarship application – the next section will be immediately useful. For those who prefer a more inductive, *emic*, or contextual approach, I recommend you skim the next section for now. Indeed it is always helpful to familiarize yourself with literature and research connected to your phenomena of interest. Then, after you have situated yourself within the literature and the scene, you can return to these pages and write up a research proposal that can guide the rest of your data collection and analysis.

Title, abstract, and key words

Many people judge a book by its cover – and a research project by its title, abstract, and key words. Titles of research proposals have two primary goals: (a) to communicate the main topic(s) of the research; and (b) to invite the reader to learn more. To achieve the first goal, the title should be self-explanatory and include key words about its main topics, disciplinary affiliations, and methodological approach. To achieve the second – the invitational – goal, the title should be at least easy to understand and devoid of technical language, and also potentially creative or catchy. However, forgoing clarity in favor of cleverness is ill advised. I will forever be thankful to my doctoral advisor, Stanley Deetz, for gently encouraging me to modify my first single-authored article title from "Smile, You're at Sea" to "Becoming a Character for Commerce" (Tracy, 2000). The first title was fun, but cutesy, while the second is catchy, capturing with more gravity the profit motive behind cruise ship employees' cheerful display.

Many of the same suggestions about the title hold true for the abstract and for the key words. A fair share of readers will never read further than the proposal's introductory framing material. Officials at granting agencies often make immediate decisions about reviewers on the basis of key words and abstract. Given the widespread use of online search engines, you should consider listing key terms that might be employed to locate your proposal through computerized word searches. Consider:

- methodological terms (e.g. qualitative, ethnography, naturalistic, interview, participant observation);

TIPS AND TOOLS 5.1

Research proposal components

Every group, professor, granting agency and scholarship board has its/his/her own preferences for what belongs in a research proposal and for the relative length of each section. The outline below overviews the sections and page lengths I typically recommend for a double-spaced, typed, 12–15-page classroom assignment.

Title, abstract and key words (~½ page)

Introduction (~2–3 pages)
   Research purposes and goals
   Reference to key audience, terms, and approaches
   Rationale (practical, theoretical, and/or methodological)

Literature review/conceptual framework (~6–8 pages)

Research questions/foci (usually incorporated in Introduction or Literature review)

Methods (~3–4 pages) – See Tips and Tools 5.2 for details
   Researcher's role
   Background of site/participants
   IRB approval
   Sampling plan
   Sources of the data collected (e.g. participant observation, interviews, focus groups, online data, documents)
   Research instrumentation and approach (e.g. examples of interview questions, methods of transcribing, fieldnote writing)
     [the preceding two sections are often combined]
   Proposed methods of analysis

References (variable)

Budget (~1 page)

Timeline (~1 page)

Potential outcomes/findings (~1 page)

- names of disciplines (e.g. communication, sociology, criminal justice, psychology, management);
- types of context (e.g. nonprofit, education, corporation, retail, family);
- theoretical approaches (e.g. feminist, critical, interpretive, poststructural).

Finally, you should be aware of the outlet's rules regarding the length of titles, abstracts, and key words. In most cases, titles should be between 10 and 15 words – and usually not more than two lines; outlets often ask that abstracts be between 100 and 200 words. The number of key words is often limited to a range between three and five.

Introduction/rationale

The introduction and rationale provide an opportunity to quickly grab the attention of your core audience and explain why readers should care about the project. This section includes several key elements.

Purpose statement

First and foremost, the reader needs to understand the primary purposes and goals of your research. Make the goal statement obvious and explicit. It is perfectly fine to say: "The primary purposes (or objectives or goals) of this research project are..." Revisiting this statement repeatedly is crucial for ensuring that the project, as eventually written, actually carries out the goals framed in the introduction.

Conceptual cocktail party

Second, the introduction should identify, name, and begin dialogue with the research project's central audience – or, as my doctoral committee member Anne Sigismund Huff called this group, the "conceptual cocktail party." Just as people have their favorite friends they gather around at a party, researchers also have their dream team of scholars, activists, journalists, professionals, or public figures with whom they would like to dialogue about the project.

In the first couple of pages of the manuscript, you should name and cite four to five people whom you would love to read, respond to, or critique the project. Although these particular people may not be contacted, their names will serve as context cues for your readers, and especially for readers who have been their students, protégés, followers, and admirers. And you may get lucky. Sometimes reviewers of a grant proposal are chosen precisely because they are familiar with the scholars cited in the first few pages. If nothing else, citing these people early on lets the reader understand the types of conversations you are hoping to engage through the project, setting the tone for your rationale.

Rationale

The **rationale** is a third important ingredient in an introduction. In the rationale, the researcher clearly answers the question, "Who cares?" This is accomplished through an explanation as to why the study is significant, important, and helpful. Strong rationales are specific. They also tend to be multi-pronged, meaning that they attend to why the study is significant theoretically, practically, and methodologically.

Phronetic, contextual research that focuses on salient issues in the field usually has a built-in practical rationale. For instance, in 2009 former student Liz Cantu conducted a qualitative study on how various stakeholders made sense of mortgage foreclosures. Given the foreclosure epidemic hitting the United States at that time, Liz's study had a built-in practical rationale.

A theoretical rationale may be achieved by answering questions such as:

- How will this study build upon existing knowledge?
- How does it fill a gap?
- How might it bridge various concepts in a useful way?

It is usually not good enough to simply suggest that "xyz topic has never been studied before." Rationalizing a study on a *lack* of knowledge can invite counterarguments from your reader (a stance that you do not want to encourage). And, if a project has never been done, there might be very good reasons for it – say, the study is not feasible, or the topic is not smart or interesting. A rationale based on *need* and *added value* rather than on lack is much more persuasive. You can focus on the value of the study by discussing how the research may help settle a theoretical debate, incrementally build understanding, or problematize a long-standing assumption.

Finally, some projects have a significant methodological contribution. Given the valuable data garnered through interpretive, contextual, and naturalistic methods, certain theories or topics may be better understood solely by using qualitative methods. Indeed, qualitative methods such as interviews and participant observation can significantly enhance theories or topics that have primarily been studied through the lens of positivist paradigms or quantitative experiments, surveys, or self-reports. For example, in working with Holocaust survivors, Carolyn Ellis and her colleagues devised an interaction interview format that allowed them to actively engage and work with participants to construct their stories (Ellis, Kiesinger, & Tillmann-Healy, 1997).

When rationalizing a study because of its qualitative method, it is important to keep in mind that potential key readers are those who have studied your same topic using *other* types of research methods. Hence it makes sense to review the limitations of past research in a fair manner, without undue harsh criticism. Researchers from other approaches are human beings and, as such, will likely avoid reading, appreciating, or citing your work if it paints them in a ruthlessly critical light. As one of my colleagues, Elizabeth Richards, often advises: "Don't stand on the shoulders of giants only to pee on their heads." What she means by this is that, although well-placed critique helps us extend understanding and modify theories, researchers should not come off like ungrateful children. Instead, good writing acknowledges earlier research and highlights how the current study adds nuance, depth, and complexity. Whether or not we necessarily agree with, or like, past research, we have benefited from the fact that it sets the stage for our proposed study.

Literature review/conceptual framework

The literature review, also known as the conceptual framework, is usually the lengthiest part of a research proposal (it often makes up about one third of the final report). The literature review tells the story of the primary concepts and theories that frame the study and how these ideas have evolved over time. Researchers engaging in their first qualitative data collection project should seriously consider using a theoretical framework with which they are already familiar. Alternatively, I recommend accessing theories that are easily available (such as the frameworks described in this book) or adapting material from a similar study, always giving credit to the original author(s).

How should you select the literature to review? First and foremost, the literature review discusses past research upon which the current study builds, problematizes, or extends. So a literature review for a study of how media representations shape youths' perceptions of romantic relationships might introduce the media portrayals of heterosexual and homosexual romantic relationships, a poststructuralist conceptual lens, and then review current research on romance (Jackson & Gilbertson, 2009). Good literature reviews also define clearly the key constructs to be examined and sum up what is currently known about the topic.

Literature reviews are usually best organized by topic or issue rather than by author. The literature review should not be written simply as a series of article abstracts piled on top of one another. Rather, it's helpful to discuss key topics as if discussing the plot of a story, and to support key topics with references and examples. Providing a descriptive blurb of each referenced study is generally preferable to providing a single claim followed by a long list of citations.

Another way to think about the literature review is as a puzzle. The puzzle represents a body of knowledge. The literature review explains the existing puzzle pieces by explaining key terms, theories, and chunks of available knowledge. However, the literature review also clearly delineates a *missing* puzzle piece – and previews how your particular research study is designed to fill that gap. This approach illustrates the body of existing knowledge, but also points out what is unknown, confusing, or broken. The literature review shows that some knowledge may not yet exist – but it avoids critiquing individual past authors for failing to pursue the exact research questions proposed in the current study.

Research questions/foci

As discussed in Chapter 1, research questions are a core part of qualitative research projects. By the time you are writing a research proposal, the questions should be more specific than the guiding question from which we started: "What is going on here?" And, by the time you write the final report, research foci should be seamlessly connected to the findings. Furthermore, they should be closely associated with the title, rationale, and literature review. By the time readers have read the literature review, they should not be surprised by the research questions or foci. They should not feel as though these came out of thin air. Rather it should be clear that *of course* you would pose these questions or pursue these goals, given the rationale and story line of concepts provided so far.

Good research questions or statements of focus include language and key terms already employed and defined. For some projects, these are better placed after the rationale; for others, they emerge more naturally from the literature review. The former is often the case with problem-based phronetic studies, the latter with studies that are more theoretically derived. If you are confused about placement, consider modeling your work after an article that is particularly compelling or similar to your project. Finally, keep in mind that research questions and foci statements should guide, but not dictate, your research path. They will continue to morph throughout the data-gathering, analysis, and writing processes.

Methods

The methods section details the context, the participants, the researcher's role, the participation level, and the data collection and analysis procedures. In some cases, this section will delineate the number of researcher hours, the exact number and types of research participants, and the number of pages of transcribed data that may be expected. If the proposal is a class assignment or a thesis/dissertation prospectus, providing this information allows advising professors to provide suggestions about the planned procedures, scope, and framework.

The methods section should explain specialized qualitative words (e.g. what is an "emic approach") and should use citations to support the procedures used (e.g. you could support the idea of engaging in participant observation first, and then moving on to focused interviews, by citing successful research that has taken this approach in the past). Tips and Tools 5.2 overviews items that generally belong in the methods section.

(Data analysis methods are covered in Chapters 9 and 10, and tips of how to describe analysis methods in the final report are provided in Chapter 12.)

TIPS AND TOOLS 5.2

What belongs in a qualitative methods section?

- Researcher's role – (e.g. full participant?) and brief description of gaining access.
- Participants and sites of study – what types of participants and contextual sites are under study? Describe the context(s), number of participants, their background, and the demographics.
- Indication of human subjects review and approval from IRB – this may not require a whole section, but IRB should be noted somewhere along the way.
- The sampling plan or rationale – this may be sprinkled throughout the methods section. It explains why the context and the participants studied were appropriate given the research goals.
- Description of data collected – this includes data sources and collection procedures, such as participant observation fieldnotes, focus groups, webpages, interviews, documents. Many audiences will be keenly interested in the *number* of participants, research hours, and pages of typewritten transcribed fieldnotes, interview transcripts, or documents.
- Interview questions – these should either be embedded in the methods section or attached as an appendix.
- An overview of data analysis procedures. Although details for data analysis may not have emerged yet, it is important – especially for grant-giving and scholarship agencies – that the researcher evidences a clear plan answering the research questions, analyzing the data, and fulfilling the stated purposes.

Budget/timeline

Finally, some research proposals will call for a specific budget and timeline. This section is the place where you will delineate the necessary research materials and their costs, as well as predict how long the completion of various parts of the project will take. Do not be too conservative with your figures, as projects may often take longer and cost more than predicted. At the same time, padding the budget or timeline is ethically problematic and damages the credibility of the entire project. Tips and Tools 5.3 provides a list of items that may be especially worthwhile in the budget section.

The process of mapping out the timeline and the budget provides a good opportunity to know whether the project is too grand for the resources available. If the project seems too large, you should modify the stated goals and scope. Perhaps you need to switch your theoretical framework to focus on already familiar concepts. Possibly one of the proposed research questions can be answered through past research – and need not require your own interviews. Or perhaps the project should be broken into two or three smaller projects, or shared with a research partner.

I often recommend to students that they create a file and label it "after I've completed this class," or "after I graduate." In these files you can less anxiously compile all the great ideas you do not have time to accomplish immediately, and you'll know that these good ideas are ready and waiting when a future opportunity arises. Furthermore, for every proposal or essay, I create an accompanying "dump box" – which is essentially a computer file where I cut and paste the paragraphs, sentences, or tables that end up not really fitting

TIPS AND TOOLS 5.3

What to include in a qualitative project budget

Among other items that qualitative researchers may want to include in a budget are:

- computer equipment such as a lap-top, portable computer for fieldnote writing, digital audio-recorder, and transcription pedal;
- cost of transcribing, translation, research, or editing services;
- equipment, room rentals (e.g. for focus groups);
- researcher travel (to the site, to places for archival research, to additional granting agencies, to visit collaborators, to research conferences);
- monetary participant incentives (for interviews, focus groups, member checks/reflections, and follow-ups);
- entertainment, food, or childcare costs for the participants;
- books, on-line subscriptions, or supplies (markers, paper, posterboard);
- salary, summer support, or teaching buy-out for the researcher(s) and research assistants;
- qualitative data-analysis software (such as Dragon Naturally Speaking, NVivo, or Atlas.ti).

my emerging project. In the future, I often find a perfectly crafted paragraph that can finally see the light of day. One project's dump is another's delight!

Projected outcomes

Finally, some proposals will require a discussion of projected outcomes/results. Outcomes may be conceptual or material. For instance, conceptually, the project may help resolve a theoretical debate or increase understandings of a problem. Material outcomes, on the other hand, refer to **deliverables**, such as:

- a class paper;
- conference papers and presentations;
- external grant applications;
- scholarly articles;
- white papers;
- new class syllabi;
- a strategic plan for a new research center;
- coordination of guest lecturers.

These deliverables are material representations of the research project.

Together with other admonitions throughout this chapter, I must emphasize how important it is to avoid over-promising projected outcomes. Although you may feel tempted to list every single finding or paper that may ever result from the research, limit yourself to outcomes that are certainly achievable within the specified time period. Fulfilling fewer outcomes well is preferable to completing a half-hearted job with many; it's better to "under-promise and over-deliver."

In summary

This chapter has overviewed the institutional review board process and the writing of the research proposal. The requirements for institutional review vary from one institution to another; but many institutions ask that you explain the rationale of the research, the research instruments, the ways you will seek informed consent and maintain confidentiality, and how the research will proceed. Depending on the vulnerability of the research participants and the scope of the project, the review process may be exempt or expedited, or it may require full-board approval. Despite the fact that some qualitative researchers have difficulties with IRB, the process can help ensure the ethics of the project and also serve as a stepping stone toward writing other types of proposals.

The second half of the chapter reviewed research proposals, which are the formalized planning documents required by many external audiences. Research proposals usually consist of a title, an abstract, and key words; an introduction/rationale; a literature review/conceptual framework; research questions/foci; a section on methods; and an overview of budget, timeline, and deliverables.

You might be wondering *when* you should write the research proposal. In most cases, its due date is externally determined by granting agencies or professors. Many qualitative researchers have been asked to submit detailed research proposals long before they have been able to immerse themselves in the scene and know exactly what they plan to study. In such cases, the best you can do is "fake it to make it"; and remember that parts of the research plan can and will be modified along the way, no matter when the proposal is due.

If you, personally, have the power to determine the timing of the research proposal, my suggestion – especially for those pursuing a contextual, problem-based approach – is to develop it about *a third of the way through data collection*. This leaves enough time to get into the scene and figure out various directions, but it also encourages you to systematically review the existing literature early enough for it to usefully guide your fieldwork, interviews, focus groups, and the remaining data collection.

KEY TERMS

→ **assent**   used instead of informed consent, with individuals who are vulnerable or have diminished capacities – such as children, the sick, and the mentally disabled

→ **Belmont report**   a statement of basic human subject principles issued by the National Commission for the Protection of Human Subjects

→ **deductive disclosure**   the indirect identification of respondents through the use and piecing together of known data

→ **deliverables**   material outcomes of a research project such as: (1) conference papers and presentations; (2) external grant applications; (3) scholarly articles; (4) white papers; (5) new class syllabi; (6) a strategic plan for a new center of research; (7) coordination of guest lecturers or; (8) a class paper

→ **exempt review**   the quickest type of review for an IRB application; this level of review pertains to studies that examine public behavior and grant anonymity to participants – for example, a study of how dog walkers communicate at local parks

expedited review   the most common type of IRB review, where signed consent or assent forms are required and the researcher maintains a record of the participants and of their personal information

full-board review   the most involved type of IRB review; it is used when the research is risky – as in observing terrorist groups – or when participants are especially vulnerable and in need of extra protection – for example they are mentally impaired

human subject protections   codes developed to protect people ("human subjects") from unethical research

informed consent   the process by which researchers inform potential participants about risks, benefits, and what else is involved in agreeing to participate in a study before they decide to do it of their own will

rationale   the part of a research paper or proposal that illustrates why your study matters and answers the question "Who cares?" from a theoretical, practical, and methodological point of view

research instruments   the tools used to collect the data; for qualitative researchers, these are the researchers themselves, together with interview questions, focus-group plans, and open-ended surveys

research proposal   a detailed plan that lays out the purpose, path, and procedures of the project

CHAPTER 6

Field roles, fieldnotes, and field focus

Contents

Qualitative Research Methods: Collecting Evidence, Crafting Analysis, Communicating Impact, First Edition. Sarah J. Tracy.
© 2013 Sarah J. Tracy. Published 2013 by Blackwell Publishing Ltd.

After receiving IRB approvals and negotiating access to a scene, researchers move from being naïve explorers to making mindful decisions about their level of enmeshment in the field. As they do so, they must also consider how best to take notes and piece together data to make meaning out of the research project.

This chapter opens with a discussion of different levels of participation or enmeshment in the field, and how each standpoint has advantages and disadvantages. It proceeds with recommendations for how to create material records of participant observation, explaining how to move from making raw records in the scene to developing typed fieldnotes with analytic reflections. The chapter discusses several ways you can best focus and narrow your data collection. It closes with a section on "following, forgetting and improvising," in which I discuss how to manage various ethical dilemmas and challenges in the field.

Field roles and standpoints of participant observation

In the early days of participant observation, one of the primary rules of fieldwork was that researchers should avoid being complete participants, as they might become so assimilated that they would be swallowed up by the culture. The fear was that they would no longer be able to notice assumptions and values specific to the group under study. Many researchers labeled this situation (which was "to be avoided at all stakes") "going native" (Lindlof & Taylor, 2011).

However, the notion of "going native" has a problematic history (Ashcroft, Griffiths, & Tiffins, 1998). The phrase originally referred to the European colonizers' fear of being acculturated into the customs of the African natives they had captured. Because the colonizers viewed their captives as primitive, they used the pejorative phrase "going native" to warn others from becoming too identified with indigenous peoples. Similarly, the expression has also been used in reference to foreign officials who became so sympathetic toward the locals that they did not adequately represent their own national interests.

This phrase, if relevant at all anymore, applies to realist approaches that assume the importance of objectivity and detachment and suggest that enmeshment with participants goes hand in hand with improperly tainting and biasing the account (Angrosino, 2005). In contrast, more interpretive, critical, and poststructural approaches suggest that a position of sympathy and identification with those under study is not categorically problematic and, in many cases, is necessary for understanding the emotionality of the scene (Goodall, 2000). Further, the whole metaphor of "going" native suggests that there is a final destination to which a researcher finally arrives and from which s/he does not move any further.

A more worthwhile way to consider one's participation in the scene is in terms of a "continuum of enmeshment" and of a potpourri of overlapping roles. Each standpoint has its own set of opportunities and limitations. Two key questions are:

1   Which standpoint of participation is most appropriate, given my research goals?
2   Given the standpoint I inhabit, what kind of data or research topics would allow me to maximize opportunities and minimize limitations?

The following section provides information that can help you to answer these two questions by reviewing types of participant observation and their advantages and disadvantages.

Complete participant

One of the most convenient places to start fieldwork is right where you are – in your own workplace, culture, social group, classroom, vacation destination, or watering hole. I use the phrase **complete participant** (Gold, 1958; Spradley, 1980) to describe researchers who study contexts in which they already are members or to which they become fully affiliated; an alternative description is "complete member researcher" (Adler & Adler, 1987, p. 67). As a complete participant, a researcher has multiple reasons to participate in the context and a variety of incentives to spend time in the field (Anderson, 2006).

Complete participation has a number of advantages. First, this role provides convenient access to a wide range of readily available data. Actors respond as if they were dealing with a colleague or friend rather than with a researcher, which may encourage candor and openness. Being a complete participant allows insight into motivations, insider meanings, and implicit assumptions that guide actions but are rarely explicitly articulated. However, given the range of meanings in any one context, complete participant researchers must "assiduously pursue other insiders' interpretations, attitudes, and feelings as well as their own" (Anderson, 2006, p. 389). Furthermore, some research foci are especially well suited for complete participation; if the goal is to understand what collective membership in a certain group *feels* like, it makes sense to become a member.

One particular type of complete participant is the **ardent activist** (Snow, Benford, & Anderson, 1986), who seeks to embrace and practice the values and ideologies of the group under study. Former doctoral student Christina Colp-Hansbury became a member of the silent war protest group Women in Black precisely in order to be able to understand what it felt like to be part of a protest group – with its attendant uncertainties and taunts from passers-by. Likewise, complete participation can be a good route to studying groups that are relatively closed or mistrustful of outsiders. When ethnic minorities study their own cultures, they are less apt to encounter mistrust and hostility, or they access only a small portion of the data – those that are deemed safe and appropriate for outsiders to see (Zinn, 2001).

Perhaps most significantly, complete participants have access to a depth and breadth of the culture's deep background that gives them a unique standpoint from which they can make connections among a span of issues that might otherwise go unnoticed. For instance, in my cruise ship research, I was able to examine the critical irony related to the customers' sexual harassment of my co-worker Kaci by linking it to the mandates "we never say no," inculcated in the staff's land-based training months earlier (Tracy, 2000). I was only able to connect these facts because I was exposed to data over time.

Despite these advantages, complete participation has limitations. The most significant challenges are those of ethics and deception. Complete participants are oftentimes covert in their research strategies – figuring that, since they are already in the scene, they will just go ahead and start collecting research data without telling anyone about it. And covert research of non-public interactions runs counter to IRB-mandated informed consent.

Despite the ethical and IRB issues, some researchers are completely secretive and never disclose that they are conducting research. Other complete participants seek permission from one or two gatekeepers but do not disclose their research agenda to all the people they encounter. At least some members in the scene may be unaware that a researcher is in their midst, and therefore they may unwittingly reveal sensitive information they would not purposefully volunteer for a published report.

When reflecting upon these ethical challenges, it is useful to consider the utilitarian question of whether the ethical disadvantages associated with covert status and deception outweigh the advantages of revealing important data or stories that might otherwise remain silent. Award-winning researcher Judith Rollins (1985) provides an eloquent explanation as to why she went undercover as a complete participant to examine the challenges faced by Black domestic workers:

> I decided that because this occupation had been such a significant one for low-income women and because so little research had been done on it despite its presence throughout the world, the understanding that might be gained by my putting myself in the position of a domestic, even in this limited way, was worth the price (Rollins, 1985, p. 15, as quoted in Hesse-Biber & Leavy, 2006, p. 252).

Indeed deception may be especially warranted when studying "up" the hierarchy, as elites have good reason to keep secrets about their interactions with the less powerful. If a researcher reveals and problematizes the status quo, power holders' high status might be disrupted. Deception, though, is not for the faint of heart. Undercover research is accompanied by significant stress and anxiety that you may be found out (Goodall, 1989). Hence, if you are new to fieldwork, especially if you struggle with social anxiety or nervousness, covert status is ill-advised.

Working "undercover" can also lead to logistical problems. Covert researchers cannot be seen taking fieldnotes and often must wait until a later time to do so. This may result in a less detailed and complex recording of the scene. Further, covert status makes interviews – particularly audio-recorded or structurally guided interviews – virtually impossible. This inability to use some ethnographic tools usually results in a less complex data set and precludes the opportunity to systematically compare similar interview responses across a span of people. Complete participation also limits the types of questions you can ask. Cultural members tend to put up with a variety of questions – even those that are stupid, blunt, or taboo – from overt researchers that they would never tolerate from regular people (Bailey, 1996). When I conducted interviews with my cruise ship colleagues, I had to spend a significant amount of time reassuring them that I was truly interested in hearing their point of view about everyday ship activities. They would roll their eyes when I asked a question such as "Where is frontstage and where is backstage on the ship?" and would say, "Sarah, you already know the answer to that." Or they would omit key points in a story that I had witnessed – leaving it to me to decide whether or how I should best fill in the details.

Another disadvantage of complete participation is that the researcher can become so enmeshed that it becomes difficult to notice the cultures' unique values (Agar, 1994). To illustrate this issue, consider the following question: "What values and behaviors are uniquely typified in a classroom?" This question would likely be quite easy to answer if you traveled to a classroom that was in an unfamiliar discipline or school. Unique assumptions and practices are instantly recognizable ("Wow, over in that *other* classroom, there is a distinct hierarchical structure, and students don't speak unless first spoken to"). In contrast, it is more difficult to assess characteristics of a classroom in which you have already been a complete participant. You may not even think of noting the way everyone freely discusses issues, or the fact that students pull their seats into a circle. When values and behaviors are familiar, they become so normalized that they are almost invisible to insiders. As Spradley (1980) warns, "[t]he more you know about a situation as an ordinary participant, the more difficult it is to study it as an ethnographer" (p. 61); in contrast, "[t]he *less* familiar you are with a social situation, the *more* you are able to see the tacit cultural rules at work" (p. 62).

This disadvantage of losing perspective may be minimized if the researcher can escape the scene or "cool out" before analyzing and coming to conclusions about the data.

By waiting several months after leaving my cruise ship job before I analyzed data, I was able to note oddities in my own behavior that I did not notice while I was in the scene. For instance, on the ship I "chose" to cut my hair to distinguish myself from other employees and to get more mentions in the passenger comment cards. At the time, this felt like a personal, non-coerced choice. After I was out of the scene, I noticed how the "hair-cutting as a method to get more good comments" served as evidence of my thorough enculturation (some would say brain-washing). As staff, we so thoroughly bought into the idea that comment cards were currency for promotion that I never thought to question why other types of evaluation were not used. In short, the break I took between observation and analysis allowed me time, space, and perspective to examine my own discursive construction in the field and provided a valuable standpoint from which I could critically reflect upon my role as an acculturated cruise ship employee.

Play participant

Some of the most renowned ethnographies have been conducted by what I call the **play participant** – also known as the "participant as observer" (Gold, 1958, p. 220), the "active participant" (Spradley, 1980, p. 60), or the "active member researcher" (Adler & Adler, 1987, p. 50). I use this description because it memorably suggests a stance in which fieldworkers *play* at becoming active members engaging in a range of cultural activities, but their membership is improvisational and unbound by many formal norms of the scene – they can opt in and out in ways unavailable to a complete participant. Play participants watch and do what others are doing, "not merely to gain acceptance, but to more fully learn the culture rules for behavior" (Spradley, 1980, p. 60). They shadow, which means they not only watch but follow around, eat, spectate, and play with participants (Gill, 2011). At the same time they keep one foot outside the scene by consistently taking fieldnotes and intermittently leaving. Their research is explicit rather than covert.

The close enmeshment of play participants within the context often encourages them to closely understand participants' values. However, play participants are just as likely to take on the role of the **controlled skeptic** (Snow et al., 1986), in which the researcher becomes close to the scene and asks questions in a polite, curious, and naïve manner yet maintains skepticism. This role is common among researchers who examine religious organizations or political interest groups (Gordon, 1987; Shaffir, 1991).

The play participant's role has a number of advantages. These include becoming close and emotionally connected with those in the scene. Play participants are able to go beyond reports that rely on the five senses – of what they see, hear, taste, touch, and smell – to what they also intuitively *feel*. At the same time this can be uncomfortable, which some might say is a disadvantage that arises from being so attached (even if playfully) to the scene. I felt these advantages and disadvantages keenly during a situation in which I "played" as participant in a correctional officer defensive tactics training session – an issue explored in Consider This 6.1.

As illustrated, the play participant's role gets close enough to the scene for the play participant to be able to *feel* along with participants – a situation that has many of the same advantages and disadvantages as that of the complete participant. However, the play participant also has some advantages the complete participant does not. For instance, because their research is explicit, play participants can consistently make detailed and verbatim data recordings of interactions in the scene. The practice of consistent critical reflection through fieldnote writing provides analytic distance and helps to ensure that researchers do not become so fully acculturated that they are unable to detect the context's values, behaviors, and customs.

CONSIDER THIS 6.1

Why "playing" = learning

The following narrative, drawn from my research with correctional officers, illustrates how being a play participant can provide important insight that is unavailable to those who just stand at the periphery or never get involved. As you read this narrative, ask yourself: What are the advantages of being a "play participant?"

One of my primary sources of correctional officer data collection was attending an annual week-long in-service training alongside officers. As part of our physical defensive tactics training, I learned how to take down, hold, cuff, and apply pressure points that would cause maximum discomfort with minimal damage. I practiced these techniques on others and felt others practice them on my own body. I viscerally learned the importance of these techniques as measures to quickly and professionally de-escalate violent situations in the jail.

At the end of the week we put into practice all of these physical defensive tactics. The trainers, dressed in bright red padded suits, played what they called the "bad guys" and acted out scenarios in which a group of three or four officers had to react. We were all quite relaxed and excited to have the opportunity to "beat up" our trainers.

In the middle of the second scenario (which I observed from the sidelines), the mood changed. In this scenario one of the "bad guys" pulled a (plastic) knife on one of the officers. None of the officers in training saw the knife, and the trainer proceeded to "stab" one of them. The stabbed officer stopped in his tracks, nervously laughed, and announced to the other officers, "I'm dead!" The other trainees halted their defensive tactics activities and hung their heads in embarrassment.

Suddenly, one of the trainers yelled sternly: "You're still going – just because one of you is dead doesn't mean you stop!" The atmosphere instantly changed from playful to serious. It could have just as easily been me who failed to spot the knife. Together with the others, I felt humiliated and terrified. In a flash of a plastic knife, I experienced the high stakes of defensive tactics. I knew in my heart, my head, and my body that the training was not just a game. If officers – or even volunteers like me – handled these incidents incorrectly, they could be hurt or killed. In that moment, the potential repercussions of jail and prison violence became real at a gut level.

Furthermore, play participants can escape and cool out from fieldwork that can be hot, intense, draining, and emotional. During these cool-out periods they have time to write up their notes in detail, review past research related to their emerging findings, and talk with colleagues and peers. Finally, because everyone in the scene is aware of the research, it is easier to depart from the scene and terminate the field research (a topic covered in detail in Chapter 14).

The biggest challenge of play participation is consistently maintaining trust and reassuring others that the research is essentially harmless. Play participants must endear themselves to the group and keep group members apprised of their ongoing activities. Think of it this way: if you want to "play" with other people who do not know you – whether it's playing tennis, a card game, or pick-up basketball – the insiders get to say whether you are allowed to play or not.

Successful play therefore requires an ongoing process of negotiation in which the researcher is aware both of the task and of the relational concerns, and attends to various members' needs

CONSIDER THIS 6.2

When playing is uncomfortable

The fieldnote excerpt illustrates the difficulties of negotiating a play participant's role. As you read it over, ask yourself: What are the disadvantages of playing along with participants on their terms and in their space?

I'm observing the work release unit at Nouveau Jail during shift change. The second-shift officers appear and the friendly day-shift officer leaves to go home. A white officer in his mid-thirties, Ben Jewel, enters the officer booth and says to me: "I vaguely remember you from one of our roll calls." The other officer enters, a husky Hispanic man named Billy, who appears to be about 22 years old. I recognize him from a fleeting interaction several weeks ago. He is loud and sarcastic. I hope he and Ben are okay with my presence. They were not expecting me. They showed up for work, and I was there.

   I give them informed consent forms, and they both immediately start mocking them. Billy says: "Uhh, scary, I'll never sign anything." I am concerned that they will not sign the forms. At the same time, they do not ask me to leave. Maybe they just don't care? I hang out and watch. Forty-five minutes later, Ben signs the informed consent form. As he hands it to me, he offers amicably: "Seriously, if you have any questions, just let me know." Billy continues to ignore the form and my presence. How am I supposed to know whether I should stay if he refuses to even acknowledge me? I feel paralyzed, uncertain of what I should do next.

   Billy has not yet looked me in the eye. He goes on about his business, and I bow my head and pretend to doodle. In my peripheral vision, I see Billy stand up and walk toward the corner where I am sitting. I refuse to look up. But then, BOOM!! He slams the cupboard next to me. I jump. He chuckles a bit.

   After a while Billy begins to warm up. He tells stories about camping and his latest girlfriend. Rubbing his hands together, he says of his upcoming camping plans: "I'm going to get some." Although I am somewhat repulsed by his "get some" comment and my ego is bruised from feeling ignored, I proceed to engage Billy in an extended and quite pleasant conversation about camping. Moments later, he signs and returns the informed consent. The rest of our time together is affable and comfortable. It just took an hour and forty-five minutes to get there.

and expectations. Play participants may sometimes act cooler – more unfazed, naïve, tough, less offended, or shocked – than they actually are. For example, in his ethnographic study of firefighters, Scott (2005) explains that, to maintain trust and camaraderie as "one of the guys," he would display neutral responses, or even laugh at humor he found offensive – a field dilemma disclosed by many ethnographers who study masculine work settings (e.g. Collinson, 1992). Play participants will experience ways of being that are not comfortable and may refrain from making comments or judgments they would readily make in their own in-circles – something that is illustrated in Consider This 6.2's narrative reflection.

Focused participant observer

A third type of field-work role is one I call the **focused participant observer**, also called "observer as participant" (Gold, 1958, p. 221) or "reactive" observer (Angrosino, 2005, p. 732). I use this phrase to refer to an observer who enters a scene with an explicit researcher status and a clear agenda of what data to gather in the scene. This approach is usually associated with controlled studies, in which actors agree to respond to the researcher solely in regard to issues predetermined in the research design.

Structured interviews without long-term participation are a common method of data collection for focused participant observers. For example, Studs Terkel's (1974) famous book *Working* is made up of essays in which a wide variety of people describe their jobs. He was interested in hearing about members' work, but he did not hang out with them over the long term or observe them.

The fieldwork of focused participant observation is highly structured and often conducted for short time periods. A good example is a study of "elderspeak" – a type of patronizing talk to older people – in nursing homes (Williams, Kemper, & Hummert, 2003). The researchers wanted to gauge the effects of an intervention program designed to reduce nurses' elderspeak. To this purpose, the research team recorded field data before and after the intervention and then analyzed them for evidence of key characteristics of elderspeak, such as terms of endearment ("sweetie" or "big guy"), inappropriate collective pronouns ("are *we* ready for *our* breakfast?"), exaggerated intonation, simplified vocabulary, and shorter sentences than normal. As Williams and colleagues explain:

> We obtained speech samples of each CNA [certified nursing assistant] interacting with residents by using wireless receivers that transmitted to a recording station. The transmitters were attached to the CNA's uniform with a small microphone that could be switched off and on. We recorded each CNA for 1 to 2 hr, until we obtained five recordings of conversations of adequate length with participating residents. We obtained five interaction segments for each aide before and after training to provide a representative sample. We compensated CNAs $10 for participation in each recording session. We archived the recordings in digital audio files, and later transcribed them, coded them for elderspeak measures, and rated them on emotional tone. (Williams et al., 2003, p. 244)

Through this method, the researchers focused their data-gathering energies.

The primary advantage of focused participant observation is that it provides a clear plan for data collection – which makes it a common approach in granted or funded research. The time commitment for participants is usually short, predictable, and circumscribed. Because participants know how long they need to be involved in the study, researchers can avoid the ongoing negotiation issues associated with more enmeshed roles. Focused participant observers also have a good idea, in advance, about which data will "count" as being part of the study. Williams and her colleagues (2003) knew that they had to record the nurses just long enough to gather several interactions with patients. Terkel's (1974) interviews took fascinating turns and twists, yet he remained focused on issues of work.

Although focused participation has a number of advantages, it also has some limitations. The participants have fewer opportunities to reveal various facets of their identity. The briefer the contact between researchers and participants, the greater the likelihood for misunderstanding. Researchers rely more heavily on their own interpretations of what they hear and see, and they are less motivated to ask about participant interpretations. Furthermore, because researcher–member interactions often occur only once, the data are more likely to provide a one-time snapshot rather than complexities over time.

Finally, because the researcher chooses a specific focus *before* data collection begins, the analysis is not *emic*, but rather assumes a deductive, *etic* approach. This may be appropriate if the researcher already has a fair amount of background knowledge on the scene – as was the case with Williams and her colleagues, who had already conducted a series of elderspeak studies. However, focused participation can be problematic for those who are new to the topic or context. This stance assumes that researchers know what data to collect before they familiarize themselves with a scene or people, and this may allow important data to go unnoticed.

Complete observer

The fourth main field research role is that of **complete observer** (Gold, 1958), also known as the "unobtrusive (nonreactive)" observer (Angrosino, 2005, p. 732), the "passive observer" (Spradley, 1980, p. 58), and the "peripheral member researcher" (Adler & Adler, 1987, p. 39). This role is similar to that of the complete participant, in that the research is usually covert and participants do not know they are being studied. However, rather than participating in the scene, complete observers stand at the periphery, merely watching the scene unfold in front of them. A complete observer is kind of like a "secret shopper," who furtively evaluates a cashier or a shopping experience from afar, on the strength of a one-time experience. Complete observers watch scenes as if they were watching a movie or a performance. They are at the periphery, and participants are generally unaware of being studied. Contexts for complete observation may include watching a parade, a festival, or a group of protestors.

The primary advantage of complete observation is ease of access. One can learn a lot through complete observation. Although I would argue that gaining permission and negotiating trust are often enjoyable activities in which you can learn a lot about the scene, some researchers view such activities as hassles that just delay data collection. Indeed, studies that employ complete observation of public spaces almost always have "exempt"-level review from institutional review boards. For these reasons, complete observation can be a quick way to become acquainted with qualitative methods.

As an initial research activity, I often ask students to simply hang out in a public space, observe, and take notes. This can be particularly helpful if you do the observation in partnerships or in small groups. Even if the observation is made in a short amount of time, a powerful lesson will emerge by comparing and contrasting different people's observations of the same scene.

Despite the advantages of being a complete observer, this detached role also comes with limitations. Like the complete participant, the complete observer usually cannot be obtrusive or obvious in data collection. In some public scenes, such as a coffee shop, a researcher might get away with taking notes. However, taking notes in some scenes without permission – like when you are watching an airport security line, or when you are visiting a friend for dinner – may raise the attention of participants or encourage inquiry (although speaking or texting into your smart phone may not).

Probably the largest risk of complete observation is the researcher's level of detachment and separation from the context. Complete observers do not engage in the explicit questioning of actors in the scene, and therefore they have limited access to participants' motivations or feelings. Furthermore, they spend only fleeting time with any one actor. Without data from long-term immersion or interviews, it is easy for researchers to misunderstand the action and to overlay their own interpretation on it. Misinterpretation may come as a result of simple ignorance of important local details. Returning to my earlier mall example, a secret shopper (or a complete observer researcher) might negatively evaluate a cashier who keeps checking his telephone throughout a transaction. However, a more enmeshed researcher might have background that helps to explain the cashier's behavior – perhaps the employee has promised his pregnant and overdue wife that he will be instantly available if she goes into labor, and that's why he keeps checking his phone even as he works.

Misinterpretations by complete observers can also be due to **ethnocentrism** – the tendency to consider one's own culture as normal, natural, and right and therefore to judge data emanating from dissimilar groups as odd, problematic, or of less importance. While ethnocentrism is a risk in *all* types of research, when researchers are involved in distant or short-term field interactions, they are rarely forced to account for their own bodies, identities, or research goals in relation to the scene. If you find yourself in a complete observer role, I encourage you to become more enmeshed over time. Angrosino (2005) argues that the most modern and progressive qualitative researchers approach data collection as a dialogue of equal collaboration that celebrates multiple and contradictory voices. Such an approach is difficult – if not impossible – in the complete observer role.

In this section I have reviewed four levels of field-work enmeshment, namely those of the *complete participant, play participant, focused participant observer* and *complete observer.* Each type of participant observation has advantages and disadvantages. The key is to be aware of them and to choose a role that most closely aligns with your comfort level, the scene, and the goals of the research.

Writing fieldnotes

In addition to considering the pros and cons of different participant observation standpoints, another significant part of fieldwork is mindfully recording and making sense of the data through **fieldnotes**, the textual domain for later research reports. Fieldnotes serve to consciously and coherently narrate and interpret observations and actions in the field, offering creative depictions of the data observed (Wolcott, 2005). The fieldnote writing process is methodological and systematic, yet also playful and inventive. This section reviews how to move from participant observation to head notes, raw records, and formal, typed fieldnotes.

Raw records and head notes

The fieldnote process begins with what I call **raw records**, also called jottings (Emerson, Fretz, & Shaw, 1995), scratch notes (Sanjek, 1990), and condensed accounts (Spradley, 1980). Raw records are the first, unprocessed notations of the field. I use the phrase "raw records" because it relates to their fresh nature, yet it is broad enough to relate to records that are handwritten, electronically jotted, or audibly recorded. Depending on the type of participation in the scene, these records will be taken more or less obtrusively. There is the classic joke that participant observers have small bladders, because of their frequent trips to the nearest restroom (Fine, 1993). Indeed, covert fieldworkers regularly sneak away – to their cars, to the bathroom, or to some other back-stage area – to record raw observations and reflections.

Overt observation allows for explicit and detailed raw notes. Nonetheless, researchers should learn to use shorthand or mnemonic codes in order to take down information in an efficient and less obtrusive manner. Goffman (1989) suggests that researchers take notes on acts or events that are different from the ones they are currently watching. In other words, he would suggest that researchers avoid frantically scratching down notes in the midst of a

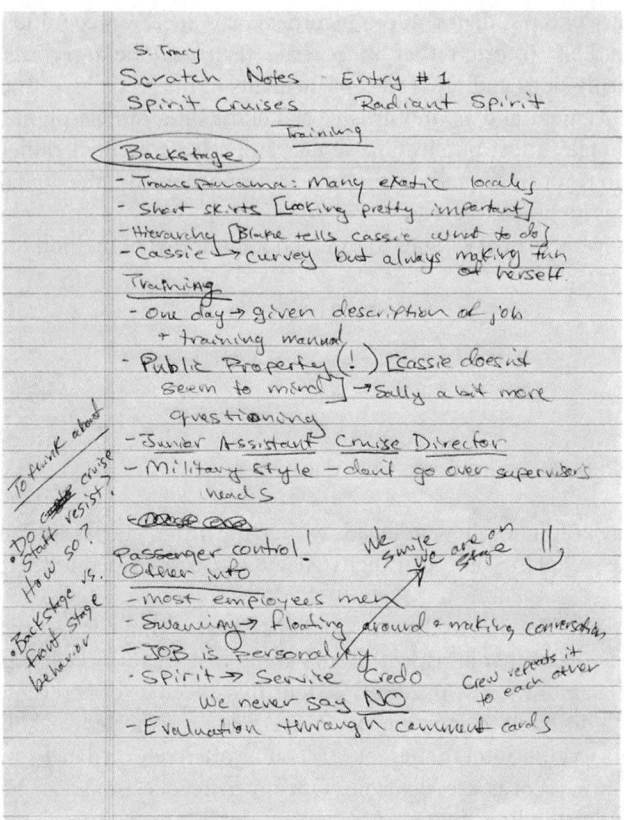

Figure 6.1 Raw records can take a number of printed or audible forms. Here is a snapshot I took of some scratch notes I scrawled on a notepad during my cruise ship research (they were later expanded into formal, typewritten fieldnotes).

particularly revealing, sensitive, or embarrassing activity. By waiting for a minute, until participants begin engaging in something more harmless and mundane, they will likely feel less sensitive about someone taking notes.

I have relied on large and cheap yellow notepads and a pen for my raw records (see Figure 6.1). Other options include writing on napkins, one's hand, or a piece of table cloth. More technologically savvy alternatives include lap-top computers – especially tablet computers that recognize and transform one's handwriting into type. However, computers can malfunction, break, be stolen, and be heavy to carry – so sometimes a minimalist method is optimal. I am usually quite overt with my note-taking. Actors may indeed change their behavior when they know they are being watched. However, I have found the advantages of detailed raw records to outweigh the disadvantages of obtrusiveness. Regardless of method, I recommend recording the time of day intermittently as you collect data. Doing so helps you to later ascertain the saturation of activity. For instance, did you observe for a long stretch of time making relatively few notes (very little saturation), or did you take extremely detailed notes in a short time period (high saturation)?

Some researchers take along a camera and/or a video-recorder. Photos and video can provide a vivid and detailed recording, documenting the exact set-up or the participants in attendance, but they have the downside of relinquishing anonymity. Indeed, exempt IRB studies often require that data are not connected to participants – and this may preclude the use of photos or recordings that identify specific members or sites. The advent of instant Internet uploads has further resulted in people being sensitive and cautious about digitized data collection.

With the popularity of smart phones, digital audio recorders, and speech recognition software, more researchers audibly record rather than write their raw field records. Researchers may also (with permission) audibly record participants in the scene. Creating audio records can be quite convenient and as unobtrusive as talking on a mobile phone. Despite these short-run advantages, most publication venues still rely on written rather than audio presentations. Audio recordings that remain forever "trapped inside" the digital device may not be as useful as written field records.

No matter your approach, several primary issues to think about in terms of method for raw records include:

1 efficiency;
2 reliability and durability;
3 personal comfort;
4 organizational skills;
5 the way you personally make sense of and learn from data.

For some researchers, a file drawer full of yellow notepads with handwritten entries will be easier to work from, while other scholars will prefer digitized audio files uploaded to their computer or MP3 player.

Of course, sometimes researchers find themselves in situations where taking raw records is next to impossible. Does this mean that all is lost? Some argue that "fieldwork that is never written up is wasted" (Delamont, 2004, p. 225). I concur that specifics of an event, interaction, or activity are much different from memories. Nonetheless, memories can still serve as useful data. Researchers writing autoethnographic accounts often rely on data from previous years, for which no raw records are available. One's own recollections can be especially valuable data for understanding the construction of identity over time or for examining retroactive sensemaking. However, for supporting claims about an *in situ* event, interaction, or activity, real-time field records are invaluable.

In cases where raw records are not feasible, *headnotes* are the next best option (Emerson et al., 1995). Headnotes are "focused memories of specific events, as well as impressions and evaluations of the unfolding project" (Lindlof & Taylor, 2002, p. 159). For example, when I was working on the cruise ship, I made mental notes to remember certain passenger comments. Once late at night in the dance club, a passenger caught me yawning and said: "Hey, you can't do that." I instantly smiled and apologized. Later that night, I expanded upon this headnote by writing about it in my field journal.

Because memories fade so quickly, headnotes should be recorded as soon as possible – whether that's by writing oneself a text message or by scratching it down on a napkin. Many researchers audibly record headnotes while commuting home after a field visit, and they supplement them with additional memories that emerge over time. Others may strengthen and check their memories with people who were present in the scene, or they may stimulate their memories with archived documents, emails, letters, or interviews. No matter whether researchers are relying on raw records, headnotes, or a mixture thereof, they should transform these into formal fieldnotes as soon as possible.

Formal fieldnotes

Fieldnotes are the material representation of the field-work event and, over time, they become equated with the scene's actors and actions. Fieldnotes heavy with descriptions – rich, thick, and detailed – allow the researcher to re-enter the context and revisit those relationships, even years after an initial field visit. In order to ensure that you write high-quality fieldnotes, it's important to plan time, preferably within 36 hours of the field visit, to write up raw records. After more than a day and a half, the codes, snippets, and shorthand in raw records fade and become confusing. In the gap of time between field visit and fieldnote writing, researchers should avoid talking to others about their experiences. When we have a conversation prior to writing the fieldnotes, the subsequent fieldnotes invariably become a record of that conversation rather than a record of the raw data and of our initial interpretations. In other words, once we narrate, subsequent narrations become (re) presentations of earlier narrations.

So, how do you start a fieldnote?

Researchers should gather raw records, open a new document, save the file under a standard and recognizable name (e.g. Cruise Ship Disco_1-1-1996 midnight-2 a.m.) and create a document header that includes pertinent information helpful for future identification (e.g. New Year's Celebration and Drunken Aftermath). A header should also note the location or source of the data as well as the field visit's date, time, and day of the week. I also include the date when the fieldnote was typed up from raw records, so that I can later evaluate the accuracy of the data. The longer the time between field visit and fieldnote write-up, the lower my confidence in its accuracy. The header also includes the number of field hours represented, which eases the computation of the total field hours. Finally, the fieldnote title serves as a reminder about its focus or contents – for instance "A Busy Booking Evening." An example of a fieldnote header is provided in Researcher's Notepad 6.1.

Fieldnote writing may be loose and informal. The goal is to write quickly rather than force a consistent or prescribed style. Most fieldnotes will never be read by anyone but the researcher. Do not spend a lot of time editing. When you include fieldnote data in the final report, you will have time to clarify, edit, and beautify the notes.

Fieldnotes are most user-friendly when they employ a cogent organizational structure. Some researchers start with a "high point" of their field visit and then work around it. Others construct "real-time" fieldnotes, which begin with concluding interpretations of the field and then work backwards, showing how these conclusions were reached. Another option is to use a mixture of "sketches" (a "still-life" verbal depiction of the scene), "episodes" (an account of the action that moves through time, often with a climax), and "fieldnote tales" (series of episodes that are interwoven) (Emerson et al., 1995).

Even with all these potential organizational structures, my advice for those new to fieldnotes is to adopt a chronological order, inserting the time of day – in boldface type –

RESEARCHER'S NOTEPAD 6.1

Fieldnote header

Fieldnotes – Nouveau County Jail
June 18/19, 1999 – Friday/Saturday
11:30 p.m. to 3:30 a.m.
4 hours
Fieldnotes typed June 20, 1999
"A Busy Booking Evening"

several times throughout the full fieldnote. Inserting the time of day in fieldnotes eases the process of searching and finding events that you remember occurring at a certain point. Creating topical "subheads" likewise makes for clear organization, easy searches in the text, and a more inviting reading and analysis. A good way to conclude the fieldnote is with a "to do/observe/ask next time" list. I also recommend the creation of an ongoing **cast of characters file** as a separate document. In it researchers can create ongoing descriptions of various people in the scene. The best character depictions move beyond the common indicators of social categories (merely labeling the participant as a "tween," "cougar," "junkie"), to give complex characterizations. Not even superheroes are all good or all evil (or all of anything, for that matter).

Qualities of good fieldnotes include clarity, economy, vividness of style (the use of analogies, imagery, and metaphors), richness and detail, explication of tacit knowledge, showing rather than telling, dialogue, noticing data as evidence, and the inclusion of one's own interpretations (with measured tentativeness). The following section expands on these qualities.

Economy versus detail

Two of the most common questions from students about fieldnotes are: How long does it take to write fieldnotes? And how long should they be? For me, writing fieldnotes usually takes up the same number of hours as my fieldwork session – so four hours in the field on Friday means I spend four hours on Saturday or Sunday fieldnote writing. However, writing time will vary depending on the density of the data observed and your own writing speed.

How long should fieldnotes be? Lindlof and Taylor (2011) advise that "a standard rule of thumb is 10 double-spaced pages of writing for every hour of participant-observation" (p. 158). Goffman (1989) suggests slightly fewer pages – three to five single-spaced pages for every hour in the field. I say, it depends. On the one hand, detailed and comprehensive fieldnotes set the stage for a resulting qualitative product that is robust, lush, and meaningful. On the other hand, longer is not always better. Fieldnotes that are overly meticulous become cumbersome and daunting. Goffman (1989) suggests that researchers avoid writing too much, or they will never want to read and analyze the data. So, take stock. If *you, the researcher*, are bored or intimidated by your own fieldnotes, this is a clue that something has gone seriously awry. Miles and Huberman (1994) go so far as to say that, "unless something has an obvious, direct, or potentially important link to a research question, it should not fatten your fieldnotes" (p. 25).

The length and detail of notes should relate to the stage of analysis. In the early stages, fieldnotes include a detailed discussion of everything, in a child-like stance of ignorance. In those initial field visits, research questions are quite broad ("What is going on here?"), and fieldnotes should record a wide range of issues. Early fieldnotes should include as many "minor" events as possible, as these can end up turning into major building blocks for later arguments. As the research narrows, fieldnotes can and should become more focused.

Showing (and using dialogue) versus telling

In addition to balancing detail with economy, fieldnote writers endeavor to *show* rather than merely *tell about* the scene. By "show," I mean that the scene is described in enough detail, so that readers may come to a conclusion about its meanings on their own. This contrasts with the author *telling* the reader the conclusion to begin with. Consider the difference between the following explanations of a party:

- *Telling* The party was festive, and people were enjoying themselves, except for Alec, who seemed extremely bored.
- *Showing* The party began with an explosion of brightly colored balloons and crepe paper. People smiled, waved hello, clinked glasses and clapped each other on the back. Then, out of the corner of my eye, I saw Alec's eyes glaze over.

The first description *tells* the reader how to make sense of the situation, whereas the second *shows* the scene in so much detail that readers can make their own conclusions. Showing requires more words than telling. Hence researchers must make tough decisions about which parts of the data to show rather than tell.

High-quality fieldnotes also elaborate upon **tacit knowledge**. Tacit knowledge is cultural knowledge that is never explicitly articulated, but is revealed through subtleties of shared cultural meaning such as eye rolls, smirks, and stolen glances. Understanding tacit organizational power relations, for instance, requires more than accessing the official organizational hierarchy document or asking an informant: "Who's in charge?" Instead, tacit knowledge about power relations is revealed by who eats lunch with whom, by the employees' tone of voice when they talk with one another, and by who is invited to (or left out of) certain meetings. Expert qualitative researchers richly describe this tacit knowledge in their fieldnotes – rather than merely summing up and telling about it through abstract generalizations. Doing the first means avoiding overused clichés such as "clammy hands," "gut-feeling," "ate like a horse." Fieldnotes should also explicate simple evaluative labels; for instance, rather than merely judging an event as "mind-numbing," "exciting," or "fascinating," fieldnotes should illustrate how and why these conclusions make sense.

Indeed, fieldnote descriptions should use concrete, multi-sensory details and action. Spradley (1980) suggests that researchers "reverse this deeply ingrained habit of generalization and *expand, fill out, enlarge*, and give as much *specific detail* as possible" (p. 67). Using active verbs instantly enlivens the fieldnote without taking up much space (compare the inactive sentence "She *went* to the window" to the active "She *skipped* to the window"; or "He *put* on his coat" to "He *threw* on his coat"). Verbatim dialogue and description of nonverbal communication are vital, especially for scholars focused on human interaction. Dialogue, *in situ*, creates some of the most fascinating and convincing data available, as it effectively shows the interaction without a specific prompt from researcher (say, an interview question).

Even small snippets of dialogue and indigenous *in vivo* **terms** – sentences or phrasing directly from the field – can enliven a research report. Quotation marks should set off this language in fieldnotes. In fieldnotes, I recommend using "double quotations" to denote direct quotations of verbatim dialogue, and 'single quotations' to indicate words you do not have an exact record of, but remember bits and pieces (or the other way round, if you write in UK English). Quotations identify that the language comes from the field, *in vivo*, rather than from the researcher's own disciplinary lexicon.

Making the familiar strange and the strange familiar

The idea of "making the familiar strange and the strange familiar" is a recurrent theme in a range of interpretive arts, ranging from artistic photography to modern advertising. The phrase itself goes back to poets, romanticists, and semioticians, who argued that the function of art is estrangement (Hawkes, 1977). Photos of mundane objects encourage intense admiration when their depiction is strange, off-center, and quirky. The passer-by pauses, cocks her head, and wonders, "Is that an apple? Huh, I never saw an apple look like that before. Cool." On the flip side, advertisers know that to garner sales of strange and exotic foods – say, antioxidant-rich goji berries – they can make the berry seem less foreign by pairing it with good old cornflakes. Likewise, fieldnotes should describe routine activities in ways that renew perception, making the scene fresh and unexpected. When faced with "common sense" or the "same old, same old," good fieldnote writers problematize taken-for-granted beliefs and question everyday activities. By doing so, they reveal cultural assumptions underlying the scene.

For example, imagine that a fieldworker observes a classroom. At first glance, nothing seems spectacular or noteworthy. The seats and lectern are arranged the same way they are "always" arranged. However, a good fieldworker makes this familiar arrangement strange by pointing out peculiarities or curiosities about this ordinary classroom. The researcher might note that all seats are facing forward and are packed so closely together that students bump arms. Nonetheless, the seats are situated quite far away from and at a lower level than the instructor, who stands behind a lectern, on stage. This observation provides enough vivid detail to set up and help explain why, for instance, students in this classroom may feel close affinity with their classmates and whisper to them during lectures, but feel quite disconnected from the instructor. If the researcher would have just noted, "typical lecture-hall set-up," then the familiar would not have been made strange, and the resultant interesting description would be lost.

In addition to making the familiar strange, good fieldworkers also make the strange familiar. In other words, they take issues that may seem bizarre and help the reader see how they are also familiar and commonplace. For instance, consider the somewhat odd event of a big holiday celebration in a women's prison. By including intense detail in fieldnotes – about misbehaving visiting children, card-making activities, traditional dinner, and incessant talk about "I'm so full, why did I eat so much?" – the researcher can show how this somewhat incongruous situation of celebrating Christmas behind bars is actually quite familiar. Through the detail of fieldnotes taken on a cruise ship in 1995 and in a prison in 1999, when I reanalyzed the data years later, I found that holiday activities in these two total institutions were actually quite similar.

Noticing the data as evidence

Early on in the research process, researchers often do not know *why* they are taking notes or *what* they are looking for. Like police investigators, fieldworkers collect data in the hope that they will be meaningful down the road. For these data to have *meaning*, the researcher's role must also change, metaphorically speaking, from crime-scene clue gatherer to lawyer compiling evidence that supports a certain argument. In the process, it is also important to note the *lack* of evidence. Granted, *an absence of evidence is not necessarily the evidence of absence*. In other words, just the fact that something expected seems to be missing from the scene does not mean that it is actually missing or that it does not exist (if you are not able to find or collect a piece of evidence, it does not mean that that piece does not exist). However, missing data can be telling, especially when paired with other data. Good fieldnotes include information about what is missing or absent in the scene.

Keep in mind that gathering evidence is not about mere facts, but requires building a *narrative argument* specific to its purpose. The type of evidence needed to support an argument will differ depending on the audience's standards and notions of credibility. Some audiences will be convinced through rich imagery, while others will want facts and numbers, and others will desire visual figures and drawings. Regardless of these variations, a key goal of fieldnote writing is to go beyond listing various pieces of evidence to *plotting* how these bits may fit together in terms of stories or claims. Consider This 6.3 provides reflective activity on noticing data as evidence.

Good fieldnotes not only record observation, but also include analysis. The next section provides guidance on how best to include early interpretations into fieldnotes.

CONSIDER THIS 6.3

Noticing the data as evidence

The following fieldnote is excerpted from my cruise ship research.

Backstage behavior

The cruise staff members are the picture of hospitality in the passenger areas. They consistently smile, say hello, and watch their language. However, they are very crude backstage. This is especially true in the officer's mess hall at dinner. Examples: William will speak graphically about passengers on board whom he finds sexually attractive. People talk badly about naturalist Susie, saying she is gross and disgusting. In fact one cruise staff member imitated her "ever-present nose boogers" by stuffing a bit of bread up his nostril. This brought gales of laughter from the other members of the table.

Sexual jokes and innuendo, inside jokes [*most of which I still don't understand*], and cussing dominate mealtime discussion. Today, at lunch, cruise director Tim and assistant director Pedro were joking about something that I didn't understand. Pedro looked over and said: "Look, Sarah doesn't even get it… good Sarah, don't come down to our level." [*I expect they would expect, however, that eventually I would be able to "come to that level" and joke along with everyone else.*]

1   What claims might you begin to make from these data? In other words, how might these data serve as evidence for certain claims?
2   Explain the evidence (or lack of evidence) that support such claims.
3   What other types of data would be helpful to more convincingly support such claims?
4   Now, take a look at *your own* fieldnotes or other data display (e.g. a map of the scene) and consider how you might begin to notice the data as evidence.

Analytic reflections

One of the primary differences between qualitative research and journalism is that researchers explicitly capture their own reactions, doubts, potential prejudices, frustrations, and interpretations of the scene. In other words, qualitative researchers go beyond recording "who, what, where, when, and how" to explaining notions of "why," "how does this make me feel," "how does this relate to my research questions," and "what's next." These reactions can be captured in a number of ways.

Some fieldworkers keep separate diaries or journals (Sanjek, 1990) to provide autobiographical notations about the "experiences, ideas, fears, mistakes, confusions, breakthroughs, and problems that arise during fieldwork" (Spradley, 1980, p. 69). Most field journals never make it to public scrutiny. However, they certainly can be published, with or without the author's express permission. Fifteen years after Malinowski died, his private field diaries were published – which detailed his racial prejudices, sexual fantasies, drug use, soul-searching, and homesickness (Malinowski, 1967).

Another way to capture reflections in the field – and one that I believe is very helpful for maintaining consistent self-reflexivity and transparency – is by sprinkling **analytic reflections** throughout fieldnotes. I use this as an umbrella term to include commentary about researcher insecurities, fears, or uncertainties; the way others are relating to the presence of research; initial theories or gut reactions about the scene; and interpretations related to research interests. Analytic reflections may come in a variety of forms, such as (a) brief reflective bits of writing, known as "analytic asides"; (b) more

TIPS AND TOOLS 6.1

Fieldnote writing tips

1 Write up fieldnotes quickly after the participant observation and before talking about the scene with others.

2 Include an informative and standard header and file name, which easily help you identify and organize the fieldnotes.

3 Choose a cogent and inviting organizational structure. Include time and topical headers/notations.

4 Create a cast of characters with a rich, multi-faceted description.

5 Use a free-flowing style, write quickly, and do not bother with close editing early on.

6 Show rather than tell.

7 Make the strange familiar and the familiar strange.

8 Write in rich detail, with lots of background, context, action, and sensory imagery.

9 Avoid clichés, evaluative labels, and lackluster language.

10 Use dialogue and quotations to indicate direct or indirect quotations and *in vivo* language.

11 Balance the level of detail with economy and focus.

12 Mindfully consider how the data serve as potential evidence for claims that connect with research questions. Ask yourself: how might these data build upon, extend, or conflict with current understandings?

13 Use analytic reflections to document uncertainties, opinions, and emergent interpretations.

14 Do not let analytic reflections dictate the filter through which you will evaluate all future data. Describe first. Analyze second.

15 Consider the significance of fieldnote content. If your fieldnotes seem dull and meaningless to you, your analyses will likely be boring and insignificant to others.

16 Conclude fieldnotes with a "to do/observe/ask next time" list.

17 Ask yourself: do these fieldnote data suggest a slightly different research direction, or different foci? If so, revisit and rework guiding research questions.

elaborate reflections on specific events or issues, known as "commentaries"; or (c) sustained analytic "in-process memos," which are often written after completing the day's fieldnotes (Emerson et al., 1995). Researchers may set off such reflections from the rest of the fieldnote – in italics, in brackets, in colored type, or with marked-up comments.

When the time comes for a more formal analysis, these analytic reflections are invaluable – as they track the path and growth of claims over time. Furthermore, analytic reflections are kind of like your own, personal backstage – where you get to ruminate, complain, confess your temptations, and air your opinions. So, go ahead and write down that "I felt totally sick today," or that "Tonight's observation seemed to question my stereotypes." These reflections will keep you honest in terms of evaluating – and perhaps counter-biasing – your fieldnotes in the future. Keep in mind that analytic reflections are not conclusive judgments, but loose interpretations that leave room for myriad possibilities. Maybe the guy you first thought was an "arrogant jerk" just went through a divorce. Maybe your initial stereotypes are completely off base. Maintaining tentativeness is crucial for allowing the data to guide the analysis meaningfully.

Tips and Tools 6.1 provides some general tips to consider when you are writing fieldnotes. As you consider these tips, I also encourage you to revisit excerpts of fieldnotes provided in Researcher's Notepad 4.3, Consider This 6.2, Consider This 6.3 – as well as the longer fieldnote excerpt in Appendix A.

Fieldnote wrap-up

In summary, fieldnotes are characterized by a number of qualities such as clarity, vivid imagery, detail, economy, and piecing together the data as evidence. At the same time they are tentative about early interpretations. I know that some of these tips may seem counterintuitive, or even contradictory. How can fieldnotes be detailed but not wordy? How can researchers piece together evidence and make claims, but also remain tentative?

If you are feeling these contradictions, then you are not alone. Be assured that dealing with the inherent paradoxes of fieldnote writing becomes easier with practice. Ambiguity and confusion are clues that you are doing something right, as "the strength of ethnography is to be found in the working-out of the contradictions and dilemmas" (Eastland, 1993, p. 121). When you are finished writing a fieldnote, take a breath and pat yourself on the back for accomplishing a key component of the research process.

Also, take time to ensure that you electronically back up and save multiple copies of your work. In addition to saving the document on a password-protected computer, I recommend saving a back-up, printing out hard copies, and arranging them chronologically in a binder. Storing fieldnotes in multiple places guards against theft, computer glitches, and researcher meltdowns. Hard copies also provide a mental boost – as they materially illustrate the hard work involved in participant observation.

Focusing the data and using heuristic devices

The first few forays into the scene are marked by "getting to know you" rituals, tours, and introductions. For those first visits, I encourage you to be intuitive in choosing what to pay attention to. Ask the participants what they think is most important in the scene, and follow their lead. Also, pay attention to your own instincts. Do not try to "save the best for last." Rich data are often fleeting.

After you have been in the scene for a while, though, you might begin to wonder: *What data should I collect next?* After examining favorite issues or people, researchers should consider visiting the periphery. For instance, in the 911 research project, I was able to gather valuable comparison data by shadowing affiliated groups such as paramedics, ambulance dispatchers, firefighters, and police deputies. Indeed, one of the best ways to understand a scene is to compare the typical with the unique/extraordinary on the one hand, and with the peripheral/marginal on the other. Three types of data collection – (a) typical/representative; (b) negative/disconfirming; and (c) exceptional/discrepant – have exceptional pay-off together (Spradley, 1980). In particular, the theories that emerge from the first category can be verified, nuanced, and clarified by using the second two categories.

After you have been in the field for a while, **heuristic models** – conceptual tool kits that stimulate further investigation, learning, and thinking – can also help you become more systematic. Examples include many of the analysis strategies offered in Chapter 10 (so, if you're stuck on where to analyze data next, read ahead), as well as those presented in Chapter 3 in the form of established theories and models.

For instance, many ethnographers have turned to the *organizational cultural approach* in order to study their data, and in doing so they have focused their data collection on the scene's **rituals**, which are defined as meaningful cultural practices or sets of activities performed at regular intervals by members of various groups. Rituals often include verbal **scripts** – in which the verbal action is planned, memorized, and routinized

(Pacanowsky & O'Donnell-Trujillo, 1983). The ritual could be as elaborate as the Balinese cockfight (Geertz, 1973), or as inane as one factory worker stealing another's fruit at break time (see Roy, 1959 for a hilarious description of "banana time"). The collection of rituals and scripts provides valuable data on how the participants display their cultural membership and temporally pace the scene through their talk.

There is no one "right" heuristic for any scene. However, if you are stuck on where to focus next, I encourage you to consider heuristic theories, models, or questions – such as the following, that can guide your field visits:

1   SPACE/SCENE   How is the physical space or place set up? What does this say about the group?
    a   Where is **frontstage** (where people are on display or watched)?
    b   Where is **backstage** (where people feel protected from watching eyes; only available to insiders)?
2   OBJECTS AND ARTIFACTS   What material artifacts are present and what do they signify?
3   ACTORS AND AGENTS   Who are the people involved? What is their status? How do they claim attention?
    a   ROLES AND TYPES How are people classed into certain categories?
4   ACTIVITIES, EVENTS, RITUALS, AND CEREMONIES   What are the common sets of related acts and activities? How are they patterned? What do these activities signify about the group?
5   INTERACTIONS   Who interacts with whom? What does this say about participants?
6   TIME   How is time structured? What are the sequences of activities?
7   GOALS/PURPOSE   What are people trying to accomplish? How are they motivated?
8   FEELINGS   How are emotions hidden, felt, or expressed?
9   POWER RELATIONS   What are the patterns or indices of power and subservience? Who is in charge? Who is subservient?
10   VALUES   In what ways are core beliefs espoused, embodied, and practiced? Do values that are formally expressed align with those informally practiced? If not, what does this signify?
11   COMMUNICATION   What types of script or specialized vocabulary mark the scene?
12   PROCESSES   What different episodes, life cycles, or socialization phases are evident?

A good place to begin is to choose several of these heuristic questions and cluster them together. For instance, a study of the student union could begin with an identification of various scenes (restaurant, store, study lounge, front step hang-out, commercial area). You could then note multiple activities such as eating, shopping, flirting, studying, and protesting. Within each scene there are different roles for the various actors (students, faculty, employees, security guards, regulars, visitors), all of whom use different vocabularies and scripts. And, depending on the time of day or time of year, one is likely to observe different types of rituals, meetings, and ceremonies.

After starting from a wide angle of description, the researcher should eventually narrow down through **selective observation**, which involves "going to your social situation and *looking for differences among specific cultural categories*" (Spradley, 1980, p. 128). For instance, during selective observation, you might ask how different groups of actors react to different events, or how people's feelings differ depending on the goal. Or the focus could be placed on how certain *roles* in the system have varying resources in relation to power. For instance, Cliff Scott and I focused on the role of "frequent flyers" – a derogatory phrase used by firefighters and other emergency responders to label citizens who call the police for routine health problems – and how frequent flyers are taken less seriously than callers who live in the ritzy part of town (Tracy & Scott, 2006).

Furthermore, as fieldwork progresses, researchers become more attuned to specific issues of interest. For example, a researcher who is in the early stages of examining street life in a downtown area may write long and detailed fieldnotes about everything. However, after weeks of fieldwork, this same researcher should choose a point of focus – say, street performances. In the final stages of fieldwork, he may further narrow this focus to public drunkenness. Because public drunkenness is a relatively rare performance, he may have to spend many hours in the field, but he should spend less time writing about the handful of drunken incidents observed.

There is no one right way to use the heuristic tips provided in this section. Participant observation can certainly be guided by a rational check-list of "things to see." However, such lists should serve only as starting points. As you narrow down, I encourage you to keep your research questions close at hand. They are your constant compass. Review them and revise them after you have been in the field. Another way to focus is to decide what you *will not* be studying. The only way to open up the door to depth is to close the door on never-ending breadth. It's a trade-off, and a good one.

FOLLOWING, FORGETTING, AND IMPROVISING

The last few chapters have provided tips for easing off your navigation into participant observation and fieldnote writing. My goal has been to move beyond theoretical discussions of methodology and ideological concerns, in order to focus on the self in the scene and on what to do once you arrive there.

Providing practical participant observation and fieldnote advice is a tricky endeavor. Indeed, "the biggest problem novices find when preparing for ethnographic fieldwork is that the methods books are not explicit enough about what to observe, how to observe and what to write down. It is very hard to describe in words how to observe" (Delamont, 2004, p. 225). My desire has been to discuss what researchers actually can do in the field to increase their opportunities for good data collection. Of course, despite all this advice, participant observation is fraught with ethical dilemmas and challenges that require you to play with the "rules" and improvise.

One primary dilemma is how involved you should become in the scene. Some believe that the overall task of fieldnotes is to create a detached and objective account of one's experience. Others believe that detachment is not only impossible, but unethical. Angrosino (2005) believes that the most progressive participant observers empathetically ask questions that emerge from connections and concerns among poor and marginalized people, and that fieldworkers should serve as advocates and spokespeople, to help empower underprivileged causes and communities.

Whether you subscribe to the detached or to the involved approach, it makes sense to carefully consider the ethics of fieldwork. Common ethical missteps include claiming to observe when you actually just participated (or vice versa); claiming to have observed a conversation when it is hearsay; depicting orchestrated events as spontaneous; or using without permission data from overheard conversations or from misdirected emails (Punch, 1986; cf. Lindlof & Taylor, 2011). Many ethical challenges are ambiguous. For instance, how much should researchers divulge about their research interests? Most institutional review boards desire researchers to be completely transparent with participants. However, this becomes problematic when field participants try too hard to "help" and just tell you things they think you want to hear. I found this to be the case with a handful of correctional officers. After they read my consent form, which listed as foci emotion and burnout, they kept talking about stress. These data were difficult to evaluate, because I did not know whether their stories were just a response to my stated interests or whether they would have complained about burnout anyway.

Participants may also try to hide things, tell lies, or keep secrets. Lies and secrets are not necessarily "bad" and "inaccurate" data. Indeed, people largely live and act in line with the stories they tell – whether or not the stories depict a material reality accurately. However, many researchers want participants' stories to reflect a verifiable reality. One way to increase your chances of getting beneath external pretenses is to conduct long-term participant observation. Façades are hard to keep up over time, and members usually become less guarded after researchers prove themselves as trustworthy and friendly. Goffman (1989) suggests another tactic. According to him, participants are more likely to be truthful when they are surrounded by an audience of peers. In consequence, you might consider asking participants to recall certain incidents when they are in each other's presence (although one could argue that this could lead to other types of deception or to boasting).

Despite good intentions and diligence, another participant observation dilemma is that most researchers end up with field data that are never written up into formal fieldnotes. This may be due to lack of funding, to the researcher's laziness, or to the fact that the data are so emotionally painful that the fieldworker does not have the heart to revisit them. Many times, though, researchers just lack the planning or the time to write up the data. When fieldnotes are not written up, the researcher faces questions about how best to reference such data – if at all – in the final research report. Is it ethical to count these data as field hours, or to draw on incidents that never made it beyond headnote memories? How about years later? My recommendation is to be transparent to the reader. Autoethnographers frequently make use of data that were never transformed into formal fieldnotes. However, the reader has a right to know the method by which the data were transformed, narrated, and analyzed – and in many cases participant observation is much more useful when written into full fieldnotes.

If you routinely find yourself without time or resources to write fieldnotes, you should consider ways to fund your research. Although little funding exists for basic descriptive research, participant observation that is connected to public health or social problems – such as examining drug addiction, AIDS, and mental illness – is increasingly common (Gans, 1999; Goffman, 1961a). A grant that provides release time from other responsibilities will provide more time for writing.

Finally, another challenge is to figure out how and where to cut and narrow down. Fieldnotes can never tell the entire story; but it can feel as though you were lying through omission when you only tell a snippet here and there. Ethnographers should feel consoled by remembering that there are second chances, in future fieldnotes or articles by themselves – or even by other researchers. I encourage you to create a file with "ideas for future research." This file is not only helpful for planning future projects, but it can be referenced when you write the "future directions" section of the current project.

While some researchers suffer from having too many interesting data, others suffer from just the opposite – a lack of significance. If you are faced with this problem, I encourage you to modify the research approach, travel a bit further, change your vantage point, or just visit your fieldsite at a different time of day. If you still cannot find an interesting story, it's time to take a hard look in the mirror. Have you ever noticed that the same people regularly tell stories that are clever, ironic, or interesting? Are these people inherently exposed to more interesting lives and situations? Perhaps. But, more likely, they have an eye for detail, they are able to point out situations that contain absurdity or humor, and they have a mind to dig below surface assumptions and values, to highlight what is interesting or ironic.

So, if you're having trouble finding significant or interesting stories in your fieldwork, take a critical look at your own fieldwork and writing practices.

- Do you need to read more widely and come into the scene with a more complex set of sensitizing concepts?
- Could your fieldnotes benefit from lush detail or verbatim quotations?
- What is your mood and energy level when you're observing and writing notes?
- Do you need to be more courageous, flexible, or opportunistic?
- How much time are you devoting to the process?

The success of participant observation and the quality of fieldnotes reflect more on the researcher than they do on the field. Be passionate, generous, diligent, disciplined, and curious, and likely the data will become richer and the field more giving in return.

EXERCISE 6.1

Fieldnotes

Write a set of fieldnotes that represent at least four hours of participant observation and reflect tips and guidelines for good field records and observation. Provide an updated rendition of your guiding research question(s)/foci at the top of the fieldnotes.

In summary

Participant observation and fieldwork are arts to which full books have been devoted (Emerson et al., 1995; Sanjek, 1990). In this chapter we have examined how to best structure a process that can feel ambiguous and scary. We first explored different standpoints for participant observation in the field, each one of which has its ups and downs. Furthermore, we traveled through best practices for creating headnotes and raw records.

Raw records should be transformed quickly into formal, typewritten fieldnotes. As discussed, good fieldnotes are marked by several best practices, such as showing rather than telling, balancing efficiency with detail, including analytic reflections, seeing data as evidence, including verbatim dialogue, and making the familiar strange.

The chapter closed with a discussion of how researchers can focus and narrow their data collection. Researchers can consider a number of different heuristic questions and focus their data on various roles, rituals, scripts, or power differences. Becoming more selective in data collection and fieldnotes is necessary for pushing your rich descriptions toward focused claims, explanations, and storied plot lines.

Finally, the chapter concluded with a section on "following, forgetting, and improvising" in which I discussed various ethical dilemmas associated with fieldwork. Indeed, sometimes the best advice for fieldwork is to just get out there and *do it*. Sometimes *acting* and *improvising* are the most rational and worthwhile ways to learn. If you feel uncertain about fieldwork, you know you have joined millions of qualitative researchers before you. As the renowned ethnographer Michael Burawoy once told me: "If you're not suffering and anxious and insecure about your participant observation, then I suspect you're not doing it right."

KEY TERMS

→ **analytic reflection**   an umbrella term to include commentary about researcher insecurities, fears, or uncertainties the way others are relating to research presence and initial theories, gut reactions and interpretations about the scene

→ **ardent activist**   a researcher who not only seeks to understand, but also embraces and practices, the values, and ideologies of the group under study

→ **backstage**   an area where people feel protected from watching eyes only available to insiders

→ **cast of characters file**   a document that catalogues the ongoing descriptions of various main people or characters in the scene

→ **complete observer**   a researcher who observes from the periphery, watching the scene unfold in front of them without participants aware of the research

→ **complete participant**   a researcher who does participant observation in contexts in which they are already members or becomes fully affiliated

→ **controlled skeptic**   a researcher who becomes close to the scene and asks questions in a polite, curious, and naïve manner, yet maintains skepticism

→ **ethnocentrism**   the tendency to consider one's own culture as normal, natural and right and therefore, to interpret, judge and measure data emanating from dissimilar groups as odd, problematic or lesser than

→ **fieldnotes**   the textual notes used as the basis for later research reports they consciously and coherently narrate and interpret observations and actions in the field

→ **focused participant observer**   a researcher who enters a scene with an explicit researcher status and a clear agenda of which data to gather in the scene

→ **frontstage**   an area of the scene where participants are regularly on display or watched

→ **headnotes**   mental notes or detailed memories of specific events in the field that the researcher commits to memory and writes up at a later time.

→ **heuristic model**   a conceptual tool kit that stimulates further investigation, learning, and thinking

→ ***in vivo* terms**   terms, sentences, or phrasing directly from the field or from participants

→ **play participant**   a researcher who becomes an active member in the scene, engaging in a range of cultural activities, also called a participant as observer or active participant

→ **raw records**   the first, unprocessed notations taken in the field either audibly or in print

→ **rituals**   meaningful cultural practices or sets of activities that are performed at regular intervals by members of groups

→ **scripts**   verbal sequences in which action is planned, memorized, and routinized

→ **selective observation**   observation that occurs when the researcher goes back to the field with specific phenomena in mind and gathers more data on these selected issues

→ **tacit knowledge**   cultural knowledge that is never explicitly articulated, but is revealed through subtleties of shared cultural meaning such as eye rolls, smirks, and stolen glances

CHAPTER 7

Interview planning and design
Sampling, recruiting, and questioning

Contents

Qualitative Research Methods: Collecting Evidence, Crafting Analysis, Communicating Impact, First Edition. Sarah J. Tracy.
© 2013 Sarah J. Tracy. Published 2013 by Blackwell Publishing Ltd.

Interviews are guided question–answer conversations, or an "inter-change of views between two persons conversing about a theme of mutual interest" (Kvale & Brinkmann, 2009, p. 2). However, they differ from other conversations by having a specific structure and purpose. Interviews are common practice in a variety of situations, including therapy, police investigations, marketing focus groups, philosophical/ Socratic dialogues, medical exams, and opinion polls. Although people tend to think of interviews as dyadic face-to-face interactions, interviewing can occur in small groups (such as focus groups) and through various mediated contexts. As you consider the role of interviews in your own research, it is helpful to think about how interviews complement other types of qualitative research – a topic explored in Consider This 7.1.

CONSIDER THIS 7.1

Yin and yang: taijitu

People who practice yoga can choose from a number of different styles, such as Bikram (hot) yoga, Vinyasana (flow) yoga, and Restorative (relaxing) yoga. Although every type of yoga is committed to physical and mental self-awareness, each practice is uniquely characterized by its relative emphasis on "yin" versus "yang" or vice versa. Yin and yang are commonly depicted as constituting together the spherical taijitu. Yin (the dark portion) refers to aspects of submission, while yang (the light portion) refers to principles of creation and strength. Each force works together with the other in cyclical fashion, and seeds of one are found in the other, so that neither is dominant. In other words, they complement each other as a dynamic system and interact to create a greater whole (Brons, 2009).

What do yin and yang have to do with qualitative research? If practicing fieldwork is the yin of qualitative methodology – characterized by the researcher's submission to emergent ideas and by her/his letting the context determine the foci of study – then interviewing is the accompanying yang – with its active recruitment of participants and design of specific questions and dialogues (see Figure 7.1). There are aspects of each that flow together in any qualitative study, but some studies emphasize one more than the other.

Figure 7.1 Taijitu: Depicting yin and yang. Interviews and fieldwork complement each other, interviews acting as the more obtrusive, strong, "yang"-like component, and fieldwork acting as the more submissive and free-flowing "yin." They are not opposites, and seeds of one can be found in the other.

Because interviews are researcher-generated and created, they require a fair amount of planning and strategic thinking. This chapter provides the nuts and bolts of planning and designing interviews. The chapter opens with discussing the unique value of interviews and then reviews various types of interviews: structured and unstructured, individual, group, face-to-face, mediated, and focus-group interviews. The chapter also explores ways in which researchers can strategically make choices about interview sampling, venue, and size. Perhaps most importantly, the chapter provides guidance on how to write, structure, and order interview questions and dialogue.

The value of interviews

Qualitative interviews provide opportunities for mutual discovery, understanding, reflection, and explanation via a path that is organic, adaptive, and oftentimes energizing. Interviews elucidate subjectively lived experiences and viewpoints from the respondents' perspective – a concept introduced in Chapter 3 as *verstehen*. Although interviewer and interviewee are, in many ways, conversational partners and may even be(come) friends (Oakley, 1981), the interviewer almost always has more control than the respondent in terms of dialogue direction and topical emphasis. This difference in power also means that the interviewer has an obligation to treat the respondent and the resulting data with ethical care.

Interviewing, on the one hand, is like having "night-vision goggles" (Rubin & Rubin, 2005, p. vii), because interviews enable the researcher to stumble upon and further explore complex phenomena that may otherwise be hidden or unseen. However, interviews are as much about rhetorically constructing meaning and mutually creating a story as they are about mining data gems. Meaning is created *between* participants rather than being held in the minds of the interviewer or interviewee and swapped back and forth (Tripp, 1983). Indeed, interviews are not neutral exchanges of questions and answers, but active processes in which we come to know others and ourselves (Fontana & Frey, 2005). Researchers, therefore, must examine not only *what* data are collected in an interview, but also *how* the interview is accomplished through active negotiated interaction (Holstein & Gubrium, 1995).

Approximately 90 percent of all social science investigations rely on interviews (Briggs, 1986). As noted by Lindlof and Taylor (2011), this is so for several good reasons. Through interviews, the respondents can provide their opinion, motivation, and experiences. They may tell stories and narratives – complete with dramatic plot lines, heroes, and villains. Such stories frame the way participants understand the world, delimiting opportunities and constraints for action. Through interviews, participants can provide **accounts** – or rationales, explanations, and justifications for their actions and opinions. Interviewees can reveal their specific vocabulary and language and explain why they employ certain clichés, jargon, or slang. Interviews are especially valuable for providing information and background on issues that cannot be observed or efficiently accessed. Some issues – such as sexual activity, drug addiction, bathroom or locker-room habits, childhood discipline, violence, and death – are generally off limits or unavailable for participant observation study.

Interviews may also access information on past events, rare occasions, dastardly deeds, clandestine trysts, disasters, celebrations, or buried emotions. For instance, if you are researching coal mine safety, interviews provide opportunities to ask participants about a past explosion, their emotional response, and whom they blamed. Interviews are especially helpful for acquiring information that is left out of formal documents or omitted from sanitized histories, which reflect power holders' points of view.

If the topic of study is very specific – for instance, the child adoption process experienced by people beyond the age of 45 (rather than adoption in general) – interviews serve as an efficient method to "get to the heart of the matter" by comparison to more open-ended participant observation. However, just because interviews are efficient for accessing certain populations or topics, the interviews still need to be transcribed – a process that, as I describe in Chapter 8, can take as long as, or longer than, typing up fieldnotes.

Interviews are also very valuable for strengthening and complicating other data. In conversing with interviewees, you have the opportunity to bring up observations or hearsay, and to ask interviewees to verify, refute, defend, or expand. Did you observe something in the field that seemed abusive, unexpectedly compassionate, or puzzling? Interviews provide a forum for probing. Similarly, interviews create the opportunity to test hunches and interpretations about the scene. Indeed, as I discuss in greater detail below, the best qualitative interviews go beyond collecting data to interpreting and analyzing them, even within the interview itself.

As you ponder the value of interviews for your own research project, keep in mind that they are more than just a tool for wrenching data from a participant. Indeed, new and empathetic approaches to interviewing suggest that we should never treat "the interviewee as a 'clockwork orange,' that is, looking for a better juicer (techniques) to squeeze the juice (answers) out of the orange (living person/interviewee)" (Fontana & Frey, 2005, p. 696). Rather, interviews are an art that requires study and practice, and their conduct will affect research relationships that flower (or wilt) as a result.

As artistic creations, interviews call for researchers to critically reflect on their role, identity, and subjectivities (Roulston, de Marrais, & Lewis, 2003). Self-reflexive interviewers consider how their subject positions might impact the interview process and its results. Amy Pearson (2012), for instance, took stock of how her thin feminine body was viewed as "suspicious" when she engaged interviews with employees of the historically masculinized environment at the National Park Service. Her subjective position as a young female academic may have encouraged participants to disclose less sexist viewpoints than they may have done otherwise. Amy directed our class in a self-reflective exercise that is adapted in Exercise 7.1.

EXERCISE 7.1

Self-reflexive interviewing

1   Write down obvious, physical traits/demographics that your participants might see or notice during an interview. Consider asking a partner to expand on this list (as sometimes we don't recognize things about ourselves that are obvious to others).

2   Now reflect and write about other qualities/characteristics of yourself and your interviewing style that will become visible during the interview process.

3   How do you foresee these traits and qualities impacting and influencing the interview process? The data obtained? Your relationship with the participant?

Clearly, interviews have a lot of value. Because they are often perceived as simply "conversations," you may be tempted to jump into them without much design or planning. However, given the time, resources, and "sunk costs" of interview scheduling, conducting, and transcribing, some advance planning can really pay off in the long run.

Who, what, where, how, and when: developing a sampling plan

A **sampling plan** is the design for how to specifically choose sources for your data. I introduce the notion of sampling here, in the interview chapter, because sampling is a necessary step in terms of choosing people to interview. However, sampling can also refer to choosing specific locations, times of days, various events, and activities to observe in fieldwork. Hence the following discussion of sampling is broad enough to apply to both interviewing and participant observation. Even if you enter a research study with a very general question like "what is going on here?," you should strategically consider what data will match your emerging research goals.

Good qualitative researchers, at the very least, engage in **purposeful sampling**, which means that they purposefully choose data that fit the parameters of the project's research questions, goals, and purposes. For example, in her groundbreaking study of emotional labor, Hochschild (1983) wanted to understand employees who were required to show certain emotional fronts as part of their job. Many employees manage their external emotional façade to some extent. However, she purposefully chose to study flight attendants and bill collectors, because she believed they were the "toe and heel" of emotional labor professions and would reveal a broad range of emotional work. A variety of sampling options are listed in Tips and Tools 7.1. In the next section I review types of sampling plans and provide advice on how to choose the best sample for your study (see Patton, 2002 for more information).

Random samples

In **random samples** every member of a group has an equal opportunity to be selected. Random samples are popular among researchers who desire to make statistical generalizations to larger populations; such is the case in political polling and census taking. Random samples are usually not employed by qualitative researchers who more often aim toward depth of analysis over breadth of coverage.

Keep in mind that "random sampling" is not what the colloquial expression "randomly choosing the data to study" would imply. For instance, a random sample of surviving American World War II veterans over the age of 80 living would ensure that *every single veteran* who met these sample criteria had an equal opportunity of being chosen for the study – even those without a telephone listing or Internet access. Acquiring such a sample requires much more work, time, money, and diligence than, say, hanging out at a nursing home and haphazardly (or "randomly" in the colloquial use of the word) knocking on doors to find participants. Indeed, the result of the "haphazard knocking" approach is actually more accurately described as a convenience sample.

Convenience/opportunistic samples

One of the most common sampling plans is the **convenience** or **opportunistic sample**. These samples are chosen because, in short, they are convenient, easy, and relatively inexpensive to access. Many research studies sample college students for this very

TIPS AND TOOLS 7.1

Sampling plans

All researchers should strive toward a *purposeful sample*, in which data and research questions/goals/purposes complement each other. Which combination of the following purposeful sampling plans meets your research goals, resources and timeline?

Type of Sample	Purpose
Random	Creates an equal opportunity for all the members of a certain population to be chosen
Convenience/Opportunistic	Appropriate when time and money are scarce, but may indicate laziness
Maximum Variation	Includes the entire rainbow of possible data. Helps to ensure the inclusion of usually marginalized data
Snowball	Expands in size as the researcher asks study participants to recommend other participants
Theoretical Construct	Helpful for testing and finding gaps in existing theory
Typical Instance	Focuses on the routine, the average, and the typical
Extreme Instance	The most/least/best/worst of a certain category. Can be valuable and interesting, but also time-consuming
Critical Instance	Focuses on data that are rare, under-studied, or strategically bounded to the argument at hand

reason. Good ethnographers live full and complex lives, and they rightfully turn to their personal networks for research inspiration, resources, and samples of convenience. However, there is a difference between making full use of one's networks and just avoiding hard work.

Good samples align with the research project goals. Convenience samples are most appropriate when the priorities are speed and low cost. For example, if a researcher examining friendship needs a data set in three weeks, then the best option may be to offer undergraduate students extra credit for research participation. However, in many cases, a convenience sample just doesn't cut it. A researcher studying friendship, for instance, could learn a great deal by talking to senior citizens who have maintained friendships over a lifetime, to middle-aged racquet ball buddies, or to little children who could share stories about their play group or imaginary friends. Such data would surely enrich and complicate assumptions about friendship – and likely be much more interesting than the data collected solely among undergraduate students. Furthermore, many reviewers instantly write off convenience samples as lazy and not credible.

Maximum variation samples

A **maximum variation sample** is one in which researchers access a wide range of data or participants who will represent wide variations of the phenomena under study.

Researchers may even specifically recruit underrepresented or marginalized groups, so that their views can add complexity and breadth.

For example, this strategy was used by Foss and Edson (1989) in their study of women's choices about changing their names after marriage. The authors purposefully recruited three groups of women. Group one included women who adopted their husbands' names; in group two they kept their birth names; in group three they chose hyphenated or new names. To reach these three groups, the authors had to make a concerted effort to recruit women who kept their birth names. They felt the extra effort was worthwhile because their sample variation was necessary for illustrating the complex nature of post-marital naming decisions.

Snowball samples

Another method for reaching difficult-to-access or hidden populations is **snowball sampling**. Researchers begin by identifying several participants who fit the study's criteria and then ask these people to suggest a colleague, a friend, or a family member. Just like a snowball rolling downhill, snowball sampling plans can expand quickly. Noy (2007), in his study of backpacker tourists, makes the point that snowball samples are often well poised for investigating organic social networks and marginalized populations.

However, one downside to snowball samples is that they can quickly skew to one type of group, clique, or demographic (as participants tend to suggest others who are similar to themselves). Furthermore, snowball samples may quickly get out of control. A potential solution is to recruit a handful of participants who represent a maximum variation, and then to generate several smaller snowballs from that diverse initial sample.

Theoretical-construct samples

Theoretical-construct samples are those that recruit participants or collect data because these meet certain theoretical characteristics or conceptual frameworks. For example, Ashforth and Kreiner's (1999) theoretical construct of "dirty work" includes three different types: physical, social, and moral. A researcher could use theoretical-construct sampling by specifically recruiting employees who engage in *physical* dirty work (say, ditch-diggers or crime scene investigators); employees whose work is marked by *social* stigma (undertakers or asylum workers); and employees whose work falls in Ashforth's and Kreiner's category of *morally* dirty work (prostitutes or casino owners). As a result of these choices, the sample would fit the theoretical construct.

Theoretical-construct sampling is also appropriate for participant observation data. For instance, a researcher interested in social support among a group of Weight Watchers could purposefully focus the data collection on three different types of support (Albrecht & Adelman, 1987): (a) instrumental support (an exchange of time, resources, or labor) through making healthy food for one another; (b) informational support through researching and circulating brochures that listed local fitness classes; and (c) emotional support through listening and providing compassion when others talked about their struggles with eating.

Theoretical-construct sampling is a systematic and credible approach. However, qualitative researchers who wish to *build* theory themselves also need to attend to data that do not easily fit into already developed theories. Rather than solely imposing the theoretical construct upon the data, qualitative researchers who also attend to an emic or interpretive approach will also consider how emergent data extend or critique extant theory – a topic we return to in Chapter 9.

Typical, extreme, and critical instance samples

Other research projects employ **typical instance sampling**, in which interviewees are chosen because they are typical of the phenomenon under examination. For instance, an advertiser may want to reach the "typical" underground commuter on the London Tube; therefore s/he would research the demographic characteristics of commuters who ride the tube – their age, gender, ethnicity, and average minutes traveled per day – and then choose interviewees who fall into the most typical categories.

Typical instance sampling is also worthwhile in participant observation. Because human beings are naturally attracted to the odd and unusual, observing mundane activities ensures that research claims represent a range of activity. For example, Trujillo (1992) used his background as a pitcher, his affinity for baseball parks, and his attending games as a fan to explore the culture of baseball by studying typical baseball regulars: fans, umpires, ticket takers, ushers, and managers.

On the flip side, some researchers purposefully sample data that are rare, unique, odd, and deviant. This is called **extreme instance sampling**. For example, scholars interested in happiness may choose to interview people who are especially resilient, energetic, and long-living (Lyubomirsky, 2008), and those interested in crisis sensemaking may purposefully examine tragic disasters (Weick, 1993). In choosing such samples, researchers can explore the limits of existing theories and potentially develop new concepts. Extreme instance sampling is especially appropriate for research on crimes, communication problems, extreme acts of altruism or heroism, and other rare phenomena. While extreme instances can be quite valuable and interesting, researchers should keep in mind that this type of sampling can take significant time and effort. Finding (and even knowing what equates with) "extreme" requires first gathering and then sorting through a lot of "typical" data.

Similar to, and sometimes overlapping with, extreme instance sampling is **critical incident sampling**. This approach is appropriate for exploring data related to incidents that (or people who) are unique given the research being pursued. Some researchers repeatedly focus on specific critical incidents – like renowned sociologist Dennis Mileti, who studies social behavior in the chaos produced by natural disasters, such as the Loma Prieta earthquake in California (Mileti & O'Brien, 1992). The data obtained may not necessarily represent the "extreme" valence of an issue, but they are interesting because of their rarity or strategic connection to the larger argument.

A good critical case also permits logical deductions in the form: "If this is (not) valid for this case, then it is not valid for any (or only a few) cases" (Flyvbjerg, 2011, p. 307). For example, imagine you are a researcher studying the demise of traditional dinnertime rituals. You could purposefully choose a critical sample of families who might be *most likely* to practice traditional dinnertime rituals (e.g. religious or well-to-do families with children of elementary-school age, a stay-at-home mother, a working patriarchal father who arrives home at 5 p.m., and a functional dining room). You might find that *even these families* do not engage in traditional rituals like saying a family prayer before dinner. In choosing this critical case, you might be able to play with the claim that, "if dinnertime rituals are fading even in this critical sample, then such rituals are likely disintegrating among most families." In short, choosing a critical sample can help with transferring claims to larger populations in the long run (for more on this, see Flyvbjerg, 2011).

Determining the best sample

So how and when should you determine the best sample? Qualitative researchers conducting interviews or focus groups (without participant observation) usually design a sampling plan at the onset of their projects. Their research questions determine the type of populations and people who can most appropriately provide data about the phenomena of interest.

For example, researchers at the Project for Wellness and Work–Life at Arizona State University wanted to understand men's opinions about gender roles at work and at home. Additionally, we were curious to know how their attitudes intersected with work–life policies and with challenges related to women's workplace. Given the goals of the study, the criteria for participants were: (a) to be male; (b) to be in a high-ranking, gate-keeping executive position; (c) to be romantically partnered; and (d) to have children of one's own (Tracy & Rivera, 2010). In this study we determined the sample before recruiting participants and gathering the data.

When participant observation occurs before the interviews, a strict sampling plan may be unnecessary (and restrictive) in the project's beginning stages. When you are new to the field, it is fine just to hang out and see what emerges as interesting. After being in the scene for a while, it makes sense to revisit research goals and systematically design the sampling plan. The process is similar to visiting a foreign land or a national park. On your first few visits, just wander around and appreciate whatever comes your way. But, if you are short on time and want to enjoy several specific experiences (be they a jazz concert, a waterfall, or a talk about cultural history), plan your visit likewise.

How many interviews are enough? The answer is an unabashedly ambiguous "[a]s many as necessary to find out what you need to know" (Kvale, 1996, p. 101). Sample size is critically important for researchers who need statistical power to generalize, but quality is usually more important than quantity for qualitative research. Not enough interviews will result in shallow and stale contributions. Too many will result in a paralyzing amount of data, which discourage transcription and penetrating interpretations. In my semester-long doctoral methodology courses, I generally suggest five to eight interviews as pedagogically valuable – but this decision is tied to the course's specific goals and time constraints.

The answer to "how many" depends on the richness of data gathered from other sources, on budget, and on timeline, as well as on your access to software or research help in transcribing and analyzing the data. Interviewing is no small task. Even after interview design and question development, I estimate that each one-hour interview equates to 15 total research hours when you consider the time devoted to planning, scheduling, conducting, organizing, transcribing, and analyzing. So think long and hard about the number of interviews that are necessary.

Indeed, the contrast between the initial enthusiasm and the eventual snafus, exhaustion, and challenges that come with interviews is distinct! Researchers should begin analyzing and interpreting data along the way. Ask yourself: Have the data provided rich contributions to research goals? If not, then more interviews are warranted. Can you predict what your interviewees will say? Some would say that this might happen after as few as 12 interviews (Guest, Bunce, & Johnson, 2006). If so, you have likely reached data saturation (a topic to which we will return in Chapter 9), and additional interviews will bring fewer and fewer insights.

Interview structure, type, and stance

Interviews are conversations with a purpose, and, depending on this purpose, interviews should be organized in different ways. Here I discuss a variety of interview structures, types, and stances. I encourage you to think about the advantages and disadvantages of each type in the light of your particular research project and goals. For examples of actual interview and focus group excerpts, you can refer to Researcher's Notepad 8.1 and Appendix C.

Structure of interviews

Some interviews are tightly structured, ordered, and planned, whereas others are free-flowing spontaneous and meandering. **Structured interviews** generally use an **interview schedule** – a list of questions that are repeated in the same order and in the same wording, like a "theatrical script to be followed in a standardized and straightforward manner" (Fontana & Frey, 2005, p. 702). Indeed structured interviews often include questions that have a limited set of response categories (e.g. "Sometimes? Always? Never?").

Structured interviews are advisable when you want to compare and contrast data across a large sample. Furthermore, because the interview schedule serves as the primary research tool, structured interviews are popular when you employ research assistants – for instance in large-scale telephone interviews, which have a stimulus–response format. Research assistants (or professionals at research firms) can be trained to ask questions uniformly. As long as they do not deviate from the script, the disadvantages of the interviewer not having a complex understanding of the topic at hand are reduced.

The downsides of highly structured interviews are their lack of flexibility and depth. Because interview schedules encourage the researcher not to deviate from the script, they simultaneously discourage the interview from probing or picking up on emotional cues like hesitations, fluctuations in vocal tone, or other nonverbal expressions. Such an approach assumes that respondents answer truthfully and singularly the first time a question is asked. As such, a structured interview "often elicits rational responses, but it overlooks or inadequately assesses the emotional dimension" (Fontana & Frey, 2005, p. 703).

Unstructured interviews are more flexible and organic in nature. The interviewer enters the conversation with flexible questions and probes, or maybe even with just a list of bullet points. This less structured **interview guide** is meant to stimulate discussion rather than dictate it. Such an approach encourages interviews to be creative, adapt to ever-changing circumstances, and cede control of the discussion to the interviewee (Douglas, 1985). The interviewer assumes the posture of a listener and reflector as much as – if not more than – that of the questioner. Unstructured interviews may take place during a slow point of fieldwork, over a meal or drink – or they may be planned for a specific time.

The advantages of unstructured interviews are that they allow for more emic, emergent understandings to blossom, and for the interviewees' complex viewpoints to be heard without the strict constraints of scripted questions. Furthermore, less structured interviews are likely to tap both content and emotional levels. Oftentimes the interview process itself is the venue through which researchers learn what data are most interesting and important, and flexible interview guides allow for focusing on topics that emerge as most fruitful, interesting, and important. Because questions in unstructured interviews are organic, the resulting data are more meandering and more complex, too. As Kvale notes:

The more spontaneous the interview procedure, the more likely one is to obtain spontaneous, lively, and unexpected answers from the interviewees. And vice versa: The more structured the interview situation is, the easier the later structuring of the interview by analysis will be. (Kvale, 1996, p. 129)

Given all this, it makes sense to consider your preferred methods for data analysis and to structure your interviews accordingly. If the analysis goals are very specific (e.g. answering a specific question dictated by a research grant), then structured interviews may be more appropriate.

The less structured the interview, the more skill, expertise, and knowledge are required of the interviewer. To be able to probe effectively, the interviewer must understand the research goals and know the relevant literature. In order to pick up on emotional cues, the interviewer must have skills in empathy and relating. These skills require more training than a quick overview of an interview script, and therefore unstructured interviews are inappropriate if you must rely on research assistants new to qualitative methods.

Certainly, no one level of structure is ideal for all people or situations. Some researchers thrive using several key bullet points to guide informal dialogue. However, if you are new to qualitative methods or you experience social anxiety during interviews, the need to "improvise" may be terrifying and counterproductive. Even those who think they are wonderfully spontaneous often benefit from more structure. All too many times, interviewers are thrown for a loop and find refuge in carefully worded pre-planned questions. Furthermore, including several structured questions asked in the same way across interviews provides the option of systematically comparing and contrasting data across participants, something that lends complexity to any research project.

Interview types

Different interview "types" have been introduced by various scholars, and they differ depending on the goals of the research, on the participants, on the researcher's epistemological leanings, and on the structure of the interview. Even if you never adopt one of these types of interviews in full, considering the various genres can be helpful in your project's design.

Ethnographic interviews (Spradley, 1979) are informal conversational interviews; they are emergent and spontaneous. They usually occur in the field and sound as though they were a casual exchange of remarks. However, in contrast to other fieldwork conversations, the ethnographic interview is a conversation that is specifically instigated by the researcher and may not have occurred otherwise. For example, during breaks at home parties, Riforgiate (2008) asked consultants about ways in which they balanced work, life, and family responsibilities.

It makes sense to purposely seek out ethnographic interviews or discussions when people are otherwise unoccupied. I spoke with correctional officers when they were bored during graveyard shifts. Riforgiate (2008) interacted with participants as they set up their makeup, jewelry, or kitchen supplies. Former MA student Sundae Schneider-Bean interviewed tourists when they were waiting in line at the airport or sitting in a lobby waiting for their tour bus to arrive (Schneider-Bean, 2008). Participants in such contexts often welcome ethnographic interviews to pass the time.

Informant interviews (Lindlof & Taylor, 2011) are another common type of interview. Despite the pejorative connotations of the word, informants are not always "snitches" or "moles." Rather, the qualifier "informant" is used here to characterize participants who are experienced and savvy in the scene, can articulate stories and explanations that others would not, and are especially friendly and open to providing information. Finding good informants usually requires a long-term relationship. Furthermore, for reasons of ethics and credibility, ethnographers should seek out insight from a variety of informants rather than relying on just a few to speak for the entire culture (see Joralemon, 1990 for a cautionary tale of relying on a single informant).

In the course of his three-year field research project on wheelchair rugby, Lindemann (2010) traveled the country with disabled rugby players, befriending them, serving as a physical aid, helping with equipment during practices and games, and generally "hanging out" off court, at parties and bars. The conversations that arose from interactions with his informants proved invaluable data about the ways these athletes communicated their masculinity in the context of disability.

Respondent interviews are those that take place among social actors who all hold similar subject positions and have appropriate experiences, which attend to the research goals. This could include a group of volunteers, children, breast-feeding moms, or professionals. In contrast to informants (described above), who have a unique depth and breadth of experience and feel articulate about a range of cultural issues, respondents are relied upon to speak primarily of and for themselves – about their own motivations, experiences, and behaviors. Respondent interviews may be particularly worthwhile when attempting to understand similarities and differences within a certain cultural group. Montoya (2012), for example, interviewed a series of Latino male entrepreneurs in order to understand workplace socialization across generations (or inter-generational relationships).

Narrative interviews are open-ended, relatively unstructured interviews that encourage the participant to tell stories rather than just answer questions. Stories might relate to the participants, their experiences, or the events they have witnessed. One type of narrative interview is the **oral history** (Dunaway & Baum, 1996), which queries those who eye-witnessed past events for the purpose of (re)constructing history. Oral histories often focus on the experiences and perspectives of marginalized group members, whose views may otherwise be hidden or written out of formal accounts. For example, Davis (2007) interviewed Black women who witnessed and survived the 1921 Tulsa Race Riot.

Life-story interviews (Atkinson, 1998) or **biographic interviews** (Wengraf, 2001) also elicit stories. In contrast to oral histories, which focus on a specific event, life-story approaches ask interviewees to discuss their life as a whole, their memories, and what they want others to know. Life-story interviews may be particularly interesting to conduct with members of your own family or with famous personalities who have caught the public imagination. They can also provide understanding – and perhaps even empathy – for people who may otherwise be seen as socially aberrant or undesirable. For instance, Oleson (2004) makes a revealing examination of serial killers' life-stories.

Researchers may also choose to examine how interviewees' answers are created within discourses and power relations – a type of interview I call discursive. A **discursive interview** pays attention to large structures of power that construct and constrain knowledge and truth – and to how interviewees draw upon larger structural discourses in creating their answer. For example, Rivera & Tracy (2012) found that Hispanic border patrol agents tell stories of feeling compassion toward undocumented immigrants, in part because the immigrants remind them of their ancestors. A discursive interview picks up on the fact that participants' compassion emerges from and intersects with larger discourses of race, class, and myth – for instance the myth of the American dream. In turn, the interviewer probes the meaning of this discourse, critically examining the interview's data in light of societal structures and myths.

Interview stances

Interviews vary according to the interviewer's power, emotional stance, and extent of self-disclosure. Some believe that interviewers should always be up front and truthful, sharing their opinions and motivations for the study. In contrast, others argue that covert interviewing methods and shielding one's true feelings are no different from the usual deceitfulness that marks everyday life (Douglas, 1985). The very common interview stance of **deliberate naïveté** (Kvale, 1996) lies somewhere between these extremes. It asks interviewers to drop any presuppositions and judgment while maintaining openness to new and unexpected findings.

Traditional realist notions of objective research suggest that interviewers should be in control, create a style of interested but objective listening, and avoid evaluating, befriending, teaching, comforting, or confronting. Others question the desirability of a detached model of control. For instance, in **collaborative/interactive interviewing** (Ellis & Berger, 2003) interviews are jointly created, so that the researcher and the participant are on an even plane and can ask questions of each other. Ellis, Kiesinger, and Tillmann-Healy (1997), for example, used such an approach when they dialogued about eating disorders and employed this exchange to better understand bulimia and the paradox of expecting a thin body in a society where food is so abundant. These reflexive co-constructed interviews are helpful tools in a variety of research projects, including autoethnography.

Indeed, interviews are not just dialogues in which participants give (their ideas) and the researcher takes (the participants' ideas as commodified data). One way in which researchers may give back is in the form of providing advice, education, and insight on a certain issue or topic. **Pedagogical interviews** not only ask participants for their viewpoints, but encourage researchers to offer expertise in the form of knowledge or emotional support. A researcher interviewing targets of sexual assault, for example, might show insight into the fact that all types of people have been victims of assault and that participants are not to blame for their situation.

Rubin and Rubin (2005) proffer a model for **responsive interviewing** that suggests that researchers have responsibilities for building a reciprocal relationship, honoring interviewees with unfailingly respectful behavior, reflecting on their own biases and openly acknowledging their potential effect, and owning the emotional effect of interviews. Feminist researchers (Reinharz & Chase, 2002) also advocate that the researcher and the respondents work together to create the narrative in a way that can benefit the group.

This is quite similar to Oakley's (1981) **friendship model of interviewing**, a feminist type of interviewing in which participants are treated as intimate friends rather than as objects. This approach suggests that researchers can and should show their human side, answer questions, and express feelings. They need not try to act in an unbiased way or to avoid sharing their opinion. Rumens (2008), for instance, used this approach when interviewing gay men about how they understand, value, and give meaning to their workplace friendships with women. He learned that gay men are quite inventive in their friendships with female co-workers, in ways that challenge typical workplace relationships.

Choosing a friendship approach for interviewing requires special care and reflection. Most interviews are not marked by a completely reciprocal interaction of two equal partners. Whenever an interviewer defines the situation, introduces topics, and deliberately steers the course of the conversation, this equates with an asymmetry of power. Researchers must prepare for the obligation that comes with such power and consider carefully how they might ensure that participants are treated ethically and fairly.

While some interviews are marked by empathy and compassion, others are marked by confrontation. In **confrontational interviews** (Kvale & Brinkmann, 2009), the interviewer deliberately provokes confrontation and divergence of interests. The interviewer may contradict or challenge the interviewee and, in doing so, highlight their differences of opinion. Confrontation is ethically questionable when you are interviewing participants

TIPS AND TOOLS 7.2

Interview structure, types and stances

Interviews can vary in their structure, in their type, and in the interviewer's stance. Which combination is best suited for your study? Why?

Interview Structures	Interview Types	Interview Stances
	Ethnographic	Deliberate naïveté
Structured	Informant	Collaborative/
Unstructured	Respondent	interactive
	Narrative (oral history, life-story, biographic)	Pedagogical
		Responsive/friendship
	Discursive	Confrontational

who are traumatized or hold relatively low power positions. However, such an approach may be warranted in situations where social justice is at issue – especially when the participant is powerful, especially confident, or otherwise belongs to an elite. Indeed, relatively secure interviewees may actually welcome the intellectual and identity challenges that come with confrontation. One word of warning, though: if you choose to challenge, you should also prepare for counterattack – and be able to deal with it good-naturedly, without defensiveness. Further, I recommend leaving the most confrontational questions for the close of the interview – a tactic we will address in the next section.

Tips and Tools 7.2 reviews the interview structures, types, and stances discussed above.

Creating the interview guide

As noted in regard to interview structure, interview schedules are standardized scripts of questions, whereas interview guides refer to less formal lists of questions, which are more flexibly drawn upon depending on the situation and the participant. Both these tools represent *what* questions will be asked, the interviewers' general *manner*, and the *order* in which to ask them. Most researchers engaging in contextual interpretive, critical, or post-structural approaches rely on interview guides rather than on schedules.

Before writing interview questions, it makes sense to revisit your overall research questions, the literature, and – for those engaging in other data collection – the data collected thus far. These sources can serve as a springboard for interviews – suggesting themes of interest to explore. Researchers should also consider the extent to which interviews will be designed to (a) explore new themes; (b) attempt to test emergent hypotheses; (c) explore feelings and opinions; or (d) gather factual data. Answers to these questions will help determine question content, type, and order. Exercise 7.2 provides a brainstorming exercise that can help as you begin thinking about how interviews may extend and contribute to your research project.

EXERCISE 7.2

Strategizing interviews

1   What topics would you like to address (theoretical, practical, methodological)? In other words, what do you want to know that the current literature and data collection doesn't fulfill? Consider your conceptual framework.

2   How does your response to question 1 align with one or more of your guiding research questions? Consider tweaking research questions as necessary.

3   What contributions do you hope interviews might provide?

4   What are several interview questions that will help in pursuing such a contribution?

5   What type of interview sample is best poised to help achieve these contributions?

Wording good questions

As you move into interview design, it is important to keep in mind that interview questions cannot be asked the same way as research questions. Research questions often include abstract theoretical constructs, whereas interview questions must be simple, jargon-free, and attend directly to the interests and knowledge of interviewees. For example, one of my initial guiding *research questions* in my 911 call-taker study was: "What vocabulary is used by call-takers, and how does this help call-takers manage stress in their job?" If I had asked call-takers this as an *interview question*, they likely would have furrowed their brow and thought to themselves, "What the heck does she mean by 'what *vocabulary* do we use'?"

Furthermore, a number of interview questions may attend to any one research question. The model in Researcher's Notepad 7.1 distinguishes between research questions and interview questions inspired by a study of emotional deviance with judges (Scarduzio, 2011). Emotional deviance relates to behavior in which employees' emotional expressions are different (or deviate) from organizational norms – for example, when a funeral director giggles, or a waiter rolls his eyes in exasperation. The model in Figure 7.2 indicates how interview questions are written differently from research questions, and also how certain interview questions may attend to more than one research question.

In addition to being aware that interview questions are asked differently from research questions, some general tips can help ensure that the former lead to good data (Seidman, 1991). Generally speaking, good interview questions have the following characteristics:

1   They are simple and clear. They avoid acronyms, abbreviations, jargon and scholarly talk.

2   They are not double barreled but rather inquire about one thing at a time. For instance, rather than asking, "In your opinion, what are the advantages of buying electric vehicles and solar panels?" a better tactic is to divide this into two questions: one about electric vehicles, the other about solar panels.

3   They promote answers that are open-ended and complex. In most cases, yes/no questions should be followed by "Why?" or "In what ways?" or, better yet, they should be reworded so as to encourage a more fine-grained answer (e.g. "To what extent is…").

4   They are straightforward, neutral, and non-leading. For example, rather than asking: "Don't you appreciate the way your spouse looks out for you?" – it is better to ask: "In

RESEARCHER'S NOTEPAD 7.1

Research questions versus interview questions

Model

Figure 7.2 Research questions and interview questions are not one in the same. This diagram – based upon Jennifer Scarduzio's (2011) research – provides one example about how they may differ yet relate to one another.

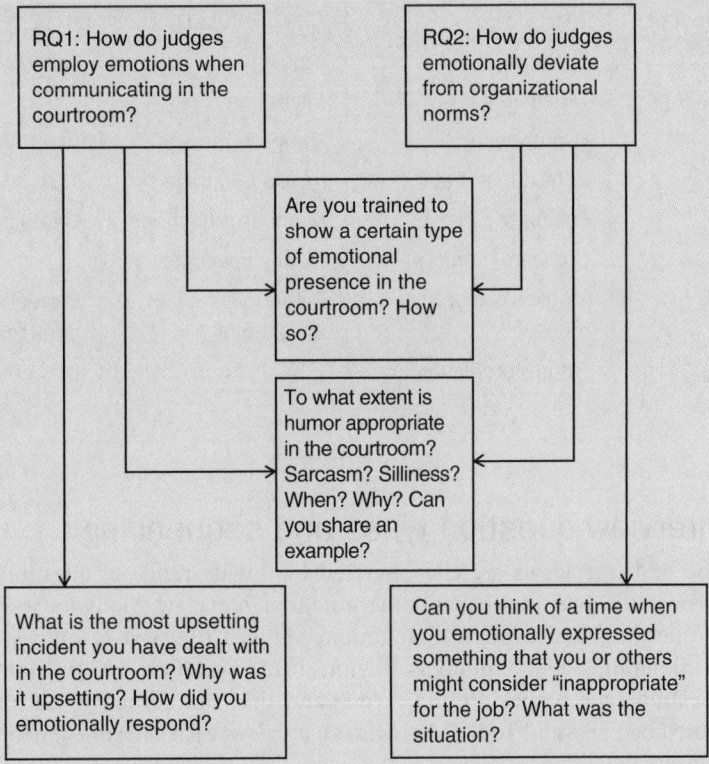

what ways do you feel your spouse looks out for you? Do you appreciate this behavior? Resent it? Have another reaction? Why?"

5   They uphold rather than threaten the interviewees' preferred identity. For instance, if the research participant views herself as a social justice activist, it is better to ask "How do you think your volunteer efforts affect the local voting turnout?" than "Do you really think that simply volunteering impacts voting turnout?" Of course, later in the interview, especially if you want to penetrate a front or to play devil's advocate, this more threatening question may be appropriate.

6   They are accompanied by appropriate follow-ups and probes (e.g. "Can you give an example," "Tell me a story about that," or "How might you go about doing x?").

So, now that we have overviewed tips for good questions, let us review the most common types of questions.

TIPS AND TOOLS 7.3

Interview question types

Interviews can make use of a number of types of questions. This table lists a variety, some of which are best placed in the opening, while others generate open discussion, others direct the interviewee to particular answers, and others are well poised to close the interview.

Opening Questions	Generative Questions	Directive Questions	Closing Questions
Informed consent	Tour	Closed-ended	
	Example	Typology	Catch-all
Rapport building	Timeline	Elicitation	
	Hypothetical	Data referencing	Identity enhancing
Experience	Behavior/action	*In vivo* language	
	Posing the ideal	Member reflections	Demographic
Factual issues	Compare/contrast	Devil's advocate	
	Motives/others' motives	Potentially threatening	Preferred pseudonym
	Future/prediction		

Interview question types and sequencing

The best interviews are characterized by a wide range of questions. Here I walk you through the question sequence in a potential interview. Along the way I provide examples of questions and explain their unique value. I use past resources as guides (Kvale & Brinkmann, 2009; Lindlof & Taylor, 2011; Spradley, 1979). However, many of the question-type names are my own – and they are coined to be intuitive and easy to remember. Tips and Tools 7.3 provides a preview; each category contained in it is described in more detail below.

Opening the interview

The first few minutes of an interview should break the ice and set expectations. Researchers can confirm the length of the interview by saying something like this:

> Thank you for agreeing to meet with me today. I have us scheduled for an hour together. Does that still work for you? I want to honor our time constraints today. Therefore, while I encourage you to elaborate on your answers to my questions, there may be times when I redirect, so that we may be sure to cover all the issues within the hour.

As you open the interview, keep in mind that **informed consent** is usually required by IRB for audio-recorded interviews. Given the influence of first impressions on the rest of the interview, researchers should practice how they will introduce informed consent and should provide time for the participant to read over the form and ask questions. This is a good stage to jot down some fieldnotes about the interview context, nonverbal communication, the appearance of the interviewee, where the interviewee chose to sit, whether the interviewee arrived on time, and any other interesting data that will not emerge in an audio recording.

Once the expectations have been set, the first questions should **build rapport**, helping the interviewee feel comfortable, likeable, and knowledgeable. In order to engage respondents immediately, questions should be non-threatening, open-ended, and very easy and inviting, such as: "When did you decide to become a math major?"

Good interviews often begin with open-ended **experience questions** that will prompt the participant to tell stories – which later questions can refer to and follow up on. For instance "How did you know you wanted to be a father?" or "What is your most vivid athletic experience ever?" During these first few moments, you might also consider – briefly – sharing your own story, as mutual self-disclosure can help bring you closer to, and create affinity with, your participant and mitigate real and perceived power differences. Although rapport is critical, it's important to be mindful of the allotted timeframe and to get to the primary topics of interest in short order.

Asking *what* and *how* about certain **factual issues** is also a good way to open an interview. For example, "At *what* point was your organization founded?" or "*How* does one sign up to volunteer?" Certainly, fact-based questions can also be interspersed *throughout* the interview (because a long list of fact-based questions, quite frankly, is boring). However, asking about personal opinions, feelings, and conclusions too early is a bad idea (e.g. in the first few minutes avoid something like: "Do you think this program is a good idea? Why?"). *Why* questions can be interpreted as prying or threatening. Asking *why* too quickly can also prompt the interviewee to intellectualized speculation (Kvale, 1996).

Generative questions

After opening the interview, I recommend moving to what I classify as **generative questions** – non-directive, non-threatening queries that serve to *generate* (rather than dictate) frameworks for talk. Such questions relinquish control to the respondents for the pace and exact topic of the answer. In this section, I discuss and provide examples of generative questions.

Tour questions ask the interviewee to overview familiar descriptive knowledge or memories about an activity or event. Examples might include "Can you describe a typical triathlon for me?" or "How is your household's dining room set up? Who sits where?" These questions are not only based on factual description, they also ask about the present – which is usually easier for participants to reflect upon than the past or the future.

Tour questions can be usefully followed with probes asking for **examples** such as: "You said that accidents are more common than one might expect in triathlons. Can you provide an example?" or "Can you tell me about one of your most memorable holiday dinners?" Asking a **timeline question** also adds contextual depth to tour questions. For instance you might ask" "What were the events leading up to you becoming a race director?" or "Have you always sat at the head of your household's dining table? At what point in time did this configuration become the norm in your household?"

Hypothetical questions ask interviewees to imagine their behaviors, actions, feelings, or thoughts in certain situations. For instance, "Imagine you were the head of the Olympic Games. What changes would you make to the way triathlon is raced?" or "If you were to find your child sitting in your chair at dinner, what would you do?" Such questions provide interesting insight, as interviewees imagine novel situations or roles. Hypothetical questions are usually unthreatening, as they are "imagined" situations. However, they may also elicit a philosophical rather than empirical answer about actual behavior.

In consequence, it is important also to ask **behavior and action questions**. For instance, "You said you coached your brother as he trained for his first 5 k race. What advice did you give him?" or "What have you done in the past when your child has misbehaved at the dinner table? What was the misbehavior? How did you react?" Such questions are fact-related, which usually makes it quite easy for interviewees to answer. At the same time, past behavior questions can be threatening if they bring up *bad* behavior from the past, so take care to ask about positive or neutral issues before asking about the negative ones.

Posing the ideal generates responses in which interviewees can starkly contrast reality with their wishes, dreams, and desires. I have used questions that ask, for instance: "If you could wave a magic wand and instantly have five extra hours a week to train, what would you spend your time doing?" Another option is to ask about perfection: "What would a perfect dinner time look like at your house?"

Connected to understanding reality versus one's desires or wishes is the notion of **compare–contrast questions**. These ask interviewees to consider one idea or category in relation to another. For example: "In terms of personality and motivation, what differences have you observed between triathletes and yoga enthusiasts?" or "How is your dinner routine similar to or different from the routine in your own house as you were growing up? The routine at your in-laws?" Compare–contrast questions can generate a flood of knowledge that does not emerge in simple, fact-based description questions ("Tell me about your job"). Just as fieldworkers are better able to notice the unique and interesting features of an *unfamiliar* context, interviewees often best articulate the unique features of their situation or role when they consider *contrasting* situations or roles.

Finally, asking about **motives** can include asking about feelings, actions, or behaviors. Your instinct may be to ask "why," in order to get to motives, but asking "how" may actually generate a more useful account. Katz explains that "how" questions invite

> personally historicized, temporally formatted response, while 'why?' authorizes responses formatted in the atemporal and impersonal categories of moral reasoning. Asking someone why they married someone, chose a residence, or took a job often elicits brief justifications that highlight present features of the mate, home, or work situation; features that may well have been discovered since the relationship was established and that, as current realities, are right at hand to provide an impressive documentation of the answer. Shifting the question to how one got that job, found that residence, or got together with that mate commonly turns the discussion toward 'the long story' that traces how networks of social relations and detailed processes of social interaction worked to shape the respondent's present status. (Katz, 2001, p. 445)

So one might ask "How were you attracted to endurance sports?" or "At what point do you discipline your child when they misbehave at the dinner table? How do you make that decision?" Asking "how" from our participants allows us as researchers to answer "why." As Katz notes: "If research subjects can reliably report why they do the things we want to understand, who would need us?" (p. 445).

Of course, you might ask the participant to reflect upon **other people's motives**. For example, you could ask: "Why do you think younger endurance athletes push so hard at the beginning of a race, even when that means bonking out at the end?" or "Why do you think your wife sits in the dining chair closest to the television?" Although such questions can provide fascinating data, they can also encourage participants to blame, philosophize, or guess, so they should be used sparingly.

Finally, after you ask about past and present experiences, interesting data can emerge through **future prediction questions**. Just as it sounds, these questions ask interviewees to forecast future events, feelings, or behaviors. Although this can lead to some philosophizing, future predictions valuably explore the interviewee's hopes, dreams, worries, and fears. Examples might be: "Where do you envision your athletic ability to be ten years from now?" or "When you're retired, what do you think will be your most vivid memories of dining with your family?"

Directive questions

While generative questions encourage broad and open-ended answers, most researchers also hope to elicit *specific* areas of information during interviews. **Directive questions** structure and *direct* interviews (Lindlof & Taylor, 2011). Such questions put more control in the hands of the interviewer and can be more complex, threatening, or difficult for the interviewee to answer. As such, these questions are best asked after trust and rapport have been built.

The simplest type of directive question is the **closed-ended question**, which, like a survey question, asks respondents to choose among two or more potential answers. These could include "yes/no" questions such as: "Are you registered to race an Ironman triathlon in the next year?" They can also include questions with multiple but not infinite answers, such as: "Which day of the week do you most enjoy going out to dinner?" Sprinkling in one or two closed-ended questions can provide wonderful data from which to compare and contrast the participants. Furthermore, depending on the number of interviewees, the closed-ended data may also be appropriate for statistical analyses.

Typology questions ask respondents to organize their knowledge into different types or categories. For instance, a typology question could ask: "What are the most common race-day rituals you see triathletes engage in?" or "What types of dinner-time routines regularly occur at your house?" Using prompts is especially important for encouraging participants to articulate a range of categories or types. For example you might say: "Okay, so one dinner routine is reciting a prayer and another is that you all help clear the table. What other types of routines usually happen at dinner?" Typology questions encourage the development of lists of strategies and categories. Indeed, entire essays and manuscripts can be organized around typologies (something we will return to in Chapter 10).

Elicitation questions use a picture, a video, a text, or an object in order to prompt and elicit discussion. Elicitation is often used in focus groups when, for instance, members watch a commercial, pass around a new kind of toothpaste tube, or evaluate various print brochures. Using material objects or images to elicit verbal reflections serves to structure and drive the interview in specific ways. Elicitation need not be elaborate. It can be as simple as pulling up a website and asking, "What do you think about the way this organization describes itself?"

The researcher can provide a visual – for instance by asking interviewees to react to a photo of a perfectly coiffed nuclear family eating their Thanksgiving meal. Or interviewees can choose their own object – for example, asking a participant to pull up, review, and reflect on her recent email activity, or to discuss a favorite image hanging on her wall. One step further is asking participants to create and discuss a certain object. Such was the case when my colleagues and I asked targets of workplace bullying to draw pictures of "what bullying feels like" and then explain their pictures (Tracy, Lutgen-Sandvik, & Alberts, 2006). Elicitation approaches can spark creativity, moving respondents from solely textual information to considering the visual and material (Harper, 2002). Furthermore, through the embodied process of playing with visual materials, participants may provide a more realistic response than the one collected through words only (Prosser, 2011).

Data-referencing questions are those that refer to data collected in the past. In his research with quadriplegic rugby players, for instance, Lindemann (2008) observed players faking a more debilitating level of injury than the one they actually lived with. During interviews he brought up this practice and asked his respondents to explain. In interviews, participants sheepishly explained that "some" rugby players occasionally performed a higher injury level so that they would have an advantage on the rugby floor. During these interviews, Kurt also learned that the quad rugby players referred to this injury-faking behavior as "sand-bagging." This *in vivo* **language** – Latin *in vivo* means "in the living (being/organism/situation)" – is distinctive or unique to a certain population or context. Kurt asked his respondents what "sand-bagging" meant to them. Answers to *in vivo* language questions can be extremely illuminating, especially when explanations of such language are compared and contrasted across participants.

Another directive type of question comes in the form of asking participants to reflect on your analyses about the data and research. In **member reflection questions**, the interviewer posits a certain understanding of the data collected thus far and asks the respondent to comment upon it. For example, in my 911 research, I asked: "On the basis of my fieldwork so far, it seems that one reason 911 call-takers cannot be very empathetic is that empathy takes time, and a main goal of the job is to collect facts as quickly as possible. What do you think about my interpretation here?" Member reflections allow participants to give an opinion and shape the emerging analysis. Such questions should be reserved for near the end of the interview (so as not to influence earlier generative questions) and are best directed to particularly articulate or reflective informants.

Another type of question that is better placed near the end of an interview is the **devil's advocate question**, in which the interviewer takes a deliberately skeptical view of the respondent's position or answer. This type of question rests on the presumption that engaging others in an argumentative process will provide valuable data. Interviewers "play" devil's advocate when they adopt an oppositional viewpoint. Alternatively, they may frame the devil as an anonymous other – for example by saying something like: "I heard a police officer say that it's not that hard to be a 911 call-taker. So what makes your job so difficult?" Such a question may prompt the respondent to explain, for instance: "Yes, police officers have to be out in the field, but call-takers have to deal with citizens calling 911 for the first time. They're distraught, don't know the system, and sometimes treat us like secretaries, and that's why dealing with them is emotionally so exhausting." Playing devil's advocate, in this case, clarifies the issue.

Several notes of caution regarding devil's advocate questions: First, they are best used with respondents who are confident and relatively high-power – people who are comfortable explaining themselves without feeling threatened. Second, there is a fine line between *playing* devil's advocate and acting like a confrontational know-it-all. Without good rapport and trust, and without an accompanying level of nonverbal playfulness, devil's advocate questions are ill-advised.

Speaking of sensitive questions, the end of the interview is a good time for other types of **potentially threatening questions**. Leaving personal or political questions for the end is advisable because, first, they may be less problematic if good rapport is already built and, second, if these questions do cause offense, at least other questions have already been asked and answered. Examples of potentially threatening questions include asking people to reflect on their mistakes, their vulnerabilities, or their weaknesses. For instance: "What do you wish you would have done differently in terms of disciplining your children?" Such questions should be accompanied by supportive nonverbal communication and probes that are considerate and pay heed to the respondent's specific identity needs (e.g. to be seen as expert, powerful, moral, or likeable).

Closing the interview

Several questions are common at the close of the interview. **Catch-all questions** can effectively capture and tie together loose ends or unfinished stories. For instance one could ask: "Is there anything you wish people knew about your position that you haven't told me already?" or "What question did I not ask that you think I should have asked?"

This is also the time for **identity-enhancing questions**, which encourage the respondent to leave the interaction feeling smart, expert, well liked, and appreciated. Such questions are not about ingratiation; rather they extend good will and allow participants to feel pleased about their role in the research. They might be of the form: "What advice would you give to someone who is thinking about their first triathlon?" or "What did you feel was the most important thing we talked about today, and why?" Answers to these questions can also guide future interviews.

Opinions differ about when and how to ask **demographic questions**. Some believe they should be asked at the beginning, in case the interviewee terminates the interview prematurely. However, demographic questions tend to be boring, and therefore can interfere with developing rapport. Further, demographic questions can be sensitive and offensive because, by definition, they label and categorize. Of course, some demographic questions may be necessary for routing questions to come (thus the answer to "Do you have children?" may stimulate a possible question about parenting) – and, if asked as part of another interview question, a demographic question is unlikely to feel threatening. Hence my recommendation is to intersperse demographic questions throughout the interview. However, if you have a long list of them, I recommend placing them at the end. Another option is to create a short printed survey.

A good way to close the interview is by expressing gratitude and reassuring the respondent of confidentiality. This is also the time to let the participants know that their data will be kept safe and confidential. As part of this process, you might ask the participant if s/he has a **preferred pseudonym** – which you can do by saying something like: "I'm going to be using fake names when I write up these data. I can make one up – or is there a name that especially suits you?"

Interview question wrap-up

In summary, interview guides can include a large range of questions. I encourage you to experiment with different types, as they all can work in different ways with each interviewee. Although I have provided suggestions about ordering, the way you sequence and word questions depends on the respondents' earlier answers and expressed comfort level, which is communicated both through their words and through nonverbal indicators such as eye contact, fidgeting, and verbal fillers. Throughout the interview it is crucial to listen carefully and to attend to nonverbal cues and to the fact that their meaning might vary depending on the context. For instance, a head nod could mean: "I understand"; "I agree"; "I'm ready to proceed"; "I like this question"; or just "I'm ready to get out of here and, if I nod, maybe we'll be done faster."

Researchers should also consistently check in with participants by strategically using **follow-ups** and **probes** (Kvale & Brinkmann, 2009). Following up can be as easy as saying "Uh huh," "Oh," nodding, or shrugging. Such responses can encourage the interviewee to

EXERCISE 7.3

Interview guide

Prepare an interview schedule or guide for use with your participants.

1   Identify (a) the ideal sample; (b) the type (or types) of interviews you are likely to engage in; and (c) the stance(s) that you will take (see TIPS AND TOOLS 7.2).
2   Explain why these approaches are most appropriate for your research.
3   Then, write out the actual queries and probes in the order you foresee, identifying the types of questions (aim for a mix and see TIPS AND TOOLS 7.3).
4   Provide an updated rendition of your guiding research question(s) at the top of the exercise.

continue or to change course. Through *probes*, interviewers pursue questions to a deeper level. Probes may include pre-planned follow-up questions, or they can be created on the fly, by repeating a portion of the respondent's initial answer and asking for clarification. Silence can also be an effective probe. Oftentimes, all that is needed for the respondent to reflect is the time and space to do so.

Exercise 7.3 provides an assignment that will help you develop an interview guide.

In summary

This chapter has discussed the value of interviews and how best to develop a purposeful sampling plan that will attend to key aspects of the research study. There are a number of sampling strategies to choose from: random samples, convenience/opportunistic samples, maximum variation samples, snowball samples, theoretical construct samples, typical, extreme, and critical instance samples. Developing a strategic sample of the right size is integral to answering research questions.

Interviews vary in proportion with their level of structure (formal or informal), each level having advantages and disadvantages. Researchers can choose from a variety of interview types (informant, respondent, ethnographic, narrative) and of interview stances (naïveté, confrontation, collaboration). One of the most important parts of qualitative data design is developing a formal interview schedule or a more improvisational interview guide. Many decisions must be made regarding the sequence and types of questions asked and the way probes and follow-ups will be delivered so as to ensure good data, and also to make the interviewee comfortable.

As should be obvious from this chapter, good interviews – although they may sound like simple conversations – require strategic thinking and planning. Taking care of such planning is crucial not only in order to ensure useful data, but also because interviews are intrusive and overtly directed by the researcher. Circling back to our metaphor of yin and yang, at the beginning of this chapter, it is important to spend time "warming up" in the stages of interview planning and design before jumping into the practice of questioning participants. Doing so will go a long way to support the successful embodiment of the actual interview – a topic we turn to in the next chapter.

KEY TERMS

accounts rationales, explanations, and/or justifications given by participants to explain their own actions and opinions

behavior and action questions questions that ask about specific past instances and behavior

build rapport building rapport should occur during the beginning of the interview. The first few questions should help the interviewee feel comfortable, likeable, and knowledgeable

catch-all questions questions that can effectively capture and tie together loose ends or unfinished stories

closed-ended questions like survey questions, these questions ask respondents to choose among two or more potential answers

collaborative/interactive interviewing (Ellis & Berger, 2003) jointly constructed interviews among two or more people who, together, act as researcher and research participant

compare–contrast question a type of question that asks interviewees to consider one idea or category in relation to another

confrontational interview a type of interview where the interviewer deliberately provokes confrontation and divergence of interests with the respondent

convenience *or* opportunistic sample the most common form of sampling, participants are selected because access to their population is easy and inexpensive (e.g. college students)

critical incident sampling a process similar to extreme instance sampling. This type of sampling is appropriate for exploring data related to unique or difficult-to-find incidents or people

data-referencing question an elicitation question that asks interviewees to reflect on data collected in the past

deliberate naïveté (Kvale, 1996) an interview stance that asks interviewers to leave at the door any presuppositions and judgment and to preserve an attitude of openness toward new and unexpected findings

demographic questions basic questions that ask about identity characteristics (sex, race, class, sexual orientation)

devil's advocate questions questions in which the interviewer takes a deliberately skeptical view of the respondent's position and asks for justification; they are usually placed near the end of the interview

directive questions an umbrella label for the types of questions that direct interviews toward providing specific responses

discursive interview   a type of interview that asks the participants to consider larger structures of power that construct and constrain their knowledge and attitudes

elicitation question   a directive approach that uses a picture, a video, a text, or an object to prompt and elicit discussion

ethnographic interview   an informal conversational interview; it is emergent, spontaneous, and usually occurs in the field

examples   specific instances designed to illustrate an answer

experience question   a question that prompts participants to tell stories that later questions can refer to and follow up on

extreme instance sampling   the purposeful sampling of data that are rare, unique, odd, and/or deviant. This type of sampling is the opposite of typical instance sampling

factual issues   fact-based "what" and "how" questions

follow-ups   strategic verbal and nonverbal ways to affirm an interviewee's response and to decide where the interview will proceed

friendship model of interviewing   (Oakley, 1981) an interview stance in which participants are treated as intimate friends rather than as objects

future prediction question   a question that asks interviewees to forecast future events, feelings, or behaviors

generative questions   an umbrella label for non-directive, non-threatening queries that generate but do not dictate frameworks for interviewee's responses

hypothetical question   a question that asks interviewees to imagine their behaviors, actions, feelings, or thoughts in certain situations

identity-enhancing question   a question in which the respondent can leave the interaction feeling smart, expert, well-liked, and appreciated

informant interview   an interview with participants who are experienced and savvy in the scene, can articulate stories and explanations that others cannot, and are especially friendly and open to providing information

informed consent   consent from the participants that verifies that they understand their rights and that participation is voluntary

interview   guided question and answer conversation between researchers and participants

interview guide   a list of flexible questions to be asked during the interview, which are meant to stimulate the discussion rather than dictate it

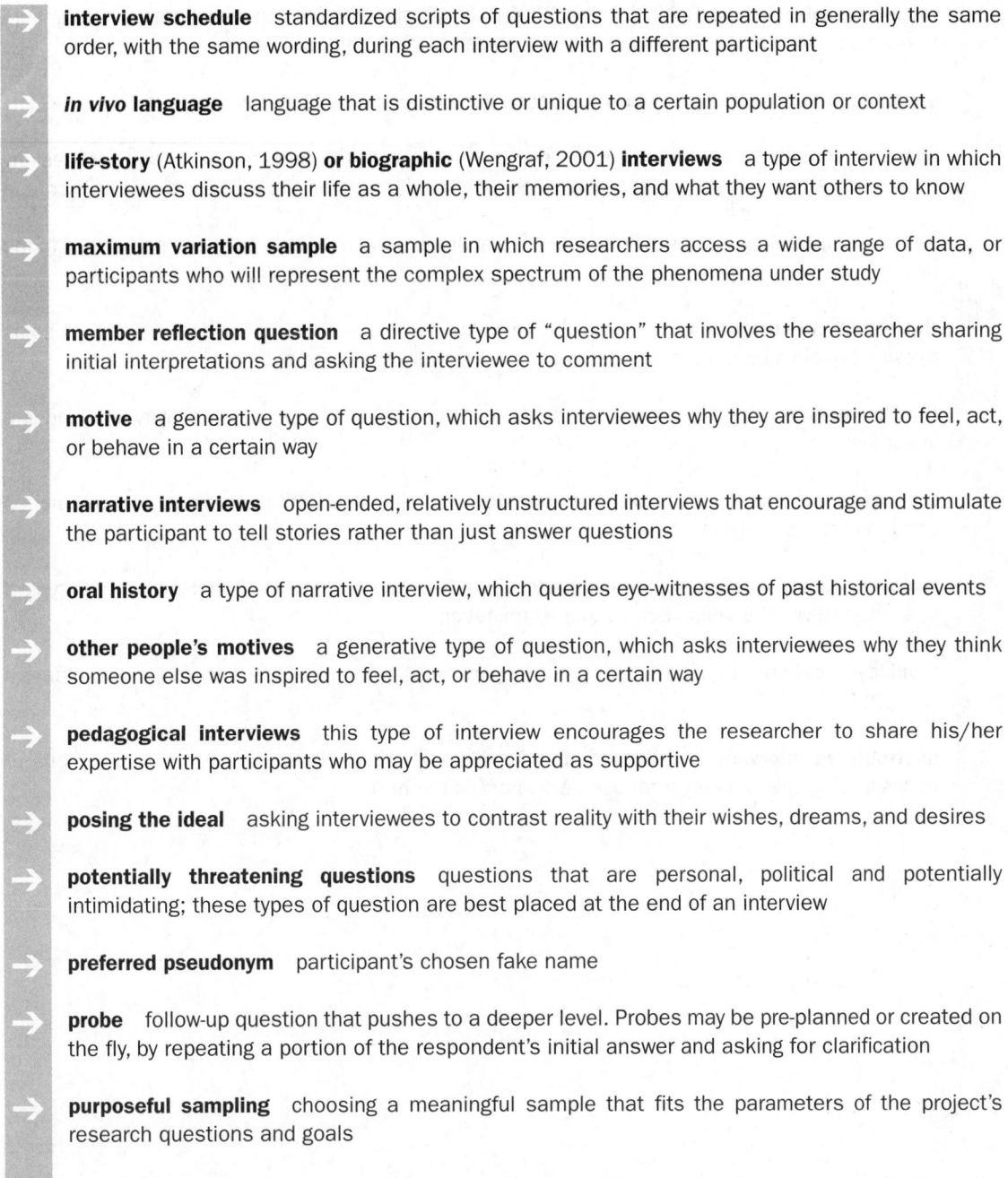

interview schedule   standardized scripts of questions that are repeated in generally the same order, with the same wording, during each interview with a different participant

***in vivo* language**   language that is distinctive or unique to a certain population or context

life-story (Atkinson, 1998) **or biographic** (Wengraf, 2001) **interviews**   a type of interview in which interviewees discuss their life as a whole, their memories, and what they want others to know

maximum variation sample   a sample in which researchers access a wide range of data, or participants who will represent the complex spectrum of the phenomena under study

member reflection question   a directive type of "question" that involves the researcher sharing initial interpretations and asking the interviewee to comment

motive   a generative type of question, which asks interviewees why they are inspired to feel, act, or behave in a certain way

narrative interviews   open-ended, relatively unstructured interviews that encourage and stimulate the participant to tell stories rather than just answer questions

oral history   a type of narrative interview, which queries eye-witnesses of past historical events

other people's motives   a generative type of question, which asks interviewees why they think someone else was inspired to feel, act, or behave in a certain way

pedagogical interviews   this type of interview encourages the researcher to share his/her expertise with participants who may be appreciated as supportive

posing the ideal   asking interviewees to contrast reality with their wishes, dreams, and desires

potentially threatening questions   questions that are personal, political and potentially intimidating; these types of question are best placed at the end of an interview

preferred pseudonym   participant's chosen fake name

probe   follow-up question that pushes to a deeper level. Probes may be pre-planned or created on the fly, by repeating a portion of the respondent's initial answer and asking for clarification

purposeful sampling   choosing a meaningful sample that fits the parameters of the project's research questions and goals

random sample   a sample in which every member of a group has an equal opportunity to be selected for participation in the study. This type of samples is rarely attained in qualitative research; it is more common in statistical studies

respondent interview   interview that takes place across a range of social actors who hold similar positions and have the appropriate experiences, attending to the research goals

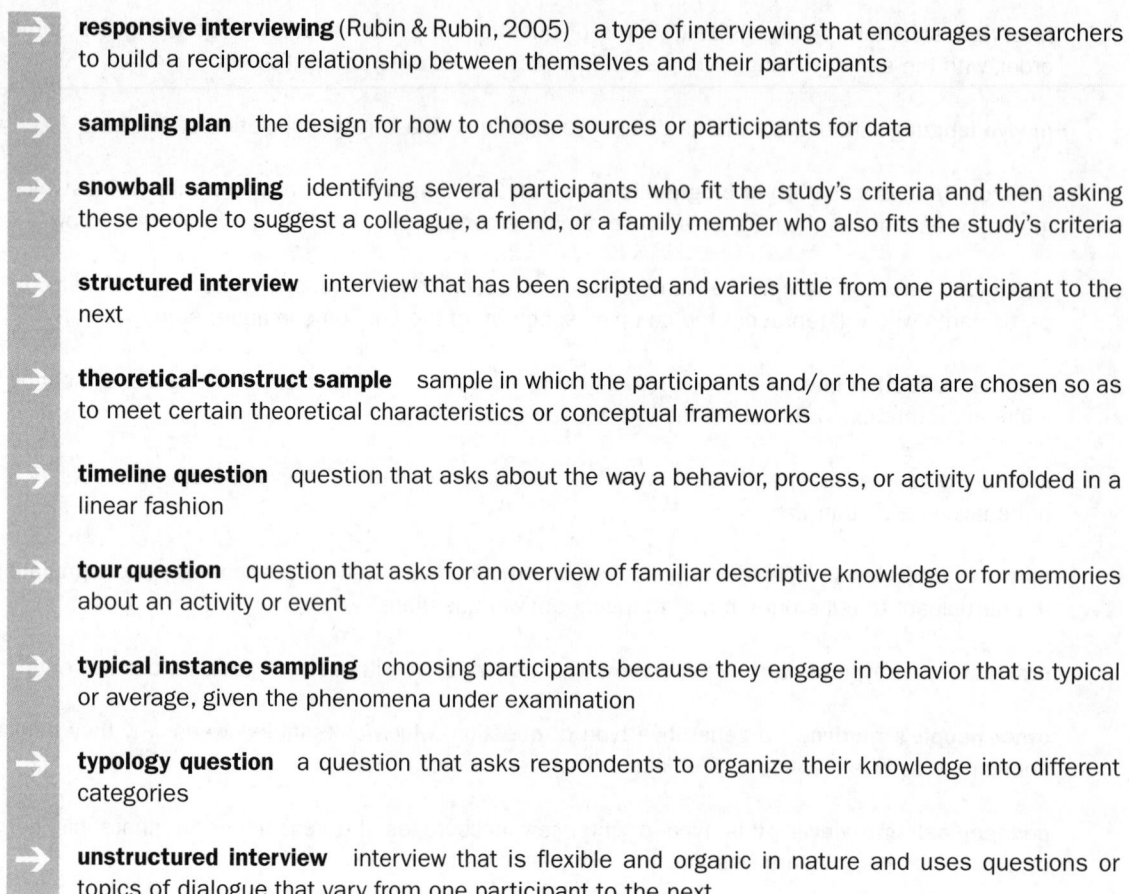

responsive interviewing (Rubin & Rubin, 2005)   a type of interviewing that encourages researchers to build a reciprocal relationship between themselves and their participants

sampling plan   the design for how to choose sources or participants for data

snowball sampling   identifying several participants who fit the study's criteria and then asking these people to suggest a colleague, a friend, or a family member who also fits the study's criteria

structured interview   interview that has been scripted and varies little from one participant to the next

theoretical-construct sample   sample in which the participants and/or the data are chosen so as to meet certain theoretical characteristics or conceptual frameworks

timeline question   question that asks about the way a behavior, process, or activity unfolded in a linear fashion

tour question   question that asks for an overview of familiar descriptive knowledge or for memories about an activity or event

typical instance sampling   choosing participants because they engage in behavior that is typical or average, given the phenomena under examination

typology question   a question that asks respondents to organize their knowledge into different categories

unstructured interview   interview that is flexible and organic in nature and uses questions or topics of dialogue that vary from one participant to the next

CHAPTER 8

Interview practice
Embodied, mediated, and focus-group approaches

Contents

Negotiating access for interviews

Conducting face-to-face interviews

Technologically mediated approaches to interviewing

The focus-group interview

Overcoming common focus group and interviewing challenges

Transcribing

In summary

Qualitative Research Methods: Collecting Evidence, Crafting Analysis, Communicating Impact, First Edition. Sarah J. Tracy.
© 2013 Sarah J. Tracy. Published 2013 by Blackwell Publishing Ltd.

For one bizarre week during graduate school, I was paid $25 an hour to act out dating scenarios with a man I'll call Jeff. Jeff was twice my age and suffered from extreme social anxiety. His wealthy parents had gathered together a team of professionals, including a psychologist, a nonverbal communication professor, and a sex therapist. The nonverbal communication professor knew of my experience in improvisational comedy. Apparently that, coupled with my relative good humor and willingness to work on the cheap, made me an attractive addition to the team.

Jeff's parents desperately wanted their son to get married. This meant he needed to overcome his social awkwardness and learn to flirt, talk, and date. They decided that the best way for him to learn these skills was to fly us all to Aspen, CO for the peak week of the season (between Christmas and New Year's), to engage in intensive training with their son. Each day of that memorable trip we engaged in a host of role-play scenarios during which Jeff and I acted out initial conversations, first dates, casual flirtation, and follow-up phone calls. Depending on the scenario, I was instructed to act interested, flippant, rude, shy, irritated, and so on.

All the while, the psychologist, sex therapist, and nonverbal communication expert observed, took notes, sighed, coached, and furtively traded vexed glances. They watched Jeff vacillate, in an uncanny combination of acting defensive, childlike, belligerent, earnest, and gawky. We realized early on that it would be a challenge to help Jeff land a single date, let alone get permanently hitched. Every evening in Aspen, Jeff and the trio of senior experts attended snazzy parties (arranged by Jeff's parents) while I stayed behind at the hotel, coded videos from the day's session, and dined solo on expensed room service. Over the week, Jeff only very marginally improved and we heard bleak and ambiguous reports about his future love life. I never heard about him after that holiday break.

I tell Jeff's story here because the skills required for interviewing are in many ways similar to the skills of dating and interpersonal interaction. Both can be taught – to an extent. And the more you practice the better you can get. However, there are no standard rules, and some people just seem more attuned to it than others. People often jump into both types of communicative interchanges (dating and interviewing) without preparation. Yet successful interviewing, like dating, is so much more than a formula, and what comes very easily to some people is extremely difficult for others. Even with a wonderful script and lots of coaching, a competent interviewer must have the skills and the personality to listen, learn, and instantly adapt. Any conversational move, just like a chess move, changes the entire game.

This chapter focuses on conducting the actual interview. It opens with a discussion about how to recruit interviewees – a topic that is curiously skipped over in many qualitative research guides. Then I move to topics such as how to develop rapport, engage ethically with the participant as a human (and not as an object), and follow this up in ways that facilitate additional data collection and analysis. The chapter discusses various interview formats – face to face, mediated, one on one, or group. Additionally, it explains how to set up, coordinate, lead, and conduct a focus-group session. Finally, it provides information on transcription and transcription symbols.

After reading this chapter you should feel more confident about conducting interviews and focus groups. Indeed, just as with any interaction, interviewers should not paralyze themselves with worry. To be a good interviewer, you need not be perfect or omniscient, as there are few deal-breaking pitfalls. However, asking questions and getting answers – just like dating – can be much trickier than it first seems.

Negotiating access for interviews

When it's time to do interviews, researchers first need to find people who are willing to talk to them. In other words, access goes beyond getting the "okay" from an organizational gatekeeper: researchers must find people who are prepared to give up their time and their stories and must in turn accommodate participants' routines, rules, and schedules. This means learning to deal with rejection and being flexible.

Researchers can do several things to encourage participation. If you are already in the field and want to interview people in this same context, participants may readily agree to an interview. This is especially true if you have already made a good impression. On the flip side, if you have made a bad impression or no impression at all, this can work against recruiting interviewees, as they may wish to avoid you, or they think that additional research is a waste of time. That said, even if you have spent hours hanging out with participants in a specific field context, you will learn very different things in an interview.

In order to encourage participation, it's important to frame the interview in a way that makes sense to participants and to tap into their expertise and interests. Many people like to talk about themselves. Further, just like in dating, it makes sense to chat and warm them up a bit before the "interview ask." This may mean interacting via email, informally hanging out in the field, and showing interest in their lives (e.g. if you hear they like to cook, share your favorite recipe). This is a relationship you are trying to build. Treat it that way.

Of course, some relationships are more difficult than others. Past research documents the difficulty of enticing certain populations to engage in research – for example people who are financially advantaged (Adler & Adler, 1987), or elites (Undheim, 2003). Denial of access is exacerbated when the research is perceived as intruding upon the interviewee's private sphere or impinging upon his/her vested interests (Renzetti & Lee, 1993). For example, past research suggests that elite men can be suspicious of research they perceive to be feminine or feminist in nature, private, or politically delicate (Pini, 2005). Likewise, they are unlikely to participate in research that might reveal a weakness (Butera, 2006). This information is not meant to scare you off from interviewing certain populations. In contrast, I share it as consolation. If you have trouble, for instance, encouraging wealthy politicians to talk to you about sexual harassment, then you should not take it personally! On the flip side, if you get access to these populations, realize that your data may be especially valuable and rare.

As you recruit interview participants, if you have IRB permission to keep participant records, you should add their information to your contact log, as discussed in Chapter 4. Developing a systematic way of scheduling and confirming the interview is an important step toward successful recruitment. The best scheduling method depends on the audience. Some people may need to schedule several weeks ahead, whereas others may not plan anything more than several days (or hours) ahead.

For interviews that are set up more than a day or two in advance, a reminding phone call, a text, or an email are of the essence. In this confirmation, you might provide a tip about how the participant can identify you (e.g. "I'll be the one wearing a red scarf and carrying a water bottle with Bikram Yoga on it") and what to do if something comes up at the last minute (e.g. "I'll be checking my cell phone, so please text this number if anything happens"). Taking a few minutes to confirm can save hours of traveling, sitting, and waiting.

Conducting face-to-face interviews

In the following section I discuss several topics associated with face-to-face interviews (see Figure 8.1). Good interviewing is more than just asking good questions – it is creating a logistically feasible and comfortable interaction that will encourage an engaging, honest, and fun dialogue. For examples of actual interview and focus-group excerpts, see Appendix C.

Figure 8.1 Face-to-face interviews provide the opportunity to create rapport and to collect both verbal and nonverbal data. Considering issues of access, space, privacy, and comfort can help the interview go smoothly. © Tetra Images/ SuperStock.

Interview logistics

One of the first decisions every interviewer must make is where to hold interviews. Although some of this information may seem commonsense, too many researchers have glossed over these "easy" issues and wasted valuable data. Good locations are characterized by:

- access (available parking, reasonable commuting time);
- quiet space without a lot of distractions;
- actual and perceived safety (the place is well lighted – perhaps a public space);
- adequate privacy (especially from co-workers, family, or friends who may be implicated in the interview);
- comfort (temperature, comfortable chairs, etc.);
- availability of electricity if required for a lap-top or audio recorder.

When deciding on locations, I encourage researchers to come up with several good options and then ask participants what works best for them. I have successfully held interviews in my office, as well as in classrooms, restaurants, coffee shops, parks, and break rooms at the interviewee's workplace.

Connected to the choice of location are decisions about audio recording. Effective audio recordings require that (a) the voices are audible and (b) the recording technology is functioning correctly. I encourage you to test out your audio equipment in the proposed location *before* the interview. Clattering dishes, whirring coffee grinders, and a gentle breeze may seem just fine until you find out that the voices are muffled and difficult to transcribe. During the interview, it makes sense to have an unobtrusive method for verifying that equipment is working. I also encourage taking some notes during the interview as information about nonverbal communication enhances the transcription. Further, such notes will be invaluable if the audio recording is corrupted or lost.

Once the time has come for the interview, researchers should arrive early at the location agreed upon. This leaves time to retest the audio equipment and review the interview guide. When the interviewee arrives, don't be surprised if you feel nervous. Participants usually feel nervous too. Smile, shake their hand, thank them, and, depending on the location, offer to get them something to drink or eat (and allow time for this in your interview window).

The interview should begin with a briefing that includes a description of the interview's purpose, length, and topics covered. This review should include an explanation about confidentiality and a presentation of the consent form. Make sure to set aside time for these activities, as well as for a debriefing at the end of the interview. These pre- and post-interview discussions can take 15–20 minutes, so if you think the interview questions and answers (Q&A) will last 45 minutes, then the entire session may last a little over one hour.

While the interviewees are reading over the consent form, I encourage you to take fieldnotes about when and where the interview occurred, the participants' appearance or disposition, their facial expressions, and anything that may constitute valuable background. For instance, in my interviews at various restaurants with correctional officers, I made a note of the direction in which participants sat during the interviews. I found that most of them sat facing the door, or at least facing out toward the room – which illustrated how correctional officers perform surveillance and watchfulness even when they are outside work. When the consent form is signed, it is time to reference the interview guide and begin.

Why good interviewing is so much more than asking questions

Many qualitative research books focus only on creating good interview questions. However, conducting an interview is much more than that. Inspired by and building upon interviewer qualification criteria set by Kvale (1996, p. 148), I suggest that good interviewers are:

- knowledgeable about the topic and the person – especially if the participant is well known or belongs in an elite group;
- gentle and forgiving – allowing interviewees to pace and respond the way they desire, and providing smooth transitions between topics;
- sensitive – paying attention to the emotional tone, in addition to the message;
- open-minded and not quick to judge (verbally or nonverbally);
- probing – not taking everything at face value, but rather asking critical questions about inconsistencies;
- attentive – supportively listening and referencing earlier answers;
- interpreting – clarifying and extending the interviewee's answers (e.g. "when you say abc, do you actually mean xyz?").

As should be obvious from this list, characteristics like listening, following up, clarifying, and interpreting are crucial parts of interviewing. Throughout the conversation, interviewers condense and interpret the meaning verbally, providing space for the interviewee to further reflect and reword. This changes the interview from a stimulus–response tool into a conversation that produces meaning. Such a dialogue ideally encourages participants to explore new relationships and to generate novel insight.

For instance, during interviews with male executive gatekeepers (Tracy & Rivera, 2010), near the end of several interviews, the interviewer (Jason Zingsheim) gently pushed the executives on their initial responses, which suggested that *workplace flexibility* was the primary and best solution for the parents' work–life balance dilemmas. He asked: "Are there other things, besides flexibility, that could happen at home or work that would make it easier for parents to balance work and life?" Such a question encouraged the participants to examine critically their own taken-for-granted assumptions about gender and parenting and how these assumptions informed organizational policies. As a result, some executives began to consider how the division of labor at home made it more difficult for women than for men to succeed at work. In this way the interviews provided a space for learning and for the transformation of meaning. In other words, *the interviews did not just uncover information, but produced meaning.* The participant, too, became a researcher and an interpreter.

In addition to providing verbal interpretation, it is important to consider your own nonverbal communication. In most situations, facial expressions and body language should communicate warmth, acceptance, and neutrality. The participant may talk about something that the researcher finds shocking, disgusting, or devastating. While I do not suggest inauthenticity, the interview is designed primarily as a platform for the participants' feelings and thoughts, not for the researcher's opinions. Showing shock or judgment will likely limit the interviewee's trust and level of disclosure. Relatedly, interviewers should be careful about their note-taking practices (Patton, 2002). As in taking fieldnotes, if you suddenly begin scribbling more than normal, the participant may believe you are especially surprised or pleased by his answer. It makes sense to introduce note-taking at the beginning of the interview, as just another part of the process.

At the close of the interview, researchers should express appreciation for the interviewee's time and expertise. Being specific about your gratitude is a gift. For instance, rather than just saying "Thank you for your time," it may be even better to say: "Thank you so much, you really provided some fascinating information on (x, y, or z) that I haven't received from others." You can also offer to send them a transcript of their interview (which may, in turn, serve as a vehicle for further data collection and follow-up).

Finally, before the interviewee leaves, turn off the audio recorder. Depending on the situation, you might ask whether there are any last issues that the participant would want to bring up, now that the recorder is turned off. If the participant begins talking about something especially valuable, you might gently say: "This is really insightful and important information. Is it okay if I include it along with my other data?" This will allow the participant to manage the extent to which this extra information can be used as data.

After saying good-bye, there are still several things to accomplish immediately after the interview (Patton, 2002). First, verify that the audio recorder did in fact work. If it did not, immediately begin recording or writing your memories of the interview. Even if the recorder worked, take any additional notes about the scene that would not be evident in the audio transcription. This might include the participant's nonverbal reactions to various questions, or any type of disruption that may have occurred during the interview.

For example, half-way through one of my interviews with a female correctional officer, she stood up and began looking out of the window of the fast-food restaurant. She suddenly walked away from our table and toward the window, claiming that she had seen someone outside who looked like an inmate wearing "prison greens" waiting by the bus stop. This incident – which added to the growing mound of data about officers' high levels of suspicion and paranoia – was muffled on the audio recording and useful only because I took notes about it immediately following the interview.

These tips will hopefully provide you some behind-the-scenes advice about how to conduct face-to-face interviews. Of course, some interviews take place over the phone or email, or are otherwise technologically mediated – a topic we turn to next.

Technologically mediated approaches to interviewing

Mediated interviews are interviews that do not occur face to face, but rather via technological media such as a telephone, a computer, or other hand-held device. Certainly face-to-face interviews have the clear advantage of providing rich information in terms of nonverbal communication. However, in many cases – whether due to geography, cost, disability, social anxiety, or refusal to meet in person – mediated interviews prove a valuable vehicle for interviewing (see Figure 8.2).

Mediated interviews can be **synchronous** and **asynchronous** (Ayling & Mewse, 2009). In synchronous methods, all the parties meet and talk together at the same time (as in face-to-face methods). Synchronous methods include telephone or webcam conversations and Internet text-based chat. Asynchronous methods are those in which the two parties can participate in the interview at different times. Examples include emails, Internet forums and bulletin boards, or social networking sites. Finally, some mediated approaches – like text messaging – can be either asynchronous or synchronous. In what follows I share some views on the strengths and weaknesses of mediated interviews.

Strengths of mediated interviews

One of the primary strengths of mediated interviews is their ability to cost-effectively reach participants who are distributed across a wide geographical area or otherwise unavailable. A face-to-face interview requires coordination in time and place – and what is convenient and comfortable for one member may not be so for the other. In mediated interviews, each individual can participate in a space of his/her own choosing. For example, O'Connor and Madge (2001) conducted interviews with mothers of newborn babies using online conferencing software, a synchronous method. Such an approach not only allows for comfort, but provides opportunities to study populations otherwise unavailable. One can also conduct mediated focus groups through online services. For example, "IdeaScale"

Figure 8.2 Modern technology provides options for conducting interviews via telephone, computer, and other media venues. Plugging in this way has advantages and disadvantages by comparison with face-to-face options.
© Oliver Rossi/Corbis

(http://ideascale.com/) – used by President Barack Obama in 2009 to generate ideas for creating value and saving money in government – was built to channel discussions among 25 or more people. Online programs such as these allow broad audiences to contribute to the collection of qualitative data.

Mediated approaches can also encourage increased engagement and sharing. Follow-up interviews that ask participants to reflect on initial interpretations may be more thoughtful when the researcher sends information via email to begin with, and the interviewees have time to really think about the data before responding. Participants are also more likely to be open with a complete stranger when they communicate online rather than face to face (Joinson & Paine, 2007). If the researcher is studying an online community, participants will certainly feel most familiar, comfortable, and safe in that same context. Furthermore, for research on intimate, traumatic or potentially shameful topics, mediated approaches can be especially worthwhile. Ayling and Mewse (2009) found that chat room interviews are most appropriate in eliciting rich dialogue with gay men who use the Internet to find sexual partners.

A primary strength of asynchronous approaches is that they are flexible about the time and level of detail they allow the interviewee to devote to each answer. Some interview questions are complex. Asynchronous interviews slow down the communication process and provide space for participants to thoughtfully consider the question, reflect on their response, and compose a thorough answer (Paulus, 2007). Also, the process of typing, re-reading, and editing can encourage respondents to be more direct in their answers.

Another potential advantage of mediated approaches is that they can even out power differences and encourage full participation from all members. As noted by O'Connor (2006):

> In a virtual interview, the speed of typing dominates the interaction rather than the most vocal personality, which changes the rules of engagement and has the potential to disrupt traditional interviewer/interviewee power relations. This represents an important advantage of virtual interviews, particularly in the group context. Those individuals who are shy and reticent to speak in face-to-face in group interactions may find the virtual environment a liberating one in which they can "speak." (Online resource)

In addition to providing avenues for voice, communicating via cyberspace can help participants better control their self-presentation; therefore such participants may be more sociable and friendly than they would be in person (Nguyen & Alexander, 1996).

Another advantage is that approaches mediated through text supply data otherwise unavailable in face-to-face approaches. The level and quality of the participants' demonstrated grammar and spelling skills serve as data in themselves. Additionally, the response offered by members of some populations (e.g. the deaf, people with a vocal disorder/disease, or speakers with a heavy accent) may be much richer and complete when it can be given textually rather than verbally. Furthermore, computerized translation tools may facilitate data collection with participants who do not speak the interviewers' language. Again, participants who are shy or worried about their social desirability may be less anxious and more authentic in virtual approaches (O'Connor et al., 2008).

A last advantage of mediated approaches is that, ironically, mediated interviews sometimes require the researcher to purchase less equipment than traditional interviews. Of course, mediated approaches require a computer and a web connection, or a phone. However, interviews via text, email, or online services like "Skype" do not require audio recorders, batteries, or transcribing pedals (a topic to which we return in the close of this chapter). Indeed, such interviews save researchers the time and cost of transcription, because the textual data are self-transcribing (Mecho, 2006).

Disadvantages of mediated interviews

Mediated interviews also have some significant downsides. First and foremost, they provide mediocre embodied or nonverbal data by comparison with face-to-face approaches. Rich cues such as facial expression, physical appearance, tone of voice, odor, laughter, and even the place where the participant chooses to sit are less evident in mediated approaches. Granted, facial expressions can be communicated to some extent via webcams. However, emailed emoticons and abbreviations – such as smiley faces and LOLs – are a poor substitute for the real thing. Furthermore, people are less likely to use symbols to indicate negative emotions such as frowns, eye rolls, tears, or sarcasm – cues that represent invaluable data. The lack of two-way nonverbal communication diminishes the interviews' co-construction of meaning.

Second, mediated interviews require the respondent to have sufficient technological expertise and access. Even participants who say they are computer savvy may still have difficulties downloading an emailed interview guide, filling it out, saving it, and returning it via an attachment (Illingworth, 2001). Because young, educated, and affluent people tend to have more access to technology than older, less educated, or poorer individuals, mediated interviews may skew the study's sample or leave out important information.

Another disadvantage of mediated approaches is participant distraction. Because no one is "watching," respondents may be tempted to engage in other activities simultaneously – such as driving, housework, eating, or checking email. They may also ask others how to respond – or they have so much time to think about their response that it ends up being very different from the ways in which they normally present themselves. Even synchronous phone or webcam calls can be complicated by differing time zones (Kazmer & Xie, 2008) – which can increase the possibility that respondents are sleepy, intoxicated, or cranky. These distractions may be particularly problematic in group interviews of the "conference-call" type, in which some participants zone out as others carry the conversation.

Another disadvantage, especially for asynchronous approaches, is participant attrition. Participants drop out of email or web forum interviews for a variety of reasons, such as inconsistent computer use, disconnection from a certain web service, or the deletion or loss of interviewer messages, which are routed to their "junk" email boxes. People also drop out when responding seems too time-consuming. Especially for slow typists, writing takes longer than talking. Indeed, mediated interviews move the "time cost" of transcription onto the participants' shoulders (Kazmer & Xie, 2008).

Computer-mediated or text-message interviews can also compromise confidentiality. Textual interaction is saved in multiple spaces – not only on the researcher's and the respondents' computer hard drives, but also on various computer servers, and perhaps on various (public or semi-public) websites or forums along the way. Certainly, this repeated documentation can be beneficial if one copy is lost or corrupted. However, a major disadvantage is that privacy can be breached more easily when the data are stored in so many locations (Murray & Sixsmith, 1998).

Additionally, when participants have a mediated copy of their interview, they are more likely to share it with others. If the raw data are publicized, they can impact future data collection – as happened in a case in which a participant posted her complete interview transcript to her personal website (Kazmer & Xie, 2008). This resulted in other participants being aware of the interview questions and reading another participant's responses before their own interviews.

Cleaning and organizing mediated interview data also takes longer than expected. The most fallacious reason for choosing mediated interviewing is that "it's easier." Certainly, textual mediated interviews do "self-transcribe." However, data are not magically formatted and easy to read, as they appear on screen; they must be printed or saved in a systemic fashion (e.g. via the participant's name, interview date, or round of data collection). The organization of mediated data can take significant time; it includes steps such as masking information for confidentiality, importing data into a database, cleaning up fonts, handling various types of attachments, and guarding against computer viruses sent via email (Kazmer & Xie, 2008).

Finally and perhaps most obviously, a disadvantage of virtual approaches – especially when respondents are chosen via website chat rooms – is that of identity verification. It is impossible to ensure that participants are providing their true identity. So, while a researcher may think she is interviewing the mother of a newborn child, it is possible that she is interviewing a lonely retiree seeking out intelligent conversation. Interacting with the participant multiple times can help lower this possibility.

Tips and Tools 8.1 provides a summary of the strengths and disadvantages of mediated interviews.

TIPS AND TOOLS 8.1

Mediated interviews: advantages and disadvantages

Strengths of mediated interviews	Disadvantages of mediated interviews
Cost-effective access to geographically distributed or otherwise unavailable populations	Decreased availability of nonverbal and embodied data
Increased engagement, thoughtfulness, and sharing, especially for intimate, traumatic, or shameful topics or member reflections	Sample limited to those who have technological access and expertise
Provides spelling and grammar data	Increased possibility of respondent distraction
Encourages the voice of participants who hold low-power positions, suffer from social anxiety, or are physically unable to verbalize their thoughts	
Self-transcribing	

And for asynchronous textual approaches in particular...

Allows time and care for the interviewees to provide a thoughtful response	Study attrition – more participants "drop out"
	Typing or texting answers can take longer for participants
	Participant may carefully construct a desired presentation
	Comprised confidentiality of data
	Data cleaning takes more time than expected
	Identity verification is complicated

As researchers make decisions about mediated interviews, they should consider the context and the participants' comfort with certain technologies. Telephone interviews can be an excellent choice if participants enjoy talking on the phone. Likewise, queries sent via email may be the best route for reaching busy professionals who can respond to questions sporadically over the course of several days.

However, if you are leaning toward mediated approaches simply because they seem easier, let me again ring the warning bell. In many cases mediated interviews can take at least as much planning, logistical work, and data cleaning as face-to-face approaches. But, more importantly, the beauty of qualitative research is largely about the messiness, energy, and feelings that inherently emerge when multiple bodies meet together in relationship. When an embodied relationship is missing, you miss out on the vigor, liveliness, and wonderful chaos that mark face-to-face qualitative research.

The focus-group interview

One particular type of interview deserves its own section – and that is the **focus-group interview**, a group interview with 3 to 12 participants and marked by guided group discussion, question and answer, interactive dialogue, and other activities. The phrase was originally coined to refer to the practice of focusing in on very specific questions after having completed considerable research (Merton, Fiske, & Kendall, 1956, as cited in Fontana & Frey, 2005). Focus groups have a long history in market research, but they can also be material for excellent qualitative research.

The value of focus groups

In addition to providing a less expensive and time-consuming way to reach a larger number of participants, focus groups are valuable for several reasons. First, they are ideal for producing the insights that are known to result from group interaction. In a phenomenon known as the "group effect" (Carey, 1994) and the "therapeutic effect" (Lederman, 1990), focus-group participants show less inhibition, especially when they interact with similar others. Their talk exemplifies "a kind of 'chaining' or 'cascading' effect in which each person's turn of the conversation links to, or tumbles out of, the topics and expressions that came before it" (Lindlof & Taylor, 2011, p. 183). The group effect produces insightful self-disclosure that may remain hidden in one-on-one interviews. As such, focus groups can effectively explore emotional experiences.

For example, in a research project with people recovering from drug addiction (Malvini Redden, Tracy, & Shafer, 2012), focus groups created a synergy that stimulated memories, experiences, and ideas. Participants' experiences are validated, extended, and supported by similar others. Indeed, in hearing each other talk, focus-group participants learn from, and support, one another. In this way focus groups can be transformative – raising participants' consciousness about certain issues, or helping them to learn new ways of seeing or talking about a situation.

Because of the cascading effect, focus groups are also valuable for generating a wealth of vernacular speech *in vivo*, which is specific to the group at hand. For instance, Lederman and Stewart (2003) used focus groups as a method to help formulate effective language for a health communication campaign related to domestic violence on college campuses. Accessing language *in vivo* is also useful for developing subsequent interviews or questionnaires. If researchers are considering focus groups as one out of several data-gathering methods, I recommend conducting them *after* engaging in some participant observation, but *before* conducting more focused dyadic interviews or questionnaires. This moves the research, in turn, from a wider to narrower scope.

Another interesting perk of focus groups is that they basically serve as a mini interaction laboratory, allowing the researcher to observe how ideas interact with and cascade from one to another, and the extent to which people are able to articulate their ideas (as they must grapple with others' interruptions, starts and stops, and compete for floor time). Watching the ways ideas emerge through talk is especially valuable for scholars interested in communication and group interaction. For instance, in workplace bullying focus groups (Tracy, Lutgen-Sandvik, & Alberts, 2006), we were able to see how some individuals could more persuasively and credibly tell their stories by commanding floor time. Seeing this competition for floor-time helped us to better understand how a busy workplace environment (with a cacophony of competing voices) can make it difficult to tell a credible story about workplace bullying.

Focus groups also facilitate creative types of data-gathering that go beyond open-ended questions. For instance you can ask participants to jointly poll or rank various issues by saying:

> Today I have heard the following reasons why people take the bus to school: (1) cost; (2) convenience; (3) meeting new people; and (4) because you can multitask. Which of these is the most important reason? Who thinks cost is the most important reason? Okay, I see that 6 out of 10 are raising hands.

Polling can clarify certain issues' importance and can lead to a lively discussion if participants debate the rankings. Relatedly, the focus group leader can break up interaction by providing one or more written surveys; these can be aggregated by a discussion assistant and then shared to generate reactions from focus-group members.

Another creative approach consists in asking the participants to come up with metaphors or comparisons for the topic at hand. For instance you might say: "Fill in the blank. The campus shuttle bus is like a _____." or "If you were to describe the campus shuttle as a movie character, who or what would it be?" Participants might respond by saying the campus shuttle feels like a party bus, a sewer, a study hall on wheels, or that it's kind of like comedian Will Ferrell, because you never really know what you're going to get, and it's oftentimes bizarre. These comparisons emotionally illustrate how people envision a certain issue; they access how people feel about, approach, or frame particular ideas.

If you are working with an especially gregarious group, you could ask its members to perform typical scenarios associated with the topic and/or try to "sell" something related to it. For instance, if you were conducting a focus group about political candidates and their campaign commercials, you could ask the participants to watch several campaign commercials, critique them, and then act out more effective commercials.

Finally, artistic approaches provide an invaluable path toward accessing left-brain creative and visual knowledge. Artistic approaches – whether by molding clay, assembling blocks, or drawing pictures – are especially restorative for studies on the experience of trauma or pain. In our focus group on bullying, we asked participants to draw a picture in response to the question "What does workplace bullying *feel* like?" The method produced unanticipated results in terms of providing an outlet for the expression of complex and subtle information that was difficult to verbalize; essentially it acts as a "catalyst for members of teams to 'say the unsaid' both on an emotional/psychological and on a political level" (Tracy, Lutgen-Sandvik, & Alberts, 2006, p. 156).

When to use focus groups

Focus groups are appropriate for your research project if your topic could benefit from the group effect. However, there is another issue to weigh: the extent to which the participants share a significant experience in common. Good focus groups require strategically combining participants with similar others. For example, in studying the way different people watch television, Adams (2000) divided his participants into three age brackets: (a) 18 to 24 – representing a group comfortable with new technology and relatively unfamiliar with a time when the major networks controlled virtually all viewing; (b) 25 to 43 – representing the so-called "ideal demographic" age for network television viewers; and (c) 44 and up – an audience with heavy ties to the traditional broadcast structure and more resistant to change (p. 82).

Likewise, focus groups are well poised for learning how certain groups react to a similar issue or shared experience. Group interaction aids respondents' recall and stimulates embellished descriptions of jointly experienced events (disasters, celebrations, riots, other historical events) or reactions to a common product, commercial, or health campaign. Pairing individuals with clashing world views in the same group can certainly provide insight on opposing opinions. However, focus groups become unwieldy and disjointed if participants do not share a reference point. Let me give you an example to illustrate.

Imagine you are trying to better understand how a variety of people respond to a single type of public transportation (say, the campus shuttle bus). In this situation, a focus group with shuttle bus users may be ideal. All participants have a common touchstone, so questions can be focused on their reactions to and evaluations of that shared topic. If, however, you are interested in how individuals use a variety of different public transportation options, then one-on-one interviews may be more appropriate (for example one interview with an avid bus rider, another with a bicycle commuter, and another who van-pools with co-employees).

Indeed, if you are investigating topics in which each participant has individually differentiated experiences, focus groups are not the best route. When group interviews do not have a shared starting point, they are less of a joint dialogue and more just a group of people competing for talk time. Additionally, if the topic is contentious, embarrassing, shameful, or unlawful, focus-group participants may disclose less, due to confidentiality concerns. Although you, as a researcher, can promise confidentiality, focus-group participants are not similarly bound.

Planning the logistical details of focus groups

Like planning and hosting a party, focus groups require a combination of event planning and organizational skills, crowd control, graceful introductions, and sustained good cheer. In Tips and Tools 8.2 I provide a table of tips for managing the logistical details of focus groups, drawn from my own experiences and other sources (Edmunds, 1999; Greenbaum, 1994; Krueger & Casey, 2000; Lederman, 1990; Lindlof & Taylor, 2011). I list these tips in roughly chronological order.

Conducting the focus group

The big day has arrived and it's time for all of the focus-group planning to come to fruition. Focus groups are the equivalent of qualitative researcher workouts. As for any big event, researchers should arrive well rested, with a good breakfast and warm (possibly caffeinated) beverage in hand. Here I overview suggestions for the big day.

TIPS AND TOOLS 8.2

Planning a focus group

Format	Determine the most effective format, considering both face-to-face and technologically mediated options.
Length	90 minutes is usually ideal; 60–75 minutes with children or senior citizens; longer periods may be acceptable if they are interrupted by an activity or lunch. Beware of fatigue, both for the participants and the researcher(s).
Number of participants per focus group	The group effect can be captured with as few as 3 participants, and multiple voices can still be engaged with as many as 12; 6 to 9 participants is ideal. Over-recruiting is helpful, as 10–20 percent of participants may not show up.
Payment/compensation	Market research focus groups almost always motivate participation through payment. Depending on length, complexity and sample, $35–$100 is appropriate for granted academic research (via cash or gift card).
Strategic groupings	Consider if complementary or argumentative interactions would be more appropriate for the research.
Facility	Dedicated focus-group facilities can be costly, yet so much more convenient and reliable than make-shift locations. Issues to consider include: 1 the room size and desired table and chair set-up; 2 availability and positioning of various technology tools (video projectors, pen/paper/markers, whiteboard, flip charts); 3 refreshment options: is there a kitchen or adjacent break room available? 4 waiting room area for guests: this is especially important for focus groups in which members will have a care-giver or driver accompanying them, or children in tow. Consider providing the service of a licensed care-giver.
Accessibility to participants	Respondents must be able to feel comfortable in the facility. Focus groups can be held in participants' home turf, such as a company conference room or dorm lounge, instead of a traditional focus-group room. Weigh accessibility with confidentiality/privacy. Venues convenient for the researchers (e.g. college campuses) are often inconvenient for the participants.

Focus-group responsibilities	A team of researchers and assistants can help ensure the success of focus groups. Roles include: **1** HOST(S) someone who will direct and welcome participants (e.g. leading them from parking to building), coordinate refreshments, and provide payment; **2** MODERATOR a competent and credible speaker who is familiar with the interview guide and can effectively manage group dynamics; **3** FIELDNOTE RECORDER someone who will watch, take notes, and provide input to the moderator regarding group dynamics; the fieldnote recorder can be positioned behind one-way mirrored glass, or to the side of the room; **4** TECHNOLOGY ASSISTANT someone who will manage and monitor the audio-visual equipment, set up white boards or easels; this person can also transfer notes between the fieldnote recorder and the moderator.
Screening questionnaire	Conducting a mini-survey before the focus group can ensure that participants meet the desired characteristics. The screening questionnaire may also include demographic queries and open-ended questions that gauge participants' attitude, level of self-disclosure, and articulateness.
Moderator script/question guide	As an interview guide, focus-group scripts should be planned in advance. Key elements are described in the following section.
Confirmations	Contact participants (and provide transportation directions) several times before the focus group, including the night before. Confirm more participants than needed; expect no-shows. Confirming attendance is more than worth it, considering the costs of reserving a space, purchasing refreshments, and the research hours. Focus group "do overs" are extremely expensive.

First, prepare the venue for the event ahead. This includes hanging clear signs (or deploying hosts wearing bright-colored tee-shirts) that direct participants to parking and the focus-group locations. Any (preferably non-perishable) food should be set out in advance, with trash cans nearby. The technology assistant should arrive early, double-check the recording equipment, and have a back-up plan in case something malfunctions midway through. Set the temperature so that participants will be comfortable and alert, and remember that the room will warm up as the group gathers.

As participants arrive, greet them warmly, provide informed consent and name-tags, and invite them to help themselves to refreshments. Depending on confidentiality concerns, you might encourage participants to choose a pseudonym (or even a number) for their name tag. This way their name is hidden during the focus group – both in any recordings and from other participants. If desired, you can link this with other contact information after the fact. Due to all these introductory activities, there is usually a

15- to 20-minute time-lag between the time when participants are asked to arrive and the time when the focus group begins.

Once the participants are seated, the moderator provides a focus-group overview that generally includes a self-intro, the general purpose of the research, and the specific objectives for the day. This is also a good time to explain interaction ground rules. Ground rules vary by group, but they may include the notion that "there is no right answer" and that a variety of input is sought. You might also ask participants to monitor their talk time and to make adjustments if they find themselves speaking much more or less than others. I also let participants know that I may jump in every once in a while, to encourage quieter respondents or to redirect conversation if we are going off on a tangent. Participants can also be reminded to speak clearly and one at a time. And, just like in a movie theater, alert participants to fire exits and bathroom locations and remind them to silence hand-held devices.

Focus-group leaders should also discuss confidentiality and informed consent. In this discussion, I remind participants that the session will be recorded (releasing those who are not comfortable with this) and I disclose if members of the research team are behind glass. This is the time to collect any unsigned informed consent forms. Furthermore, I explain that the research team will keep the data confidential, but that we cannot guarantee that co-participants will do the same. Nonetheless, I tend to ask participants to show via a head nod that they will agree to keep the information in the focus group confidential.

Moderating the focus group

Several practices are particularly helpful for moderating focus-group dialogue. Knowing the discussion guide inside out allows topics to be addressed as they arise naturally. At the same time, moderators should consider how they might tactfully dissuade or refocus tangents. Moderators should consider carefully the way they dress, and how their identity or demographic characteristics might influence the participants. For instance, when working with former drug addicts, we recruited moderators who were from the same cultural group as focus-group members, in order to promote mutual trust and understanding (Malvini Redden et al., 2012).

Moderating also requires a mix of listening and leading. Moderators do not take frenetic notes (this is what fieldnote recorders do), but rather they gauge the tone of the group and refer back to comments made earlier in the discussion. This includes following up on nonverbal reactions (e.g. "Sabrina, I saw you nodding your head when Bill was talking. Say a little bit about what you are thinking") and providing positive and supportive feedback – especially if topics are complex or emotionally sensitive. Listening also includes clarifying, paraphrasing unclear comments, and probing for more detail when necessary ("Why do you feel that way? Can you provide an example?").

Good humor, along with avoidance of jargon, judgment, or "acting like the expert," will go a long way toward making others feel comfortable. At the same time avoid too much head-nodding, as that can discourage those who disagree from speaking up. Summarizing what is heard in the group and then asking group members to comment provides a breather, as well as an accuracy check. Another important role for moderators is to encourage balance in talk time – reminding those who interrupt that "the audio recorder can only access one voice at a time" – and to "hold that thought." Encouraging contributions from those who are talking less also ensures that one person or a small coalition does not dominate.

Strategic breaks in the focus group provide opportunities for focus-group team members to give each other feedback. Some researchers take a break after opening questions in order to allow natural unprompted conversations to evolve in the group. Breaks should be provided at least every hour.

Moderators should close the focus group by asking participants to keep the focus-group information conversations confidential. Other effective wrap-ups include asking respondents what they learned from their participation or what they were most surprised about. Soliciting advice regarding questions to ask in future groups can also procure insight. As focus-group participants disperse, a member of the team can thank them and provide compensation.

As focus-group participants leave, you may feel so exhausted that you want to follow them out the door. Nonetheless, it is important to take a half hour or so to debrief after the focus group, noting initial reactions and making a "to-do" list for things to do differently next time. I encourage researchers to audio-record this debriefing, as significant insights and reactions are easily forgotten. In addition, a team member should organize a spreadsheet and enter into it the participants' information from their screening questionnaires. Information should also be collected and organized for whoever will transcribe. The transcriptionist should ideally have access to the audio recording, the moderator's script (providing the focus group's general path), and video recording (so that notations can be made about nonverbal behavior). An example of a moderator guide is offered in Appendix B, and it illustrates one way a focus group may unfold.

Overcoming common focus group and interviewing challenges

No matter how much experience or planning goes into them, challenges still emerge in interviews and focus groups. Here I discuss some of the most common interviewing challenges (Kvale, 1996; Roulston, de Marrais, & Lewis, 2003). By considering these issues in advance, researchers can prepare for them and expect them, knowing that they are not alone.

One of the primary challenges comes in the general category of unexpected participant behaviors. Sometimes interviewees act in ways that are strange or defy expectations. Participants can arrive late or leave early. Differences in time orientation may be especially salient when interviewing those from different cultures. Some participants eat, smoke, or chew (gum or tobacco) during the interview, muffling their voice.

Researchers' own actions and subjectivities can negatively affect the interview. Interviewers can get tired, nervous, or forgetful, and in the process, fail to provide adequate overviews or cogent transitions. They may talk too much, interrupt, or fall short of listening attentively. Or, they may sum-up their participant's talk using problematic **formulations** – "statements in which speakers paraphrase prior utterances through preserving, deleting, and transforming information produced by other speakers" (Roulston et al., 2003, p. 659). For instance, maybe the participant provides a complex description, and the interviewer responds by saying: "Okay, sounds like you had a bad experience, let's move on to the next question." Problematic formulations essentially put words or meanings in the interviewees' mouths that do not belong there. Researchers can attend to these challenges by listening to their own audio-recorded interviews and noting if they hear themselves talking too much, laughing too hard, or cutting the interviewee short. Audio recordings serve as a sharp pedagogical tool.

Researchers often have trouble in phrasing and ordering their questions. The original phrasing may sound too formal or casual. Or perhaps the interviewee goes off on a tangent that attends partially to a query; but, to access more information, the researcher must make up a new question on the spot. Sometimes, a tangent goes on for so long that the intended purpose of the study is not even addressed. The interviewee may even begin asking questions of the interviewer. On the one hand, researchers must be flexible to allow such tangents and mutual self-disclosure – as doing so allows important or significant parts of the story to emerge. On the other hand, most successful studies go into depth on one or two specific topics, rather than just skimming a wide breadth of ideas. While tangents may be helpful in early interviews, as the study progresses, researchers need to ensure that they are asking about key foci.

Another central concern for interviewers is being unaware of how to probe and follow up. Kvale (1996) offers some good advice, giving the example of an interview with a pupil who stated: "I am not as stupid as my grades at the examinations showed, but I have bad study habits" (p. 32). So how might an interviewer follow up?

> Reactions could then be on a factual level: "What grades did you get?" or "What are your study habits?" – questions that also may yield important information. A meaning-oriented reply would, in contrast, be something like, "You feel that the grades are not an adequate measure of your competence?" (Kvale, 1996, p. 32)

Other ways to follow up on this question could be:

> Silence; Hm, mm; Can you say more about that?; Could you give some examples about what you're saying?; Is this similar to other people?; Can you talk more about grades and their relation to being stupid?; Are you sure you have bad study habits?; Do you think grades are a good judge of smarts or stupidity? (Kvale & Brinkmann, 2009, p. 139)

As is evident in these examples, probes may ask for greater depth or ask about facts, feelings, deeper meanings, clarifications, or comparisons. Following up may also include your own disclosures, as personal examples can help develop rapport and comfort.

Emotional participants can also pose challenges. When interviewees show strong emotion, researchers may feel frozen or guilty, thinking, "Oh no, I made my participant cry (or get angry or something else)." In such situations interviewers might attempt to show compassion by recognizing, relating, and (re)acting (Way & Tracy, in press). Recognizing comes in attentive listening and watching for signs of pain or distress. This can only be done if you actually look at and sincerely listen to your participant. Relating refers to identifying and trying to see the world empathetically through your participant's eyes, if only for a moment. And (re)acting can be as simple as a pat on the hand, a sympathetic nod, or offering a drink of water.

When she was interviewing targets of workplace abuse, Pamela Lutgen-Sandvik attended to upset participants by giving them some time to breathe, passing them a tissue box, and offering words like: "I can tell that this was a really painful situation for you." This practice of providing assistance, advice, and education when appropriate was so common in her research, she actually put a name to the approach – **remedial–pedagogical interviews** (these are detailed in Researcher's Notepad 8.1). Such empathetic approaches emphasize morality and attempts to restore sacredness and humanity to the research process (Fontana & Frey, 2005).

On the one hand, challenges lie in talking with traumatized interviewees. On the other hand, some interviewees appear pompous, aloof, or might even seem as though they are lying or creating an inauthentic front. Lying is a rare but distressing problem. Rubin and Rubin (2005) offer several tips to help researchers who encounter distorted or politically correct responses. First, they suggest that, to recognize distortions, fabrications, and omissions, researchers should "build redundancy into the design by asking the same question in different ways… If you encounter inconsistencies, you can ask about them

RESEARCHER'S NOTEPAD 8.1

Remedial–pedagogical interviews

By Pamela Lutgen-Sandvik, in her own words

Researchers often face moral challenges when they interact with participants who have experienced (or are experiencing) trauma. Namely, is it ethical, in the name of science, to ask people to relive painful experiences? In such situations, researchers can help participants deal with the pain by providing emotional support (remedial) and offering expert knowledge (pedagogical).

Remedial   I use the term *remedial* because it suggests support without the patronizing connotation of an expert "who knows all." The term remedial, unlike the terms therapeutic or counseling, avoids implications that the interviewee is sick and needs to be cured. I consciously decided to use a remedial approach in my workplace bullying research because remaining emotionally detached felt immoral. I took a cue from Lofland and Lofland's (1995) question, "Is it ethical to see a severe need for help and not respond to it directly?" (p. 63). I could not remain silent and act as if I did not hear participants' pain and implicit requests for support. Interviews were laced with exchanges marked by support and validation. The following dialogue illustrates such an exchange between a female target (CA) and me (PS):

CA   I'm grateful that you're doing this work. Because, I wonder, "Is it just me?"
PS   Right. You wonder, "Am I just crazy?"
CA   Right.
PS   And, did I just bring this on myself?
CA   Well, it's easy to think that way, because … it's so shaming.
PS   And the bully often tries to make you think it's you.
CA   Boy that's for sure. The bully *does* make you think it's you! Then with the lack of support, with co-workers, it's like they're marked.
PS   It's the same kind of stuff that many people say.
CS   Yeah. It does make you feel like, like there's something wrong with you.
PS   And what that means is that it *isn't* you.
CS   Yes, yes. Yeah, I get that one.

In an earlier exchange, this woman said she thought she "was losing it" and that she "must have done something to" draw the bully's negative attention. I reframed her language to help counteract this self-doubt and self-blame. I checked for understanding while reassuring her that she wasn't alone and that past research showed her feelings to be quite common. In doing so, the interview was also pedagogical.

Pedagogical   My interviews included an educational aspect in which I shared findings from bullying research, including information on the prevalence of bullying and reassuring targets that they had not brought abuse upon themselves (e.g. "Research has yet to identify a specific type of person or personality that is more or less likely to be bullied"). The following excerpt illustrates the pedagogical features of interviews:

DB   I don't know. Do things like that happen? I know they don't happen in the real world like that. I keep thinking if we were like Microsoft …

PS   This happens all over the place. There doesn't really seem to be a specific industry or career where it is more likely.

DB   It does? I'm not crazy?

PS   It does. I've talked to engineers, to professors in universities, to librarians, to school teachers.

DB   Oh my God. It goes on everywhere? I mean, that's so weird. Why would anybody do it?

PS   It doesn't happen in every workplace, but it does happen more often than one might think. A recent study indicates this happens to nearly 30% of US workers sometime during their careers and about one out of ten workers at any given time.

DB   Huh, well, I guess I'm not going crazy. I mean, just knowing what it is, I mean knowing it's *bullying*, that was so powerful.

These excerpts illustrate the emotionally counteractive, educational dynamics present in remedial–pedagogical interviews – designed to help participants talk and learn through a dialogue marked with active listening, support, dignity, and respect.

politely" (p. 73). Another tactic for verifying the facts is to ask the same question to multiple people. If you let interviewees know you're talking to others, they may be less likely to fabricate or exaggerate.

At the same time, an inconsistency in the data among different interviewees is not necessarily a problem. A multiplicity of interviewees necessarily results in a multiplicity of views. Indeed, in **polyphonic interviewing**, multiple voices of the respondents are reported separately rather than collapsed together by the interviewer, and differences in perspectives are highlighted rather than glossed over (Krieger, 1983). Although the actual interview process may look the same for those engaging polyphonic interviewing, the write-up or presentation of the results would highlight the sample's differences and inconsistencies.

Fibbing is not "all bad" either, because, when people do lie, this may provide important clues to meaning. For example:

> Criminologist David Luckenbill wanted to find out the income of young male prostitutes he was studying but felt they were exaggerating how much they earned. Toward the close of the conversation, Luckenbill asked his interviewees if they could give him change for a $10 bill and learned they did not have enough cash to do so. Luckenbill realized that his interviewees were lying about their income, but rather than discounting what the interviewees said, concluded that these young men so wanted to justify their occupation that they greatly exaggerated their earnings . (Rubin & Rubin, 2005, p. 72)

As illustrated in this example, participants may lie for strategic reasons, and their half-truths may create an opportunity for valuable and otherwise inaccessible insight. Furthermore, if you suspect that participants are lying, you should critically examine your own research practices, asking yourself if a certain question or interview tone might motivate participant dishonesty.

As reviewed, the actual embodiment and conduct of interviews can include a number of potential challenges. It is one thing to talk about these challenges, and another to actually deal with them on the spot. Past student Jennifer Scarduzio created an embodied activity, duplicated in Exercise 8.1, which provides an opportunity to role-play interview challenges before encountering them in the real deal.

EXERCISE 8.1

Role-playing interview challenges in a fishbowl

Rationale   One cannot really understand the challenges of interviewing until one practices it. This activity asks participants to practice an interview in a "fish bowl," while the rest of the group watches and offers advice.

Materials   One 3 × 5 index card for every student; note-paper; basket or bowl.

Participants   On an index card, write your own name and provide a description of an ideal interviewee for your respective project. The description can be basic or detailed. On a separate piece of paper, write 2–3 potential interview questions for this ideal interviewee.

Leader   Write on small squares of paper 8–10 challenges that might occur during an interview. Fold them and place them in the middle of the table or in a basket. Examples include:

1 go off on a tangent;
2 one word or short response;
3 peeking at interview guide questions, trying to look ahead;
4 offended by the question;
5 distracted during the interview (e.g. cell phone, computer, eating);
6 don't understand the question, need it to be clarified;
7 emotionally upset (crying, angry, etc.);
8 interviewing the interviewer more than being interviewed;
9 refusing to answer the question;
10 appearing to lie or distort the truth.

Place two chairs at the front of the group and have the leader select a participant to be the interviewer.

Then ask for a volunteer (someone comfortable with improvising) to act as the interviewee, and provide this person with the interviewer's description of the ideal interviewee. This volunteer should also choose a square of paper from the bowl (a square that has one of the challenges written on it).

In front of the rest of the group, the interviewer proceeds to ask the interviewee the questions they just crafted.

The interviewee will answer the questions, embodying the characteristics of the interviewer's ideal interviewee while also trying to improvise the interview challenge (e.g. going off on a tangent).

While the interview is taking place, the leader will call "freeze" to stop the interview at key points and will ask the audience questions such as: How could the interviewer rephrase that question? What are some strategies for responding in this situation?

The leader will unfreeze the situation, allowing the interview to continue, hopefully integrating some of the tips provided by the audience.

This can be repeated many times over and with different interview pairs and different challenges.

Transcribing

One of the most important parts of transforming embodied interviews into usable data is transcribing – or creating typewritten records from audio recordings. Granted, transcribing is not a requirement; listening repeatedly to participants' voices can be an effective method for early analysis. This has become easier with digital audio files that can be transferred to a range of devices (computers, PDAs, car stereos, MP3 players). Listening to interviews while commuting, running, or gardening can get you very close to the data. That said – because most publication venues are visual rather than aural, and most people find it easier to examine printed rather than auditory data – most researchers create printed transcriptions (and expect their students and peers to do the same). This section overviews the analysis role of transcribing, the most common transcribing symbols, and how the detail of transcription depends on the study's overall goals.

There seems to be a myth among students and researchers that transcribing is an awful job. However, transcribing can be a fascinating and sometimes even fun experience (Bird, 2005). Seriously. Transcribing is time-*consuming*, but not time-*wasting*. Just by listening closely, you will quickly identify ways to improve question wording, tone, and pace. Many researchers have been instantly motivated to improve their interviewing skills after hearing themselves interrupt or repeat themselves by using the same phrase ("wow," "really?" "fascinating"). Furthermore, transcribing is a key part of the data analysis process. Transcription facilitates the close examination of data, which is so imperative for interpretation.

There is no such thing as "universal" transcription symbols. Even those researchers working from the same theoretical field (such as conversation or discourse analysis) do not always agree on transcribing conventions. No matter what the level of detail is, it is smart to create a key or legend so you remember weeks, months, or years later whether, for instance, ellipses refer to pauses or to omitted words, or whether brackets refer to contextual information or to summaries. The symbols provided in Tips and Tools 8.3 are synthesized from a few common charts (Kvale & Brinkman, 2009; Silverman, 2001), coupled with my own examples.

Is more detailed transcription always better? No. Qualitative research demands flexibility, and transcribers use what works for them and their audiences. Just like fieldnotes, transcriptions are human constructions, and how they are constructed depends on the goals of the larger research project. Conversation and discourse analysts interested in the detailed features of talk – including its pace, sequence, intonation, pauses, interruptions, talk-overs, and volume – will use a very specific form of transcribing, catalogued by a plethora of conventions and symbols (Atkinson & Heritage, 1984; Jefferson, 1992; Tracy, 2001). Some researchers make detailed summaries of interviews and only transcribe key quotations (e.g. Miller, 2007). If you are interested in issues of marked nervousness, conversational dominance or recalcitrance, humor, or uncertainty, using a high level of transcription detail can be extremely valuable. For instance, in our study of male executives discussing work–life (Tracy & Rivera, 2010), we paid special attention to verbal disfluencies (e.g. "umms," "ahhs"), pauses, questioning, and talk repairs. Sigmund Freud might have us think that such disfluencies categorically reveal unconscious desires or secrets. However, modern linguistic research suggests that disfluencies are just as likely to cue emotional arousal, stress, anxiety, embarrassment, deception, or added cognitive load – such as talking about something very complicated or never considered before (Erard, 2007). These talk junctures may instead indicate resistance, change, and flickers of transformation. Appendix C provides different examples of transcribed interview or focus-group excerpts, and an explanation as to why this level of detail was appropriate to the study's goals.

Many people are interested in how much time they should budget for transcription. On average, one hour of audio takes a good typist about four to five hours to transcribe and results in 20–25 single-spaced typewritten pages (Kvale & Brinkmann, 2009). However, this time varies. It may take only a couple hours to transcribe one hour of a single voice (e.g. a speech), or up to eight hours for a one-hour focus group. Transcribing takes longer when the recording has multiple speakers, background noise, or when participants have accents

TIPS AND TOOLS 8.3

Common transcribing symbols

Explanation	Symbol	Example
Stretched sound, syllable, word	Colon(s) : ::	But I re:ally wanted a milkshake.
Emphasis	*Italics*	She should have *asked* me what I wanted.
Brief pause (less than 2 sec)	(.) parens surrounding period	Well (.) I don't care if it's cold outside.
Longer pause (specified seconds)	(#) parens surrounding number of seconds of pause	I prefer chocolate ice cream because (4), hmmm, (2) I'm just a chocolate person.
Transcriber comments about context	((words)) double parens around comment	I gave you a five dollar bill, so you owe me two fifteen. ((participant talking with and getting change from the cashier))
Transcriber uncertainty about what said	(unclear word) parens around the unclear word	I (subscribe) to an (anti) fruit and vegetable diet plan most the time.
Statement that fell in vocal pitch	. Period	Healthy food seems boring to me.
Statement that rises in vocal pitch	? Question mark	Why should I eat healthy when I'm just going to die anyway?
Animated speech	Exclamation point!	I'm so excited for my new juicer!
Vocal noises	(SOUND OF NOISE) parens around all caps	(GULP) Juicing is healthy? Hmmm, I may need to boycott it then. (LAUGHTER)
Contiguous utterances	= Equal sign	*Interviewer*: It seems your health practice and health rhetoric don't exactly match=*Respondent*: =I kind of have a split personality
Speech overlap	[Single left bracket	*Interviewer*: Why did that paradox develop? *Respondent*: [I think I am kind of a rebel at heart.
Abrupt cut-off word or sentence	- Hyphen	Well, just because I'm a paradox-
Comparatively high volume	CAPS	I am SO TIRED of the conflicting information we get about nutrition.
Audible outbreaths, including laughter	hhh (the longer the more hs)	It's kind of funny, hhh, that, hhh, even though I don't care about health food, I'm a rule follower in other parts of my life.

Explanation	Symbol	Example
Audible inbreaths, including surprise	.hhh (period then hs)	.hhh Oh my gosh! I can't believe you said that!
Words omitted from sentence	[...] three equally spaced dots (ellipse) inside brackets	When I exercise, especially when I swim [...] I get ravenous later in the day.
Sentence omitted from excerpt	. [...] four dots (or rather full stop and ellipse in brackets, with space between)	A question is when I am going to eat. [...] My trainer says to eat within 20 minutes after a workout.
Multiple sentences omitted from excerpt	// double slash	Milkshakes are my decadence. // And the very best flavor of all is peanut butter chocolate malt.
Words written by transcriber (for clarification, summary, or confidentiality)	[replacement or additional words]	My favorite is the Dairy Queen [on the west side] because my nana [grandma] used to take me there when I was little. [Participant goes on to talk more about going to Dairy Queen with her grandparents].

or speech impediments, or they speak quickly or incoherently. Over time, it becomes easier to distinguish different voices from each other, recognize speech patterns, and understand the importance of nonverbal cues. Transcription does get easier and faster with practice!

Why does transcribing take so long? Simply because typing takes longer than speaking. Furthermore, the transcriptionist must make careful analytic choices about the notation of laughter, pitch, volume, tone of voice, sarcasm, silence, and various contextual details. Of course, if the desire is just to get down the words, then transcription is much quicker (and if nonverbals are not important, an email or a chat-based interview format may be just as valuable). Finally, transcribers consistently make choices about punctuation and the right homonym (e.g. did the participant mean "their," "there" or "they're"?).

Transcribing decisions profoundly impact the meaning of the data, and this is why researchers should carefully consider the disadvantages of not transcribing the data themselves. Researchers who pay a professional to transcribe must be prepared to shell out more than $100 for an hour-long interview and double that for each hour of a focus group. Further, researchers should remember they will still need to allocate time for reviewing transcripts for accuracy. The process of **fact checking** transcripts consists in listening to the recordings while simultaneously reading over transcripts and stopping along the way to input corrections or modifications, and this usually takes longer than the recording time at least by one half. Fact checking transcripts is imperative for accessing good data. Transcriptionists, especially if they are unfamiliar with the research, can easily make errors. For example, they might mistake "labor market" for "layer market" or write "it just makes sense," when the speaker said "it doesn't make sense."

No matter who does the transcribing, the activity is eased by accessing the most up-to-date equipment. This includes a transcribing pedal (also called a treadle switch) and headphones. The pedal allows transcribers to start, stop, rewind, and replay the recording with their feet, so that fingers remain on the keyboard, typing away. Multiple speed playback capabilities are also helpful. Several software programs can play digital audio files controlled by mouse-clicks (and can be found via an online search of "transcription software"; they are also embedded within many qualitative data analysis software programs, as described in Chapter 10).

Increasingly, researchers are using voice-recognition software such as "Dragon Naturally Speaking" to assist with transcription (http://www.nuance.com/dragon/index.htm). Because voice-recognition software works best when trained to a single person's voice, most researchers use it by listening to the audio through a headset, and then restating the words into a microphone hooked to the computer. The software then detects and transcribes the transcriber's voice. Because voice-recognition software is quite computer-intensive, transcribers should use a USB microphone, which bypasses the computer's soundcard; they should also use a computer with plenty of memory and a fast processor.

In summary

In this chapter we discussed the nuts and bolts of conducting an interview. We discussed the advantages and disadvantages of technologically mediated interviews, as well as of one-on-one versus group interviews. Focus groups require logistical coordination similar to managing any other big event. Although they take much planning, focus groups are an effective method for understanding groups' feelings and for reaching a lot of participants in a concentrated period of time. We also discussed several key challenges in interviewing and how to overcome them. The chapter closed with a discussion about transcribing.

After reading this chapter, you might be thinking, "Wow, interviews are a lot of work." Indeed, they do take time, effort, practice, and skill. Kvale (1996) outlines the various emotional phases that mark an interview study, suggesting that researchers begin with enthusiasm and become quickly engaged in the project. Midway through, they often face a period of sobriety and must summon patience to carry on. As challenges emerge, patience may turn to aggression and feelings of stress. Near the end of the study, interviewers often feel exhausted.

Indeed, the interviewing process can be draining. Hence it is not uncommon for those who have the resources to ask research assistants to conduct interviews and transcriptions. Some people view interviews as semi-skilled labor, in which outsourced professionals or assistants simply implement the interview guide. It is slightly better when interviewers are given some background on the purpose of the interview and on the project. This knowledge represents a tool box of skills from which the trained interviewer can draw.

Ideally, though, researchers should conduct their own interviews and focus groups. Indeed, interviewing can be one of the most exciting and fulfilling parts of qualitative research. Furthermore, when the interview is seen as an art, we see that it requires a host of skills and qualified judgment. Those who are truly expert in the craft – think Hugh Downs, Katie Couric, and other legendary journalist interviewers – have uncanny intuition, creativity, and the ability to improvise. Furthermore, interviewers may have special expertise that can help provide the interviewee with support and helpful information. The most important aspects of an interview, such as tone of voice, pauses, timing, laughter, and nonverbal expressions, are acquired, honed, and perfected only through practice. I hope you'll take up the challenge. A well-conducted interview is a beautiful thing.

KEY TERMS

→ **asynchronous interview**   a type of technologically mediated interview in which the two parties can participate at different times (e.g. email)

→ **fact checking**   researchers' reviewing of interview or focus-group transcripts for accuracy

→ **focus-group interview**   a group interview with 3 to 12 participants; it is marked by guided group discussion, question and answer, interactive dialogue, and other activities

→ **formulations**   statements through which speakers paraphrase prior utterances and in this way preserve, delete, and transform information produced by other speakers

→ *in vivo* **speech**   speech that is genuine and specific to a group in its local context

→ **mediated interview**   interview that is not taken face to face but rather via technological media such as a telephone, a computer, or a hand-held device

→ **polyphonic interviewing**   the multiple voices of the respondents are reported separately rather than collapsed, and differences in perspectives are highlighted rather than glossed over

→ **remedial–pedagogical interview**   a type of interview developed by Pamela Lutgen-Sandvik, which provides support and education when appropriate

→ **synchronous interview**   a type of technologically mediated interview in which all parties meet and talk together at the same time; it is similar to the face-to-face interview and can be conducted through telephone, webcam conversations, and Internet text-based chat

CHAPTER 9

Data analysis basics
A pragmatic iterative approach

Contents

Qualitative Research Methods: Collecting Evidence, Crafting Analysis, Communicating Impact, First Edition. Sarah J. Tracy.
© 2013 Sarah J. Tracy. Published 2013 by Blackwell Publishing Ltd.

estimate that at least 80 percent of qualitative articles say something like, "I used a version of grounded theory and the constant comparative method for analyzing my qualitative data." Qualitative researchers' reliance on grounded theory has made the two sociologists credited with its creation, Barney Glaser and Anselm Strauss, very famous (Glaser & Strauss, 1967), and has also supported the careers of Juliet Corbin (Strauss & Corbin, 1990) and Kathy Charmaz (Charmaz, 2006), who have extended and reinvented grounded methods.

Why does grounded theory continue to exert such influence on the qualitative landscape? It provides a systematic and rigorous framework for researchers who desire an inductive, emic approach to data analysis. The researcher begins from individual cases and from incidents in the data, and these develop progressively into more abstract categories and theories. Researchers continually return to the field and strategically sample data that fill in the blanks and the weak spots of the emerging theory. Grounded theory is marked by simultaneous involvement in data collection and analysis, its most important basic rule being: "*study your emerging data*" (Charmaz, 2006, p. 80). In grounded analyses, the study's emphases develop from the data rather than from research questions or existing literature. Indeed, grounded studies are marked by delaying the literature review until after the data are collected.

Although countless numbers of qualitative researchers refer to a grounded approach, few subscribe to grounded theory in its entirety, or even know the details of its origination and transformation. Students are sometimes surprised to learn that, after Glaser and Strauss's co-authorial success, the two later criticized each other and parted ways in the late eighties (Kelle, 2005). Furthermore, researchers who cite grounded theory often do not realize that its original Glaserian focus on generating explanations of behavior most readily aligns with positivist and realist approaches, whereas later Straussarian versions are more constructivist, pragmatist, and commensurable with critical, interpretive, postmodern, and social justice approaches (see Charmaz, 2011 and Morse et al., 2009 for discussions of grounded theory's historical transformation).

Although I, along with the majority of qualitative researchers, owe a debt of gratitude to those who developed and extended grounded theory, the problem-based approach of qualitative data analysis discussed throughout this book is best described not as grounded, but as **iterative**. An **iterative analysis** alternates between emic, or emergent, readings of the data and an etic use of existing models, explanations, and theories. Rather than grounding the meaning solely in the emergent data, an iterative approach also encourages reflection upon the active interests, current literature, granted priorities, and various theories the researcher brings to the data. Iteration is "not a repetitive mechanical task," but rather a reflexive process in which the researcher visits and revisits the data, connects them to emerging insights, and progressively refines his/her focus and understandings (Srivastava & Hopwood, 2009, p. 77).

This chapter lays out pragmatic and easy-to-understand methods for analyzing qualitative data by using an iterative (alternating emic/etic) approach. The chapter begins by discussing how to organize data so as to make them simple to read and absorb. I then discuss options regarding manual versus computer-aided data analysis. Then I review key aspects of iterative data analysis, explaining how to pragmatically code data into descriptive first-level codes and analytic second-level codes. After several coding cycles, I discuss how to lay out a loose analysis plan, how to consider various focused data analysis strategies, and how to develop codebooks and analytic memos. The analysis practices presented in this chapter will increase your chances of creating an artful, insightful study.

Organizing and preparing the data

Qualitative data analysis is heavy stuff, giving your brain's gray matter quite a workout. If you have been reading and re-reading the data along the way, recording analytic reflections, and transcribing or reviewing transcriptions of interviews, the analysis process has already begun. That said, in order to get the most from the focused analysis stage, it makes sense to systematically organize and prepare the data. Think of yourself as a celebrity chef on television cooking a meal. By prepping your ingredients first, when it's "go" time you can focus your precious energy on fine-tuning the harmony of flavors and creating that perfect presentation – rather than having to shuffle around finding, chopping, and measuring.

Indeed, the beginning stages of data analysis are quite similar to the organizing and heavy lifting process associated with any research paper. If you have already formatted and labeled your data and created contact sheets and lists of pseudonyms, the data prepping process will be eased. Analysis activities also include gathering, ordering, (re)labeling, printing, and sometimes reformatting the data.

Prepping all the raw materials, including fieldnotes, interview transcripts, key documents, and links to various electronic files and websites, can be exciting yet overwhelming. You will have to make tough decisions about what to include for any one particular analysis. For instance, perhaps you gathered all of an organization's training manuals, but you have decided that these manuals do not directly impact your particular study. Or perhaps a research assistant archived 12 months of chat-room discussion, but the current paper will only focus on the most recent two months. Qualitative data are precious, and carefully archiving them will streamline future analyses. At the same time, do not feel beholden to analyzing closely all the data you archive.

During the organization phase, I encourage you to reflect on the ways in which you, personally, best process the data. Are you addicted to your lap-top? If so, organize the data into intuitively named computer files that you will be motivated to read every time you turn on your computer. Or, if you use multiple computers, consider saving the data on a secure server, which is easily accessed from a variety of locations. Some people prefer working with hard copies, which means it's time to put your printer into overdrive and to organize the data into clearly labeled binders.

Different organizing schemata have advantages and disadvantages. A popular schema is to order the data chronologically, interspersing fieldnotes, interviews, and documents by their date of collection or construction. Chronological organization has the benefit of showing the trajectory of your analysis, illustrating how the data were collected and interpreted over time. Furthermore, chronological ordering eases analyses that are interested in correlation and causation – something we will discuss in greater detail in Chapter 10.

You may also organize your analysis using the *type* of data as a criterion – for example, by placing fieldnotes in one file, interview transcripts in another, and so on. Data can also be organized by *source*. This schema may be appropriate if you have researched a family and you possesss interview, fieldnotes, and diary data linked to each family member. Likewise, if the demographic attributes of a certain participant are salient, such as gender, race, age, profession, or region, organizing the data according to these *attributes* could make sense (e.g. all the data from lawyers in this binder, teachers in the other binder).

As should be clear, the organizing process is an interpretive activity. When the data are organized in a certain way, they implicitly encourage the researcher to notice some comparisons and overlook others. As a case in point, in my correctional officer data I created five binders:

1 chronological fieldnotes from the jail;
2 chronological fieldnotes from the prison;
3 chronological interviews with jail correctional officers;
4 chronological interviews with prison correctional officers;
5 both prison and jail data gathered from supervisor interviews, correctional officer training fieldnotes, and official training documents.

This organizing schema encouraged me to make distinctions between prisons and jails, but it made me more likely to overlook key differences between male and female officers, for example. Furthermore, my original organizational process spurred me to examine contradictions between informal organizational norms (found in binders 1–4) and formally espoused organizational values (found in binder 5). In short, the organization of the data influences the issues interpreted as salient. Of course, there is no one perfect way to organize. Just realize that your system will impact your analysis – and consider organizing your data in a way that might be most meaningful down the line.

The organization process may seem tedious, or even boring. However, I encourage you to relish in its mindlessness. Organizing can be done sporadically throughout the day, with a baby in your lap or the tunes blaring. Just do it. Without a well-organized data set, analyzing and writing will feel about as inviting as trekking through an overgrown jungle.

Analysis logistics: colors, cutting or computers?

Coding refers to labeling and systematizing the data. Coding can be accomplished by using a variety of materials – paper and colored pencils, an Excel spreadsheet, or computer-aided qualitative data analysis software. Each approach has advantages and disadvantages and is personal to every researcher and project. The best approach for one person will not be right for another, and what works for one project may be clumsy for another. Here I briefly review coding options that are popular among those new to qualitative research.

Manual approaches

If you are drawn to creative craft projects, manual coding may be perfect for you. A manual process begins by gathering hard copies of all the data, preferably with wide margins and lots of white space, then marking up the text with pens, pencils, highlighters, and markers, and finally cutting, pasting, hole-punching, piling, and stringing together the data. Before the availability of computers and word-processing software, this type of manual approach, including the process of writing data summaries on key sort cards with punch code numbers on the edge, was quite common (Podolefsky, 1987).

Indeed, early in his career, my doctoral advisor Stanley Deetz analyzed qualitative data using Q-sorts – a modification of traditional factor analysis (McKeown & Thomas, 1988). This entailed noting down various subjective events and characteristics on cards, intuitively placing them into piles with a common conceptual relation, and interpretively naming them. He would then use needles and ribbons to pull out information embedded in the cluster that suggested a certain intersectional interpretation.

Manual cutting and pasting is still useful in today's era of computers. Indeed, Saldaña describes an activity called "tabletop categories," in which participants

> [f]irst code the data in the margins of hard copy, cut each coded "chunk" of data into separate pieces of paper, pile them together into appropriate categories, staple each category's pile of coded data together, label each pile with its category name, then explore how they can be arranged on a tabletop to map the categories' processes and structures. (Saldaña, 2009, p. 188)

RESEARCHER'S NOTEPAD 9.1

Manual coding visual display

Figure 9.1 Manual coding methods can include visually linking codes, ideas, and theories. The canvas pictured here was created and photographed by Karen Stewart (2010) as she analyzed her data from The Burning Man Festival.

Such an approach is especially valuable among those new to qualitative analysis and for anyone who is attracted to touching the data physically and seeing it.

Likewise, tracking codes and ideas on a large white board or canvas and using different colors and arrows can be an aesthetically effective analysis method. Former doctoral student Karen Stewart used a large stretched canvas and illustration markers to record her thoughts as she moved from data to writing her narrative and visual analysis of the Burning Man Festival (Stewart, 2010). Researcher's Notepad 9.1 (Figure 9.1) pictures the canvas she filled in, little by little, as she made sense of her data.

I used a manual approach to analyze emergency 911 fieldnotes and interviews in the early 1990s. I printed out all the data and used differently colored pencils to draw marginal lines, stars, exclamation points, and notes next to the data associated with certain codes. Some data had multiple colors/codes connected to them – because they referred to a number of issues. After marking up all the data, I then created a locator sheet. I wrote the name of the code (a process described in more detail below) at the top of the locator sheet – like "sarcasm" – and then I listed the various pages within the data that were associated with a specific code, like "June 5 fieldnote, p. 7, bottom"; and "Jenny Interview, p. 3, middle."

I kept the locator sheet and the piles of marked-up data on hand as I wrote the resulting paper. When I desired data connected to a certain code, I checked out my locator sheet and paged through the relevant fieldnote or interview transcript to find the appropriately color-coded piece. As I "used" different data in my writing, I crossed them off on my locator sheet, which directed me to a different datum the next time. This worked quite well, but analysis is eased through the use of computers.

Computer-aided approaches with everyday software

The onset of advanced computers and easily accessible word-processing and spreadsheet software has made analyzing the data more efficient. Here is a story that presents one way of using everyday software to analyze data.

By the time I was working on my dissertation in the late 1990s, I color-coded the data right onto my computer screen, just changing the font to a certain hue or highlight to correspond with a certain analytic theme. Double- or triple-coding a datum was creatively accomplished through layering highlights, color, and fancy fonts. After color-coding all 700+ pages of correctional officer data, I kept these coded documents open and created a new document titled "Analysis Breakdown." There I created a bolded heading for each theme and then copied and pasted under each heading the data of the relevant color, drawing them from all the various fieldnote and interview documents. This resulted in an analysis breakdown document more than 100 pages long, which I then printed out in color.

When writing the dissertation, I kept the hard copy of the analysis breakdown document at my elbow and would refer to it to find examples of data associated with a certain code. I also kept it open on my computer screen, so, depending on the length of the data segment, I could either just retype that segment from the hard copy or conduct a computerized word search and copy and paste it into my writing. Compared to my 911 process, this approach was faster than paging through the original data fieldnotes and interview transcripts, especially since I had so many pages of data.

In addition to using word-processing programs, many researchers also have easy access to spreadsheet programs like Excel. Although spreadsheet programs are designed for numeric data, qualitative researchers can also use them to store and count key bits of data. I personally have used Excel to track research participants and their demographic data (as described in Chapter 4). Other researchers have found creative ways to use Excel headings in labeling and sorting certain analytic themes (Meyer & Avery, 2009).

Because most researchers have handy access to word-processing and spreadsheet programs, these are quite popular in qualitative data analysis. However, for more complex analyses, or if you are considering more than one qualitative data analysis project in your career, I recommend investigating more advanced and specifically designed qualitative software – which I overview in Chapter 10. After considering your data analysis technology, it's time for data immersion and primary-cycle coding.

Data immersion and primary-cycle coding

About three quarters through the data collection, I recommend that researchers submerge themselves in the entire breadth of the data by reading and re-reading them, listening to them, and thinking about them. During this **data immersion phase**, I suggest – in contrast to Glaser's (1992) take on grounded theory – that researchers should talk to others about their data and emerging findings. Talking to others about your data aids in sensemaking and in considering a variety of interpretations. In all immersion activities, the goal is to absorb and marinate in the data, jotting down reflections and hunches, but reserving judgment.

Good open-ended questions to ask are: "What is happening here?" or "What strikes you?" (Creswell, 2007, p. 153). Any corpus of rich data can be analyzed in multiple ways, so it's important to stay open to multiple meanings. The question is not "What is *the* story?" – but rather "What is *a* story here" (Weick, 2001, p. 461). If you have the luxury of time and breadth, throw a wide net. Answering these questions begins the process of coding.

Codes are words or short phrases that capture a "summative, salient, essence-capturing, and/or evocative attribute for [...] language-based or visual data" (Saldaña, 2009, p. 3). Coding is the active process of identifying data as belonging to, or representing, some type of phenomenon. This phenomenon may be a concept, belief, action, theme, cultural practice, or relationship. The first activities of coding processes have been called "open coding" and "initial coding" by grounded theorists (Charmaz, 2006; Glaser & Strauss, 1967) and "first cycle coding" (Saldaña, 2011). The phrase "open coding" suggests that in these initial cycles you are trying to open up meaning in the data. Saldaña's (2009) notion of cycle captures the circular reflexive process that marks qualitative data analysis. For our purposes, I'll use the phrase **primary-cycle coding** to refer to these initial coding activities that occur more than just a single "first" time. The data might be read and coded several times during this primary stage.

Primary-cycle coding begins with an examination of the data and assigning words or phrases that capture their essence. Those who use a manual approach could write the code in the margin, and those who use Microsoft word-processing software could type the code in the "comment" function or in another column. Here is an example of first-cycle coding from my 911 fieldnote data:

Call-Taker (CT) Tiffany hangs up from a call, rolls her eyes at CT Brittany beside her, and says: "God, some people are sooo retarded!"	"RETARDED"
Tiffany then mimics the caller, sing-songing in a high-pitched voice:	MIMICKING
"I've been dating this guy for a week, and I let him use my car. He's in prison, but I don't know his last name." Laughing, Brittany goes on to tell a story about the "schizoid" who called earlier about his	SARCASM LAUGHING "SCHIZOID"
neighbor's sprinkler hitting the sidewalk. She says to me, "So many people call us for things that are not real emergencies!"	"REAL EMERGENCY"

Primary-cycle codes are usually, but not always, also **first-level codes**. First-level codes focus on "what" is present in the data. They are descriptive, showing the basic activities and processes in the data (e.g. LAUGHING; MIMICKING). Some researchers suggest that using codes that are gerunds (words ending in "-ing," like "laughing" rather than just "laugh" or "fun") serve to helpfully highlight action in the scene (Charmaz, 2011). First-level codes require little interpretation and first-level coding might even be delegated to a research assistant who knows little about the research project ("Please highlight all the data in which participants are laughing and this will be considered under the first-level code LAUGHING").

In these primary cycles of coding, imagine that you are a journalist who has arrived first at the scene of an accident. The goal is to detail the "who, what, and where," not to provide an analysis of *why* the accident happened or of *how* to figure out blame (don't worry, these interpretations will come later). Keep in mind, too, that you can double- and triple-code the same datum if several codes relate to it. For instance, in the 911 excerpt above, some of the data could have been additionally labeled with codes such as STORY-TELLING or EYE-ROLLING.

As you travel through the primary cycles of coding, try to transform general codes into ones that are more specific and active. FRUSTRATED may change to EYE-ROLLING, and HUMOR may change to SARCASM. Primary-cycle codes may also make use of the actual words or phrases within the datum itself (e.g. as illustrated by words in quotation marks in the excerpt above: "RETARDED," "SCHIZOID," "REAL EMERGENCY"). These are called *in vivo* **codes**, and they use the language and terms of the participants themselves (Strauss, 1987). *In vivo* coding is especially useful for researchers interested in the local jargon, slang, and vocabulary of a certain community.

Throughout the coding process, researchers use the **constant comparative method** (Charmaz, 2006) to compare the data applicable to each code, and they modify code definitions to fit new data (or else they break them off and create a new code). For example, you may begin with the code "LAUGHTER," but over time you might want to add to this conceptual bin data that don't exactly fit the code LAUGHTER (e.g. a bad joke that no one thought was funny). Through the constant comparative process, you may decide that this bin should be named ATTEMPTED HUMOR rather than LAUGHTER. The constant comparative method is circular, iterative, and reflexive. Consistently reviewing your codes and their explanations and slightly modifying them or creating new ones along the way helps with avoiding "definitional drift" as you code your data (Gibbs, 2007).

How detailed should you be during these primary cycles of coding? Both *lumping* your data into large bins and *fracturing* them into smaller slices have advantages and disadvantages (Bazeley, 2007). The 911 data excerpt above is fractured, almost each line being labeled with its own code. Fracturing takes a lot of time but provides a vivid, multi-textured picture of the data. In contrast, the entire excerpt could have been lumped together with a code like "GOSSIPPING ABOUT CALLERS." Such a code is just as "correct" and would have been much quicker. However, lumping large swaths of data into big general categories may not lead to as insightful interpretations as fracturing the data into smaller slices, each with a more specific code.

Lumping versus fracturing is a matter of degree and personal style. Those who first fracture the data into small pieces, each with its own code, usually connect these bits into larger categories during later coding cycles. In contrast, those who lump first usually make finer distinctions later. If in doubt, I encourage more detailed fracturing first, and lumping second. As one particularly wise long-distance runner once told me: "There are no shortcuts in life or training. You either pay early or pay later, and later usually costs more." The same might be said for coding data. Coding activities that are painstaking in earlier cycles can pay off in terms of intellectual creativity and theoretical contribution in later cycles.

What data should be coded first? Many qualitative experts suggest first coding those data that are typical or interesting in some way, and then moving on to contrastive data. The initial data texts coded will influence the resulting coding scheme, so choose texts in these early stages that represent a range of the data available. Also, an iterative approach does not require that the entire corpus of data be put through a fractured and detailed primary-coding cycle. Indeed, after you have read through all your data a few times and conducted line-by-line open coding on a portion, it is time to take a deep breath and consider some focusing activities.

Focusing the analysis and creating a codebook

As you engage in primary-cycle coding, it is helpful to create a list of codes and a brief definition or representative example of each – especially if the codes are not self-explanatory. Depending on the detail of your primary-cycle coding and the breadth of your data, this "start-list" (Miles & Huberman, 1994) of codes may range from 30 to 300 and over. As you become more focused, it's wise to develop a systematic **codebook** – a data display that lists key codes, definitions, and examples that are going to be used in your analysis. Codebooks are like "legends" for your data, helping you meet the challenge of getting your head around pages of transcripts, highlighting, and scrawling. Codebooks are especially crucial when you are working in a team, among different people coding the same data set – something I cover in more detail in Chapter 11, in relation to inter-coder reliability.

The codebook can morph throughout the data analysis process. It serves as a chronological map registering how the codes emerged and changed over time (re-save new versions with the date of modification). Codebooks are also helpful for explaining the data analysis process to instructors, advisors, supervisory committee members, and external reviewers. Indeed, they are often appended to books, theses, dissertations, and grant reports.

Unlike a long list of codes that may develop in first-cycle coding, codes in the codebook should be more limited in scope. Codebooks can be elaborate or simple, and usually the more team members who are coding the data, the more detailed the codebook must be. For example, Bernard and Ryan (2010, p. 99) provide a detailed example of a very codebook that includes:

short description of code;
detailed description of code;
inclusion criteria (features that must be present to include data with this code);
exclusion criteria (features that would automatically exclude data from this code);
typical exemplars (obvious examples of this code);
atypical exemplars (surprising examples of this code);
"close but no" exemplars (examples that may seem like the code but are not).

If you are coding the data on your own or with just one partner, the codebook may be more streamlined. Researcher's Notepad 9.2 contains an excerpt from a codebook used to analyze male executives' viewpoints on gender, work, and life (Tracy & Rivera, 2010). This particular project resulted in a standard journal-article length manuscript, and the codebook included a total of 22 codes: 15 first-level and descriptive ones, 7 second-level and more analytic – a distinction I discuss in more detail in the next section. I have found out that it is difficult for me to keep my head around more than 25 codes during any one analytic project. This number will vary from person to person, but it's important to realize that, when you (or members of your research team) cannot hold the corpus of code definitions in short-term memory, high-quality analysis can suffer.

In addition to creating a codebook, it is wise to frequently return to research interests/ questions and the research proposal. Because most researchers are under time and subject constraints, many of us pursue analysis directions that align not only with themes emerging in primary coding, but also with ones that mesh well with research goals, experience, and deadlines. Indeed the most promising analysis directions are inductively poignant and at the same time offer new or underexplored insight, connect up with research priorities, make use of past expertise, and meaningfully interact with existing research.

Throughout the analysis, revisiting research questions and other sensitizing concepts helps you to ensure they are still relevant and interesting. Original research interests are merely points of departure and other, more salient, issues may emerge in the data. After some primary-cycle coding, researchers should reconsider the best direction

RESEARCHER'S NOTEPAD 9.2

Codebook excerpt

Abbre-viation	Code	Definition/Explanation	Examples (Hypothetical – Unless Otherwise Indicated Through Direct Quotes)
First-level [descriptive] codes			
Tr-Self	Traits – set interviewee apart	Answer to question about what has set the interviewee apart from other employees, as a leader, and/or about any other characteristics the interviewee attribute to his career success.	My education; I am always working.
PolSug	organizational policy suggestions for work–life	Answer to the question: What could organizations do to make work–life balance easier or to help women in their on-ramping? Any other information interviewee offers concerning ways in which organizations could make work–life easier.	Flexibility; telecommuting; day care; giving more sick days.
WL-Fut	Future work–life balance	Descriptions of how interviewee thinks his children will manage work–life balance	I think they've seen that mom's staying home works well in our marriage, so they'll likely do the same.
Second-level [analytic] codes			
Private	Privatization of work–life policy	When asked about organizational policy, interviewees provide an answer about their personal beliefs, practices, experiences, and situations	When asked in general about women going to work, respondent talks about how hard it is to find good day care; interviewee is asked four times about workplace policy before he says anything (in earlier answers he spoke about private familial views and practice).
Choice	Choice – women's work	Statements suggesting that interviewees view women's work as more of a "choice" than of a necessity and therefore think that women have only themselves to blame if there are work–life problems.	"I don't think my daughter will choose to go to work." I think women should stay home with the children.
Off-OK	Off-ramping OK	Statements that suggest interviewee thinks that it is acceptable (and even praiseworthy) for women to leave the work world when they have a baby	I applaud women who leave work in order to take care of children.

of the analysis, rework research questions/foci, and educate themselves on literature that frames new directions.

Consider the popular "answer and question" televised game show Jeopardy. Jeopardy contestants must consider hints given in the form of answers and only then come up with a question that fits those answers; on this analogy, qualitative researchers should consider their primary-level codes to be similar to "hints" or "answers," and then they should go back and fit them with relevant or interesting research questions. For example, given the codes of "privatization of work–life policy," "women's work framed as choice," and "off-ramping OK" in the male voices codebook above, a good research question might be something like: "Why do women continue to face challenges in terms of work-life balance?" Of course, any group of codes, when combined in different ways, could answer any number of questions. Hence the researcher should choose to focus on the questions (and corresponding codes) that are of the greatest significance, interest, and value. Consider This 9.1 illustrates a brainstorming activity designed to help focus the data analysis.

CONSIDER THIS 9.1

Focusing the data analysis

1   Which literatures or theories am I already acquainted with?
2   Given the data I've collected, read, and coded so far, what are some interesting themes or issues?
    a   Do these themes meaningfully intersect with the literatures and theories that I am already acquainted with (= answer to question 1 above)? How so?
    b   In what ways do these themes intersect with literatures and theories that pair well with qualitative methods (= as discussed in Chapter 3 and elsewhere)?
    c   In what ways do these themes intersect with literatures or theories that I'm unfamiliar with, but am drawn to and willing/have time to learn more about?
3   What is my conceptual cocktail party (in other words, with whom am I entering into dialogue through this study?). Name specific scholars if possible, and, if not possible, specific disciplines or sub-disciplines.
4   Who are the potential audiences of my study?
    a   Who would benefit, appreciate, and learn from this study and why?
    b   Who do I want to notice and read this work?
5   Given this discussion, what would be two to four primary areas of literature or theory that may best situate and contextualize my study?
    a   What are the gaps, controversies, or unanswered questions in these literatures?

Now, take a look at your research questions.

1   How could my research questions/foci be improved so as to provide an intuitive and logical link between the framing literatures/theories and the data? Rework/modify.
2   Given this exercise, what would be some of the ways to modify, redirect, or narrow additional data gathering practices?
    a   Are there interview questions that now seem more pressing than others?
    b   Are there samples (of data or people) that would help flesh out the emerging analysis?

Secondary-cycle coding: second-level analytic and axial/hierarchical coding

In **secondary-cycle coding**, the researcher critically examines the codes already identified in primary cycles and begins to organize, synthesize, and categorize them into interpretive concepts. Secondary-cycle coding moves beyond first-level descriptive codes to analytic and interpretive **second-level codes** – which are similar to what others have called "focused" codes (Saldaña, 2009). Rather than simply mirroring the data, second-level codes serve to explain, theorize, and synthesize them. Second-level coding includes interpretation and identifying patterns, rules, or cause–effect progressions.

Second-level codes often draw from disciplinary concepts, and this is why being well read is crucial for analyzing the data with complexity. For instance, I have used a second-level code "INCONGRUITY HUMOR." This code draws directly from humor theory and means that, when topics are contrasting, ironic, or incongruous, we find them funny (Tracy, Myers, & Scott, 2006). For example, incongruity marks the following joke: "A sandwich walks into a bar. The bartender says, 'I'm sorry, we don't serve food in here.'" The humor is tied, in part, to the incongruity of the idea of a sandwich walking around in a pub. A code INCONGRUITY HUMOR can only emerge and be understood by reading and knowing the humor literature.

If you apply disciplinary concepts as second-level codes, it's important to make sure these particular concepts are the best there can be for explicating the data; and, if they are not, find other concepts that are. I remember a vibrant data session with Karen Myers and Cliff Scott in which we tried to make sense of the purposes and consequences of humor among human service workers. In one memorable data analysis session, we made decisions about whether certain data were related to a second-level code SUPERIORITY HUMOR or rather ROLE DISTANCING. These codes are similar in that they are both about differentiation, but the first is about differentiation from another person or group (Lynch, 2002), while the second is about differentiation from one's own role (Goffman, 1961b). Interpreting which of these concepts made the most sense for the data analysis was crucial for creating precise and credible analytic claims.

The creative process of developing second-level codes may also include **prospective conjecture**, in which researchers consider novel theoretical juxtapositions and borrow from other fields, models, and assumptions (Hallier & Foirbes, 2004). With regard to the humor project, Cliff, Karen, and I had already reviewed the data in terms of concepts from past humor research. As we were discussing the emerging analysis, though, something in our guts told us that humor was accomplishing something more complex than the functions delineated in past research. Over several hours we filled the chalk boards with notes, read and rehashed the data, paced the room, and tested out various ideas on each other (Tracy, 2012).

We pressed the limits of the existing literature and considered various theories that might explain better what was going on. Somewhere in this dialogue, Cliff suggested that our participants' humor might be serving as a type of organizational sensemaking (Weick, 1995). Karen and I furrowed our brows, Cliff explained further, and we began pulling examples to see how sensemaking played out. Aha! In that ephemeral moment our interpretation came together. In short, through prospective conjecture, we melded research about organizational sensemaking with humor theory and came up with the second-level code HUMOR AS SENSEMAKING – which, we argued, was a primary contribution of our research project (Tracy, Myers, & Scott, 2006).

Whereas first-level codes are generated by the data, the researcher uses first-level codes coupled with interpretive creativity and theoretical knowledge to generate second-level codes. This is why it is very difficult to delegate second-level coding activities to someone who is not an expert on the data, the framing literature, and qualitative data analysis methods. It's quite simple to ask a research assistant to code certain data LAUGHTER at first level, but it's a much more difficult and interpretive task to code data HUMOR AS SENSEMAKING. This second-level coding requires understanding how superiority humor contrasts with incongruity or tension relief humor (Lynch, 2002), as well as how sensemaking communicatively plays out in a group.

In addition to creating analytic codes, in second-cycle coding researchers begin identifying patterns or groupings of codes within the data. For instance, they might identify codes that continually reappear in the data and link them together in a specific way. **Axial coding** (Charmaz, 2006) is the process of reassembling data that were fractured during open coding (Strauss & Corbin, 1998). This process, which I more intuitively relate to **hierarchical codes**, includes systematically grouping together various codes under a hierarchical "umbrella" category that makes conceptual sense.

For instance, imagine you were doing a research project that analyzed behavior at family dinners, and the following first-level codes emerged continually in the data: (a) PRAYER/ BLESSING; (b) WHAT I DID AT WORK; (c) WHAT I DID AT SCHOOL; (d) CLEARING THE TABLE. These first-level codes could then be categorized into a larger hierarchical code. If you were a researcher interested in rituals, for instance, all these codes might be grouped within a code "DINNERTIME RITUALS." If you were interested in comparing expectations from children versus parents at the dinner table, you might group the first two codes into "PARENT RITUALS" and the latter two into a hierarchical code "CHILDEN'S RITUALS."

Gradually, throughout the activities of analysis, researchers move from emergent and descriptive coding to more focused and analytic coding. In the process they come to better understand how their data analysis significantly attends to salient research foci/questions. At this point, researchers should also better understand which data will be most important for the analysis. Certain data, even if they are already collected, may only tangentially relate to the evolving research interests, and therefore they should be syphoned off, for use in a different project.

Meanwhile, second-cycle coding activities may suggest that additional data need to be collected to flesh out an emerging code or explanation of what is happening in the scene. In these cases, the researcher should go back to the field to gather more data about the issue – a practice called **theoretical sampling** (not to be confused with **theoretical construct sampling**, which was discussed in Chapter 7). This phrase, "theoretical sampling," comes from grounded theory, in which researchers gather data in order to inform an emergent theory in the data. You know you have gathered enough data when new pieces add little, if any, new value to the emergent analysis – a state called **theoretical saturation** (Glaser & Strauss, 1967). Strauss and Corbin (1990, p. 212) elucidate this point, explaining that data collection is sufficient when:

(a) no new or relevant data seem to emerge regarding a category;
(b) the category is well developed in terms of its properties and dimensions demonstrating variation; and
(c) the relationships among categories are well established and validated.

Another good question to ask is this: "Does the emerging analysis attend to my research foci in an interesting and significant way?" If not, this may suggest the need for more data. It might also suggest the need for additional synthesizing activities – a topic we turn to next.

Synthesizing and making meaning from codes

Throughout the coding process, it's important to record your emerging analysis thoughts and ideas systematically. The bright ideas you have one day inevitably fade over time, and you can save yourself from duplicating work by keeping a record.

First, I recommend creating a document that records all of your analysis activities, chronologically. I call this document "methods section draft." It need not be pretty. Just the date and a discussion of what you accomplished in terms of analysis (e.g. week of June 5, read all of my data and made marginal notes; week of June 12, organized fieldnotes into three binders and began line-by-line first-cycle coding; week of June 19, the following 20 first-level codes emerged...). This "methods draft" document will be invaluable as you are asked to recreate and describe your analysis process in subsequent papers, articles, or grant reports. Without such a record, rigorous iterative analyses can be difficult to remember and explain – which results in that all too frequent platitude, "I repeatedly read over my data and central themes emerged." Blech!

Second, qualitative researchers should write **analytic memos** both as a part of the analysis process and as an analysis outcome. Analytic memos are "sites of conversation with ourselves about our data" (Clarke, 2005, p. 202) and a place to "dump your brain" (Saldaña, 2009, p. 32). They are a longer version of the fieldnote's **analytic asides** (discussed in Chapter 6), and they are usually focused on the meaning of codes and on the connections among them. They can be written in long hand, in a journal, or they can appear as a separate set of documents saved in regular word-processing software or as a file in qualitative computer software systems. Analytic memos call for free writing, creativity, and writing as a method of inquiry (Richardson, 2000b). In other words, memo-writing is one of those activities where you write first and understand later. Researcher's Notepad 9.3 provides an example of a couple analytic memos.

Analytic memos help researchers figure out the fundamental stories in the data and serve as a key intermediary step between coding and writing a draft of the analysis. Although they can take many forms, analytic memos are often characterized by one or more of the following features (Charmaz, 2006):

(a)   they define the code as carefully as possible;
(b)   they explicate its properties;
(c)   they provide examples of raw data that illustrate the code;
(d)   they specify conditions under which it arises, is maintained, and changes;
(e)   they describe its consequences;
(f)   they show how it relates to other codes;
(g)   they develop hypotheses about the code.

Analytic memos are very helpful for thinking through how codes relate to each other. Indeed, in secondary-cycle coding, it is important to go beyond merely comparing and contrasting the data, to also examining it for antecedents and consequences of various codes. Reflecting on and making hypotheses about these linkages is crucial for understanding process, action, chronology, explanation, and causation.

Researchers continue to revise claims and hypotheses as they gather and analyze more data. Confirming data strengthens the emergent claim. Researchers should also play devil's advocate with themselves through the process of **negative case analysis**. Such a practice asks researchers to actively seek out deviant data that do not appear to support the emerging hypothesis, and then revise arguments so they better fit *all* the emerging data. Negative case

RESEARCHER'S NOTEPAD 9.3

Analytic memos

Miriam Sobré-Denton (2011) studied an international university student group called "INTASU." Along the way, she wrote a number of analytic memos that helped her tease out the importance of cosmopolitan identity and various communicative features as international students made sense of their place in the host culture. Here are two unpublished examples.

Cosmopolitan identity (4/2/09)

It strikes me that when people discuss being members of INTASU during their interviews, they seem to be often talking about a culture of unbelonging – that is, people who feel that they really don't fit in anywhere, fit in with INTASU. This often seems to stem from having moved about often from a young age, being bicultural (as with Bahil, Ella, and Jonah) or simply having been exposed to multiple cultures and constantly striving for self-recognition. This can even be seen in the American members of the group (i.e. John, Lauren), in that there is a certain risk taking and need to fit in with others on the fringes that characterizes members of INTASU, regardless of nationality. Specifically, I am interested in how such members realize aspects of their international or cosmopolitan identities through this group, and whether this relates to the descriptions of INTASU as "home" or "family."

Bitching (4/8/09)

Based on last week's class discussion of bitching as part of graduate school, it made me think of how INTASU members may complain about the host culture (America) as a way of bonding with other members of the group, adapting/adjusting to the host culture, and creating social support. Everyone is feeling the same way, and although bitching may be counterproductive, it is a central activity in this kind of group organization. Something to think about: How does this relate to cosmopolitanism?

analysis discourages the practice of cherry-picking data examples that only fit early explanations and ignoring discrepant evidence. As such, negative case analysis helps to ensure the fidelity and credibility of emerging explanations.

In addition to the analytic memos, midway through secondary-cycle coding, I encourage researchers to create a **loose analysis outline** that notes the primary research questions/foci and the potential ways the emerging codes are attending to them. Do not worry too much about whether this analysis plan is complete or right. Rather, view this plan as merely an outline that will assist you in further coding and writing. In creating this plan, think critically about the scope of the particular analysis project at hand – are you writing a 30-page paper, a thesis, a dissertation, or a book? The analysis plan should have the same scope. You need not include every single interesting direction. Indeed, think of your codes and analytic memos as the raw ingredients that you get to choose from in order to make up the outline. Choose only the ingredients that will create the perfect dish for this occasion.

For example, in our work–life research project with male executives (Tracy & Rivera, 2010), we created a loose analysis outline that included a number of first-level and second-level codes. In determining the most promising codes and emergent claims, we went back

Loose analysis outline
Male voices project

This unpublished outline helped generate Tracy & Rivera, 2010.

Issues motivating the study

1 Women's advancement in organizations has stalled.
2 We have little research about work–life balance from men's viewpoints.
3 Men in past research have espoused work–life policy and family as important; however, we don't know how/if their viewpoints about gender and work–life in the private sphere intersect with public work–life considerations.

Guiding questions motivating the analysis

What are male gatekeepers' attitudes about work–life balance and male and female roles in regard to life and work? How might their talk about gender and work–life in the private sphere and in regard to their own family help us understand their attitudes and practice of work–life policies in the public sphere?

Potential themes that emerged in coding that might answer these questions

1 Men privatize work–life policy (when asked about policy, they answer in relation to their personal beliefs and situation). Therefore, it makes sense to look at their private views on these things…
2 Myth that flexibility = sufficient work–life policy
3 A conflation of child care with doctor's visits and child care
4 An absence of understanding as to how the (uneven) division of domestic labor (negatively) affects women's ability to be productive at work
5 How does a spouse have an effect on one's own career success?
    (a) spouse needed for daughter;
    (b) spouse needed for son;
    (c) the idea that a daughter's spouse (the future son-in-law) might be valued in terms of how much he supported her in her career was a bit foreign – many interviewees did not even answer the question as it was intended
    In the course of some interviews, it seems that just hearing about the connections between these issues increased interviewees' sophistication of understanding work–life.
6 Women were appreciated as nurturers, supporters, sounding-boards (how does this align with description of best employee?):
    (d) what participants appreciate from wives;
    (e) what participants appreciate from employees (generic);
    (f) what participants appreciate from female employees.
7 Working women are often framed as adopting a "choice" rather than acting from an economic necessity (assumption that most female employees are like the interviewees' own wives?).
8 Interviewees have fairly gender-specific viewpoints on what their children will do:
    (g) career future for girls;
    (h) career future for boys;
    (i) how the offspring will manage work–life balance.
9 Women off-ramping to be at home with children – this is something to be applauded.

to our research questions and motivating reasons for the study. For this particular project, we were interested in how male executives' stories about work, life, and home could help shed light on women's workplace challenges. In the coding process we identified issues such as how participants talked about raising their children (a code we labeled GENDERED SOCIALIZATION), and how male executives spoke about women's work as a choice (CHOICE). These two codes emerged as salient in the data *and* connected to our research interests. Meanwhile, a code RELIGIOSITY seemed interesting, but not clearly connected to our current foci. Hence we saved that code for a future analysis.

On the basis of these activities we created the loose analysis outline that appears in Researcher's Notepad 9.4. The outline served to focus the analysis, and it identifies the codes that were actually most interesting or promising to pursue in the final cycles of coding. After developing this outline, we went back to the data and used the corresponding codes in a more etic, top-down manner. This outline helped us know where to focus and was integral to our progress into writing. I encourage you to create your own loose analysis outline, which should guide your secondary coding cycles as well as the writing process.

FOLLOWING, FORGETTING, AND IMPROVISING

This chapter has provided a lot of advice for analyzing and coding data. However, these rules are not written in stone. Indeed, the large variability of terms that people use for analysis – open coding, line-by-line coding, fracturing, lumping, analytic coding, axial coding, categorizing, constant comparative method, primary- versus secondary-cycle coding, and so on – indicates the wide range of ways in which different researchers have made qualitative analysis their own. Some terms and processes just resonate differently with different researchers.

I encourage you to pick up, practice, and play with the various techniques described in this chapter, and to do it in ways that make sense to you. If something seems initially uncomfortable or hard, push yourself at least to try it. As my yoga instructor says, it's often the poses we resist and hate to do that we benefit from the most. Over time, you will find that you are attracted to some analysis techniques more than to others. You will also find that some activities will be more appropriate than others, depending on the project at hand, depending on whether you're working on your own or with others, and depending on whether the goals of the project are tightly scripted or completely open-ended. Play, and have fun with it. What you learn from the journey is exactly the goal of data analysis.

In summary

This chapter reviewed the nuts and bolts of qualitative data analysis. Although data analysis, in many ways, occurs alongside research design and data collection, there are several primary activities that make up the focused analysis stage. These activities move recurrently back and forth – between considering the emergent data on the one hand and reviewing existing theories, literatures, and research interests on the other (for a flow-chart that visually depicts this whole process, peek ahead to text Tips and Tools 10.1).

First steps include organizing the data and considering various tools for qualitative analyses – both manual and computer-aided. Reading and re-reading the data helps with data immersion and transitions to primary-cycle coding, in which the researcher groups the data by descriptive first-level codes and keeps an eye out for promising *in vivo* codes (which use participants' local language). Primary-cycle codes answer the question "what's going on here?" – providing a summary of data content. Throughout coding, researchers use the constant comparative method to make modifications in the coding scheme and to create new codes.

Too many hardworking qualitative researchers drown in a self-created sea of primary-cycle codes. To avoid this common problem, I recommend several focusing activities throughout the process, including reflecting on research questions and creating a codebook. Focusing activities make visible the most promising directions for additional analysis and provide a moment for researchers to come up for air, take a look around, and get real about their goals, timelines, and expertise.

Secondary-cycle coding goes beyond asking "what" to asking "why" and "how" the data are interesting and significant. In this cycle, researchers categorize first-level codes into larger axial or hierarchical codes that serve as conceptual bins for emergent claims. They also devise analytic codes that may employ disciplinary or theoretical concepts. Such work requires interpretive creativity and therefore can be one of the most intellectually challenging – but also energizing – parts of the analysis process. This is where researchers feel the excitement of "yes, I think I may have something here!"

Several synthesizing activities assist with secondary-cycle coding and bridge to analysis and writing. Through writing analytic memos, researchers define and explain the emerging codes, providing examples of illustrative data and explanations regarding contexts where the code is likely to emerge. These reflections should ideally go beyond comparing and contrasting codes in terms of their definitional frames and borders, to unpacking the antecedents and consequents of certain codes.

This is also a time to begin making hypotheses and predictions. To ensure and strengthen preliminary claims, researchers should not only find data that support their hypotheses, but also conduct negative case analyses in which they purposefully seek out disconfirming evidence. Negative case analyses, in turn, encourage modifications and changes to claims, so they more precisely align with the qualitative evidence at hand.

After several rounds of secondary coding, researchers should return to the motivating research questions and foci. A loose analysis outline will help answer the question: "Is this study interesting and significant?" If the answer is no, this means the data collection or analysis is not yet complete. Researchers should gather additional data to fill out the emerging theoretical contribution (called theoretical sampling) until such time that the codes and emerging analysis are theoretically saturated. They may also turn back to the literature in order to get better sensitized to issues they are not yet able to appreciate in the data. Finally, they can turn to more advanced types of data analysis – a topic to which the following chapter is dedicated. Exercise 9.1 provides an assignment that will help you practice analysis.

EXERCISE 9.1

Iterative analysis basics

Choose one or more of the following activities for practicing the basics of qualitative data analysis.

Please indicate your overall research questions/foci at the top of the exercise.

1   Bring a data text (e.g. fieldnote, interview transcript, document) that you have coded (whether that be manually or through a computer program). In an addendum, explain the ways in which you created codes, the various types of codes, and their significance to your final project. For which codes do you need more data or information? How will you gather that information?

2   Develop a codebook that includes the name of the code, its explanation, and a real or hypothetical example from the data. Identify different types of primary and secondary codes, including first-level descriptive, *in vivo*, axial/hierarchical, and analytic.

3   Turn in several "analytic memos." In writing the memos, consider the following characteristics:

   a   Define the code as carefully as possible.
   b   Explicate its properties.
   c   Provide examples of raw data that illustrate the code.
   d   Specify conditions under which it arises, is maintained, and changes.
   e   Describe its consequences.
   f   Show how it relates to other codes.
   g   Develop hypotheses about the code.

On the basis of the memo(s), develop and discuss one or more primary claims that may frame your analysis. What data must you still collect in order to examine the strength and tenability of these claims?

KEY TERMS

→   **analytic asides**   brief, reflective pieces of writing interspersed throughout the fieldnotes; they are shorter and less detailed than analytic memos

→   **analytic memos**   "sites of conversation with ourselves about our data" (Clarke, 2005, p. 202) and a place to "dump your brain" (Saldaña, 2009 p. 32) about the ongoing investigation

→   **axial coding**   the process of reassembling data that were fractured during open coding; also see **hierarchical code**

→   **codebook**   a type of data display or legend that lists key codes, definitions, and examples that are going to be used in the analysis

→   **codes**   words or short phrases that capture a "summative, salient, essence-capturing, and/or evocative attribute for […] language-based or visual data" (Saldaña, 2009, p. 3)

coding   the active process of identifying, labeling, and systemizing data as belonging to or representing some type of phenomenon

constant comparative method   a method of analysis used to compare data applicable to each code and to modify code definitions so as to fit new data (or else to break off and create a new code)

data immersion phase   a phase of data analysis during which researchers read and re-read their data, talk with others about them, and marinate in the emerging findings

first-level code   a type of code that is descriptive, shows the data's basic content and processes, requires little interpretation, and focuses on "what" is present in the data

hierarchical code   an analytic bin in which smaller codes are conceptually connected; also see **axial code**

***in vivo* codes**   codes that employ language and terms used by the participants themselves

iterative analysis   a method of data analysis that alternates between emic, or emergent, readings of the data and an etic use of existing models, explanations, and theories

loose analysis outline   an outline that notes the primary research questions and potential ways in which the emerging codes are attending to these questions

negative case analysis   seeking out deviant data that do not appear to support the emerging hypothesis, and revising arguments so that they fit all the emerging data better

primary-cycle coding   initial coding activities, which begin by examining the data and assigning words or phrases that capture their essence

prospective conjecture   researchers' activity of considering novel theoretical juxtapositions and of borrowing from other fields, models, and assumptions

secondary-cycle coding   critical examination of the codes already identified in primary cycles; at this stage the researcher begins to organize, synthesize, and categorize these codes into interpretive and sometimes disciplinary concepts

second-level codes   codes that serve to explain, theorize, and synthesize the data; they include interpretation and help the researcher identify patterns, rules, or cause–effect progressions

theoretical-construct sampling   sampling in which the participants and/or the data are chosen to meet pre-existing theoretical characteristics or conceptual frameworks

theoretical sampling   activity in which researchers continually return to the field and strategically sample data that fill in the blanks and the weak spots of the emerging contextual theory

theoretical saturation   a state in which new data add little, if any, new value to the emergent analysis

CHAPTER 10

Advanced data analysis
The art and magic of interpretation

Contents

Computer-aided qualitative data analysis software (CAQDAS)

Advanced approaches for analyzing qualitative data

In summary

Qualitative Research Methods: Collecting Evidence, Crafting Analysis, Communicating Impact, First Edition. Sarah J. Tracy.
© 2013 Sarah J. Tracy. Published 2013 by Blackwell Publishing Ltd.

I vividly remember a data analysis session with mentor and co-author Karen Tracy during my first year of graduate school. Karen, an expert discourse analyst, and I sat together reading and re-reading our 911 emergency communications data. As a first year MA student, I kept offering up descriptive codes – things like "joking," "story-telling," and "making fun of callers." Meanwhile Karen kept asking patiently: "But Sarah, why is that *interesting*?" At the time I was confused about what she was soliciting. I was adept at *coding* the data, but I was not moving to a deeper level of *interpretation* – one that pinpointed why the emergent themes were significant and surprising, why they contributed to theory, attended to our research questions, or led to new insight.

Indeed, there is a difference between coding the data and interpreting their meaning and significance. Coding certainly lays the groundwork, but interpretation requires linking the emergent meanings together, or to other frameworks – and occurs not just through sitting and "thinking" but through actively writing and engaging in various other creative analytic processes. Interpretation can take place in analytic memos, second-level analytic coding, and various synthesis activities described in the previous chapter. However, read on if you desire additional analysis, inspiration, and guidance. You'll find that advanced analysis is an art, and one that can often seem magical and ephemeral.

The chapter opens with a discussion of computer-aided qualitative data analysis software (CAQDAS,) also known, more simply, as qualitative data analysis software (QDAS). CAQDAS not only eases the sorting and data management process, but also provides options for advanced interpretation. Even if you already know that you will not be using CAQDAS, this section may still provide some valuable background; but you may just want to skim it. The chapter then turns to examining seven ways of analyzing data, which are:

1   exemplars and vignettes;
2   typologies;
3   dramatistic approaches;
4   metaphor analyses;
5   visual data displays;
6   analyzing for explanation and causality; and
7   discourse tracing.

You can use just one of these strategies, or you can mix and match techniques from them that work for your project. Also, realize that this is just a sampling of the analysis practices available. You might seek out your own readings and investigation of the close analysis of talk through discourse and conversational analysis (Tracy, 1995), or the examination of life stories and their meaning making through narrative analysis (Riessman, 2008). Indeed, each analysis approach can frame an entire project or just serve as one instrument in your larger analysis toolkit.

Computer-aided qualitative data analysis software (CAQDAS)

Chapter 9 discussed how researchers can analyze data through manual cut-and-paste methods or by making use of standard word-processing and spreadsheet programs like Microsoft Word and Excel. Although standard computer programs can be easy and low-cost, these programs are not specifically designed to analyze qualitative data, and rigging them to do it can be cumbersome and inefficient. Researchers who plan to conduct a number of qualitative projects throughout their career, who have a lot of data, or who are comfortable navigating computers should investigate software programs specifically designed for qualitative researchers.

Computer-aided qualitative data analysis software (CAQDAS) is computer software specifically designed for the qualitative analysis of data. The software provides options for organizing, managing, coding, sorting, and reconfiguring data – both transcribed textual documents and digital audio/video files – in complex and fun ways. Further, it gives options for creating theoretical models that grow out of the coded data at hand.

Just as word-processing programs like Microsoft Word do not *write* a paper and presentation programs like PowerPoint do not, by themselves, *design* a slide show, CAQDAS does not *analyze* data on its own. Rather, CAQDAS *facilitates* qualitative data analysis – just as word-processing software facilitates writing and presentation software eases presentation design (see Figure 10.1).

The real advantage of CAQDAS is its capability for coding, sorting, querying, and retrieving data through the use of Boolean ("and/or/not") searches. Think of your data as all kinds of delicious food spread out over a very, very long table (so long that you cannot see the end of it). When it comes to wanting a certain food, with CAQDAS you can place an order; and, when this order is entered into the system correctly, it will pull up *exactly* the food specified. CAQDAS saves you the time of walking around this very long table and collecting one dish at a time. It also ensures that you only get the food you want, and nothing more. Extending the metaphor, with CAQDAS you can order all the foods that include "chocolate" and "pecans" but exclude any with "toffee" (of course, I have no idea why anyone would want to do that…).

Furthermore, you can write analytic memos within the software and code them just as you would code any other data file. CAQDAS is also helpful for following up on initial hypotheses. For example, one of the hypotheses made in terms of our male voices data (Tracy & Rivera, 2010) was that male executives who consistently framed women's work as a "choice" were *also* more likely to be married to women who *did not* work outside of the home. Through NVivo's data querying tools we were able to cross-tabulate the interviewees' demographic characteristics (e.g. the working status of participants' wives) with certain codes (e.g. the code "WOMEN'S WORK FRAMED AS CHOICE"), and by doing so to understand the extent to which this and other emerging hypotheses were supported, or needed to be reconsidered.

Figure 10.1 A screen shot of NVivo data analysis software. NVivo is one of several popular software programs that are invaluable in helping organize, code, and query qualitative data. Reproduced by permission of QSR International.

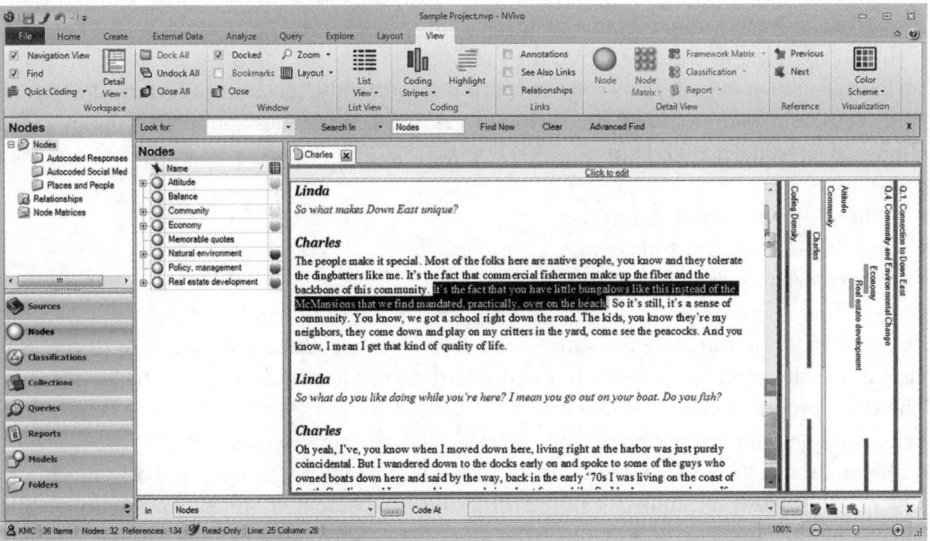

Some researchers have expressed reservations about CAQDAS, feeling that it may result in distance and alienation from the data, or promote a built-in structure for coding and building concepts (Coffey, Holbrook, & Atkinson, 1996). I have not personally discerned these disadvantages in my own research, but I have worked with people who did. For example, after using CAQDAS for most of her qualitative analysis, former doctoral student Miriam Sobré-Denton felt that it "trapped all the meaning inside the computer." Miriam chose to print out and review hard copies of all her data and codes. Then she returned to CAQDAS to assist with data queries. Certainly, CAQDAS might hide the data in some ways. However, data can also hide under stacks of binders and papers.

The primary disadvantages of CAQDAS are its cost, its availability, and its learning curve. So how do you know if it's worth the time and trouble? I heartily recommend its use if you answer "yes" to one or more of the following questions:

- Will you conduct multiple qualitative projects over your career?
- Do you have 100 or more pages of data to analyze?
- Would you like to compare or contrast data from multiple sites or interviewees?
- Are you analyzing data in a team of two or more researchers?
- Are there institutional or grant resources to support the purchase of software?

Because I have answered affirmatively to *all* these questions at one point or another, I now use CAQDAS for all my qualitative data analysis projects. I believe so much in the advantages of qualitative software that we installed it in our graduate student computer lab, and I regularly teach an advanced qualitative analysis course that trains students in its use.

Although I will not go into all the capabilities of CAQDAS here (see Bazeley, 2007; Gibbs, 2007; Lewins & Silver, 2007 for how-to guides), it is helpful to consider its many proficiencies. Software can link analytic reflections to emergent codes and documents (and these reflections can be coded themselves); compare variables (gender, region) across various cases (interviewees, multiple field contexts); link to external web material; collapse multiple codes into one (or position them in a hierarchy/typology); facilitate the creation of models that emerge from the data; provide creative analysis options for webpages, audio recordings, and social networking feeds; count the frequency of certain codes, phrases, or words; and check the consistency and reliability of data analysis when two or more researchers are analyzing the same material.

If you are interested in CAQDAS, the first step is to choose the software. Read up about various programs (e.g. Barry, 1998) and, more importantly, seek out programs that peers, colleagues, and mentors have used with success. The three most popular programs (see Gibbs, 2007; Saldaña, 2009) are:

- ATLAS.ti: www.atlastic.com
- MAXQDA: www.maxqda.com
- NVivo: www.qsrinternational.com

The next step is to purchase the software (usually at a discount for students) or to access it via a university computer lab or a free short-term trial. Then find some CAQDAS tutorials. The three programs noted above come with demonstration software, tutorials, and online help, and I have also found helpful advice via YouTube and web searches.

Manuals specific to CAQDAS can be extremely handy (e.g. Bazeley, 2007; Lewins & Silver, 2007). However, tutorials and readings become outdated quickly and many people learn computer software best by tinkering and doing – preferably in a setting where others are also working and can share tips. As in other computer software, there are multiple paths for accomplishing the same goal in CAQDAS (e.g. if you want to sort the data, you could use alternately a keyboard's function key, the right mouse click, or a drop-down menu). When you have played around on the software tutorials, it's time to import your fieldnotes, interview/focus group transcriptions, and any audio or digital files. The manuals noted above provide good advice about how to bundle, organize, and link various types of files together as you import them.

When qualitative researchers who plan on conducting more than one qualitative project in their career ask me when they should begin using CAQDAS, I smile and say, "Yesterday." Just like other software, CAQDAS is a wonderful tool even if you only understand a portion of its capabilities. Indeed, many of us use word-processing programs every day, but only use their most basic functions. You can experiment as you work, coding, uncoding, and recoding; sorting, unsorting, and resorting. Just make sure to keep back-up files. Playing with the software *is* the analysis (just like playing on PowerPoint *is* the slide-show creation process). Researchers need not wait until the analysis is figured out to benefit from qualitative software.

Advanced approaches for analyzing qualitative data

In many ways, interpreting qualitative data is an indescribably ambiguous process, filled with reading the data, reflecting on the literature, thinking, talking, note-taking, writing, and thinking some more. Although qualitative analysis can be enigmatic, something magical and artful emerges from a pragmatic set of best practices. Engaging in systematic analysis can increase the odds for ephemeral "aha" moments. I believe that researchers have a responsibility to describe their analysis path transparently – for reasons of credibility and pedagogy. Hence, in the discussion that follows, I try to go beyond providing the theory of these analysis approaches, to offering specific steps and examples of how to use them.

Exemplars and vignettes

One of the most common analysis approaches is identifying and interpreting the poignant examples that illustrate the full complexity of the data. Exemplars and vignettes serve as *embodiments* of an inductive construct or claim, or, put another way, as "rhetorical device[s] which may help the readers enter into the author's argument" (Atkinson, 1990, p. 91). They are more than just examples; rather they illustrate many, if not all, facets of the emerging analysis. In this way, exemplars and vignettes are similar; but, as I describe below, they also differ.

Exemplars are the significant and multi-faceted examples researchers *identify in the data through coding*. Indeed identifying exemplars is like finding jewels through an ongoing process of digging, sorting, coding, and reflecting. Sometimes exemplars shine brilliantly only after several cycles of analysis, when various codes get layered one on top of the next and it becomes evident that a particular data segment is meaningfully saturated by different facets of the emerging examination. Other times, the researcher knows from the moment of data collection (in the field or in the interview) that she has just witnessed a situation or heard a quotation that beautifully sums up the analysis. In such moments you might think: "Aha! Now, *this* is an exemplar of exactly what's going on in my data!!"

So, what do exemplars look like? The following story serves as an exemplar from my correctional officer research. A female correctional officer named Lorenzo shared this story as I shadowed her at Women's Minimum Prison.

> Probably the most stressful thing that's happened to me since I've been in here is taking down this inmate in segregation. I couldn't get the handcuffs off of her, and she started threatening me with them, using them as a weapon. She was saying things like, "I'm going to kill the next person that comes in here." All dressed in riot gear, we stormed the cell and pinned her, face first on the floor of the cell. She fought us like she was a 200-pound man. I still can't get the image out of my head. She kept screaming things like, "Yeah, you hurt me… hurt me… f**k me, f**k me hard." She wanted us to hurt her… and I guess we did. I've been bothered by this incident for weeks, and when someone in the facility asked me, I said that it upset me and then that got to the captain and I got a mental health referral! That's bullsh*t. I should be able to be bothered and not be labeled as unstable.

This story serves as an exemplar because it vividly encapsulates the emotional and stressful environment in which correctional officers work, and how they must deal with these situations yet appear as though they are themselves unaffected. The exemplar illustrates the intricacy of correctional officers' emotional landscape and the way they must display certain emotional fronts. It emerged as an exemplar only after several cycles of coding, as it epitomized the following codes emergent throughout the data:

- ANGER
- DISCIPLINE
- DANGER
- STRESS
- MISTRUST
- IRRITATION WITH ADMINISTRATION
- BE TOUGH
- SUPPRESSING FEAR
- STIGMA FOR SEEKING HELP.

Certainly, other field data supported each of these codes, separately. However, Lorenzo's preceding story illustrated in a complex manner this large number of emerging codes, all present together in one excerpt. As such, it served as an exemplar, embodying the following emergent argument: correctional officers work in intensely emotional environments, yet they are expected to keep their feelings to themselves.

Striking examples such as these are not only *found* through coding, but also can be purposefully *made* through a **constructed vignette** approach. A vignette is "a focused description of a series of events taken to be representative, typical, or emblematic" (Miles & Huberman, 1994, p. 81). Vignettes are similar to exemplars in that they exemplify a key argument or claim. They are different in that the researcher (re) constructs the example by purposefully collecting and piecing together data (rather than by *finding* the exemplar intact within the data). Of course, there is a large gray area between "finding" and "constructing." Oftentimes exemplars are heavily edited from interviews and fieldnotes, which makes them appear very different from their "raw" form. However, the constructed vignette is clearly "made" by purposefully collecting retroactive thick descriptions of an event or issue. The researcher chooses the situation to be described, and then asks one or more participants to discuss aspects, such as (Miles & Huberman, 1994, p. 81):

- the context;
- their hopes;
- who was involved;
- what they did;
- what happened as a result;
- what the impact was;
- why this happened;
- expectations for the future, predictions, what was learned, etc.

To illustrate how one might construct a vignette, let us consider for a moment the argument offered above: *correctional officers work in intensely emotional environments, yet they are expected to keep their feelings to themselves.* To support this argument, I could have constructed a vignette by interviewing two or three people directly about inmate take-downs. A correctional officer, and perhaps also a supervisor and an inmate, could have offered a description coming from each of their points of view. From these data a vignette could be created that described a take-down, typical things that correctional officers and inmates say during a take-down, and the facility administrators' reaction when a correctional officer feels stressed out about this type of incident.

Although using exemplars and vignettes is very powerful and these are common parts of qualitative data analysis, I also offer some warnings. In constructing vignettes, researchers literally put words in the participants' mouths; hence researchers must ensure that these words ethically belong there (Miles & Huberman 1994). Furthermore, the persuasive story-telling of these approaches can miss the distinction between chronology and causality (Sayer, 1992) – an issue that can be ameliorated through comparative data analysis (I describe it in more detail below). Finally, it's tempting to pull out only the most sensational incidents or unique exemplars. But exemplars can just as easily be mundane and typical. For instance, common and oft-repeated jokes may serve as wonderful exemplars in an analysis – showing the values and taken-for-granted assumptions of a certain group.

This is not to say that you should exclude exemplars that illustrate outlying or unique data. As discussed in relation to sampling in Chapter 7, qualitative researchers may purposefully seek out, or be presented with, "extreme" data. Shawna Malvini Redden (in press) was in the middle of conducting an ethnographic study of airport stress and anxiety in 2011, when she just happened to fly Southwest Flight 812 – a plane that blew a hole in its roof and had to make an emergency landing. You can bet Shawna knew that the data she collected during and after this horrific experience would likely make their way into an exemplar some day, illustrating the complexity of airline passenger stress, anxiety, and coping.

You, too, might be in the midst of data collection and just feel in your gut, "Yes! This situation (or story) perfectly sums up my analysis." If this is the case, it is still important to carefully code these data and perhaps engage in negative case analysis – purposefully seeking out data that would refute your emergent argument. There is a difference between exemplars – which exemplify many codes emergent in the analysis –

and outliers, which may be interesting but represent a datum that diverges from the primary meanings in the remaining data. If you are presenting outliers, your reader needs to understand this too.

Developing typologies

Another common qualitative analysis technique is the **typology**. A typology is a classificatory system for ways of doing something. For example, a typology for domestic chores might include (a) lawn work; (b) childcare; and (c) cleaning. And each of these could be broken down according to its own typology; for instance lawn work includes activities like (a) mowing; (b) shoveling; (c) raking; (d) weeding; (e) trimming; and (f) gardening. The concept of constructing a typology should be familiar, given the discussion in Chapter 7 of interview questions that elicit typologies and the explanation in Chapter 9 of second-cycle categorizing, where smaller codes are lumped together under a larger hierarchical code.

To develop a typology, researchers identify or interpretively construct a conceptual "big bin" and then connect it with "smaller" concepts, ideas, processes, or *types* that are related and hence fit into this conceptual bin. Examples of typologies could feature an endless range of topics:

- ways of being socialized into a role;
- types of technology used in this social network;
- ways in which gender issues are made salient in this organization;
- ways in which family members are motivated/frustrated;
- methods of self-disclosing in romantic relationships;
- types of idealized images of this profession;
- types of organizational rituals.

I encourage researchers to come up with their own potential typologies. The options are endless.

Typologies may make up a mere subset of an analysis. One typology used in our 911 research was "types of nicknames given to people who call 911." By identifying and grouping together the nicknames that call-takers used for callers – such as schizoid, screamer, hystero, and prankster – the typology supported the emerging argument that call-taker talk constructs an "us/them" mentality. This was one small slice of the emerging analysis.

Typologies can also frame an entire study. Orbe and Allen (2008), for instance, created a typology as an analysis framework for understanding how matters of race were studied and articulated in articles published in the *Journal of Applied Communication Research* (*JACR*) over the course of 22 years. Considering past critical feminist research as well as the *JACR* articles, the authors created a race scholarship typology of six different genres of race scholarship.

Their analysis illustrated that most *JACR* articles were associated with a genre called "white scholarship," which universalizes the white racial experience. They named another common genre as "white compensatory" scholarship; this one acknowledged the importance of race scholarship, but only in some contexts. They also noted a *lack* of articles that analyzed how "experiences of people of color and Whites are multidimensional, similar and different, and inextricably linked" (p. 206), and they named it "multifocal–relational" race research.

Orbe and Allen's typological analysis not only illustrates the way race is portrayed in *JACR*, but also provides a theoretical framework for future race research (see Isaksen, 2011). Such an analysis is only possible through interpretive creativity about typological categories and classification.

Dramatistic strategy

Kenneth Burke (1945) introduced the **dramatistic pentad** as a tool for analyzing how speakers persuade audience members to accept their view of reality as true. To fully appreciate Burke requires a lot of reading, but one quick way to relate to Burke is to consider Shakespeare's famous quotation "All the world's a stage, and all the men and women merely players." Burke views drama as the natural human condition, and the pentad offers a powerful way of analyzing the actors, action, and scenes in it.

The pentad is made up of the five elements of human drama (see Figure 10.2).

Burke's pentad is a useful analysis tool, encouraging researchers to seek data and pay attention to:

1   Act: What happened? What is going on? What are people saying and doing?
2   Scene: Where and when is the act happening? What is the background context? What happened right before and after the act?
3   Agent: Who or what is involved in performing or construing the action? Who are the actors?
4   Agency: By what means, methods, or tools did the agents act?
5   Purpose: What were the goals and motivations of the action? Why did the agents act in this way?

The dramatistic pentad offers an especially worthwhile strategy when you analyze several parallel scenes of action in different contexts. For example, you could use it to compare television-viewing behavior in a dormitory every year over the course of ten years, or to examine conflict in staff meetings across ten different organizations. The corresponding acts, agents, types of agency, and purposes (of television viewing or conflict) could fruitfully be compared over a long time or acoss different contexts.

The pentad also serves as a powerful way to map out interview data. For instance Meisenbach, Remke, Buzzannell, and Liu (2008) used Burke's pentad to better understand the progress of organizations regarding maternity leave; this is summarized in Table 10.1, which I constructed on the basis of their arguments:

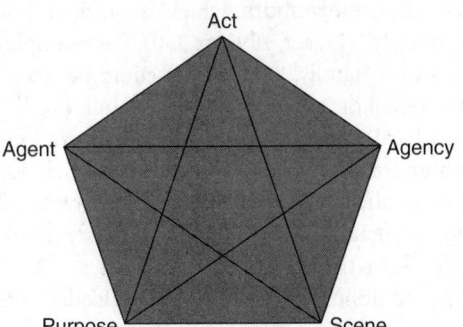

Figure 10.2 Burke's dramatistic pentad offers a powerful way of analyzing the actors, action, and scenes in the data. Courtesy of Pr. S. Wells. Reproduced from http://2009medicalrhetoric.pbworks.com/ 2009+Workshop+on+Medical+Rhetoric+- Tool+for+Theoretical+and+Archival+Research+ (SW) (accessed April 2012).

Table 10.1 Burke's dramatistic pentad offers an analysis tool for better understanding how organizations regard maternity leave.

Burke's Pentadic Element	How women talked about maternity leave in their interviews	A more progressive (but missing) way of conceptualizing maternity leave
Act	Their maternity leaves as being set up by others	Establishing and arranging maternity leaves
Agents	By human relations departments, bosses and doctors	By the mother along with the organization's representative
Agency	Through written policy	Through discussion
Scene	Within bureaucratic organizations	Within the home and organization
Purpose	In order to control and regulate maternity leaves	In order to negotiate effective and just maternity leaves

By using Burke's pentad, Meisenbach and her colleagues (2008) compared individual cases across the group of interviews and identified what was present as well as what was missing in the data.

Metaphor analysis

Most of us were introduced to metaphors in high school English class, where they were presented as a rhetorical strategy for dressing up speeches or papers. However, metaphors do more than just embellish language. **Metaphors** compare one thing (e.g. a classroom) to another (e.g. to a party, a competition, or a prison), and in doing so provide a vivid picture of how we are experiencing the scene (Lakoff & Johnson, 1980). We use metaphors regularly, usually without even thinking about it. In consequence, they are abundant in almost all types of textual data like interviews, documents, and fieldnotes.

Metaphors differ in their level of creative complexity. "Dead" or "dormant" metaphors are not even heard as metaphors, because they are so common (Grant & Oswick, 1996). For example, although "teeth of a saw" compares the saw's small sharp points to "teeth," those little points are usually called nothing but "teeth," so the metaphor is "dead": it has become literal and is not all that interesting to interpret.

Most researchers are interested in identifying **live metaphors**, which "require both a context and a certain creativity to interpret adequately" (Fraser, 1993, p. 330). For example, an organization could be like a "machine" or like a "family," and a boss could be like a "cheerleader" or like a "drill sergeant." These live metaphors conjure pictures and interpretive frameworks; the machine metaphor suggests a hard, cold, and productive organization, whereas the family metaphor invokes warmth and control from the head of household. A "cheerleader" metaphor suggests that the boss offers encouragement but may afford lower status by comparison to other organizational "main players," whereas a "drill sergeant" may get results, but he frightens new "recruits." In these examples you can see how metaphors create vibrant pictures and suggest additional metaphors ("cheerleader" → "main player," and "drill sergeant" → "recruit").

Through metaphor analysis, you might identify that your research participants are consistently framing their community as a "war zone" complete with "good little soldiers," "casualties," and "ticking time bombs." Notice how these metaphors sediment meaning in very particular ways, and how these meanings influence future action. If these participants who see their community as a "war zone" face alienated employees, they are likely to "rally the troops." However, it may be that "rallying" (bringing to order) is the last thing the "troops" (employees) need.

In other words, the "war zone" metaphor may not be sufficient for solving the problems at hand. As the researcher, you might suggest that an alternative metaphor might help participants see their options for action in a novel manner. The metaphor of community as an "organism" could bring to mind notions of health, nurturance, and symbiosis. Viewing the community as an organism suggests that "cultivating," "humoring," or "entertaining" the "stakeholders" is better than "rallying the troops." This is not to say that the "organism" metaphor is necessarily better than that of "war zone." However, different metaphors offer different possibilities for action, and an action that seems obvious in one scene may seem impossible in the other, and vice versa.

So how do you go about conducting a metaphor analysis? On the one hand, you can directly ask respondents to name metaphors – this would be something called a **forced metaphor approach** – by asking an interview question such as: "Can you provide a metaphor for what your community feels like?" However, if you ask this question, be prepared for furrowed brows. Even though metaphors are ubiquitous, most people are unclear as to what metaphors actually are (Sheenan, Barker, & McCarthy, 2004). And, even if your participants understand metaphors conceptually, people have trouble coming up with metaphoric utterances spontaneously and might just offer ones that are obvious and overused.

Alternatively, researchers can develop a list of metaphors fixed in advance and ask participants to rank them ("Would you say your community is a machine, a war zone, an organism, a patchwork quilt, or a family? Why?"). Providing a list like this circumvents the issue of "I can't think of a metaphor," but your deductive list might omit *in vivo* metaphors in use. Perhaps their community is most like a "garden" – a metaphor missing from the offered list.

Many qualitative researchers believe that the richest way to analyze metaphors is through an **idiographic approach**, which analyzes inductively metaphors that organically occur in the data (Grant & Oswick, 1996). In their everyday talk, correctional officers, for instance, offered a rich variety of metaphors to describe themselves. Among other things, they likened themselves to "professional babysitters," "glorified flight attendants," and "the scum of law enforcement" (Tracy, 2005). Researchers can also analyze the data and interpretively construct a metaphor that sums them up. For instance, when we heard targets of workplace bullying discuss their abuse in terms of having to "get over" and "suck up" a "whole line of garbage" (Tracy, Lutgen-Sandvik, & Alberts, 2006, p. 165), we created the metaphor of workplace as a "noxious substance." This constructed metaphor helped us articulate the fact that abused workers feel as though bullying poisons multiple areas of their lives.

I encourage you to identify, construct, and make meaning of metaphors in your own data. Doing so may serve as a primary analysis framework, or it can bolster some very interesting interpretations that emerge through other analysis approaches.

Visual data displays

Qualitative researchers rack up hundreds, sometimes thousands of pages of text. So how do you make sense of it? One way is through visual display. Indeed, according to

Miles & Huberman (1994), "You know what you can display" (p. 91). They believe that pages upon pages of extended, unreduced qualitative text are cumbersome and almost impossible to work from until they are situated in a table, a matrix, a network, or a flowchart. As they note: "There are many reports of anguish of trying to write text from an undisplayed database of hundreds of pages. By contrast, well-formatted displays, with data entries in which you have confidence, make writing an easier, faster, more pleasurable and productive experience" (pp. 100–101). Even if you are not convinced that data displays are the antidote for qualitative anguish, most researchers find that creating a display is another useful layer of analyzing and thinking creatively about the data.

This book has already introduced several types of data displays – including the contact information log and the participant information table (Researcher's Notepad 4.1 and Table 4.6) and the codebook (Researcher's Notepad 9.2). Data displays can take the form of a table, a list, a flowchart, or a model. Data displays help you to summarize and compare findings; to track chronology, causation, or plot; and to visualize the relationship among various concepts. Miles and Huberman (1994, p. 92) say that they also

show key data and analyses together in one small space;
help the analyst identify where further analyses or data are needed;
ease the comparison of data across contexts or data sets;
encourage the use of some version of the display in a final report.

One of the most common types of data display is the table or matrix. A **table** includes headings, with corresponding information below them, in columns. A **matrix** goes one step further; it is a two-by-two display with headings across both the top and the side. One is not necessarily better than another. Form follows function.

An in-process analysis table associated with my correctional officer research is pictured in Researcher's Notepad 10.1. I developed this display *after* several cycles of coding and writing analysis outlines. It organized the central themes and findings emerging from 722 pages of fieldnotes, documents, and interview transcripts. The columns attend to different research questions (e.g. "What are the organizational emotion norms?" or "What emotional work is done to uphold this norm?").

Tables such as the one in Researcher's Notepad 10.1 are instrumental for getting your head around the detail and expanse of the data. They may go through iteration after iteration, helping organize the data and highlight missing data (e.g. several of the cells are empty, which suggests data that still needs to be collected and analyzed). A table such as this one is helpful for communicating and procuring feedback from peers and mentors about the emerging analysis. I personally kept this table at my elbow as I drafted the dissertation, checking off various cells as I wrote. Additionally, early tables like this one provide a guiding framework from which you can later create simpler, more streamlined displays that are useful to the reader.

Indeed, Researcher's Notepad 10.2 pictures a two-by-two matrix that made it into the final research report. This matrix is much cleaner and easier to understand than the big and messy table. Providing data displays in the final report allows the reader to re-create and have confidence in the intellectual journey of the analysis. The display helps clarify and supplement the narrative text. Indeed, most of us learn differently from reading a description and from seeing a visual. And, as I discuss in Chapter 13, a variety of visual displays can enhance a written report.

Table for organizing dissertation findings

Organizational Norm	Organizational Norm in Conflict	Emotion Work to Uphold Norm 1	Emotion Work to Uphold Org Norm in Conflict	Discursive Construction/ Emotional Construction	Paradoxes Resulting from these Conflicting Norm/Emotion Work Cycles
Be nice/ friendly/ rehabilitative to inmates 1 Treat inmates with respect 2 Listen to inmates and empathize with them 3 Treat them just as you would an officer – give them responsibility	**Be custodial and don't be nice/friendly with inmates** 1 Don't be sucked in (read, inmates will always lie) 2 Don't get personal; be professional 3 You are not their friend	1 Act empathetic 2 Being a glorified flight attendant 3 Calling inmates by titles 4 The babysitting metaphor	1 Maintaining tough performances 2 Talking themselves out of being empathetic 3 Making fun of inmates 4 The scum metaphor	1 An us/them mentality (resulting in emotional suppression) 2 Wary of all inmates – (which results in thinking inmates are stupid and in making fun, which then makes rehabilitation difficult) 3 Frustration of no rehabilitation – feeling like a failure 4 Feeling powerless 5 Doubting their own job (this job sucks) 6 Celebrate when they win and inmates lose	1 Paradox: Trusting inmates (which you're not supposed to do) is only way to know what's going on 2 Be kind by not being kind 3 Be rehabilitative within an organizational structure that doesn't allow for rehabilitation 4 Respect inmates even though the justification for almost all officer duties is lack of respect and trust
Be Flexible 1 Participate 2 Think; use common sense 3 Don't be "write-up happy"	**Follow rules** 1 Follow the rules 2 Follow procedure about writing people up 3 Follow procedure	1 Dealing with arbitrary and random administrative sanctions for not following the rules	1 Appearing firm, fair, and consistent 2 Enforcing rules they don't agree with	1 Becoming unquestioning 2 Confusion/ frustration about what to do when 3 Becoming cold/ matter of fact in regard to organizational expectations 4 Guilt of upholding rules not agreed with	1 Follow the rules when they benefit the administration, which you know nothing about 2 Do your job as the rules dictate, but to do so is to become an unlikeable person
Rely on fellow workers; admin. and family 1 Rely on other officers on back-up calls 2 We have an open-door policy 3 Talk to your family about work 4 Make use of organization counseling	**Don't expect social support from fellow workers, admin or family** 1 Inform on other officers 2 Don't bring in personal problems to work – don't be needy 3 Leave work at work and home at home			1 Feeling stigmatized if they talk too much about problems – because then they're slipping into becoming like an inmate	1 Talk to admin/ be open with admin within an organizational structure that highly discourages it 2 Use medical counseling but be ready to be stigmatized for it

RESEARCHER'S NOTEPAD 10.2

Matrix display

Officer emotion labor strategies and unintended emotional consequences.

Organizational Tension	Emotion Labor Strategies	Unintended Emotional Consequences
Respect↔Suspect	Not learning details of case Being care free and laid back Framing stress as fun Story telling of crafty inmates	Officer complacency Bitterness of having to respect Joy in inmate misfortune Us/them mentality
Nurture↔Discipline	Framing themselves as societal saviors Pride in being different Not taking things personally Leaving work at work	Guilt for not helping enough Embarrassment about the job Becoming cold and unfeeling
Consistency↔Flexibility	Devising creative solutions Being strict	Paranoia Literalism/simplistic thinking Feeling disliked/badge-happy
Solidarity↔Autonomy	Choosing not to trust Choosing to trust	Confusion over who to trust Feeling weak and stigmatized Camaraderie among officers
Overall Emotional Constructions		Mistrust/Paranoia Withdrawal

Source: Tracy, 2001, p. 266

So how do you create a matrix or a table? Begin with a specific research question (e.g. "What are the rules for interaction in this context?") and consider the extent to which different groupings of data could be compared in terms of this research question (participants? contexts? time periods? types of data? emergent codes?). Then create relevant headings (e.g. "rules for interaction" might be a column heading, and different groups of participants might be the row heading). Figuring out the relevant headings is an interpretively rigorous task. However, it's easier than the next part.

Entering the relevant information in the cells takes time and intellectual creativity – and the matrix is only as good as the data within it. As you enter data, balance the importance of detail with limiting the literal size of the matrix. On the one hand, detailed entries are important for understanding the display's meaning. On the other hand, the point of a display is to help you, your co-researchers or assistants, and ultimately your reader understand a large breadth of data. I recommend that you try to fit your entire display onto a single document (even if that "document" covers an entire whiteboard). This means you probably want to avoid more than four to five headings in most tables.

Finally, pay attention to cells in which data is missing. Missing data serve as a clue that either the heading is inappropriate or you have stumbled upon an interesting invisibility in the data being studied, which might say something remarkable or unique about the context or the participants. Most likely, though, an empty cell visually cues the need for more data to flesh out the emerging analysis. Indeed, creating a cell-like display can help guard against false chronologies that are nearly invisible in the practice of narrative (or story-telling) alone.

In addition to tables and matrices, **flowcharts** can also be very helpful for making sense of qualitative data – both in the analysis and at the writing stage. Flowcharting evolved from engineering and the hard sciences to help simplify problem-solving processes. Tips and Tools 10.1 pictures a flowchart that tracks the iterative qualitative data analysis process narratively described in Chapter 9. I should point out that the very process of creating this flowchart suggested helpful ways I should modify earlier textual discussion – and indeed, as I constructed it, I went back to Chapter 9 and made a number of clarifications. In this way, flowcharting is not just about representing data; it is itself a helpful analysis and writing tool.

In Tips and Tools 10.1 and Figure 10.3 I use some of the most common flowcharting symbols (a web search on "flowchart symbols" will pull up a comprehensive list). Ovals are used to signify the beginning or ending of a process; arrows relate to the flow of logic; rectangles relate to a practice to be carried out; flattened hexagons refer to preparatory practices; and diamonds indicate decisions that must be made in order to progress.

This flowchart graphically streamlines the iterative data analysis process, but it also makes it appear simpler and much more linear than in the description offered in Chapter 9. Indeed, in reflecting upon this flowchart, friend and colleague Loril Gossett remarked – only half in jest: "If you're trying to illustrate the qualitative data analysis process, wouldn't an intricate maze be more accurate – illustrating all the dead ends and necessary backtracking?" Loril – also a qualitative expert (Gossett, 2006) – makes a good point. Flowcharts have the advantages of being memorable and encouraging to those intimidated by analysis ("You can do analysis in just a few easy steps!"), but they can also promote a myth of simplicity ("If it's really that easy, then anyone can do it!").

If you are interested in data displays, Miles and Huberman (1994) provide an exhaustive discussion. In addition to tables and matrices, they explain and illustrate the following different displays: network maps that show the interrelationships among various roles and groups (for instance they can resemble organizational hierarchical charts); time-ordered displays that track the chronological and historical flow of events; role-ordered charts that sort data by a certain set of actors and their actions in various settings (for example by answering a research question such as: "How do these three groups react differently to a variety of actions X, Y, and Z?"); and effects matrixes that track how a certain issue or intervention impacted various participant groups or contexts.

The possibilities for visual displays are endless, and I encourage you to tinker with them. One of the most fun and easy ways to perform a data display is by constructing word clouds (check out for instance the website www.wordle.net). Word clouds (like the one pictured in the next chapter, in Researcher's Notepad 11.1) graphically show the most influential words in a certain text, and therefore they may help serve as a method of analysis and display. You simply copy and paste a certain excerpt of text (whether that be an entire interview, data that relates to a certain category, a scholarly article, or something

Flowchart depicting iterative analysis process

Figure 10.3 This flowchart visually depicts the analysis process described in Chapter 9.

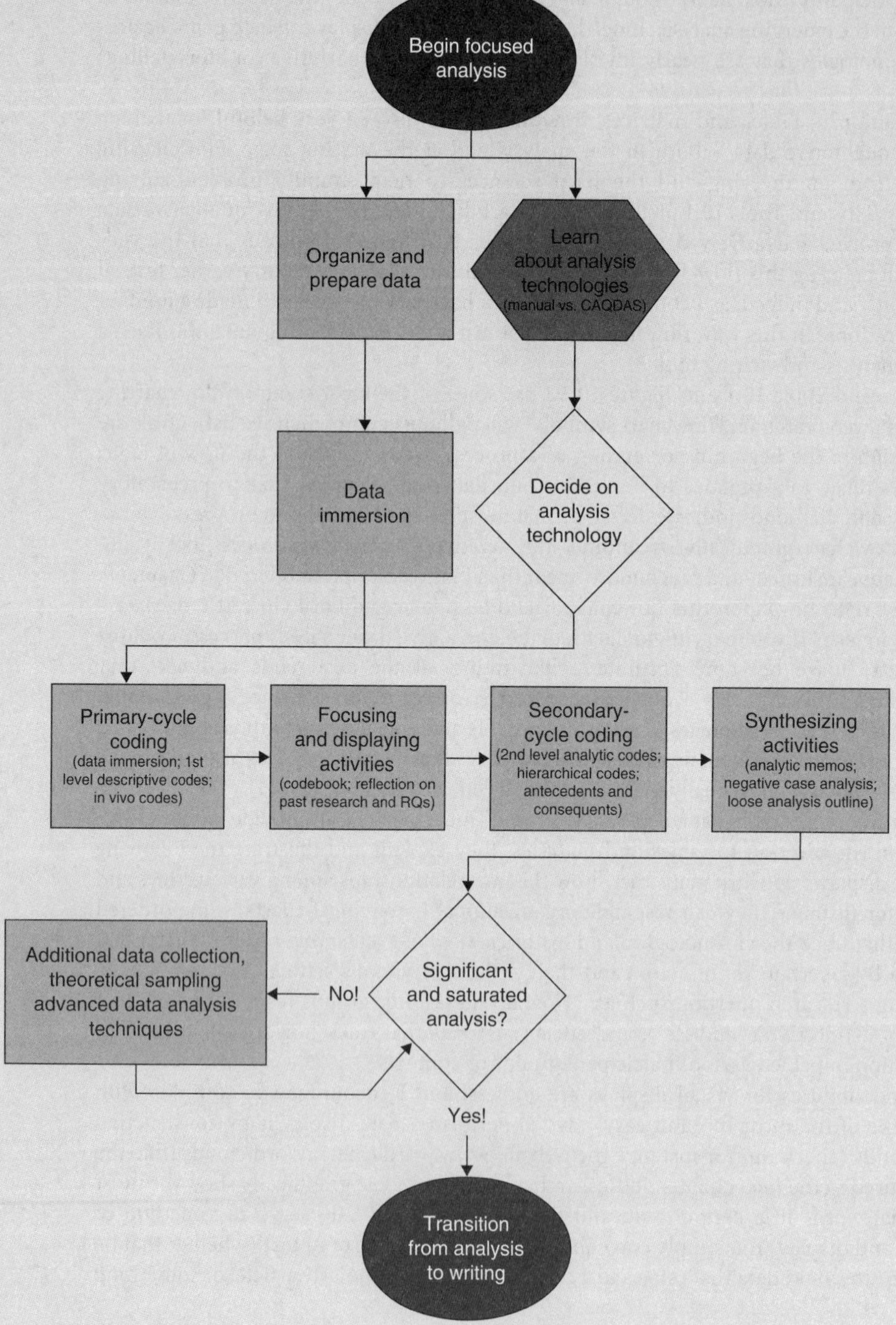

Begin focused analysis

Organize and prepare data

Learn about analysis technologies (manual vs. CAQDAS)

Data immersion

Decide on analysis technology

Primary-cycle coding (data immersion; 1st level descriptive codes; in vivo codes)

Focusing and displaying activities (codebook; reflection on past research and RQs)

Secondary-cycle coding (2nd level analytic codes; hierarchical codes; antecedents and consequents)

Synthesizing activities (analytic memos; negative case analysis; loose analysis outline)

Additional data collection, theoretical sampling advanced data analysis techniques

No!

Significant and saturated analysis?

Yes!

Transition from analysis to writing

else), and the software provides you with a word cloud that can be tinkered with in all kinds of graphically appealing ways. You might use word clouds to visualize the most influential terms in your emerging project (or in different slices of the data) – a process that stimulates further analysis and data collection. Alternatively, word clouds make fantastic visuals for papers, posters, or websites.

Most data displays go through multiple iterations, so don't aim for perfection. Furthermore, if you're not great at computer graphics, start sketching something by hand. Or check out the modeling functions available in many CAQDAS programs. Make lots of versions, date the old ones, and keep them in a file so you can see their progression over time. Toying with a visual display triggers a different part of your brain than writing prose, providing an avenue for interpretive creativity that can enhance almost any qualitative data analysis.

Explanation and causality

Qualitative data are not only excellent for answering the question "What is going on here?" but are also poised to answer questions of "Why?" and "How come?" Analyzing for causality provides valuable findings related to prediction, action, and change. Furthermore, many funded qualitative research projects aim to explain how certain interventions result in desired outcomes.

Unfortunately, too many researchers erroneously believe that qualitative data are not sufficient for explanation and that generating causal explanations requires a controlled experiment or quantitative structural equation modeling (Light, Singer, and Willett, 1990). Granted, qualitative data analysis is not designed to generate universal laws causally linking together decontextualized independent variables. However, most qualitative researchers are not interested in proposing general laws, but are rather focused on generating explanations of contextualized activity – and rich qualitative data are extremely valuable for such purposes.

Indeed, Maxwell (2004) argues that field research is far *better* than solely quantified approaches at developing explanations about **local causality** – which consists of the local events and processes that have led to specific outcomes in a specific context (Miles & Huberman 1994). For example, questions such as "How did a series of marital disputes lead to this couple's divorce?" or "Why are some teachers more successful than others at helping students to learn at this school?" or "How did this unfair workplace policy come to be interpreted as normal?" are questions of local causality.

Qualitative research, especially narratives and case analyses, is well poised for locally causal questions because it examines processes *in situ* – it elucidates "the actual connections between events and the complex interaction of causal processes in a specific context" (Maxwell, 2004, p. 256). Using a number of examples for illustration, Katz (2001, 2002) shows how qualitative data, especially when they are luminous and compelling, show not only *how* certain phenomena unfold, but *why* social life takes the forms we observe. Rich and varied data light the path for causal explanation, facilitating the ability to identify key explanations and to exclude competing theories (Katz, 2001).

Understanding causal connections requires the researcher to link antecedents (what happened before) and consequents (what happened after). Many researchers begin this process in their analytic memos (writing about the contexts in which certain issues arose, the ways various issues interrelate, and the outcomes of key issues). Several other systematic practices are also helpful for analyzing chronology and causality.

A fundamental analysis practice is to bring in the question of time. Take a look at your emergent codes and at how they overlap or co-occur. Play with a hypothesis such as "X; then Y happens" and see what data emerge to support this hypothesis. For instance, in a research study on family dinners with the emergent codes "PARENTAL DISCIPLINE" and "CHILDREN NOT EATING THEIR FOOD," a potential hypothesis could be:

X: Parental discipline at dinnertime
Y: Encourages children to not eat their food.

After examining data that might support this claim, the claim should be turned around and examined the other way (Y; then X):

Y: Children not eating their food
X: Encourages parental discipline at dinnertime.

Both of these claims make sense on their face. Hence it is important to see whether both are true, or whether the data support one more than another. It may also be that the two issues (X and Y) are just co-occurring (in other words they are linked by **correlation** rather than causation):

Children not eating and parental discipline at dinnertime often co-occur.

In such a case, you should go back to the data and examine specific (inter)actions that would link the two together in certain ways. For example, perhaps these two phenomena only co-occur when guests or visitors are present, or if it is after 8 p.m. (For a research study that qualitatively examines the effects of work–life and dinnertime battles, see Paugh and Izquierdo, 2009.)

If you are interested in examining and verifying causality, participant observation data and immersion over time is crucial. Ideally, begin playing with hypotheses relating to potential causal links while you are still in the field, so you can go back and specifically collect data about them as well as look for counterfactual evidence through negative case analyses. In the example above, for instance, you might specifically try to compare these issues using the criteria of who is present and at what time dinner is served.

Indeed, making predictions about "why" is greatly enhanced through the use of comparative data – the same event either at two different times or in two different places (Katz, 2001). Comparative evidence addresses how a certain phenomenon progressed both *with* and *without* the presence of different issues and outcomes. Drawing on one's direct experience of other cases can make it easier to "identify the relevant causal processes in an exceptional case" (Maxwell, 2004, p. 253). For instance, in the dinnertime example, the researcher could examine cases in which parental discipline (X) and children not eating (Y) are *both* evident and compare them to cases in which these issues manifest themselves in dissociation from each other (e.g. where dinnertime discipline (X) is *absent* or is linked to *contrasting evidence*, such as of children eating more (Z)). Multi-site and multi-case analyses are not the only way to draw comparisons. Examining existing literature and data about 'typical' settings or individuals of the type studied can also yield such comparisons.

Generating causal explanations of a scene can also be strengthened and verified through member reflections. You might create a flowchart and/or a narrative about the process, present it to participants, and ask for their feedback about the linkages and explanations proposed. In this process you could also design interventions (e.g. "Parents, I encourage you to begin dinner with some lively self-disclosures about your own day and with non-threatening questions for your children, rather than disciplining them at the table"). You can then make predictions that are based upon your hypotheses (e.g. "In families that attend to my recommendation, children will eat more of their vegetables") and investigate how they evolve. In addition to these general tips, researchers interested in causality might consider an emerging qualitative data analysis approach called discourse tracing.

Discourse tracing

Complex data sets sometimes require complex tools for their analysis. The method of **discourse tracing** is specifically designed for qualitative researchers who want to analyze critically data from multiple structural levels regarding events or situations that *change over time* (LeGreco & Tracy, 2009). Topics prime for understanding change through discourse tracing include policy change; the succession of a leader; militaristic action; relational turning points; new technologies; or a natural disaster. However, various parts of discourse tracing can be used even if you are not interested in change, but you want to analyze the ways different levels of discourse influence one another (e.g. see Way, 2012).

At the micro level, discourse tracers examine everyday fleeting talk and interactions – both in the form of what is said and in the form of what is left unsaid. At the meso level, discourse tracers collect mid-level formal policies and procedures (which are often documented on websites or training sessions/manuals), as well as patterns of behavior sanctioned by some type of formal authority (Way, 2012). Then, at the macro level, discourse tracers consider larger laws, societal myths, and enduring ideologies that are visible in the form of popular culture artifacts and articulated in the media. The analysis focuses on how these different levels of discourse interact with one another as a process; specifically, it studies how these discourses are formed, interpreted, adopted, used, and appropriated by various audiences. An unpublished example of micro, meso, and macro sources from Malvini Redden's (in press) airport research is found in Researcher's Notepad 10.3.

An example of a research question appropriate for discourse tracing is the following: How has the experience of airport security lines changed since the terrorist attacks of September 11, 2001? To attend to this question, appropriate micro-level data might include interviews with passengers and security personnel about airport security procedures before and after 9/11, media reports over the years about what counts as a security breach, and observing security lines today (Malvini Redden, in press). Appropriate meso-level data would be various airports' policies about security and repeated rules of the type "take off your shoes," and analysis could compare these admonitions among themselves. Finally, macro-level data could be federal laws, policies, or procedures related to the Transportation Security Administration (TSA) and consideration of the impact of societal myths and ideologies on security line behavior (e.g. "good passengers are compliant passengers").

Discourse tracing evolves through several analysis steps. First, researchers identify a "rupture" or turning point in the data. In the example above, the September 11 terrorist attacks and the resulting creation of the Department of Homeland Security and TSA serve as the rupture point. However, the rupture need not be so dramatic. For instance, a researcher interested in family dinner rituals might identify a rupture/turning point as the moment in which a formerly "at-home" parent began full-time public employment. The researcher could then examine how dinner rituals changed due to the parent's new employment.

Step two of discourse tracing is gathering together all of the micro, meso, and macro data and ordering it chronologically. As mentioned in Chapter 9, the method of organizing

RESEARCHER'S NOTEPAD 10.3

Micro, meso, macro sources

Shawna Malvini Redden (in press) was interested in the ways micro, meso, and macro sources affected airport security lines policed by the US Transportation Security Administration (TSA). What follows is just a sampling of her sources.

Analysis Level	Data Type	Data Sources
Macro	Formal Texts	Directives from the Department of Homeland Security
	Supplemental Texts	Transportation Security Administration Policies
	Media Sources	*CNN, MSNBC, New York Times*
	Pop Culture Texts	Blogs like *The Cranky Flier*; the film *Up in the Air*
Meso	Formal Texts	TSA policies/signage/directives for passengers
	Participant Observations	Security procedures in practice, TSA training
Micro	Localized Texts	Individual airport policies, signage, photos
	Participant Observations	My personal travel in airports
	Formal Interviews	65 interviews (half employees, half passengers)
	Informal Interviews	50 conversations (mix of employees and passengers)

qualitative data has significant ramifications for its analysis. Ordering the data chronologically is indispensable for detecting the emergence of social processes across time and context. Chronology also helps discourse tracers document "what's there," "what's *not* there," as well as how practices change or become routinized over time. It may become evident, for instance, that certain meso-level policies ("Everyone must take off their shoes to go through airport security") negatively impact everyday micro-practices (this policy might produce grumbling passengers, or an unsafe back-up of security lines). This might help the researcher see how the policy actually works against intended macro-level structures (e.g. that the TSA was designed to help improve, not jeopardize airport security and efficiency). Additionally, a chronology allows researchers to see how some entities (e.g. the potential terrorist) are privileged as more influential than others (e.g. sporadic travelers), and where there may be possibilities for change.

Step three of discourse tracing asks researchers to consider how certain outcomes were affected, impacted, or constrained by particular policies, decision points, or practices along the way. To do this, discourse tracers iteratively consider past research and emergent codes (as in the analysis process described in Chapter 9) and create **structured questions** designed to lift specific answers from the data. This use of structured questions is different from that of grounded approaches, in which themes emerge through multiple readings. Discourse tracers use the multiple readings and codes in order to purposefully devise questions to ask of the data. Such an approach is clearly iterative – it begins with emergent readings of the data, but then it asks questions that will be laid on top of the data, in an etic fashion. For instance the researcher might ask and seek out answers in the data to questions such as: "How does fear motivate security?" "What rationales are given for airport security policies?" "How do these transform over time?" Discourse tracing asks the researcher to view the data set as a text that can be systematically questioned. As such, structured questions ask questions of all the data.

Let us return to the everyday dinner example, to produce further illustrations. If you were examining the dinner rituals of ten different families, you might compare and contrast every single family or, alternatively, group them in some meaningful way (e.g. conservative religious families; liberal–activist families; indifferent families). A structured question at the micro level might ask: "What are this family's dinnertime routines?" (The answer to this could be found in participant observation and interview data.) A structured question at the meso level might be: "What are the parents' philosophies about gender roles?" (The answer to this might be found by examining the doctrines or common practices of their religious or activist groups.) And a structured question at the macro level might be: "How does society portray ideal parenting decisions revolving around dinnertime?" (The answer to this could be found by analyzing the advertisements or television shows watched by the family, and how these programs promoted certain family roles and dinnertime expectations.)

Discourse tracing is especially well poised for researchers who are:

1   working with multi-level (micro, meso, and macro) data;
2   comparing various contexts or cases; and
3   interested in change over time.

However, discourse tracing techniques such as chronological ordering and structured questions can be helpful even if you are not dealing with this level of complexity. Structured questions, for instance, need not refer to multiple levels of discourse; and they can be useful even when you are examining a single body of data rather than making comparisons across different cases. If you are interested in discourse tracing, I highly encourage you to access additional resources (e.g. LeGreco & Tracy, 2009; Way, 2012).

FOLLOWING, THEN FORGETTING THE RULES

Despite the systematic analysis practices reported herein, researchers often feel stymied when asked to describe transparently how they analyzed their data. And, ironically, it may be the most expert qualitative analyzers who have the greatest difficulty in articulating their data analysis decisions. Flyvbjerg goes so far as to say:

> Researchers do not need to be able to formulate rules for their skills in order to practice them with success. [...] There is nothing which indicates that researchers at the expert level [...] use context-independent rules in their best scientific performances, even though they might depict it as such when they get around to writing their scholarly articles or memoirs. (Flyvbjerg, 2001, p. 34)

Indeed analysis is a creative and messy process – one in which researchers attempt to harness their instincts and hunches, so that they may come to significant, or even groundbreaking insights about the data. DeGooyer (2003) identifies these ephemeral moments as "poignant organizing episodes" in which various strains of inquiry come together to transform the direction of the analysis. The type of iterative data analysis practiced by qualitative researchers includes a range of tacit skills that are extremely difficult to put into words. They are skills that are learned through experience.

In summary

This chapter reviewed techniques for advanced qualitative data analysis. It opened with a review of specifically designed computer-aided qualitative data analysis software and of how such software can help in systematically coding, querying, and building theory from qualitative data. The chapter then reviewed seven types of data analysis, namely (1) exemplars and vignettes; (2) typologies; (3) dramatistic approaches; (4) metaphor analyses; (5) visual data displays; (6) analyzing for explanation and causality; and (7) discourse tracing. Each of these approaches can frame an entire analysis. However, techniques from each of them can be used in almost any project. Furthermore, the approaches may provide creative inspiration, with a beginning and an end, during a process that sometimes feels never-ending.

In articulating these analysis approaches I tried to be as practical and concrete as possible, presenting best practices that lead to insightful interpretations. Exercise 10.1 provides a class assignment that encourages you to play with these analysis approaches. So now that you've read about them, it's time to practice them – and if you find yourself feeling like you're in a maze, with lots of dead ends and backtracking, know that you haven't taken a wrong turn. Analysis is not about finding the "one right path." Analysis is about playing, thinking, returning, and cycling through the maze enough times, and with enough creative attention, to be able to recognize a significant and interesting path along the way.

EXERCISE 10.1

Advanced data analysis/interpretation

1 Develop a table, matrix, or flow-chart. In a 2–3-page narrative, unpack this visual display. What types of explanations can you begin to make on the basis of the display? On the basis of the display and its accompanying narrative, discuss (in about one page) the data you still need to collect in order to better flesh out the matrix or the network.

2 Choose one or more of the creative analytic processes of metaphor analysis, exemplar/vignette analysis, typologies, or dramatistic approach. Then do a show and tell. *Show* how you applied the approach to your data – applying it to actual data. Then interpret how this approach helps to attend to interesting or significant meanings or to key research questions.

3 Play with causation. What are you finding in terms of "X; then Y" in your data? Turn it around: is "Y; then X" a better explanation? What evidence do you have to support your explanation? What types of additional data would be needed to falsify the claim (e.g. to do a negative case analysis)? What types of data would you need to bolster the claim? Across your own cases or by drawing from existing literature, what types of comparisons are available or can be arranged, in which one of the issues is absent or controlled?

4 Practice discourse tracing.

   a Briefly describe your case or research issue.

   b If applicable, define the case chronologically (using a rupture or turning point for guidance).

   c Describe data that connect to the issue – relating to the micro, meso, and macro levels of discourse.

   d If applicable and you are interested in change, order your data chronologically and read over.

   e Create 2–3 structured questions based on the literature and on emergent themes, and apply those questions to the data.

   f What do you know about the case now, through this process, that you didn't know before?

KEY TERMS

computer-aided qualitative data analysis software (CAQDAS) computer software that is specifically designed for sorting, coding, organizing, managing, and reconfiguring qualitative data also known as qualitative data analysis software (QDAS)

constructed vignette "a focused description of a series of events taken to be representative, typical, or emblematic" (Miles & Huberman, 1994, p. 81)

correlation non-causal relation between two variables or concepts (the two are associated, but one does not cause the other to occur)

discourse tracing a method designed for qualitative researchers who want to critically analyze data from multiple structural levels (micro, meso, macro) and how events or situations change over time (LeGreco & Tracy, 2009)

dramatistic pentad a tool introduced by Kenneth Burke, which asks researchers to pay attention to act, scene, agent, agency, and purpose in order to understand persuasion and action

exemplars significant examples capturing multiple codes that the researcher identifies in the data

flowcharts visual charts for displaying and making sense of qualitative data that include boxes and arrows

forced metaphor approach gathering metaphors from participants by directly asking them about the metaphors they use

→ **idiographic approach to metaphor analysis**   inductively analyzes metaphors that emerge from the data organically or naturally

→ **live metaphors**   metaphors that require both a context and a certain creativity to be adequately interpreted

→ **local causality**   a type of causality that suggests that local events can lead to specific outcomes. Qualitative research is well poised for elucidating connections between contextual events and causal processes

→ **matrix**   a visual data display that has headings across both the top and side – a two-by-two display

→ **metaphor**   a traditional figure of speech in which one thing is compared to another strictly speaking metaphors differ from comparisons (similes and analogies) in that the comparison is implicit in the former, explicit in the later. Metaphors provide a vivid picture of how we are thinking about the scene or experience

→ **structured questions**   a tactic of discourse tracing for querying the data text and lifting out specific answers

→ **table**   a visual data display that includes headings and the corresponding information, given below in columns

→ **typology**   a classification system for ways of doing something

CHAPTER 11

Qualitative quality
Creating a credible, ethical, significant study

Contents

Qualitative Research Methods: Collecting Evidence, Crafting Analysis, Communicating Impact, First Edition. Sarah J. Tracy.
© 2013 Sarah J. Tracy. Published 2013 by Blackwell Publishing Ltd.

Potential audiences for qualitative work include professors, friends, colleagues, article reviewers, governmental agencies, newspaper editors, policy makers, or lay people. These audiences are drowning in information coming from all directions – newspapers, advertisements, television shows, social networking sites, email accounts, movies, podcasts, blogs, and more. Scholarly reading is just one small slice of this material. Even so, professors review hundreds of student assignments each year, and these compete with exploding numbers of journal articles, policy briefings, memos, strategic reports, and white papers – to say nothing of novels, films, and other media.

With so much information clamoring for attention, a key question is: "How can an inquirer persuade his or her audiences that the research findings of an inquiry are worth paying attention to?" (Lincoln & Guba, 1985, p. 290). In other words, how do you make your qualitative project attractive, credible, and likely to be taken seriously? Indeed, what ought a qualitative study do? How do we identify high-quality qualitative work?

This chapter addresses such questions and describes how to identify and create quality in qualitative research. First, the chapter reviews common criteria for quality in positivist research and discusses current thinking about the distinguishing characteristics of qualitative goodness. Then it moves into an affirmative discussion of the ways qualitative researchers can strive for valuable, ethical, and inviting work.

The criteria controversy

Devising criteria for scholarly quality is one type of social and humanistic knowledge; therefore such criteria are not "discovered," but *constructed*. As Guba and Lincoln (2005) advise: "No matter how real, natural, or objective they may seem, criteria are social products created by human beings in the course of evolving a set of practices to which they (and we) subsequently agree to conform" (p. 269). Criteria are human-made filters that necessarily restrict some types of knowledge as they legitimate others; in consequence, criteria are subjective, ever-changing, and sometimes problematic. In order to lay the groundwork for discussing qualitative quality, it is important to understand yardsticks for quality that non-qualitative researchers often use and may mistakenly impose upon qualitative work.

As discussed in Chapter 3, the positivist paradigm still reigns supreme in many scholarly circles. Such an approach assumes a true and empirical reality, complete with knowledge that is "out there," waiting to be discovered with specific research instruments, which have been validated through replicated use. Good research from this approach connects specific variables with specific outcomes, so as to make predictions and statistical generalizations. Such research aims for **objectivity**, which means that researchers take measures to protect the data and their own analysis of them from being tainted by subjective biases and individual points of view. The notion that research should be "objective" suggests that knowledge-building is best accomplished through measurement devices that are detached from any particular investigator – and that objective scientific procedures will result in the development of facts that can be systematically evaluated.

Another common positivist notion related to quality is **reliability**, which refers to the stability and consistency of a researcher, research tool, or method over time. Reliable studies are those that can be replicated in exactly the same way, no matter who is conducting the study. A reliable instrument always works the same way. For example, a reliable scale measures weight consistently, no matter who is reading it and no matter in what context, who or what is on the scale, and so on. You would not trust a scale that weighed you at 140 pounds now and at 180 pounds one moment later (unless you happened to pick up a small child or a packed suitcase in between). Reliability is important in the world of scientific measurement – the home of quantitative devices like thermometers and scales.

A third index or criterion of scientific quality is that a study should have **formal generalizability** – a property that refers to the capacity of findings to be transferred from one study to another and to make predictions about how these findings relate to other populations or contexts. For instance, if something happens over and over again (when a baby releases a spoon, it drops to the ground), we predict that it will continue to do so in the future, despite the person's age and context. In order to produce a formal generalization, researchers gather a sufficient amount of data to support a claim in a certain population, they ensure that they have an appropriately randomized sample, and then they statistically calculate how these same findings are true across other populations. By doing all this, they show that the findings of a particular study apply not only to the distinct people envisaged in that study, but also to others. Generalizing always involves a leap of faith, because it predicts future behavior – and also, of course, because it takes knowledge generated in one context and applies it to others, as explained above. However, given a representative (or random) sample containing sufficient data, one can statistically generalize the findings of a smaller group onto another group – in cases like, say, voting patterns.

While these three criteria – objectivity, reliability, and formal generalizability – are very useful in much quantitative research, they do not serve as criteria for most qualitative research – especially the kind that emerges from interpretive, critical, and postmodern approaches. Most qualitative researchers question the very notion of objectivity or consider it to be a **myth** – a powerful story or legend that collectively justifies a certain social practice or institution, but is false or without proof. Seale (1999) argues: "Knowledge is always mediated by preexisting ideas and values, whether this is acknowledged by the researchers or not" (p. 470). Karen Tracy (1995) contends that objectivity is an inappropriate value criterion because it assumes a single world to be known, and therefore it assumes that researchers can actually access the replicability and accuracy of one's observations. I agree; certainly, measures may be taken to reduce one's biases or to or account for them, but completely objective and bias-free research is impossible for anyone.

Second, traditional conceptions of reliability have little application to qualitative research, because most qualitative studies are composed of a single analysis, made at a given contextual moment in time. Because socially constructed understandings are always in process and necessarily partial, even if the study were repeated (by the same researcher, in the same manner, in the same context, and with the same participants), the context and participants would have necessarily transformed over time – through aging, learning, or moving on. Hence traditional notions of reliability used in qualitative research are not only mythical, but downright problematic – the "consequence is rather that the study is no good" (Stenbacka, 2001, p. 552).

Formal generalizations – although important for predicting political races, television show ratings, or strains of the flu virus to include in a vaccine – are, similarly, ill suited for qualitative research. This is the case for two reasons. First, most qualitative researchers purposefully trade large or randomized samples for in-depth studies of fewer people or instances – and they often choose to study the unique and the strange rather than the mundane. Therefore the type of sample that would be necessary for reaching formal generalization is rarely desired by qualitative researchers. Second, historically and culturally situated knowledge is ephemeral and always in transformation. Therefore, even if a random

TIPS AND TOOLS 11.1

Eight "big-tent" criteria for excellent qualitative research

Criteria for Quality (end goal)	Various Means, Practices and Methods Through Which to Achieve
Worthy topic	The topic of the research is: • relevant • timely • significant • interesting
Rich rigor	The study uses sufficient, abundant, appropriate and complex • theoretical constructs • data and time in the field • sample(s) • context(s) • data collection and analysis processes
Sincerity	The study is characterized by • self-reflexivity about subjective values, biases, and inclinations of the researcher(s) • transparency about the methods and challenges
Credibility	The research is marked by • thick description, concrete detail, explication of tacit (nontextual) knowledge, and showing rather than telling • triangulation or crystallization • multivocality • member reflections • inter-coder reliability (when collaborating on data-analysis)
Resonance	The research influences, affects, or moves particular readers or a variety of audiences through • aesthetic, evocative representation • naturalistic generalizations • transferable findings
Significant contribution	The research provides a significant contribution • conceptually/theoretically • practically • heuristically • methodologically
Ethical	The research considers • procedural ethics (such as human subjects) • situational and culturally specific ethics • relational ethics
Meaningful coherence	The study • achieves what it purports to be about • uses methods and procedures that fit with its stated goals • meaningfully interconnects literature, research questions/foci, findings, and interpretations with each other

Source: S. J. Tracy, 2010. Qualitative quality: Eight "big-tent" criteria for excellent qualitative research. *Qualitative Inquiry*, 16, 837–851. Reproduced with permission from Sage

sample could be found, most qualitative researchers would agree that contextualized knowledge, by definition, cannot generalize to other (quite different) scenes in the future.

If positivist criteria are a poor fit for qualitative research, what are qualitative researchers to do? Some qualitative scholars have argued that trying to delineate unvarying research standards is problematic, fruitless, and even silly (Bochner, 2000; Guba & Lincoln, 2005; Schwandt, 1996). I certainly understand that "studies need to be understood and evaluated on their own terms" (Deetz, 2001, p. 38). That said, I believe that criteria can nonetheless be useful in helping us to study, practice, and perfect a method, especially when we are first learning it. Criteria help us to answer the question of whether findings are sufficiently authentic – trustworthy and related to the way others construct their social worlds – and secure – which means that people may act on their implications, for instance to construct social policy or legislation (Guba & Lincoln, 2005).

Hence I developed an expansive "big-tent" approach to criteria for qualitative quality, differentiating the end goals of good research from the mean practices that researchers take to get there (Tracy, 2010). This eight-point conceptualization for obtaining quality in qualitative research serves as a pedagogical tool, promotes dialogue among researchers from various paradigms, and encourages the viability and credibility of qualitative research with a variety of audiences. Tips and Tools 11.1 summarizes the model, and the rest of the chapter discusses how you might design your research so as to attend to these markers of quality.

Worthy topic

The first criterion for qualitative quality is worthiness of the topic. As discussed in earlier chapters, a **worthy topic** can emanate from disciplinary or scholarly theories, relevant or timely social events, or priorities of the particular sample or context of study. Research topics may be worthy because they reveal an aspect of life that has been overlooked, misunderstood, or mistaken, or because they provoke transformation or elicit emotion in the reader.

Particular worth may be found in research that it is counterintuitive, questions taken-for-granted assumptions, or challenges well-accepted ideas. This type of research contrasts with studies that (re)document a phenomenon that is already well established and accepted. Certainly, there is value in strengthening and duplicating studies in order to understand how they may change or remain stable over time. However, worthy studies also point out surprises – issues that shake readers from their commonsense assumptions and practices (Murray, 1971).

Rich rigor

A second marker for quality is **rigor**, which refers to the care and effort taken to ensure that the research is carried out in an appropriate manner. Rigor asks whether researchers have applied due diligence and done their homework. In short, have they put in the time, effort, and thoroughness to practice their craft effectively? The *means* to achieve rigor are multiple and varied. However, rigorous practices include:

- collecting enough data to support significant findings;
- spending enough time in the field to gain trust;
- identifying theoretical goals that are well aligned with your sample or context;
- practicing appropriate procedures in terms of writing fieldnotes, conducting interviews, and analyzing data.

Conducting rigorous research means practicing the discipline and having the motivation to move beyond data and analysis methods that are merely convenient and comfortable. Students completing a course in qualitative methods sometimes want a bit more specificity, so let's consider what qualifies as reasonable parameters for a "rigorous" research assignment in a qualitative methods course.

A scan of recent North American syllabi over the last ten years shows that, depending on the level of the class, students are often asked to spend between 10 and 40 research hours (time to be spent in the field or gathering data from participants) for a course-long project. Qualitative undergraduate projects tend to include about 15 research hours, graduate projects about 25 research hours, master's theses about 80 hours, and dissertations over 100 hours. These numbers reflect what many professors seem to believe is "enough time" to become acquainted with qualitative methods and to create an appropriate study at each student's instructional level.

Despite this "rule of thumb" practice in relation to research hours, there are notable exceptions. If data are new, unique, or rare, not as much time is needed to make a valuable contribution. For instance, two recent articles – one with male executives about work–life balance (Tracy & Rivera, 2010), and another with male professors about being targets of sexual harassment (Scarduzio & Geist-Martin, 2008) – rely on 13 and 4 interviews respectively. Why comparatively so few? Because the data in these studies – despite the limited sample size – are unique. Most studies of work–life balance and sexual harassment are completed with women, and high-ranking men are largely absent from the literature. If these two studies had interviewed women instead of men, they would have likely needed larger interview pools in order to make a significant contribution.

Decisions about how much data to collect also intersect with the "density" of the data. Karen Tracy and I made use of one hundred hours of participant observation data, seven interviews, and a handful of training manuals for the claims we made in our article on emotional labor at 911 (S. Tracy & Tracy, 1998). In contrast, our study of rudeness and face threat during 911 calls relied primarily on *only two* 911 incidents (K. Tracy & Tracy, 1998). The analysis of the data in this second article was *extremely detailed* – taking in the elements of the talk sequence one by one rather than pulling them globally from the emergent themes. When they proceed by this method, some articles may use only a small slice of the data.

Granted, articles using small amounts of data may still emerge from a larger data set. In Scarduzio and Geist-Martin's (2008) study of four sexually harassed male professors, their larger study included 41 interviews. In our 911 research, the two "critical incident" rude calls emerged from an analysis of seven interviews, 100 hours of participant observation, and 650 audio-taped archived calls. Clearly, there is no magic number for the amount of time in the field. The most salient issue to consider is whether the data collected will substantiate meaningful or significant claims.

In terms of rigorous data *analysis*, the reader deserves an explanation about the process by which the raw data were transformed and organized into the research report. As discussed in Chapters 9 and 10, methodology sections should detail the systematic process of sorting, choosing, and organizing the data, whether these operations were accomplished through dialogue with others, through the use of qualitative data analysis software, or by creating piles of cut and pasted data. If there are multiple researchers, authors should also discuss how they worked together meaningfully in analyzing the data (this will be discussed in more detail below, in

EXERCISE 11.1

Gauging worth and rigor

1 In what ways is your study's topic worthy? Consider issues of:
   a theoretical relevance
   b practical application
   c opportunity for social transformation
2 In what ways is your study interesting? How does it solve a problem or puzzle? How does it provide something new and surprising?
3 Is your study sufficiently rigorous? Given the topic and the contribution you hope to make, what other things might you do to ensure due diligence in terms of:
   a collecting appropriate and sufficient data?
   b spending enough time in the field?
   c adopting appropriate data collection and analysis practices?

relation to inter-coder reliability). As you are finishing up data analysis and have reflected on Exercise 11.1, it makes sense to pause and ask yourself some questions about your emerging study's worth and rigor.

Sincerity

A third marker of qualitative quality is **sincerity**: this means that good qualitative research is genuine and vulnerable. Researchers share their goals, hopes, and mistakes, and they discuss how these backstage issues have implicated the fieldwork, the participants, and the data analysis. Vulnerability demonstrates openness to the life experiences of others, as well as a willingness to share aspects of your own experiences. Sincere researchers are approachable rather than self-important and friendly rather than snobbish. They consider not only their own needs but also those of their participants, readers, co-authors, and potential audiences. Sincere researchers are honest, kind, and self-deprecating. They foster sincerity through two practices discussed below: self-reflexivity and transparency.

Self-reflexivity

Self-reflexivity, as discussed throughout this book, is an honest and authentic awareness of one's own identity and research approach, and an attitude of respect for participants, audience members, and other research stakeholders. Practices of self-reflexivity include sharing one's motivations to conduct a certain study and engaging in practices that promote self-awareness and exposure. By sharing these practices, readers can feel assured that researchers have considered their role and impact in the scene.

Self-reflexivity encourages writers to be frank about their strengths and shortcomings, substantiating "their interpretations and findings with a reflexive account of themselves and the process of their research" (Altheide & Johnson, 1994, p. 489). Self-reflexive practices inform all stages of a project, beginning with heightened awareness in the early stages of the research design and progressing to later stages of fieldwork, analysis, and writing. Self-reflexive researchers consider how their bodies and intentions impact the types of data, relationships, and trust available to them (González, 2000).

Several practices are associated with the "doing" of self-reflexivity. Self-reflexive researchers make notes about others' reactions to them. They also include themselves in the write-up of the research. Using the first person voice (e.g. "I said," or "They reacted to me by…") is not only allowed, but encouraged. Using the first person, "I," reminds the reader of the researcher's presence and influence. In contrast to mainstream journalism, self-reflexive ethnography requires explicating the *process* or *way* of knowing and *how* claims were developed (Altheide & Johnson, 1994).

How much disclosure about self-reflexivity is enough? Like a good spice, a small dose of self-reflexivity in a published research report can go a long way. Geertz (1973) made the case that he was "never […] impressed by the argument that, as complete objectivity is impossible in these matters (as, of course, it is), one might as well let one's sentiments run loose" (p. 29). Too much inward autobiographical detail about complaints, anxieties, wishes, or dreams can flood and overwhelm the text – unless, of course, the point of the text is to document these issues. In most research reports, it makes sense to "recognize our connections and write about them, but mainly as these connections further illuminate the reader's understanding of the cultural event, place or practice" (Krizek, 2003, p. 149). Through a balanced approach, authors can include themselves in the scene, but not so much that it squeezes out other important objects of study (Denzin, 1997).

Transparency

Another key part of sincerity is being honest and open about the activities by which the research transpired – a feature called **transparency**. If you were only able to obtain access to a scene because your parent works there, then, to be transparent, you should share this fact with your audience. If you had to "re-create" half of the fieldnotes because a computer glitch deleted them, it is not transparent to lump the description of this fieldnote data with the rest. In short, transparency demands that research processes – which may include interactions within the context, the methodological design, analysis practices, and relationships with participants – should be self-critically and openly delineated (Altheide & Johnson, 1994; Seale, 1999).

Other issues to consider in terms of transparency are the type of field role participation, fieldnote practices, and the level of detail in transcription. Transparency suggests that authors reveal mistakes or surprises and explain how research goals and questions changed due to external constraints or unexpected challenges in the field. Readers should also know whether the research was funded, by whom, and how/if such funding shaped or determined the research design or analysis. Finally, transparency demands being up front about other people's role in the research and acknowledging help from colleagues, participants, or student assistants. Appreciating others and acknowledging the limits of one's own role through transparent processes such as these are certainly key practices of sincerity – something pictured in Figure 11.1 (in Researcher's Notepad 11.1).

RESEARCHER'S NOTEPAD 11.1

Sincerity word cloud

Figure 11.1 Sincerity is a key characteristic of qualitative quality; it is made up of a number of intersecting practices, as pictured in this word word cloud that I created at www.wordle.net

Credibility

Credibility, a fourth marker for qualitative quality, is a common term that people often use without any clear definition. For example, public speakers learn to "establish credibility" by sharing their expertise or research on a topic and by persuading the audience that they are believable. For our purposes, **credibility** refers to dependability, trustworthiness (Lincoln & Guba, 1985), and expressing a reality that is plausible or *seems* true (Tracy, 2010). Good ethnography provides "a credible account of a cultural, social, individual, or communal sense of the 'real'" (Richardson, 2000a, p. 254). If a report is credible, readers feel confident in using its data and findings to act and make decisions. Qualitative credibility is achieved through

- thick description;
- triangulation or crystallization;
- multivocality and partiality;
- engaging in member reflections with participants.

Thick description

Thick description is achieved by explicating contextual meanings specific to the cultural group at hand (Geertz, 1973), and by providing lush material details about people, processes, and activities (Bochner, 2000). Such detail gives a complex and expansionistic depiction. In qualitative research "things get bigger, not smaller and tighter, as we understand them" (González, 2000, p. 629).

Related to thick description and concrete detail is the ability of qualitative research to tap into **tacit knowledge**, which is considered to be the body of implicit meanings floating just below the surface. In other words, tacit knowledge is the "largely unarticulated, contextual understanding that is often manifested in nods, silences, humor, and naughty nuances" (Altheide & Johnson, 1994, p. 492). If you think of an iceberg (like the one responsible for sinking the Titanic), all you may see is its top tip, sticking out of the water. This tip is akin to explicit and visible knowledge. However, the largest and most powerful part of an iceberg lies underneath, covered by water. This huge base is like tacit knowledge. Reaching tacit knowledge requires digging below the surface, to understand the importance of what is not said and how implicit core values of the group are driving action – even, or especially, when these norms cannot be easily articulated.

In order to recognize and get tacit knowledge, researchers need to spend time in the context and acquire experience of it. Just as an experienced sea captain can appreciate the difference between an iceberg and sea ice that is just skimming the surface, a researcher who has been in the field for a long time can begin to recognize the places to probe for tacit knowledge. This process includes examining the *absence* of talk and activity. Additionally, engaging in comparative research in a different but related scene is a poignant way to understand the assumed values of a certain group, system, or organization.

Crystallization/triangulation

Gathering multiple types of data seen through multiple lenses is another key way to achieve credibility. In short, findings are stronger when researchers gather their data through several sampling strategies, use more than one investigator in the field, engage multiple theoretical positions in data analysis, or use contrasting methods of data collection. This practice was originally called **triangulation**, refers to using multiple points in geographical navigation. Imagine trying to locate a museum on a map. Knowing its street name is a fine start, but additional data points – the cross-street, the postal code, or how far away it is from your hotel – can make it even easier to find it. The concept of triangulation was born in realist paradigms that aimed at ridding research of bias and at finding convergence on a single reality (or point on the map). The idea was that, when many data points converge, the findings are more credible (Denzin, 1978). One practice often associated with triangulation is that of **inter-coder reliability**, discussed in Tips and Tools 11.2.

Inter-coder reliability is only desirable when the researchers are claiming to code the data similarly. That said, there may be good reasons for two researchers to code data quite differently on purpose. Indeed multiple data points, theoretical constructs, or different researchers may appropriately come up with results that are different from one another rather than convergent. Does this mean that the research is not credible? Not necessarily. Data analyzed and gathered by two different researchers may differ because of the researchers' age, race, gender, or past experience, and both viewpoints could shed important insight. Likewise, researchers may find one organizational value espoused in some data sources, such as interviews and training documents (e.g. that good employees tell the truth). Meanwhile they may discover in participant observation that "good" employees regularly fudge the numbers or tell white lies. Findings from both data texts may be equally "true" and show the complexities of the scene.

Indeed making use of multiple data points and researcher points of view, even when they do not converge, is still a practice toward qualitative credibility. The notion of **crystallization** refers to such a practice while avoiding the realism associated with the term "triangulation." The multiple facets of crystals "reflect externalities *and* refract within themselves, creating different colors, patterns, and arrays, casting off in different directions. What we see

TIPS AND TOOLS 11.2

Inter-coder reliability

Although the overall concept of reliability is not usually applicable to qualitative research (as discussed in the opening of this chapter), inter-coder reliability is important when a team of qualitative researchers want to ensure they are coding and classifying data from a single study in a similar way.

In such cases, they engage in practices to ensure inter-coder reliability. Inter-coder reliability can be calculated in a variety of manners, the most common of which are percent agreement, Scott's pi (p), Cohen's kappa (k), and Krippendorff's alpha (a) (see Lombard, Snyder-Duch, & Bracken, 2002, for a review). Different disciplines and journals have varying expectations for computing inter-coder reliability. In what follows I describe how to engage in inter-coder reliability via percent agreement:

1   Through dialogue and consultation, collaborators create a common coding scheme.
2   Collaborators work together coding data to try to become consistent in their understandings.
3   Collaborators separate and, working independently, analyze the same subset (usually at least 10%).
4   Collaborators come back together to compare their coding and to compute inter-coder reliability.
   a   This is calculated by taking the number of codes that the researchers agreed upon (e.g. 9) and dividing it by the total number of pieces of data coded (e.g. 10).
   b   The higher the agreement rate (9/10), the more reliable (or consistent), the analysis. An agreement rate of 90 percent or higher is considered appropriate by post-positivist qualitative researchers (Miles & Huberman, 1994).
5   When collaborators reach an appropriate agreement rate, they may then assume that they are coding the data similarly, and therefore they can break up the rest of the data and analyze them independently.

depends upon our angle of repose" (Richardson, 2000b, p. 934). Through crystallization, as this notion was developed by Ellingson (2008), researchers are encouraged to engage in multiple types of data collection, at multiple points in time, with multiple co-researchers, in order to construct a multi-faceted, more complicated, and therefore more credible picture of the context.

Multivocality

One way of practicing crystallization is through **multivocality** – the inclusion of multiple voices. This means analyzing social action from a variety of participants' points of view and highlighting divergent or disagreeable standpoints. Multivocality also requires that authors be self-aware of how their own and their participants' subjectivities vary in the field – in terms of race, gender, age, education, class, or sexuality. Credibility is enhanced by considering how these differences play a role in conflicting intentions or in narratives of contextual practices and performances. For instance, different groups may have very different explanations and assessments of humor. Some may find a joke harmless and fun, while others may find it mean-spirited and divisive.

Writing a multivocal analysis can be facilitated through collaboration with research participants. As described in Chapter 3, participatory, action, autoethnographic, and feminist approaches seek out and include participant input along the way. By taking all these factors in, researchers can better ensure that their voices are represented in multi-faceted ways, nuanced, and ultimately more credible in the final report (Ellis, 2007).

Member reflections

In relation to multivocality, researchers can also include participants in the analysis of data and findings. I use the phrase **member reflections** to refer to occasions that "allow for sharing and dialoguing with participants about the study's findings, providing opportunities for questions, critique, feedback, affirmation and even collaboration" (Tracy, 2010, p. 844). Such a practice includes sitting down with your participants and sharing in-process analyses or conclusions, making note of their reactions, and including these reactions in further cycles of data analysis.

Member reflections are different from *member checks*, *member validation*, and *host verification* (Lindlof & Taylor, 2011) – all practices that emphasize the need for *correspondence* between the researcher's findings and the participants' viewpoints. Rather, member reflections suggest that participant feedback is valuable not as a measure of validity, but as a space for additional insight and credibility. Through the collaboration and elaboration that occur as a result of member reflections, new data are produced that "throw fresh light on the investigation and [...] provide a spur for deeper and richer analyses" (Bloor, 2001, p. 395).

Through member reflections, researchers may also appreciate the extent to which their findings are understandable and meaningful to the participants, themselves. In the reflection process participants can react, agree, or point out problems with the analysis. Providing opportunities for member reflections is not only ethical – especially when participants have dedicated significant patience, time, resources, and energy to the project – but also speaks volumes about the study's credibility.

What if members disagree with the findings, or dislike their own portrayal in them? Does this mean the research is less credible or valid? Perhaps, but not necessarily. Authors must be comfortable with critique and disagreement from a range of audiences, especially if they subscribe to paradigms that view the world as contested and constructed. Good researchers pay attention to the variety of reactions received, incorporating them as they continue to gather, analyze, and write. At the same time, they should not automatically change the direction of their analysis because participants disagree; "members' responses to researchers' accounts are provisional and subject to change" (Bloor, 2001, p. 391). Depending on the season, time of day, or context, they may protest at one point but certify findings at another. Researchers should create options for input and consider it as they analyze the data and write up the final report.

Resonance

A fifth key marker of qualitative quality is **resonance**, considered to be the feature of the text that meaningfully reverberates and impacts an audience. Many people erroneously assume that formal generalizability is the only way to achieve resonance. Most qualitative researchers, rather than trying to prove the generalizability of research through statistics, ensure that their research resonates by choosing specifically revealing cases or contexts of study. As Flyvbjerg notes:

> One can often generalize on the basis of a single case, and the case study may be central to scientific development via generalization as supplement or alternative to other methods. But formal generalization is overvalued as a source of scientific development, whereas 'the force of example' and transferability are underestimated. (Flyvbjerg, 2011, p. 305)

Indeed, as I discuss here, resonance can be achieved through several different practices.

Transferability and naturalistic generalization

When readers intuitively believe that research findings correspond to something significant in their own world, then resonance has been accomplished through **transferability**. For instance, if readers of my cruise ship research relate its emotional labor and burnout findings to their own situation (e.g. to their work in a restaurant or in a theme park), they are *transferring* the findings. Transferability is different from formal generalizations, in which the researcher engages in randomized sampling and "objective" scientific practices to generate context-free and formally generalizable knowledge.

Qualitative researchers also achieve resonance by helping readers feel as if they have been there. The concept of **naturalistic generalization** (Stake & Trumbull, 1982) refers to this process – in which readers appreciate a study's findings and then intuitively apply them to their own situations. For example, Geertz (1973) claims that Balinese cockfighting practices are symbolic of the culture's overall concerns with violence and status. These claims rest upon data that Geertz describes so thickly and richly that readers can viscerally feel and understand how the implications of the data might transfer – or naturalistically generalize – to their own culture (e.g. how sports such as football symbolize violence and status in US culture).

Naturalistic generalizations can actually have more impact than statistical generalizations, because participants feel as though they have made their own useful applications rather than been told by the author what meanings to accept. Indeed, Stake and Trumbull argue that, compared to formal knowledge, the readers' "practice is guided far more by personal knowings, based on and gleaned from personal experience" (p. 5). So how might researchers write their report so as to make it transferable and naturalistically generalized? As I explain below, a qualitative researcher can communicate the impact of her findings by writing so aesthetically that the reader can imagine and personally transfer these findings to a range of familiar contexts.

Aesthetic merit

Another means toward resonance is that of writing a text with **aesthetic merit** – in other words making it imaginative, artistic, beautifully written, and capable of emotionally affecting the reader (Goodall, 2008). Have you ever read something so moving that you laughed out loud, cried, felt sick to your stomach, or felt inspired to change the world? If so, then the text has aesthetic merit. It engaged your feeling and interpretive response. It was not boring.

For qualitative researchers, writing an excellent research report requires not just the basic qualities of clarity and organization. Aesthetic writers use a variety of literary and evocative styles, including personal narrative, storytelling, and emotional approaches that help readers tap into their own bodies (Holman Jones, 2005). Aesthetic texts are interactive, descriptive, and evocative (Scarduzio, Giannini, & Geist-Martin, 2011) – they move the "heart and the belly" as well as the "head" (Bochner, 2000, p. 271).

One such text is Ronai's (1992) layered account of exotic dancing. Carol Rambo-Ronai returned to her former job as an erotic dancer, conducting an autoethnography. She made use of Ellis's (1991) emotional sociology and called upon her own emotional experience as a method to describe, examine, and theorize. Ronai's raw emotions in the field helped her to understand and explain how stripping led simultaneously to feelings of power and powerlessness, repulsion and superiority. Readers feel what Ronai feels as one client paws at her on stage, another attempts unsuccessfully to stick his tongue down her throat, and another cat-calls her in the parking lot. Her writing invites readers to see, taste, touch, and smell that men's club, complete with a nicotine sheen on its walls. Through a conscious self-examination of her felt emotions, Ronai vividly shows how erotic dancing impacts private and social experiences. Certainly she succeeds in terms of Richardson's (2000a) evaluative question about good qualitative research: Does this affect me emotionally or intellectually?

A focus on aesthetics does not preclude rigorous scientific practice. Rather, it means that researchers understand that the way they creatively construct their literary tale impacts the resonance of their research report. Richardson (2000a) explains that "creative arts is one lens through which to view the world; analytical/science is another." She says that "we see best with both lenses focused and magnified" (p. 254). Aesthetic merit opens a beautiful path toward achieving resonance by provoking vicarious emotional experience in the reader (Ellis, 1995).

Significant contribution

We have now covered five key characteristics of qualitative quality. A sixth – which can make or break publication in academic journals – is the significance of the study's contribution. Significance is largely judged by whether the findings extend, transform, or complicate a body of knowledge, theory, or practice in new and important ways. In short, significant research serves to "bring clarity to confusion, make visible what is hidden or inappropriately ignored, and generate a sense of insight and deepened understanding" (Tracy, 1995, p. 209).

This insight or deepened understanding need not be huge, but it must impact the current knowledge landscape. Making a significant contribution requires familiarity with the broad literature, delving deeper into a particular issue, reading and learning as much as possible about that issue, finding its boundaries, and then pushing those limits to see how the area might benefit from more research. (Matt Might, http://matt.might.net/ provides a captivating visual metaphor in his illustrated guide to getting a PhD http://matt.might.net/articles/phd-school-in-pictures/.) After all this reading and boundary pressing, researchers engage in their own original research, with the hope that they may press the knowledge boundaries a little bit further. That little incremental addition, or dent in the knowledge boundary, is a significant contribution. It's a gift of your research to the body of knowledge – one that readers can learn from and use in their own future research.

Theoretically significant research extends, builds, or critiques disciplinary knowledge, helping to explain social life in unique ways. At its most basic level, theoretical significance may come in the form of applying an established theory in a new context. For example, Baxter (1990) identified three key dialectical tensions to help explain the development of romantic relationships. Since that time, dialectical theory has been applied hundreds of times to other settings, to explain relational contradictions amongst friends, family members, and co-workers. Applying existing theory to a new context is usually an adequate contribution in undergraduate student papers or theses. **Conceptual development**, however, goes a step further: research *builds* theory beyond the existing literature and offers new and unique understandings. Conceptual development is more difficult than simply applying existing theory to a new setting. Yet achieving the former is required in most graduate-level theses and dissertations, as well as in scholarly publications.

For instance, let us consider a study of burnout in a group of professionals (say, among attorneys). The researcher might begin with the original conceptualization of burnout that emanated from Maslach's studies with social service professionals (Maslach, 1976). Using the data gathered from attorneys, the researcher could discuss that burnout among professionals has some similarities with Maslach's notions of burnout, but is also somewhat different. Through the research, the authors may suggest that another concept – say "tedium" – better captures the unique stress and burnout that occurs among professionals (Pines, Aronson, & Kafry, 1981). This study builds upon past research burnout, but it offers a new concept of tedium, which is potentially useful to future researchers.

Speaking of future researchers, **heuristic significance** is the quality of research that prompts curiosity in others, moving them to act, perform additional investigations, or examine how the concept might play out in a different context or group. As an example of heuristically significant research, we might examine Lutgen-Sandvik's (2003) cycle of workplace abuse. Once this model existed, other communication scholars became interested in issues of workplace bullying, civility, and dignity – and this later research investigated abuse in a variety of workplace settings, looping back and extending Lutgen-Sandvik's model. Likewise, one can find out that the concept of compassion has great heuristic significance; and one reaches this insight by tracing its history, from compassion fatigue (Figley, 1995) to a process of noticing, feeling, and responding (Kanov et al., 2004), to a process of noticing, connecting, and responding (Miller, 2007), and then to a process of recognizing, relating, and (re)acting (Way & Tracy, 2012). Across these various studies the concept has changed and progressed, hopefully in a way that more precisely and richly explains the practice of compassion at work.

One way authors may bolster heuristic significance is by specifically discussing new directions or questions for research, suggesting what we still do not know and how researchers might attend to such issues in subsequent studies. Furthermore, writing about the research in an engaging and accessible manner may prompt an entire range of potential audiences, including lay people and policy makers, to act upon the findings.

Speaking of affecting a range of audiences, research may also offer **practically significant research** contributions through helpful and useful insight in the day-to-day life of key stakeholders. The phronetic, problem-based contextual approach described in this book is specifically designed to result in findings of practical significance. For example, on the basis of her ethnographic study of the ways employees manufactured a mood of innovation, Elizabeth Eger (formerly Rush) (Rush, 2010) offers a number of recommendations for mood interventions that are more fulfilling and energizing than the exhausting and depleting practices she witnessed at her research site. Such research certainly succeeds in enabling "the training or calibration of human judgment" (Schwandt, 1996, p. 69) and "the capacity for practical wisdom" (p. 70).

EXERCISE 11.2

Gauging significance

1 In what ways will your study extend, complicate, or build theoretical knowledge? How about methodological practice?

2 In what ways might your study lead to heuristic significance, encouraging future researchers to take up this area of research and study?

3 In what ways does your research implicate everyday practice? What practical tips could lay people derive from your study?

Phronesis and practical wisdom are also related to the ways the research may help transform an injustice or help others learn how to replicate a liberating environment. Lather (1986) offers the notion of **catalytic validity** to specifically refer to research that provides a political consciousness that catalyzes/moves cultural members to act. Action researchers, as discussed in Chapter 3, team up with research participants to examine issues that are contextually important and to provide findings that are helpful to cultural members. Action research allows such members to work with experienced researchers in order to critique status quo problems and to cultivate notions for transformation.

Finally, **methodological significance** is achieved when methodology is approached in a new, creative, or insightful way. For instance, one might take a theory or a concept that has mostly been studied quantitatively, through experiments or self-report surveys, and study it instead through participant observation, interviews, or focus groups. New methods may not only offer fresh theoretical insight, they may sharpen and strengthen that method. One might engage in what Richardson (2000b) refers to as "creative analytic practices" – approaching insight through dance, performance, and art. Or researchers might practice alternative analysis activities – such as asking a participant to take pictures on a disposable camera, write captions for these pictures, and then talk through their meaning with the researcher. Methodological significance provides insight in terms of our craft skills associated with collecting, managing, and analyzing data, and, given the rich texture of the qualitative landscape, this is an area ripe for expansion.

Ethical research practice

The seventh characteristic I will discuss in terms of qualitative quality is that of ethics. Ethical research practice is a thread throughout this entire book, in the form of self-reflexivity, access, participation, interviewing, fieldwork, transcription, and writing. That said, ethics is so important for quality that there is good reason to highlight it separately here. Practicing ethics in qualitative research requires consideration of (a) procedural rules and procedures; (b) the specific ethics of the context we are studying; and (c) the ethics of working – sometimes quite closely and intimately – with research participants.

Procedural ethics

Procedural ethics refer to ethical actions that are prescribed by certain organizational or institutional review boards (IRB) as being universal or necessary. IRB requirements, as discussed in Chapter 5, are:

- do no harm;
- avoid deception;
- get informed consent;
- ensure privacy and confidentiality.

We have already discussed the importance of transparency and honesty. Procedural ethics likewise encompasses the importance of accuracy and of not misleading the reader through omission, exaggeration, or inappropriate attribution. Procedural ethics also refers to consent: "Weak consent usually leads to poorer data: Respondents will try to protect themselves in a mistrusted relationship, or one formed with the researcher by superiors only" (Miles & Huberman, 1994, p. 291). Creating and cultivating trust with participants is imperative. Some believe that small measures of deception are acceptable when their potential social benefits are clear (Sales & Folkman, 2000). Nonetheless, members must know that their participation is voluntary and understand how to opt out.

Participants also have a right to confidentiality. In order to protect participant identity and privacy, researchers should secure research data (for example by storing them in locked offices or on password-protected websites) and strip them of identifiers before sharing them with co-researchers, assistants, readers, or audience members. Stripping qualitative data of identifiable material can be tricky. Researchers should carefully consider how certain actors might be identified even if their name is a pseudonym: if you share a story about an "elderly boss who stole from the company," participants may be able to quickly deduce identity if there is only one "elderly" boss. Procedural ethics about confidentiality and anonymity encourages researchers to carefully consider how they portray (or strategically conflate) sensitive data.

Situational ethics

Whereas procedural ethics provides universal edicts for all research, **situational ethics** refers to ethical issues that arise in specific contexts or sample populations. Everyone can think of acts that may be ethical in some situations or with some people, but not in other situations with other people. For instance, secretly videotaping a famous American preacher whose sermons are regularly televised has different ethical implications from secretly videotaping a medicine man celebrating an intimate ceremony in a developing world.

Situational ethics focuses on reasoned considerations about the specific situation (Fletcher, 1966); therefore it treats predetermined moral principles – such as those upheld by institutional review boards – as flexible guidelines rather than unassailable edicts. A situational ethics like utilitarianism, with its concern with "the greater good," motivates researchers to ask whether the potential benefits of the research outweigh its costs. Likewise, researchers may consider the extent to which the study's potential findings justify ethically questionable practices. Consider This 11.1 raises questions that urge reflection upon such issues. Certainly, there are no quick fixes here; but, as Ellis (2007) notes, a situational ethics asks that we "constantly have to consider which questions to ask, which secrets to keep, and which truths are worth telling" (p. 26).

CONSIDER THIS 11.1

Recruiting difficult populations

Most workplace bullying research has studied the *targets* or recipients of workplace bullying. Information from bullies, the instigators of abuse, could be extremely valuable for better understanding and stopping the psychological abuse of employees. One of the primary challenges, of course, is how best to recruit bullies – a population that does not readily self-identify or come forward to tell their story. Explore your response to the following questions about ways it might be ethically appropriate (or inappropriate) to recruit bullies for a study about workplace bullying.

1   Would it be appropriate, for instance, to recruit bullies into an interview study with advertisements that read, "Do you have problem employees?" or "Do you have trouble controlling your irritation with your employees?" or "Do you consider yourself a tough boss?" Why or why not? What else might you suggest?
2   Would it be ethical to ask people to recall high school bullies, and then recruit those former bullies to simply "talk about their job and leadership style"?
3   Once bullies are recruited, what are the ethical implications of avoiding the "bully" label in interactions with these participants, yet using the data collected from them in an article that foregrounds workplace bullying literature?

CONSIDER THIS 11.2

Situational and relational ethics

Situational ethics and relational ethics suggest that researchers must consistently question, reflect upon, and critique their ethical decisions – and realize there is no one easy answer. Potential questions researchers might ask include the following:

• Could deception serve the greater good?
• Do the benefits of research that seeks justice for many outweigh the risk of exposing the identity of a single high-power research participant?
• What are the ethics of modifying or hiding certain information when being completely open and honest could offend or alienate participants?
• Which audiences – participants, readers, or other researchers – deserve to be most taken care of in this situation?
• Is written informed consent appropriate if participants view such consent as bureaucratic, unnatural, repressive, or intrusive?
• Should I return to my research site to share my results even if these results might offend or harm some parties? What if I no longer feel welcome there?
• How do I most ethically share data about people who are deceased, sick, or otherwise cannot provide consent or respond to the research?
• How can I best tell stories that come from the standpoint of people who are marginalized, and do so in a way that reduces the risk of those findings being misused or misappropriated?

Finally, qualitative researchers can also usefully reflect on the notion of **relational ethics**, an ethics of care that "recognizes and values mutual respect, dignity, and connectedness between researcher and researched, and between researchers and the communities in which they live and work" (Ellis, 2007, p. 4). A relational ethic means being aware of one's own role and impact on relationships and treating participants as whole people rather than as just subjects from which to wrench a good story. Related to this, the notion of **feminist communitarianism** (Christians, 2005) suggests that researchers should collaborate with their participants, keep their promises, and put relationships and communal well-being at the top of their priorities. Consider This 11.2 provides several questions that may help prompt such an ethical moral compass.

To summarize, ethical research includes the consideration of procedural rules and regulations, as well as of situational preferences and participants' needs. Ethical researchers vigilantly consider the impact of their practices *throughout* the inquiry. Ethical obligations are complex, and sometimes larger structural research goals and everyday micro-practices may conflict. Further, even if an action is permissible from the point of view of formal standards, if something *feels* inappropriate, then it probably *is* inappropriate.

Meaningful coherence

The final, and anchoring, characteristic of qualitative quality is **meaningful coherence**. In using the concept of coherence, I do *not* mean that a text cannot or should not be written in a way that is layered or intentionally jarring (this will be discussed in Chapter 12). Furthermore, meaningful coherence does not suggest that researchers cannot borrow and combine concepts from different theories. In fact, a hallmark of grounded qualitative research is the notion of novel theoretical juxtapositions and of borrowing from other fields, models, and assumptions (Tracy, 2012). Rather, by "meaningfully coherent" I mean that qualitative studies should: "(a) achieve their stated purpose; (b) accomplish what they espouse to be about; (c) use methods and representation practices that partner well with espoused theories and paradigms; and (d) attentively interconnect literature reviewed with research foci, methods, and findings" (Tracy, 2010, p. 848).

For example, if a researcher is interested in better understanding "social support," a meaningful coherent study actually examines issues of "social support," and not other concepts such as "venting" or "bitching." In this way the concept is similar to **discriminant validity** – a phrase used in quantitative research to refer to the quality of a measurement device (a survey, or an experiment) to examine the specific issue intended to be studied – and not something else. Of course, in most qualitative studies the researcher, rather than a certain measuring device, is the instrument.

Meaningful coherence is also about the logical and intuitive connection of various arguments or concepts in a single paper. For instance, an *interpretive* theoretical approach, which suggests that meaning emerges from the voices of participants, should only invoke issues of power when or if participants bring up these issues themselves. If the researchers bring in structural issues of power themselves, without participant contribution, it would be more coherent to use a *critical* theoretical approach. Researchers must mindfully synch their stated research goals with theories, their research design, and their methodology.

Here is another example. Grounded theory as originally conceived by Glaser and Strauss (1967) is quite realist in nature: it develops an overriding story or set of themes as grounded and "real" in any group of data. Hence, if a researcher espoused a paradigmatic framework of postmodernism – which views reality as fragmented and largely unknowable – it would be incoherent to reference initial conceptualizations of grounded methodology (Tracy, 2010). Certainly, distinct concepts emerging from grounded theory, like the constant comparative method or analytic memos, may be compatible with a postmodern analysis. However, the researcher should know enough about the assumptions of postmodern and grounded theory to realize that the adoption of each, whole-cloth, is not coherent.

Likewise, meaningful coherence requires that researchers demonstrate their understanding that certain ways of writing – such as Richardson's (2000a) creative analytic practices – emanate from certain paradigmatic assumptions (e.g. postmodernism). Does this mean that creative analytic practices cannot be used with a realist interpretive approach? Maybe; but maybe not. At the very least, if these two approaches were to be paired together, in order to be meaningfully coherent the author would have the responsibility of explaining how and why they played well together.

Finally, meaningfully coherent studies hang together well (Fisher, 1987). The literature reviewed establishes the context for interpreting the findings. Research questions or purposes arise logically from the literature. The goals are achieved in the analysis, and the conclusions and implications speak to issues, questions, or controversies in the literature. Incoherent studies, in contrast, may open with one literature, but have findings and implications that relate to another. In sum, after reading a meaningfully coherent study, readers should clearly understand the purpose of the piece and feel as though its findings were delivered in relation to its stated goals.

FOLLOWING, FORGETTING, AND IMPROVISING

This chapter has presented a framework for qualitative quality. However, as researchers, we sometimes may fall short, deviate, forget, or purposefully improvise. In some cases our human instrument shows its innate humanness by not being able to achieve everything all of the time.

You are not alone if you feel that trying to meet one of these quality criteria makes it difficult to reach another. Researchers are often faced with a choice between two goals, such as validity versus avoiding harm, scientific understanding versus individual rights, detached inquiry versus help, help-giving versus confidentiality, and freedom of inquiry versus political advantage (Miles & Huberman, 1994). Qualitative researchers must consistently juggle priorities. For instance, a researcher may decide to prioritize relational ethics over evocative resonance and in consequence edit out a provocative data excerpt in order to protect a participant's privacy. Another researcher may decide that it is more important to focus on theoretical rather than practical implications. A third one may break an oath of confidentiality in order to reveal an abuse of power.

In addition to continually making such tough decisions in the field, qualitative researchers must also be humble enough to examine their own actions with a critical eye. Qualitative research is not without a blemished underbelly. As discussed in Consider This 11.3, perhaps the greatest ethical problems emerge when researchers begin to believe in their own constructed lies.

CONSIDER THIS 11.3

The ten lies of ethnography

Fine (1993) reviews ten lies of ethnography – espoused qualities of ethnographers that are often illusory. Here I summarize his key points. Which of these lies have you committed? Are some more forgivable than others? Why?

Kindly	We often create the illusion that we are more sympathetic toward research participants than we really are
Friendly	We often construct the illusion that we like our participants even when we do not
Honest	We often do not tell participants the whole truth about our study
Precise	We often create the illusion of accuracy, when our fieldnotes are instead an interpretation of the events and not a reflection of what "really" happened
Observant	We often create the illusion that we recorded everything in the scene, when in actuality we only recorded certain portions
Unobtrusive	We influence the scene much more than we let on
Candid	We often leave out personally embarrassing moments in our fieldnotes, in an attempt to look good
Chaste	We often create the illusion of sexual innocence when in actuality we sometimes engage in sexual flirtations and relations
Fair	We often put up the illusion of objectivity, but we really are biased
Literary	We often construct the illusion of writing competence, but we often write in ways that are confusing for readers

In summary

This chapter has elucidated eight markers of qualitative quality. These are: (1) worth; (2) rigor; (3) sincerity; (4) credibility; (5) significant contribution; (6) resonance; (7) ethics; and (8) meaningful coherence. I encourage all researchers to strive toward these goals. There is no one answer to the question of what criteria make a qualitative study "good." Does this mean that we give up on criteria? No. Indeed, "that is like saying that as a perfectly aseptic environment is impossible, one might as well conduct surgery in a sewer" (Geertz, 1973, p. 3). Even though there is no such thing as a universally pristine, valid, and precise study, there are good reasons to strive toward rigor, ethics, credibility, sincerity, and so on.

Criteria for quality can arm us with a compass and a structure – especially when we go beyond memorizing them to actually living them – and do so vicariously, through our studying the dilemmas of others or, better yet, through our embodying their practices, talking to others about their research, and seeking advice along the way. In doing so, we may liken qualitative quality to a multi-faceted crystal (Ellingson, 2008) that attends to multiple stakeholders: "participants, the academy, society, lay public, policy makers and last but certainly not least, the researcher" (Tracy, 2010, p. 849). Researchers need to take care of themselves in the process of taking care of others. Through such self-care and resilience they may acquire the discipline and energy to engage in high-quality qualitative research.

KEY TERMS

→ **aesthetic merit**   the quality of research representations to be striking, evocative, beautiful, and creative in their style and presentation

→ **catalytic validity**   the property of research to provide practical transformative change (Lather, 1986)

→ **conceptual development**   the characteristic of a project to develop a theory beyond the existing literature and to offer new and unique understandings

→ **credibility**   the trustworthiness, plausibility, and good character of a researcher and of his/her study, which impacts the believability of the research findings

→ **crystallization**   a postmodern version of triangulation, crystallization is a feature of research that uses multiple methodological approaches, data sources, researchers and/or theories and seeks the complexities that come from this process

→ **discriminant validity**   studies that possess this type of validity essentially do what they claim they will do and address the terms and ideas they purport to expound upon

→ **feminist communitarianism**   a relational ethics that values the intimacy and collaboration between participants and researchers

→ **formal generalizability**   the property of research results to be transferrable from one study to another, through statistical generalization; this property permits researchers to make predictions on how findings would relate to other populations or contexts

heuristic significance   the quality of research to inspire others to question, probe, and explore ideas in the future

inter-coder reliability   a data analysis process in which researchers working collectively on a project ensure they are all coding data in a similar manner

meaningful coherence   this marker of qualitative inquiry asks: Does the study achieve its purpose and hang well together?

member reflections   the practice of dialoguing with participants about the study's findings; this is considered to be a method of enriching the complexity of the research (in contrast to ensuring that the researcher "got it right")

methodological significance   the quality of research to engage methodology in a unique way or to revisit a previously studied area by applying new methods and, in doing so, change the way others view "how to do" studies in the future

multivocality   the result of accessing and providing space for multiple voices to be represented in a research project

myth   a powerful story or legend that collectively justifies a certain social practice or institution

naturalistic generalization   a notion proposed by Stake and Trumbull (1982), which refers to the fact that research can be generalized by its readers and made to apply to their own research projects, scenes, or even personal lives

objectivity   an ideal of positivist research; it requires that researchers take great care to remove individual biases from their study

practically significant research   the kind of research that generates knowledge that helps its participants, assists in a social problem, or sheds light on a political issue

procedural ethics   a branch of ethics dealing with the mandated standards recognized by institutions to be universal or necessary procedural ethics is also known as categorical ethics, which deals with the standards commonly required of all research projects

relational ethics   a branch of ethics dealing with the researchers' relationships with the participants and with how the former's research and research representations might affect the latter

reliability   a goal of positivist research; reliable studies are replicable, stable, and consistent over time

resonance   a marker of qualitative inquiry; it indicates that the research is meaningful and influential for audiences and readers

rigor   a characteristic of research carried out in an appropriate and disciplined manner

self-reflexivity   a primary means to achieve sincere research, this practice asks researchers to demonstrate awareness, self-critique, and vulnerability in their research, to their audiences, and with themselves

sincerity   a marker of qualitative inquiry that requires a researcher be honest and genuine about his/her subjectivities, methods, and biases

situational ethics   requires researchers to consider what is ethical in a particular research context, where "what is ethical" includes what is worth reporting and what needs to be protected in that particular context or situation

tacit knowledge   refers to the rich understanding of a field site that a researcher gains when moving beyond the surface level toward discerning complex contexts and meanings in the scene that are masked, blurred, or unspoken

theoretically significant research   research endowed with the power to build, expand, critique, or create theory as part of its author's scholarly contribution

thick description   in-depth, contextual, and rich accounts of what researchers see (and also find missing) in their fieldwork it enables readers to be shown the scene, as it were, with their own eyes

transferability   a means of determining resonance in a qualitative study, transferability permits the readers to make connections between the findings presented in one study and those of other works

transparency   a guiding principle of sincere research, this is the quality of researchers to be frank and even critical about their own research methods

triangulation   a situation where findings from multiple types of data, researchers, or sources produce similar results, strengthening the credibility of the study

worthy topic   a topic that is particularly relevant given current social events, the political climate, or contemporary controversies, or because it reveals an aspect of life that has been overlooked, misunderstood, or mistaken

CHAPTER 12

Writing Part 1
The nuts and bolts of qualitative tales

Contents

Qualitative Research Methods: Collecting Evidence, Crafting Analysis, Communicating Impact, First Edition. Sarah J. Tracy.
© 2013 Sarah J. Tracy. Published 2013 by Blackwell Publishing Ltd.

In this chapter I cover the nuts and bolts of writing up a qualitative inquiry. The good news for qualitative researchers is that writing is an integral activity throughout the data collection and analysis process. When it's time to write the "final report," qualitative researchers have already acquired great experience through writing fieldnotes, drafting interview responses, and composing analytic memos. Even the process of transcribing keeps the fingers in the habit of moving across the keyboard – and, as we'll discuss, much of writing is just forging ahead and not being too critical along the way.

This chapter opens by overviewing several common types of qualitative tales. These include traditional/realist tales, impressionistic/literary tales, and confessional/authoethnographic tales. I then discuss the primary working pieces of qualitative journal articles, and how to interconnect them. The chapter closes with a section on "following, forgetting, and improvising," which discusses the paradox faced by qualitative researchers as they try to successfully publish their research while having to meet publication expectations that do not exactly align with common qualitative processes.

Types of tales

In many disciplines, and in most quantitative research, a distinct formula and tone characterizes most journal articles. Articles usually proceed sequentially with introduction/rationale, literature review, research methods/procedures, results, discussion and conclusion. Furthermore, they are often written from an omniscient and detached point of view. This formula and this tone are comforting for their familiarity, predictability, and tendency to sound objective and authoritative. However, many qualitative researchers find that a "one size fits all" writing formula does not adequately capture the texture of their research.

Here I review several common types of writing representations – or, as John Van Maanen (1988) would call them, "tales" – that can emerge from qualitative methods. These include writing styles that are realist and traditional, creative, impressionistic, literary, confessional, and autoethnographic, critical, and formal. Although I review them separately for conceptual clarity, they often blur into or overlap with one another. One type is not fundamentally better than the other, and each type may be appropriate depending on your goals, writing strengths, personal proclivities, and intended audience. However, keep in mind that form matters. *How* you write affects *what* you can write about – and who will care about it (Richardson, 2000b).

The realist tale

The realist tale is the most common form of research representation. In such tales the author is largely absent, in favor of an institutional or objective-sounding voice – almost like a "third party scribe" (Van Maanen, 1988, p. 64). If I were writing a realist tale, I would more likely say "my participants do (x, y, or z)" than "I saw my participants do (x, y, or z)": in the former the author is absent, whereas in the latter the author's presence is obvious. Such a tale may include lots of detail and offers the perspective of the participants, but it does so in a way that suggests that this perspective is singular, universal, and able to be known.

Through the "convention of interpretive omnipotence," the realist tale provides a clear and seemingly "true" interpretation (Van Maanen, 1988, p. 51). Certainly, the author may not overtly claim "I am all powerful, and this is the only one true way of understanding this issue and group of participants." However, certain writing conventions create this illusion. For example, realist tales create an air of certainty by using an active present tense – by saying "The teacher *asks* the student" rather than "The teacher *asked* the student." They also refer to generic *types* ("call-takers make crass jokes") rather than to specific people ("call-takers Susie and Dan made a crass joke"). Furthermore, competing interpretations and conflicting data are absent. As a result, the reader is left believing that this rendition is the one (or at least the best and most true) way of understanding the issue or the culture at hand.

Realist tales have been critiqued for the authors' failure to self-reflexively consider their own role and influence in the scene. When the author is essentially written out of the text, the reader forgets that the study represents just one particular person's interpretation of the scene. However, much recent scholarship has side-stepped this critique by writing largely traditional tales, but still using first person, rich specifics, and self-reflexivity.

Indeed, we should not judge realist tales too harshly. They have been around for a long time; they often use abundant data to make persuasive analyses; and they still constitute the most common and well accepted type of qualitative research. Furthermore, a lion's share of the most accomplished writers of other types of tales were first trained in, and practiced, traditional accounts. Van Maanen (1988) suggests: "There is, alas, no better training than going out and trying one's hand at realist tales" (p. 139).

Creative, impressionist, and literary tales

Although realist tales are the most common, the **crisis of representation** (Clifford & Marcus, 1986) encouraged scholars to question the realist tale and to begin writing in ways that celebrated the partiality and subjectivity of knowledge. The crisis of representation evolved from the postmodernist questioning of the Enlightenment's assumption that *more* information, research, and knowledge can move us closer to truth and certainty. Whereas during the Enlightenment scientists and intellectuals turned to research to unveil reality, the crisis of representation in our contemporary world suggests that research can never represent an issue or a set of participants authentically or holistically. Rather, every piece of research is only one part of the story – and may camouflage or mask knowledge as much as reveal or explain it.

The stories embraced after this crisis of representation have been called many things: impressionist tales (Van Maanen, 1988), creative analytic practices (Richardson, 2000a), the new ethnography (Goodall, 2000), messy texts (Marcus, 1994). They have also been referred to as experimental and alternative. However, I like Van Maanen's characterization "impressionistic," and also Saldaña's (2009) use of Van Maanen's phrase "literary tale," because these labels are untethered – freed from a historical chronology of what counts as "new." Further, I like them more than the other labels because I think it's too easy for critics to attack the credibility of scholarship labeled as "new," "experimental," "messy," or "alternative."

So what do these tales look like? Impressionist tales bear the literary imprint of postmodern epistemology: they convey the idea that reality is fractured, dispersed, and depends on one's perspective. They "braid the knower and the known" (Van Maanen, 1988, p. 102) by highlighting the author's role in the research. Writers of impressionist tales tend to use the first person ("I" or "we"), and through this device the text clearly suggests that the study's knowledge is dependent on the authors' experiences, timing, and standpoint. An impressionist approach assumes that a single tale can never provide *the* answer or *the* interpretation. Rather, such tales are considered successful when they open up the scene in important and interesting ways. Such tales might provoke emotional engagement (Ellis, 1991), show multiple and contrasting interpretations (Wolf, 1992), use multiple voices and points of view through polyphonic story-telling (Tanaka & Cruz, 1998) and catalyze change (Lather, 1986).

Impressionist tales focus squarely on the story, while the research methods, the author's interpretation, and disciplinary knowledge are presented only inasmuch as they move forward the dramatic tale. Participants are given names and are framed as unique characters rather than lumped together as generic types and, as demonstrated in Geertz's (1973) account of the Balinese cockfight, the assumption is that readers will learn much more from exceptional specifics than from bland generalizations.

Rather than writing deductively, with the key conclusions foregrounded, impressionist tales bring the reader along the ride – by using literary techniques such as dialogue, dramatic recall, narrative suspense, unusual phrasings, headings, and unique typefaces to recreate the experience. Even with dramatic endings, impressionist tales are always unfinished; they may conclude with questions as well as answers. A variety of provocative writing forms fall into this broad impressionist/literary category: fiction, creative nonfiction, poetry, drama, performance and theater, polyvocal texts, and layered accounts (see Goodall, 2008 for a host of examples and how-to tips for writing such accounts).

One interesting approach is **poetic inquiry** – a method in which the author extracts key words from the data and strategically truncates these words into poetic structures. Poetic inquiry, also called, "found poetry," provides an innovative way to meld the participants' *in vivo* voices with the researcher's structure and rhythm. To engage in this writing practice, researchers can construct poems through their autoethnographic recollections (e.g. Fox, 2010), determine certain words or phrases that are especially rich and telling in field data texts (Walsh, 2006), or even return interview transcripts to participants and ask them to highlight certain words or phrases they believe to be the most salient. The researcher then takes these words and structures them into a poetic style.

Poetic inquiry can highlight participants' pauses, repetitions, alliterations, and rhythms – leading proponents of the method to argue that the method uniquely honors participants' vocal style and therefore is a more accurate way of representing the data than the more traditional method of quoting excerpts in prose (Prendergast, 2009). At the very least, the poem's rhythm and structure encourage the reader to hear the data in a different, and perhaps more emotional, way. Researcher's Notepad 12.1 provides an example of one type of impressionist tale using poetic inquiry.

Many students are attracted to writing impressionist tales because they view them as more fun, playful, and personal than traditional tales. They can also be more reader-friendly for a variety of audiences – so in writing them you can be motivated by considering a future point when participants, friends, and professionals read them. Anticipating appreciation from a wide variety of audiences (besides a narrow and potentially critical scholarly audience) can serve as wonderful motivation.

Impressionist tales may also feel less intimidating because authors are not claiming to tell the whole story or one single truth. If a critic claims that you left out important parts or completely got it wrong, a postmodernist can respond: "Well, I don't believe there is a single true reality, and all stories are partial." While such a statement loosely accords with the postmodern paradigmatic foundation of impressionist tales, it should not be used as a cop-out or excuse for less than rigorous writing or analysis.

Some impressionist tales open up the scene in more important or emotionally provocative ways than others. It takes training and experience to learn how to write vivid, engaging, and aesthetic tales, which move the "heart and the belly" as well as the "head" (Bochner, 2000, p. 271). These literary skills can certainly be honed – and those interested should take specific writing courses on narrative, poetry, and creative nonfiction. But choosing to write an impressionist tale on the mythical assumption that "it is easier than writing a traditional tale" is foolhardy.

RESEARCHER'S NOTEPAD 12.1

Poetic inquiry

Johnny Saldaña practiced poetic inquiry using interview data with high school students. I encourage you to compare and contrast the two data representations. What are the advantages and disadvantages of each? How might you engage in poetic inquiry with your own data?

Below is one student's verbatim account of her first years in high school (Saldaña, 2009, p. 75):

I hated school last year. Freshman year, it was awful, I hated it. And this year's a lot better actually. Um, I don't know why. I guess, over the summer I kind of stopped caring about what other people thought and cared more about, just, I don't know. It's hard to explain. I found stuff out about myself, and so I went back, and all of a sudden I found out that when I wasn't trying so hard to have people like me and to do what other people wanted, people liked me more. It was kind of strange. Instead of trying to please them all the time, they liked me more when I wasn't trying as hard. And, I don't know, like every- everybody might, um, people who are just, kind of, friends got closer to me. And people who didn't really know me tried to get to know me. I don't know.

Source: Saldaña, 2009, p. 75

Using this excerpt as a base, Saldaña reconstructed it into the following "found poem":

> *Freshman year:*
>
> > *awful,*
> > *hated school...*
>
> *Over the summer:*
>
> > *stopped caring about what others thought,*
> > *found stuff out about myself...*
>
> *This year's better:*
>
> > *friends got closer,*
> > *tried to know me,*
> > *liked me more...*
>
> *Don't know why:*
>
> > *kind of strange,*
> > *hard to explain...*
>
> *This year's better.*

Source: Saldaña, 2011, p. 129

The confessional tale

As I have discussed throughout this book, one of the flagship qualities of good qualitative research is self-reflexivity. This means that authors should be aware of the opinions and biases they bring to the research and of the way these inevitably impact the scene and the data collected. Furthermore, they should be transparent in sharing this information with the reader. While all good qualitative research should be marked by self-reflexivity, in most articles the story of the researcher sits at the periphery. In a **confessional tale** the researcher's story takes center stage.

Confessional tales usually accompany other types of tales – as part of a section on methods, for instance, or in a book chapter that deals with topics like "how I got access," or "my timeline of the research." These backstage accounts can serve as pedagogical tools or cautionary tales (Saldaña, 2009). However, entire volumes can also be dedicated to the researcher's own story. For instance, after the death of Bronislaw Malinowski, his wife published *A Diary in the Strict Sense of the Term* (Malinowski, 1967) detailing the famous anthropologist's unexpressed feelings, frustrations, and desires vis-à-vis the Trobrianders, with whom he lived and studied. Confessional tales are packed full of stories about the researcher's motivations, foibles, and backstage shenanigans. Unlike the disembodied realist tales, confessional tales are usually marked by first-person voice. The main character – the author – is often portrayed as clever or sympathetic, if imperfect. Confessional tales are written so that the reader comes to know exactly *how* the author came up with a certain assessment or conclusion.

Confessional tales are interesting when there is something significant or noteworthy to confess – something that may have otherwise remained hidden or unknown in a tale where the author was not central character. For instance, in a confessional tale, Van Maanen (1988) shares with the reader that he was denied access 14 times to a police department before he finally negotiated access through a personal connection. This information is important, not only because it pedagogically helps ethnographers better understand and anticipate their own access challenges, but also because it says something about the secrecy of police departments and their distrust of researchers and other outsiders.

Autoethnographies, although not always confessional, present some similarities with confessional tales. In an autoethnography the author highlights his or her role in the research. And, like confessional tales, autoethnographies tend to focus on the hidden, tragic, or shameful parts of life rather than on the bright, proud, and triumphant ventures (although see the journal *Qualitative Communication Research* for a special issue, Volume 2, dedicated to autoethnographies of joy). Autoethnographies usually also shed light on some larger practical or theoretical issue, whether that be death and cancer (Vande Berg & Trujillo, 2008), bulimia (Tillmann, 2009), abortion (Ellis & Bochner, 1992), domestic abuse (Olson, 2004), or thin gay bodies and AIDS (Fox, 2007).

Autoethnographic tales mix confessional information with the narrative methods of impressionistic tales. Writing techniques include characterization, dramatic plots, flashbacks, various illustrative practices, and dialogue destined to provide an emotional charge. In Researcher's Notepad 12.2 qualitative scholar Bud Goodall describes in his own words how he made use of a seemingly simple dialogue to illustrate key meanings that emerged through his fieldwork with a rock band. The dialogue is not just a confession, it also indicates key parts of the scene's meaning. While I include this excerpt here, under confessional tales, it's important to realize that dialogue can be a powerful writing technique in any type of tale.

In addition to realist, impressionist, and confessional tales, a host of other tale "types" exist. For example, Van Maanen (1988) reviews "critical tales" that have a Marxist edge and are designed to "shed light on social, political, symbolic or economic issues" (p. 27). Indeed qualitative research lends itself nicely to unmasking power and digging beneath the surface of inequalities. Van Maanen also refers to "formal tales" as ones in which certain theories are laid deductively on top of the data, to "crunch the text" (1988, p. 120). In such writings

RESEARCHER'S NOTEPAD 12.2

Dialogue as a powerful literary tactic

By Bud Goodall, in his own words

The following dialogue is drawn from my fieldwork with the rock 'n roll band *Whitedog* (Goodall, 1991). I wrote the scene from memory one night on a barstool, but it happened so often that I pretty much had it memorized. Dave, our "Roadie," would invariably make some sort of mistake, and we in the band would assume Monty Python-ish accents to assess what punishment he should receive. This conversation attained a ritual status for band members. The following scene – a typical conversation – opens when Mike Fairbanks (aka Banks), our lead singer, enters:

> *"Hey man," I say.*
> *"Hey man," he replies.*
> *"Hey man," Drew says.*
> *"Hey man," he replies.*
> *"Dr. Bud, did Dave follow all the rules?" This from Banks, right on cue.*
> *In my best Monty Python fake-peasant British accent I say, "All but one, sir. All but one."*
> *Banks rears his eyebrows, joins in on the accent. "And which one might that be, sir?"*
> *I pretend not to want to say. "It was a very small rule, actually, sir."*
> *"Quick man, let's have it."*
> *I cover my face with my arms in a tragic gesture, say only, in a small accented voice, "the one about*
> * touching the board, sir. That one. But only that one."*
> *"I must choke him, you know."*
> *"Oh, but I wish you wouldn't, sir. Not this time. He's been, well, pitiful, sir, ever since I caught him.*
> * I chastised the bastard meself. I shouldn't think he requires choking, not today, sir."*
> *"I don't know. I still feel the need to choke him. It is a rule, you know."*
> *Drew walks over, joins in the merriment. "I think it was such a small rule that you should overlook it*
> * this time." Drew puts his hand on Banks' shoulder. "Do it for us, sir, for the good of the band."*
> *"Oh, very well then. For the good of the band."*
>
> Source: Goodall, 1991, pp. 235–236

Through this dialogue, we see the camaraderie of the band, and the way we used exclusion as a marking of status. The use of the Monty Python-ish accents by the band members (but not the Roadies) allowed for a playful interaction that put our band's lived experiences on par with those from the band on the big screen.

The dialogue illustrates how white, middle-class men "do" the business of male ritual bonding through stylized aggression. Yep, this is white boy stuff, through and through. And the band calls itself WHITEDOG. Indeed.

the data are often stripped from their context and used only insomuch as they advance or problematize current theory. Overall, there are many shades and hues of writing formats to choose from. No matter what tale you choose (or what tale chooses you), most essays have some similar sections in common – an issue we turn to next.

The archeology of a qualitative essay

In what follows I trace the archeology of a traditionally structured 15 to 35-page qualitative essay. Such essays may come in the form of a course paper, a conference paper submission, a book chapter, or – the scholar's reputational gold – the peer-reviewed journal article. Of course, qualitative scholars also write book-length manuscripts, and, if you are looking for more information on how to create book proposals and longer manuscripts, Goodall (2008) offers excellent advice.

Lindlof (2001) likens the traditional qualitative article to a "four act play" consisting of introduction/literature review, methods, findings, and conclusion. The metaphor is helpful because it emphasizes the major "working parts" of a qualitative essay. However, depending on the type of text created, the "acts" may not always unfold in a linear, deductive manner. Furthermore, different audiences call for different emphases, and sometimes the information described below may be all interweaved. Throughout the discussion below, I reference (but do not duplicate) the advice given in Chapter 5 on developing a rationale, an introduction, and a methods section. As you may remember, Chapter 5 reviews how to write the following parts:

- title, abstract, and key words
- introduction
  - research purposes and goals
  - reference to key audience, terms, and approaches
  - rationale (practical, theoretical, and/or methodological)
- literature review/conceptual framework
- research questions/issues (usually incorporated in introduction or literature review)
- methods (see also Tips and Tool 2 of Chapter 5 for details)
  - researcher's role
  - sites/participants
  - IRB approval
  - sampling plan
  - sources of data collected (e.g. participant observation, interviews, focus groups, online data, documents)
  - research instrumentation and approach (e.g. examples of interview questions, methods of transcribing, fieldnote writing)

In what follows I focus primarily on writing the methods, findings/analysis, and conclusions/implications. I encourage you to take a moment, flip back to Chapter 5, re-read, and then come back here when you're done.

Writing the framing material: title, abstract, key words

As discussed in Chapter 5, many people judge an essay by its key words, title, and abstract, so it makes sense to take care in devising these. They should serve as an invitation, written aesthetically to build interest, and you should pragmatically use key words that will be caught by targeted readers and by search engines.

Crafting the introductory framing material is a crucial structuring technique. Indeed, Wolcott (2009) suggests writing a table of contents for your project early on.

One of the best assignments ever given to me in graduate school was that of writing an abstract *before* I wrote the final paper. At first I resisted, thinking, "How in the world can I know what I'm going to write before I write it?" Then I sat down, read over the abstracts of a bunch of my favorite essays, and wrote the little sucker. After I crafted it, I realized its value as a brainstorming technique that helped me figure out how the essay might best proceed. I definitely revisited and modified the abstract later, but the decisions I made in writing the abstract were very helpful to launch the writing process.

Goodall (2008, p. 37) says that the abstract should answer these questions:

1   What is the story about?
2   What is the rationale?
3   Who is the intended audience?
4   How am I connecting to a scholarly conversation?

Perhaps more than any other part of the essay, this framing material is written for the reader rather than for the sake of the author, the theory, or the art. Good abstracts are clear, concise, and avoid technical language. They provide details rather than generalities about the paper's value and contributions. As such, they should avoid bland statements like "the essay concludes with practical and theoretical implications" and substitute them with statements like "the essay provides evidence that [*ABC*] is actually a result of [*XYZ*]. In doing so, it problematizes reigning [*ABC*] theories and suggests the inclusion of [*MNO*] in future field training." Details like this will increase the odds that others will read and make use of the research (because, who are we kidding, many people only read the abstract).

Writing the introduction, the literature review, and the conceptual framework

Early research proposals are excellent reference points for the introduction, the rationale, and the literature review. However, the trajectory of your project may have significantly morphed and transformed since the time you initially conceptualized it. Therefore I do not recommend using the research proposal as the "starting document." Open up a new document and use the research proposal as just one more touchstone resource.

The introduction gives the tone or feeling of a piece, setting the stage, piquing readers' interest, and letting them know what to expect. Beginnings should always be revisited many times, to ensure the essay is indeed delivering what it has promised. An introduction might begin with a vivid vignette or a set of small examples illustrating a paradox, a problem, or a situation that is particularly surprising, curious, or enigmatic. The introduction may "create a sense of mystery or end on a question" (Goodall, 2008, p. 67) in order to draw in readers, discourage them from flipping to the next essay, and inspire them to want to make sense of the data.

This first section should also reference key readers (your conceptual cocktail party), a rationale, a review of framing literature, concepts, and theories, and the key research problems and questions. This introductory material can also usefully foreshadow the ways the study will contribute to, extend, or problematize the literature.

Writing the research methodology and method(s)

The presentation of your methodology, research procedures, and design of the study is another key part of the essay. As reviewed in Chapter 2, methodology refers to the philosophical approach toward inquiry – for instance, explaining the value of an interpretive approach to inquiry. In dissertations or theses students may be expected to include information pertaining to their philosophical methodology, in order to support the paradigmatic underpinnings of their research. However, there usually is not space for a long discussion of methodology in traditional qualitative essays.

Rather, typical qualitative essays devote space to writing about the study's method(s) – the particular techniques used to collect, organize, and analyze data. Some people call this section "research procedures," but many call it the "method" or "methods" section. Other scholars opt to name this section by using a descriptive heading – such as "Examining the Disabled Body in Sport Participation" (Lindemann, 2008, p. 103). A heading such as this one may be more useful and vividly descriptive than a generic heading "Methods." Of course, depending on the publication venue and the editor's formatting preferences, you may have little choice on what to call this section.

In addition to the information given in Chapter 5 on what to include in the methods section, the final essay should provide a transparent explanation of the actual data collected, as well as an account of the procedures used in data analysis. In Researcher's Notepad 12.3 I give examples of tables that sum up data collection – versions of which many former students have modified and used as their own.

The methods section also explains how fieldnotes were recorded, how interviews were transcribed, and how data were organized. The reader should understand the technology that assisted with data analysis (manual or computer-aided) and should have a clear picture of how coding proceeded. The reader needs to feel confident that the data collected are substantial and appropriate for providing a significant representation. Certainly, "there are no stories out there waiting to be told and no certain truths waiting to be recorded; there are only stories yet to be constructed" (Denzin, 1997, p. 267). Nonetheless, some stories are more rigorously and transparently constructed than others.

Painting a clear path for your analysis also includes providing examples of first-level descriptive codes, second-level analytic and hierarchical codes, excerpts from the codebook, and explanations of advanced data analysis techniques. Further, the methods section might explain activities like negative case analysis, analytic memo writing, theoretical sampling, and developing loose analysis outlines (analytic activities described in Chapters 9 and 10). Finally, accompanying this discussion with appropriate citations renders a pedagogical service to those readers who want to emulate or learn more about your methodological techniques. Citing references connected to your methodological practices displays credibility and rigor – something that may be especially important for readers who are unfamiliar with qualitative methods.

Unfortunately too many articles give short shrift to methods. Sometimes, but not always, this may be a sign of sloppiness, or at least of less than optimal methodological rigor. However, it is easy to forget all the analytic activities in retrospect (and this is why I recommend keeping a document that catalogues them over time). The lack of detail can also be due to limits of space. Even when the authors provide detailed descriptions of their analysis in the original submissions, editors often ask them to pare these down. The description of methods can end up being left on the cutting-room floor – which unfortunately compromises the potential for qualitative essays to teach readers about the unique strategies and value of qualitative data (Tracy, 2012).

RESEARCHER'S NOTEPAD 12.3

Methods data display

The following tables, which I created for my dissertation work with correctional officers, summarize the data collected and the research participants (Tracy, 2001, p. 72).

Summary of the data gathered

Type of Data	Hours spent collecting data		Single-spaced typed pages	
	Nouveau Jail	Women's Minimum	Nouveau Jail	Women's Minimum
Daily duties – observation/ shadowing of officers	32	48	57	92
Officer training – participation/observation	25	8	25	20
Interviews – formal/ transcribed	~16 hours 12 interviews	~14 hours 10 interviews	212	186
Training documents	–	–	20	100
Volunteer training – participation	N/A	8	–	10
Misc. meetings with primary contacts and others associated with project	~10	~10	–	–
Subtotal	**83**	**88**	**314**	**408**
Total	**171 total research hours**		**722 total pages of data**	

Descriptive statistics of participants

Total number of participants within scope of research project	109
Extended observation and/or formal interview	67
Brief observation or informal interview	42
Organization	
Nouveau employees	64
Women's Minimum employees	42
Subjects not employed by either facility	3
Type of job	
Correctional officer	68
Administrative employee (e.g. sergeant, lieutenant, captain, sheriff, etc.)	20
Other (e.g. psychologists, office staff, chaplains, past employees)	21
Gender	
Male	72
Female	37
Ethnicity	
White/Caucasian	83
Hispanic/Latino	15
Black/African American	10
Asian American	1

Writing the findings and analysis

Typically, the most substantial and longest part of qualitative essays displays the findings in a compelling way. Saldaña (2011) prefers that the findings are front-loaded and made very clear by saying something like: "The three main findings are…" (p. 142). Indeed you should not underestimate the number of readers who will only *skim* your article. Front-loading the findings or summing them up at the end makes it much more likely that these readers will take note of your findings and consider them as they design and build their own projects.

As you develop your findings, I also encourage you to keep in mind Goodall's (2008, p. 27) 4 C's of evocative storytelling:

conflict	identifies and explains problems or controversies
connection	identification with the reader through character development
continuing curiosity	novelty and plot development: is it a page turner?
climactic satisfaction	does the ending deliver?

You should think of your findings section as an act of persuasion, and, depending on the audience, you will need to craft your findings in different ways. Here, on the basis of my own experience as well as through reading other resources (e.g. Becker, 2007; Goodall, 2008; Lindlof & Taylor, 2011), I describe six common strategies for writing findings: (1) themes/topics; (2) chronology/natural history; (3) convergence/braided narrative; (4) puzzle–explication strategy; (5) separated narratives; and (6) messy/layered texts.

Themes/topics

One of the most common and intuitive organization strategies is that of organizing the essay around several primary **themes/topics**. These themes may just emerge as the most salient ones in the data, as was the case when Karen Tracy and I organized our emotional labor article with 911 call-takers around three primary categories: (1) the emotional landscape of 911; (2) institutional feeling rules; and (3) emotion labor strategies (S. Tracy & Tracy, 1998). The first section overviewed the emotional highs and lows of answering 911 phone calls. The second reviewed the organization's feeling rules for how call-takers should express (and not express) emotion. The third section described seven techniques that call-takers used in order to manage their emotion, for example joking, story-telling, and self-talk.

Themes may also revolve around categories associated with an established theory. For instance, former student Emily Cripe analyzed breast-feeding support groups (Cripe, 2011) and organized her findings into categories already identified by past social support theory: emotional support, instrumental support, and informational support (Albrecht, & Adelman, 1987). Past theory can give you a tidy organizational structure to lay on top of the data. However, in order to *build* theory and knowledge, it's important to push the limits of existing structures. To extend understanding of social support, Cripe (2011) borrowed the concept of "communal coping," a concept typically used in groups that have to cope with a shared problem or stressor (Lyons, Mickelson, Sullivan, & Coyne, 1998). This construct helped illuminate a unique type of support, which is offered in *live interactional* support groups. The addition of this concept extended the current thinking on the social support literature and helped explain why group interaction among breastfeeding women is especially supportive. In short, some of the categories found by Cripe were based on the existing literature, while new ones emerged from the data analysis.

Chronology/life-story

A second type of organizational structure for findings is the **chronology** or **life-story** (Atkinson, 1998). A chronological structure may narrate the development of a certain process, cultural change, intervention, or family feud, whereas a life-story – like a life-story interview – tells the story of a certain person or group of people over time. Such organizational patterns are also quite common for researchers who use discourse tracing as a data analysis approach (LeGreco & Tracy, 2009). They are also helpful for topics associated with key turning points, socialization, or change.

For example, Hickey and colleagues (Hickey, Thompson, & Foster, 1988) show how a fantasy character learned to become the mall Easter bunny. In "Chronicling an Academic Depression," Jago (2002) narrated her trajectory of stress and depression as a new professor. Data may also be presented in a modified or reconstructed chronological progression. Greg Larson engaged in an 11-month ethnography of an aerospace company (Larson & Tompkins, 2005) and developed an analysis that recounted an organizational change process in which managers unwittingly subverted their own influence by communicating ambivalence about changes they introduced. This ambivalence, in turn, gave employees support in resisting the proposed changes. Chronological and life-story organizational structures such as these highlight movement and temporality and explain why something progressed in a certain manner.

Convergence/braided narrative

A third writing technique is the **convergence narrative** or the **braided narrative**, in which two or more different stories overlap and parallel each other in order to illustrate a larger story. An excellent example can be found in Rebecca Skloot's (2010) award-winning bestseller *The Immortal Life of Henrietta Lacks*. This narrative weaves together the stories of (a) Henrietta Lacks, whose cancerous cells were taken without her knowledge in 1951; (b) Henrietta's immortal (HeLa) cells and their use in medical science; and (c) the complex relationship that developed between the author, Rebecca, and Henrietta's daughter, Deborah, over the years of researching and writing the book. The interweaving of these three stories brilliantly illuminated intersections between public science and private, intimate relations and how today's medical advances are intertwined with the dark history of African American exploitation.

Writing in the form of a convergence/braided narrative usually takes more space than other writing techniques, so this technique is more often evidenced in books than in articles. Furthermore, understanding how to effectively toggle between various narratives takes significant literary expertise. Those interested in the technique are advised to seek out models (see Goodall, 2008, pp. 79–83) and be prepared for multiple rewritings and reorganizations. Indeed, Rebecca Skloot herself wrote and rewrote her Henrietta Lacks book five times before ever submitting it to an editor. As she reports in a Youtube interview

Figure 12.1 One way to organize your essay is to open it with a paradox, enigma, puzzle, or absurdity, and then to "solve" the puzzle through the paper's analysis. WoodyStock/Alamy.

(http://www.youtube.com/watch?v=hXRhoA46-eA), she modeled the braided narrative structure, in part, by watching and carefully story-boarding out similar techniques in the movies *The Hurricane* (Jewison, 1999) and *Fried Green Tomatoes* (Avnet, 1991).

Puzzle explication strategy

A fourth popular way to structure the findings – and one complementary to the phronetic approach in this book – is the **puzzle explication** strategy, which opens with a paradox, enigma, puzzle, or absurdity (see Figure 12.1). Katz explains the value of such an approach:

> When ethnographers describe the operation of these enigmas, paradoxes, and little overt lies, they provoke curiosity about the big sociological "why?": what explains the sense of apparent coherence in the lives of the people studied? What makes it possible for them to take for granted that they live in a common social world? Why is social life not apparently coming apart at the seams constantly? (Katz, 2001, p. 453)

Provoking this type of curiosity encourages the reader forward, providing a guiding structure for the piece. It also encourages an analysis that is not only descriptive, but explanatory – unpacking a rationale for something that initially seems puzzling or absurd.

I used this strategy in my dissertation, by beginning with a series of vignettes that depicted "puzzling performances" from correctional officers – such as their display of paranoia in public places and their joy in catching inmates' bad behavior. The rest of the dissertation tried to find the "why" behind such performances by describing the contradictions inherent in the correctional officer's work and the creative (and sometimes dysfunctional) behaviors that such officers adopted in order to meet the paradoxical expectations of their workplace. I used this technique so that readers might learn to appreciate why officers act in ways that, on their face, seem puzzling or inappropriate.

Separated text

A fifth organizational structure is the **separated text**, in which the analysis and the theoretical information are separated from the more descriptive story. Such an approach is quite common in case studies (see e.g. Keyton & Schockley-Zalabak, 2009). The first part of case studies usually consists of a descriptive narrative that illustrates a problem, potential solutions, and leaves the actual resolution to the reader (Ellet, 2007). These descriptions are typically written without a lot of scholarly language, so they may be easily understood and analyzed by professionals and students alike. Oftentimes a case study is accompanied by a theoretical analysis that identifies scholarly concepts, and these help the reader make sense of the case in more complex ways. For instance, a case study about compassion among border patrol agents is written in a creative nonfiction style, but it is followed by discussion questions that tap into theoretical concepts such as dirty work and race relations (Rivera & Tracy, 2012).

Separating the descriptive text from theoretical analysis is also practiced for reasons of aesthetics and evocativeness. Stewart (2010) used such a technique in her visual narrative of the Burning Man Festival. Her manuscript opens with a scholarly introduction explaining the importance of narrative inquiry. It then breaks into a visual narrative devoted to photos and accompanying creative nonfiction that describes the transformative nature of the Burning Man experience in an evocative way. Along the way she uses footnotes to link the story to rhetorical and narrative theory. She closes the piece with a theoretical and methodological discussion.

This separation technique is especially valuable for authors who aim their work at various audiences of readers. In Stewart's (2010) project, some readers are primarily drawn to the Burning Man story and photographs, while others are attracted to its theoretical contributions (and therefore are motivated to read the additional excerpts and footnotes). The cross-exposure to both tales encourages audiences to find value in modes of inquiry they may not otherwise read or appreciate.

Layered/messy texts

Finally, findings sections (and entire articles for that matter) can be in the form of nonlinear layered/messy texts. Messy texts juxtapose different time periods or topics to create evocative ruptures and to hijack reader assumptions. One way they do this is through atypical visual cues, such as a series of asterisks inserted between jarring sections, like this:

* * * * *

An excellent example of a messy text is "Jarheads, Girly Men, and the Pleasures of Violence" (Pelias, 2007). The article opens by conceptually situating the forthcoming narratives in terms of power and gender. It then segues into "twenty tales of violence and pleasure" (p. 946) that jump between the author's autoethnographic stories, poems about war, and examples of violence depicted in the media, ethnographies, and novels. The narratives depict how a lone boy/man is both dominant jarhead *and* resistant girly man – alternating between subject positions of dominance, courage, and vulnerability – and ultimately suggest that it's better to be a girly man than a jarhead. The juxtaposition of these stories with the scholarly literature shows how masculinity, violence, and domination are powerfully intertwined and manifest in our social fabric.

Because **messy texts** or **layered texts** are not bound in time or rationality, they may seem easy to write (see Ronai, 1992 and Tracy, 2004 for other examples). You might think: "Heck, with a messy text, I don't have to worry about organization or transitions between sections!" However, perfecting such haphazardness in a way that creates a compelling story is no easy task. Think how hard interior designers must work to achieve mismatched "shabby chic," or how carefully hairstylists must practice before snipping the perfect tousled "shag"; in the same way, writing a messy text requires a significant amount of literary skill. Article sections must be jagged enough to rupture preconceived

EXERCISE 12.1

Which writing strategy?

As described, a number of organization/literary strategies exist for writing findings:

- themes/topics
- chronology/natural history
- convergence/braided narrative
- puzzle-explication strategy
- separated narratives
- messy/layered texts

Which of the preceding writing strategies...

1   Might be best poised for identifying problems and explaining your data?
2   Might be most appropriate for connecting with your key readers/audiences?
3   Do you feel most comfortable with or excited about pursuing as a writer?
4   Has the most potential for achieving your study's goals?

notions and evoke emotion, yet coherent enough to propel continuous reading. Certainly, such texts show in their representation that there is never a "whole story" or a set of irrefutable conclusions. At the same time, good messy texts not only ask questions, they provide valuable contributions; they go beyond inducing frustration or desperation to eliciting inspiration, hope, and courage.

Writing the conclusions and implications

An essay's conclusion serves as the last and parting impression, explaining how the study extended, problematized, or contributed to knowledge. Although their content differs from essay to essay, qualitative conclusions typically (a) summarize key findings; (b) reiterate their significance, explicitly showing how the study implicates theory and practice; (c) acknowledge limitations; and (d) point to future research directions. I discuss each of these below.

The best summaries are specific and saturated with content. They do not just reiterate the paper's headings ("first I provided research questions, then I reviewed the literature, and finally I discussed the findings"). Rather they synthesize the most important contributions of the piece. For example, on the basis of her study of emotional management in airport security lines, Shawna Malvini Redden (in press) stated in her conclusion: "The data not only show that emotions 'travel' through the airport, but also that repercussions of emotion management reverberate throughout the entire travel process" (p. 25).

Conclusions should not only summarize the data, but also tell the reader how the study links up with, extends, or problematizes existing knowledge. More than any other part of the essay, the conclusion displays the interrelationships between theory – introduced in the literature review/conceptual framework – and the data. Whereas the findings section is devoted to *showing* the claims, the conclusion *tells* the reader how their findings relate to, or build, theory.

Perhaps the study helps solve a problem, attends to a certain controversy, critiques an existing school of thought, strengthens a fledgling theory, or constructs a new one.

For example, building from the example above, Malvini Redden found that, in mandatory security line interactions, airline passengers perform unique types of emotional management, not accounted for by existing theory. Specifically, passengers suppress their irritation and uncertainty and successfully perform acceptance and compliance, so that everyone can travel efficiently through security. She proposed the concept of "emotional taxes" to describe this obligatory emotion, performed for the greater good. In doing so, Malvini Redden not only theoretically illuminated her own data, but provided a construct that other researchers could adopt in future studies.

In addition to contributing to scholarly theories or to knowledge, the conclusion may also point out practical applications. An important application from Malvini Redden's study was that customer emotion management is connected to security and organizational proficiency. Conflicts and stress in airplane security lines arise in part from the lack of explicit direction about security procedures, and this, in turn, can negatively affect the organization, its employees, and the passengers. Very often theoretical and practical implications meld into each other, but some journals ask authors to separate them into different sections.

Conclusions also include a discussion of the study's limitations. No research study is ever perfect or covers everything, and the limitations should transparently and vulnerably discuss what can be known – and also what cannot be known – from the study. At the same time, qualitative researchers should not beat themselves up for not accomplishing goals that they did not set out to achieve in the first place. For example, noting that an in-depth case study is not statistically generalizable is ridiculous, because case studies aim instead at transferability and naturalistic generalization (as was discussed in Chapter 11). In the conclusion it is more useful to set some parameters for contexts in which the findings are especially worthwhile or, alternatively, for contexts in which the findings may not be applicable (Keyton, Bisel, & Ozley, 2009).

The conclusion should also be heuristic, providing specific tips and suggestions for future research – tips that emerge from the current study. In our article examining compassion among hospice employees (Way & Tracy, 2012), we acknowledged that, because our interview data focused on communication from the viewpoint of hospice caregivers, our findings could be strengthened in future studies by examining the viewpoints of patients. As illustrated, limitations and future research can naturally be coupled together, because often the limitations pinpoint issues that can be bolstered by additional research. Developing carefully considered tips for future research is not only a gift to the readers; it may also be a gift to yourself. Indeed, you may be identifying in this way your own future research projects.

When reaching the essay's concluding sentence, readers should feel thoroughly convinced that the study has attended to its stated goals, purposes, and research questions. They should also know its limitations and perhaps feel inspired to launch their own research on a similar or related topic. If nothing else, they should feel as though their investment in the essay was worth their time. Endings are largely about "pay-offs" (Goodall, 2008, p. 86). As such, conclusions should provide some answers, even if these are tentative and raise new questions for future research. And, finally, just like good speeches, good conclusions end with a bang rather than a whimper. Keeping tidbits of data, contributions, and quotations along the way can help construct a strong conclusion (especially if you must draft it on little sleep, with a deadline looming – not that I would know anything about that…).

FOLLOWING, FORGETTING, AND IMPROVISING

The information provided in this chapter, like much advice about writing academic articles, assumes that most qualitative articles will unfold in the style of a "four act play" consisting of introduction/literature review, methods, findings, and conclusion (Lindlof, 2001). This traditional writing format is well worn, comfortable, and predictable, but teaching this style also gives me pause (Tracy, 2012).

Writing in this traditional style can be problematic, in that it perpetrates a myth of linearity and deduction. It suggests the author examined the literature and the theory to begin with, then came up with research questions or purposes, and then found data that attended to those questions/purposes – with an ultimate result of furthering knowledge and practice. However, as illustrated throughout this book, much qualitative research is inductively grounded, or at least it tags back and forth, iteratively, between past literature and more emic and emergent interests and data.

We may begin data collection with vague ideas about topics or scholarly theories of interest, but many researchers (and especially students new to research) do not know what literatures or theories will helpfully ground the piece until many of the data are already collected. We first figure out the interesting data and only then play the qualitative version of the game-show Jeopardy. In other words, many researchers first identify the "answers" of our data (in the form of fieldnotes, transcripts, codes, and analytic memos), and only then search out and construct the appropriate research questions that fit those data.

Laying the traditional four-act deductive logic at the top of an inductive or iterative research process can harm qualitative epistemology and pedagogy. Let me explain. It can harm epistemology (or knowledge-building) because it mutes the explanation of the iterative juxtapositions and theoretical laddering processes that are the hallmarks of interpretive analysis (Hallier & Foirbes, 2004). Consider the example provided in Chapter 9 as Cliff Scott, Karen Myers and I were engaging in prospective conjecture as a method of identifying the sensemaking role of humor among service workers. The deductive writing style expected by the editors and reviewers we encountered along the publication process made it all but impossible to write at length about our inductive process (Tracy, 2012). When the format of writing dissuades from such a discussion, researchers are less likely to report on their processes, and the epistemological insights that come from such reports are blunted.

Relatedly, the traditional writing style can do a disservice to pedagogy (or learning) because, when qualitative essays are written in a deductive style yet their research has been conducted in an iterative or inductive fashion, the reader has less opportunity to learn about the author's emic process. Indeed, the deductive logic of writing may actually mask the process. Let me recount an example to illustrate.

I vividly remember writing my first single-authored article about emotional labor on a cruise ship (Tracy, 2000). This was early in my career, before I was schooled in the deductive writing process. It was also before I had a head full of theories and concepts. I engaged in the data collection first, in a break between my MA and my PhD. I brought the data back with me to school a year later and organized them into the following themes – as I learned about poststructuralist understandings of control and resistance:

(a) the arbitrary and historically contingent nature of emotion labor rules on a cruise ship; (b) how emotional control mechanisms were dispersed among management, peers, and passengers; (c) the ways employees self-subordinated […] to emotion labor norms and privatized burnout; and (d) how staff identity was discursively constituted through an interplay of resistance and consent to emotion labor norms (Tracy, 2000, pp. 117–118)

In the first draft of my essay, the literature review provided background on these theories and then described my data in relation to them.

I submitted the essay to *Management Communication Quarterly*. I was happy to receive a "revise and resubmit" on the article, along with a quite supportive response from the editor. Among other suggestions, however, the editor asked that I construct and present clear research questions that emerged from the literature review, and that my findings sections then tag back to these research questions as I presented the data. I was a bit confused by this instruction, because I had not entered the data collection with specific research questions in mind (or really with any knowledge of poststructural theory whatsoever). However, like many young scholars eager to publish, I complied with the request with little complaint. In the final version of the manuscript, the literature review concludes with the following research questions (p. 99):

Research question 1   How are current understandings of emotion labor on a cruise ship historically contingent?
Research question 2   In what ways are emotional control systems dispersed among superiors, peers, and passengers?
Research question 3   How do employees play a part in their own emotional control?
Research question 4   How is cruise staff identity constituted in relation to emotion labor norms?

Furthermore, in each sub-section of the findings section I restated these questions – and by doing so I created the illusion that I collected the data for the very purpose of answering these pre-designed research question. Granted, this writing style may assist readers as they progress through the essay in a quite understandable and rational manner. Unfortunately the questions also supported the myth that, before I entered the field, I knew that these questions would arise. Including them in the "first act" of the essay suggested a deductive approach, in which the existing theories and literature drive the analysis – when in reality the data collection came first, and only later did I try to make sense of the data in terms of any types of literature or theory.

Since that time, I have attempted to present journal-length research articles in a more inductive fashion, in some cases by layering the account (Tracy, 2004) or by discussing the iterative approach in the methods section (e.g. Tracy, Lutgen-Sandvik, & Alberts, 2006).

However, in the one case where my colleagues and I attempted to present the inductive approach explicitly and write our piece inductively, editors and reviewers asked that it be reworked to a more traditional format.

So why is it important to know this story? Because providing writing advice for qualitative researchers is difficult and paradoxical. As a qualitative scholar, I recognize the problems of writing qualitative data in the traditional four-act play format – which is the norm for many journal editors and dissertation advisors. Indeed, in most cases, qualitative dissertations do not reflect the writing formats the author wanted, but rather attend to the committee's and grad school requirements (Bishop, 1999). At the same time, I tend to be a pragmatist and to realize that this traditional format is much more familiar and publishable than alternative accounts. My hope is that, over time, qualitative scholars will have the courage and numbers to cause a change in our publication expectations, encouraging a variety of formats that reflect the inductive interpretive process better. One potential way to achieve this is simply to include a layered discussion of the literature and findings, in which the author offers, to begin with, a literature review of the sensitizing concepts, then gives a taste of the data followed by a more focused discussion of the specific research direction and purposes, and next concentrates on the in-depth data analysis that led to specific theoretical and practical contributions (for a full explanation, see Tracy, 2012).

In summary

Writing marks the entire qualitative research process. However, at some point, researchers must make decisions about how to write up a final report. This chapter opened by discussing how qualitative research can be presented in a variety of tales – traditional, impressionistic, confessional. No matter the type of tale, most essays have several primary "moving parts." These include the key sections that were first presented in Chapter 5 on writing research proposals (e.g. introduction, rationale, literature review), as well as additional sections on methodology, findings, and implications. Deciding on how to write the findings depends on the audience, the writer's skills, and the goals of the analysis.

As you move into the writing process, I encourage you to keep in mind that, despite the gains of qualitative methodology, qualitative researchers still face challenges in terms of how best to write the account of an inductive or iterative process in a conventional way so as to make it listened to by others. In dealing with this issue, I've been challenged about the extent to which it is better to write in layered, iterative, and creative manners, or to write in ways that are most likely to get published in high-impact venues. Obviously it's not one or the other, but what I'm pointing out is that there are no easy answers, and this makes it difficult to prescribe best practices.

Sometimes ya gotta follow the rules before you abandon them. Indeed, when we examine the life work of some of the most accomplished performance and narrative ethnographers – people like Dwight Conquergood, Bud Goodall, and Art Bochner – we see that they wrote in quite traditional ways before turning to more creative approaches. Indeed it may be wise for novices in research to write traditionally and show that they have an understanding of the field they are entering before beginning to write in less conventional manners (Bishop, 1999). At the same time, I will forever be indebted to Bryan Taylor, accomplished qualitative scholar and a member of my doctoral committee, for encouraging me to write one chapter of my dissertation in a creative, layered format, even when other committee members were not so sure. I remember him saying: "When is Sarah supposed to learn this kind of writing if not now?" Thank you, Bryan.

The good news is that inductive and layered tales are becoming more accepted. Graduate school boards are modifying writing specifications so that students can submit theses and dissertations that push outside traditional writing regulations. Conferences like the *Congress for Qualitative Inquiry* hold workshops and feature panels of new ethnographies. Journals like *Qualitative Inquiry* and *Qualitative Journal of Communication* regularly feature impressionist tales. Richardson (2000b, p. 938) provides a helpful listing of journal outlets and book presses that are open to creative representations ethnography.

That said, oftentimes these tales are still framed as "experimental" and "alternative" – a label that places them on the sidelines of "mainstream" research. In short, political realities in the academy and among governmental grant-giving agencies continue to question the validity and credibility of impressionist representations. Those who pursue such approaches should educate themselves about the constraints and prepare for the fact that powerful audiences may accord more legitimacy to traditional tales than to impressionist and literary representations. I hope many readers will take up this challenge, but I also understand that we all gotta pay the bills.

KEY TERMS

→ **braided narrative**   writing technique in which the data are organized by overlapping multiple narratives in order to build a larger story also see **convergence narrative**

→ **chronology**   organization of the reported data according to the time sequence in which events occurred also see **life-story**

→ **confessional tale**   a style of reporting qualitative research that places the researcher and his/her experiences at the center of the story, highlighting self-reflexivity

→ **convergence narrative**   writing technique in which the data are organized by overlapping multiple narratives to build a larger story see also **braided narrative**

→ **crisis of representation**   movement originating among postmodernist scholars questioning traditional representational practices and urging formats that highlight the partiality and constructed nature of knowledge

→ **layered text**   text that juxtaposes different time periods or topics to create evocative ruptures and to hijack the reader's assumptions oftentimes sections are separated by asterisks ✳ ✳ ✳ ✳ ✳; also see **messy text**

→ **life-story**   organization of the reported data according to the time sequence in which events occurred also see **chronology**

→ **messy text**   text that juxtaposes different time periods or topics to create evocative ruptures and to hijack the reader's assumptions oftentimes sections are separated by asterisks ✳ ✳ ✳ ✳ ✳ see also **layered text**

→ **poetic inquiry**   a method in which the author or participant extracts key words from the data and strategically truncates these words into poetic formats

→ **puzzle explication**   a writing format that structures findings around a paradox, a puzzle, or an absurdity

→ **separated text**   a writing format in which the theoretical information and analysis are presented separately from a more descriptive story, for instance a case study

→ **themes/topics**   particular categories or themes that arise from the scene or from extant literature/theory and around which the reported data are organized

CHAPTER 13

Writing Part 2
Drafting, polishing, and publishing

Contents

Qualitative Research Methods: Collecting Evidence, Crafting Analysis, Communicating Impact, First Edition. Sarah J. Tracy.
© 2013 Sarah J. Tracy. Published 2013 by Blackwell Publishing Ltd.

I keenly remember a phone call from co-author (then PhD student) Kendra Rivera. I was in the midst of writing the literature review for our study of male executives and work–life balance. She was at home, drafting the practical applications section, and she needed a breather. I needed a break too, and her phone call was a welcome distraction. We were scheduled to trade drafts in an hour.

In that conversation we shared our progress and vented some of our challenges. She said, with a laugh: "I'm learning that all those cool sentences that I had read in your past articles didn't come so easily." I responded with a chuckle, trying to sound poised and unaffected rather than pleased that Kendra thought some of my sentences were "cool."

After we hung up, I went back to the draft, reviewing what I had just written. Dear God. The sentences I was re-reading on my screen were not only *not cool* but downright bulky, academically pompous, and nearly incomprehensible. Oh my. Kendra would soon be coming face to face with my "shitty first draft" (Lamott, 1994).

The cool thing is that no one (except perhaps your co-authors) ever has to see that first draft. As creative nonfiction writer Anne Lamott suggests: "Don't worry if what you write is no good, because no one is going to see it" (p. 4). But – and here's the important part – you still have to write those "no good" sentences and be okay with the fact that they are not so snazzy. It's like throwing up clay before creating a piece of pottery. If you don't first throw up the clay – ugly, gray, and as misshapen as can be – and accept it in all its ugliness, then you will never sculpt a masterpiece. Lucid arguments, gripping illustrations, and award-winning scholarship emerge from "uncool" sentences and shitty first drafts.

Helping you move from first draft to polished manuscript is what this chapter is about. I open by discussing how writing is another form of inquiry; in other words, we come to know and learn our findings and revelations through the very process of writing. I then discuss how to introduce and embed qualitative data in an essay. This includes how to choose the best data, write about it in a rich and luminous manner, and structure it so that it shows rather than tells. I also discuss several grammatical issues, explaining how verb choice is crucial for writing qualitative research reports actively and vividly. Furthermore, formatting choices, such as how to cite interviews and fieldnote excerpts and how to include visual representations, are keys for creating a reader-friendly essay.

The chapter also delves into the difficult components of writing, giving advice on how to write a lot, how to choose a publication venue, and how to navigate the revise and resubmission part of the publication process. Finally I provide insight on addressing common qualitative writing challenges. These obstacles are not signs of failure, but rather just another part of the qualitative process.

Figure 13.1 Even the most accomplished writers deal with writing block and "shitty first drafts." Having a sense of humor about it is a good first step at getting better. Cartoon from Savage Chickens (www.savagechickens.com) by Doug Savage.

Writing to inquire

By the time you sit down and begin writing sentences for the "final" report (as if any report is ever "final"), you should have lots of raw materials. These may include: the research proposal (Chapter 5) or the organized files of fieldnote and interview data; visual data displays; and a rough analysis outline (Chapter 10). All of these materials are building blocks for the final project. They also help you overcome the "final report" intimidation process. They serve as reassuring reminders that you already have accomplished a lot and have plenty to say – and also some good ideas about how to say it.

You might be tempted at this point to think that you just need to "write up" all these materials into a final essay. One of the most popular qualitative writing resources is Harry Wolcott's *Writing up Qualitative Research*, now in its third edition (2009). This book is jam-packed with writing advice, techniques and tips, and it is delivered in an accessible and friendly manner. That said, I question the "writing *up*" part of Wolcott's book title. Why?

The phrase "writing up" suggests that, before you write, you must already have the meaning, the findings, and the answers in your head. Thinking that you must first have it all figured out is bad. Very, very bad. This belief just encourages pain and procrastination. It suggests that you must wait for something really brilliant to enter your brain before you press your fingers to the keyboard. It encourages excuses for not writing – made-up things like "I've got writer's block." It emboldens you to clean the bathroom rather than write – because maybe that good idea will magically appear while scouring the toilet. Such an approach may indeed result in a spotless bathroom. However, it does not lead to brilliant writing.

If you're a qualitative researcher, the answers are never perfectly formed in the head from the start. Rather, *qualitative researchers find meaning by writing the meaning into being*. Artists' magic comes in their *process* of creation. Artists don't "paint up" their picture or "sculpt up" their statues. Likewise, qualitative researchers do not "write up." They write. And, through writing, they meander, produce crappy sentences, feel stuck, go back and edit, write some more – and through this process they come to *know*.

Richardson has written a book and several essays on how writing is not just a form of representation, but a form of inquiry. In her chapter entitled "Writing: A Method of Inquiry" in the second edition of the *Handbook of Qualitative Research* (2000b) she uses plain talk and vivid examples to explain that the form of writing is inseparable from its content and that, through writing, we learn. She also provides fantastic techniques for practicing writing as a form of inquiry. These include practices like writing the same scene from several points of view, taking the same episode and representing it as a narrative, as a poem, as a drama, and as a news story, or addressing the writing to various audiences – academics, professionals, the popular press, policy makers, or school children. Creative nonfiction writer Lamott (1994) says she gets herself to write by thinking about how her work could be a gift to someone else. Depending on the topic, qualitative researchers could frame their writing as a gift to various audiences – to participants, to an instructor, to academics, journalists, or professionals who have a stake in the topic.

Lamott (1994) also recommends viewing the writing project as a letter. Start small – as if all you need to do for the moment is write just enough to fill up a little picture frame. Lamott places a tiny picture frame right next to her computer as a visual reminder. She also quotes (p. 18) E. L. Doctorow, who once said this about writing: "It's like driving a car at night. You never see further than your headlights, but you can make the whole trip that way." Even if you prefer to plan a journey in advance, it's important to have the faith that you will be able to get there little by little. In the process, you'll come to learn the best route and the destinations that deserve the most attention.

No matter what the writing technique, a key point is that qualitative meaning comes when your fingers are moving – whether they are tapping a keyboard or scrawling over notepaper. You need not wait until you know what you want to say. The creative writing exercises Richardson (2000b) suggests make writing feel less intimidating. It's not the "final report." It's just playing. And, through play, the meaning will come.

Of course, creating an outline can help you see the journey in front of you. You might make digressions along the way, but the map gives you the courage to put one foot in front of the other and move forward. The outline helps you know that you're not writing yourself out onto a cliff and about to fall off into oblivion. With an outline in hand, when you find yourself in muddy waters, you can take a time out and relocate yourself. It also encourages you to consider how your qualitative evidence will be included in the emerging tale – a topic we turn to next.

How to write qualitative evidence

Successfully constructing a qualitative essay requires learning how to write and format qualitative evidence in a persuasive, vivid, and efficient manner. The following section gives tips and best practices for how to choose, present, and format qualitative data.

Choosing the evidence

A key question is: What amounts to good data? Identifying data appropriate for specific claims or themes begins in the qualitative data analysis process (Chapters 9 and 10). However, we often only determine what equates with "good data" when we begin writing the research report (Katz, 2002). Data that seemed mundane or irrelevant at the stage of the initial coding may become extremely valuable as arguments are constructed in prose.

As you begin to write, remember that only data that are directly linked with the study's research question(s), goal(s), and purpose(s) should end up in the essay. Resist the urge to tell the "whole story." A scan of published articles suggests that typical qualitative essays include only 1,000–3,000 words of excerpted data (three to six double-spaced pages). For most qualitative researchers, this is just a small fraction of the entire data set. Don't be surprised if it feels painful as you make decisions about which stories to include and which ones to cut. In what follows I provide advice on how to choose and format your data as evidence.

Rich, luminous, and thick evidence

One of the great values of qualitative research is that it gives rich depth to a scene or situation. It's important that this vividness does not get lost as you move from raw fieldnotes and interview transcripts to writing the final pages of the research report. As Goodall (2008) puts it, "thou shalt be descriptive" (p. 42).

Descriptive data are rich and luminous. **Rich data** provide explanations that are bountiful and generous and emerge from a variety of sources and contexts (Weick, 2007). **Luminous data** are poignant, revealing, and often characterized by enigma, paradox, and absurdity (Katz, 2001, 2002). Like glowing candles, luminous data shimmer, attract the eye, and light the path. Rich and luminous data are valuable in part because they are interesting, aesthetically pleasant, and fun to read. However, as Katz (2001) argues, qualitative researchers should avoid self-aggrandizing rallying cries that praise their "descriptions of social life as 'richly varied,' 'densely textured,' 'revealing,' 'colorful,' 'vivid,' poignant,' 'strategic,' or 'finely nuanced' [...] or as containing 'paradoxes' and 'enigmas' that fascinate the investigator and the reader" (p. 444). Katz believes that these qualitative buzz words, when used to celebrate the end goals of research, gloss the fact that these types of data are primarily valuable because they provide the means for significant understanding and explanation. In other words, radiant data are a means to an end rather than being an end in themselves.

Rich and luminous data not only show *how* a phenomena unfolded, but help to explain *why* it unfolded in *this* context or with *this* group. Furthermore, as discussed in Chapter 6, such data have the potential to make the familiar strange and the strange familiar (Lindlof & Taylor 2011; Wolcott, 2009). Qualitative data are perfectly poised to represent mundane activities in ways that renew perception. Making the familiar strange encourages the reader to pause and (re)consider preconceived notions or see a phenomenon in a fresh way. Making the strange familiar helps readers feel acquainted with foreign ideas or practices, potentially encouraging them to identify with an argument they may otherwise have written off as alien or contrary to their life experience.

Structuring the data in sections, paragraphs, and sentences

An important rule of thumb for qualitative researchers is: **show, don't tell**. This means that qualitative essays should be heavy and lush with data excerpts. Every claim should be accompanied by examples to support it. Furthermore, *show don't tell* has much to do with the chronological ordering of claims and data, as I discuss below.

Readers are much more likely to be persuaded by a certain argument if they see and understand at least some of the data *before* you ask them to buy into a certain claim or interpretation. In this way, the mantra *show, don't tell* might more precisely be understood as *show, then tell*. The structure of the essay's various sections, paragraphs, and sentences should reflect such an approach. First showing, and only then interpreting and claiming, allows readers to reach their own conclusions and discourages them from creating counterarguments before they have considered the data. If you do list a claim first, then its supporting data should follow immediately after, with linking phrases such as "for example," or "as illustrated in the following." If the supporting data are not nearby (which is sometimes the case when you preview claims in an introduction), you should specify when and where it will be found (e.g. "As will be demonstrated in the second half of this paper...").

Grammar and sentence structure also impact the ability of a qualitative account to be descriptive and persuasive. An impressive number of books provide writing advice (Becker, 2007; Bishop, 1999; Goodall, 2000; Ellis & Bochner, 1996; Lamott, 1994; Mitchell & Charmaz, 1996; Richardson, 2000b; Silvia, 2007; Woods, 1985). However, getting writing advice is kind of like getting a lecture on piano playing: it may inspire, but you really only improve by pressing your own fingers to the keys. I encourage qualitative researchers to take courses specifically focused on writing. Here I review just several writing strategies that specifically relate to representing qualitative evidence.

One technique for descriptive and efficient writing is to replace unnecessary adverbs with descriptive verbs. For instance, "Brad ran quickly" is better written "Brad bolted" (or "scampered, strode, or snaked"). Likewise, rather than concluding a piece of dialogue with "Shantelle said angrily," a more descriptive construction is "Shantelle huffed/sulked/sobbed/blazed."

Verb tense also impacts the story, especially in terms of the immediacy you desire to convey. In most cases, when reporting interview data, past tense is used to introduce interview excerpts (e.g. "she explained in the interview"). When incorporating participant observation or field evidence, both present and past tense may be appropriate, as illustrated in the following two excerpts, which are drawn from Ragan Fox's (2010) reflections of his father's Alzheimer's disease:

> The first time I hear the word "Alzheimer's," my young tongue trips over its distinctively German flavor. Do I hear a hard consonant between the "Al" and "himer" sounds? "Alt-himers?" Or is it, "Al-himers?" Maybe the woman on the news has a funny accent and is saying "old timers." [...]
>
> When my father became ill, I turned to creative writing to help me work through my anger and sadness. This would have pleased my dad, who earned a living as the author of a jewelry newsletter. Growing up, whenever we got into arguments, Dad retreated to his room and penned long, beautiful letters in which he explained his point of view and professed his fatherly love to me. He encouraged me to write, and kept large Rubbermaid boxes of all the notes my tiny, pink fingers slipped under his bedroom door. (Fox, 2010, pp. 5–6)

The first excerpt, written in the present tense, immediately invites the reader to young Ragan's side. The second excerpt, written in the past tense, provides distance, helping readers appreciate adult Ragan's most vivid memories as he makes sense of the past. Neither version is right or wrong, but they accomplish different goals.

E-prime serves as another grammatical practice that impacts the quality of qualitative presentation. Semanticists Bourland and Johnston (1991) developed e-prime – short for English-prime – as a technique for rich writing. E-prime forecloses any use of the verb form "to be," including its variants "is, was, were, are." Weick, who adopts e-prime, explains:

> This tactic, known as "e-prime" (Kellogg, 1987) means that I'm not allowed to say "Wagner Dodge *is* a taciturn crew chief." Instead, I'm forced to be explicit [and] say things like, "Wagner Dodge surveys fires alone, issues orders without explanations, assumes people see what he sees, mistrusts words, overestimates the skills of his crews." When I'm forced to forego the verb to be, I pay more attention to particulars, context, and the situation. I also tend to see more clearly what I am *not* in a position to say. If I say that Dodge overestimates the skills of his crews, that may or may not mean that he is taciturn. It all depends on other concrete descriptions of how he behaves. (Weick, 2007, p. 18)

As noted, the advantages of e-prime include more detail, specificity, and vividness.

Additionally, e-prime forces writers to specify the agent and the agent's judgment in the sentence. For example, rather than my saying "Weick's writing *is* good," e-prime translations may include: "I like Weick's writing" or "Weick won many awards for his writing." These translations indicate how the "goodness" of Weick's writing lies not in irrefutable fact, but in the eye of the beholder and within particular circumstances. The e-prime translations also beget the question "why," which calls for a subsequent explanation (e.g. "I like Weick's writing…" or "he won many awards … because he tells rich stories to illustrate claims"). In this way e-prime usefully disrupts dogmatism and "truthiness" – encouraging transparency and the backing of claims with evidence.

Despite the advantages of e-prime, many people find it difficult to write without using the verb "to be." I constructed this and the former two paragraphs in e-prime – which required intense concentration and hours of rewriting. Although writing this way takes time and effort, I encourage you to actively employ more vivid and active grammatical constructions and, at the very least, to avoid overusing the most awkward "to be" constructions – such as beginning sentences with "There is/are."

Formatting qualitative work

In constructing rich qualitative representations, qualitative scholars supplement their prose with strategic decisions regarding how to format and visually represent their work. Many students have questions about how to cite and excerpt qualitative data. Style guides published by the American Psychological Association (APA; 2010) and the Modern Language Association (MLA; 2009a, 2009b) give details on how to format quotations. Here I provide some of the basics, drawing from and expanding upon Kvale's (1996) eight tips for citing and reporting interview quotations. In what follows I repeat Kvale's primary tips verbatim (pp. 266–267), and underneath each tip I elucidate it in my own words. At the close, I provide more detail about citing fieldnotes and documents.

1 The quotes should be related to the general text.
   The author must provide a frame of reference before excerpting quotations.

2 The quotes should be contextualized.
   For example, "In response to an interview question asking [ABC], Jake explained…," or "When discussing the [XYZ] affair, Pauline retorted…").

3 The quotes should be interpreted.
   The author should explain why a quotation or excerpt is particularly interesting or relevant to the issue at hand. Show the excerpt, then explain/interpret it.

4 There should be a balance between quotes and text.
   I recommend a mix of about two fifths data, three fifths interpretation (although this differs depending on the type of analysis and on the publication venue). Additionally, the number of quotations coming from any one source should be balanced with that of quotations coming from other sources.

5 The quotes should be short.
   Readers lose interest and often skip long indented information (Bishop, 1999).

6 Use only the best quote.
   You can always mention how many other participants expressed a similar point.

7 Interview quotes should be rendered in a written style.
   Include repetitions, digressions, pauses, ums, ahs only if the linguistic form itself is important for the point being made. Otherwise edit them out.

8 There should be a simple signature system for the editing of quotes.
   The methods section should detail the principles used for editing data excerpts and should provide, if necessary, a simple list of symbols used for pauses, omissions, and so on.

You may also wonder how best to reference direct excerpts from the data. Some authors list the name, page number, and line number of the interview data in parentheses, in an endnote, or in a footnote. This provides specificity and may be especially worthwhile when the authors want to easily return to a certain datum in the revision process, when writing future reports. For this reason, creating a notation/referencing system in qualitative theses and dissertations may be helpful if you plan to publish from them down the line.

That said, most published reports do not provide this level of detail when referencing qualitative data. It can be much more efficient and reader-friendly to indicate the source of the data in a more natural way – for instance by stating things like:

"Over coffee, Johnny spontaneously indicated…"
"As I pretended to read my email, I watched the following unfold…"
"In response to my asking Rita about her favorite family ritual…"
"The official organizational memo, which I was back-copied on, read…"

These introductory phrases provide context, indicating the source of the data and the author's involvement in spurring or interacting with them.

Like literature quotations, data excerpts roughly longer than 40 words (or so) should be indented as a block, without quotation marks. Because readers often skip indented text, you should follow a block extract with an interpretation that summarizes it and its relation to a relevant claim or a certain research question. Excerpted data should be, at most, half a page in length (Saldaña, 2011). Usually the excerpt requires editing, for example ellipse – "[…]" – to indicate omitted material within a sentence, full stop and ellipse – ". […]" or "[…] ." – to indicate omitted structures or sentence(s) before or after the next grammatical sentence starting with a capital, and two slashes (//) to indicate an even larger break between the parts of the quoted text. You may also add italics for emphasis, in which case you should note "emphasis added" immediately after the quotation, in the parentheses with the reference. You can also add editorial material in square brackets [like this] inside the quotation itself, to give your own explanations (see Chapter 8 for more details on transcription symbols). Basically, the readers should be able to read the excerpt one time and immediately understand why it supports a certain claim or is otherwise connected to your paper's goals.

When excerpting fieldnotes, keep in mind that they are *already* reconstructed texts of the scene. Hence it is not uncommon or unethical to rewrite them for the final report. Indeed they usually benefit from editing and condensing before they land in the text. Further, incorporating fieldnote data right into the prose itself may be more efficient and reader-friendly than giving block extracts. For example, compare the following two excerpts from the same manuscript (Tracy & Scott, 2006). They both emerged from the same fieldnote, but one is indented as a full extract, while the rest of the field data are incorporated into the paragraph's prose – and intertwined with interpretation.

> When the firefighters arrived at the bus station, a man who appeared to be a homeless drug addict told them that he called because he was concerned about the spiders coming out of his hands.
>
> John asks the man, "Are you on crystal meth?" The patient denies it, and John responds: "Look, dude, you're shaky and a little hyper, and people on crystal meth scratch themselves to death and get wounds just like that. And then they get scabies." Firefighter Tim jumps in, yelling loudly at the patient, "SO TELL US, ARE YOU ON DRUGS?" The patient replies with tears rolling down his face, "I want to go to the hospital!" Tim fires back, "LISTEN! IF YOU'RE GONNA CALL 911 AND SAY YOU HAVE SHORTNESS OF BREATH JUST SO YOU CAN GET A RIDE, I'M NOT TAKING YOU TO THE HOSPITAL!"

The firefighters refused to take the man to the hospital, instead providing treatment on scene. His wound was cleaned and bandaged and, after Tim told the man that he had "the wrong attitude," the firefighters suggested that he walk to a special clinic designed for homeless drug addicts with chronic wounds.

When the patient walked away, Tim turned to the second author and exclaimed sarcastically, "Welcome to Bayside EMS!" The other firefighter interjected, "Yeah, if you want to do drugs, you can do them, and when you feel sad, when you hurt, we'll take great care of you so you can do more drugs." This final comment is extremely telling about the firefighters' irritation and frustration with the situation. Having to take great "care" for clients who "feel sad" is a duty that is largely connected to feminine qualities – thus challenging dominant notions of masculinity. Exacerbating this issue, the homeless man does not constitute an identity-enhancing "audience" for which firefighters are best able to perform as America's heroes (Tracy & Scott, 2006, p. 20).

As illustrated here, the fieldnote excerpt (through indentation and present verb tense) takes the reader back to the scene. The other data in prose (pulled from the fieldnote, but intertwined with the prose and interpretation) provide important information in a more efficient manner. The combination serves to show, then tell.

Learning how to efficiently incorporate qualitative data into the prose is one important part of formatting the text. Another technique for breaking up and infusing the text with meaning is that of visual representations.

Visual representations

"A picture is worth 1,000 words." This quotation may be a cliché, but visual representations are extremely valuable for instantly conveying complex, textured, nonlinear ideas. Visual evidence – photos, videos, maps, or graphic representations – can be the primary focus of, or merely a supplement to, other qualitative data (Margolis & Pauwels, 2011; Pink, 2001). Although some hard paper-publishing protocols discourage photographs because of the relatively high cost of reproduction, with more online journals available, incorporating visual data has become increasingly common.

Chapter 10 provided several examples of visual representations, including tables, matrices, and flowcharts. Qualitative scholars can also construct other kinds of images to illustrate claims and arguments. These might be pie-charts, bar graphs, doughnuts, bubbles, or a rich combination of the "smart art" offered by computer software. Specific qualitative data analysis software, and even standard data processing software, can help even the most design-challenged researchers build visual models.

As a qualitative researcher, I encourage you to think creatively about visuals that will vividly communicate the data and your emergent theory. This often means going beyond the typical box-and-arrow diagrams. For example, former student Timothy Huffman constructed a visual model to represent a key contribution in his study of homeless youth. The visual, as well as his story of coming up with it, appears in Researcher's Notepad 13.1.

Hopefully, you are inspired to consider various ways to break up and visually model your qualitative analysis. Qualitative scholars seem to love long paragraphs and page after page of prose. Too often they shy away from visual displays – perhaps because they associate them with quantitative analyses, or perhaps because they just do not have much graphic design experience. However, visual representations can significantly enhance the data

RESEARCHER'S NOTEPAD 13.1

Visual representation
Modeling volunteer motivation

By Timothy Huffman, in his own words

Are volunteers motivated to become involved because of self-serving social exchange (Cropanzano & Mitchell, 2005) or altruism (Cameron, Dutton, & Quinn, 2003)? While studying a homeless youth organization to pursue this question, I discovered that volunteers were motivated to donate their time and effort because of both selfish and selfless reasons (Huffman, 2012).

The volunteers I worked with identified personal costs and rewards (Figure 1). However, they also enjoyed using untapped resources to meet the needs of others. In other words, social exchange thinking was still present but without the self-serving bias (Figure 2). When I noticed the volunteers using terms like "grow" and "fruition," I realized they were not involved in a market exchange but rather an ecological one. They were like gardeners fostering the community (Figure 3).

One night during the analysis and writing process, I couldn't sleep and was pacing around my apartment, sketching model after model. How did it all fit together? When I finally got it, I threw my notebook down and literally jumped into the air. Literature, research, analysis, and writing started my ideas, but developing them into pictures gave them conceptual clarity. In the end, the visual improved my writing and conceptual contribution.

Figure 13.2 A model of volunteer motivation, designed by Timothy Huffman.

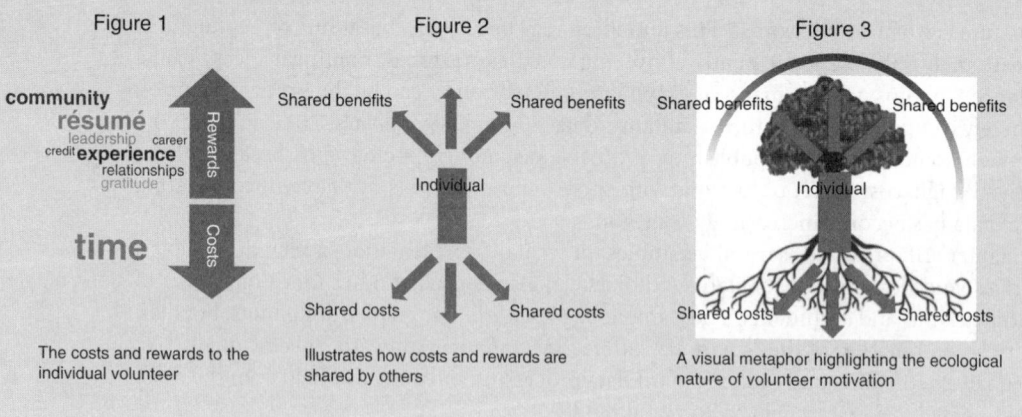

analysis. Some disciplinary audiences not only *expect* tables and models, but are *circumspect* of analyses in which these elements are absent. That said, data displays don't speak for themselves. Lofland and Lofland (1984) go so far as to say: "You do not truly begin to think until you attempt to lay out your ideas and information into successive sentences" (p. 142). At the very least, writing about visual displays clarifies meaning and prompts additional thinking.

Setting yourself up for success by considering the audience first

Who will be reading your qualitative research? Who do you *want* to read it? Synthesizing various discussions, Lindlof and Taylor (2011) delineate five primary types of readers for qualitative research. These are:

- area specialists: the scholars who regularly talk in depth about a certain issue;
- general disciplinary readers: these are not experts in the area, but they may read the piece to fuel their own creative fire and broadly expand their knowledge;
- human science readers: these mine the study's facts and findings in order to advance their own research, teaching, or grant-getting activities;
- action oriented readers: key administrators, researchers, civic leaders, and public figures who use the findings to create change, policies, or procedures;
- general readers: readers who are interested in qualitative research because it is interesting, moving, or therapeutic.

You may have a variety of these readers in mind for your audience. Or perhaps your only audience will be your professor and a kind friend or family member. In that case, the next few paragraphs may not be particularly interesting to you. However, many qualitative researchers desire specific audiences – professionals, participants, scholars, or journalists – to read and learn from all their hard work. If that's the case, then it's important to consider early on how to engage, enter, and contribute to a particular conversation. How do you do so?

To enter a conversation, you need to:

1   know what others are already saying about a certain topic or issue;
2   incorporate that information in your own formulations (even if only to dispute it);
3   demonstrate that you have listened to what they have to say;
4   contribute and add something valuable to the conversation.

Three of these four steps are more about "listening" than about "talking." Indeed, good writers, above all, are expert listeners. Did you hear that? Good writers are expert listeners. Okay, maybe, MAYBE, some people are brilliant enough (or, more likely, just loud enough), to be able to preach effectively without listening to what others are saying. For most of us, though, singing one's own tune while ignoring the harmonies around us – at least from the get go – doesn't work so well. Engaging the conversation is an excellent path to being heard, read, and published. If you don't heed the ongoing conversation, then others probably will not listen to you.

Of course, to engage the conversation, you need (a) to figure out *which* conversation is most interesting for your research; and (b) to learn *what's being said* in this conversation. The good news is that both these goals can be accomplished in the same way – by reading! If you are interested in joining a certain theoretical conversation, read up on the most germinal recent work connected to that theory. Find out *where* these scholars are publishing. If you are interested in contributing to a professional or to an applied debate, you must study (via websites, trade journals, or popular press books) the latest hot issues. And, if you find yourself running into publishing hurdles, before you begin rewriting (again!), first consider reading more, or different material.

Of course, many students pursue a qualitative project without having a particular conversation in mind. In that case, I encourage you to think about the type of work that you, personally, enjoy reading – and where that work is published and what those authors are talking about. We are motivated to write in ways that mimic the writing we like. Take a look at these articles and even consider using them as "models." I regularly encourage students to break down their favorite publications into their component parts, including the chronology and number of paragraphs or pages allotted to "doing" certain parts of the essay. Such an activity is developed in Exercise 13.1.

Another method for brainstorming writing format is to consider publication venues that are most commonly read or cited in your discipline or by your preferred readership. A journal's **impact factor** refers to the average number of citations of the articles published in that particular journal, and many people use this measure to indicate significance and prestige. Impact factor is calculated yearly for journals indexed in the Thomson Reuter's *Journal Citation Reports* – a database available via most university libraries. If you are going to do all the work associated with a rigorous qualitative study, then it makes sense to examine venues that are most likely to impact and be read by your preferred audience.

At the same time it's important to realize that the impact factor is just one out of many ways to indicate the significance of a journal or a particular article (other ways are examining

EXERCISE 13.1

Article format model

One path toward learning to write qualitative methods (or any scholarly approach) is to model one's work after favorite or exemplary essays. Just as children often begin drawing by first tracing or coloring in the lines, those new to qualitative methods need not "free-hand" their first qualitative research articles. Becoming familiar with the general contours of model essays helps you learn writing customs and to craft your piece in a format that has a successful record. Along the way, I encourage you to experiment and create your own style. Indeed, as I discussed in Chapter 12, there are downsides to following the traditional writing path, especially if such a style does not fit your methodological approach.

- Find three or four published articles that, format-wise, "do" the same thing that you want to do in your own paper.
  - For example, if you are conducting a focus-group study in which you meld two theoretical points of view, find other articles that do the same (the model article need not be on the same topic).
- Consider publication venues appropriate for your own work.
- For each "model," cite the source and create an outline of what is done in the article and the amount of space (number of pages, words, or paragraphs) allotted. For example:
  - Rationalizes the use of theory ABC as a new way of making sense of XYZ behavior (1.5 pages)
  - Bridges the two different theoretical approaches through a logical transition (2 sentences, middle of p. 4).
  - Methodology – 3 pages (pp. 11–13).
- Use the model essay's headers as a rough guide for the outline's level of detail. However, feel free to go more detailed (e.g. you may want to note the way the author made a beautiful logical transition between two theories or substantiated the use of a certain sampling or analysis strategy).
- Use these article model outlines as raw material as you determine the organizational framework of your own essay.

top hits via web searches, referencing article/chapter/book award winners, or examining the most commonly used publications in syllabi). Some researchers have made the case that qualitative methods journals and articles do not have an impact factor that matches their relative prestige because qualitative folks do not use a lot of citations. Goodall (2008) argues that, if administrators favor citation indexes and impact factors as measures of significance, qualitative scholars do themselves no favors by avoiding citations. As I heard him say in many presentations to qualitative scholars: "If we don't cite each other, we hurt each other."

Of course, some journals more commonly publish qualitative research than others. A website search using the terms "qualitative journals" nets several cross-disciplinary inventories that list these journals (e.g. the St. Louis Qualitative Research Committee publishes http://www.slu.edu/organizations/qrc/QRjournals.html). Tips and Tools 13.1 catalogues journals that have a history of publishing qualitative research in the areas of communication, media, and critical–cultural studies. The receptiveness of some of these journals to qualitative methods vacillates depending on the current editor, editorial board, and editorial policy.

TIPS AND TOOLS 13.1

Journals that have published qualitative communication research

Communication and Critical/Cultural Studies
Communication, Culture and Critique
Communication Education
Communication Monographs
Communication Quarterly
Communication Research
Communication Studies
Cultural Studies↔Critical Methodologies
Critical Studies in Media Communication
Discourse and Society
Ethnography
Field Methods
Health Communication
Human Relations
Human Communication Research
International Journal of Communication
International Journal of Qualitative Methods
International Review of Qualitative Research
Journal of American Culture
Journal of Applied Communication Research
Journal of Broadcasting & Electronic Media
Journal of Communication
Journal of Contemporary Ethnography
Journal of Ethnography
Journal of Family Communication
Journal of International and Intercultural Communication

Journal of Language and Social Psychology
Journal of Mixed Methods Research
Journal of Organizational Ethnography
Journal of Personal and Social Relationships
Journal of Popular Culture
Kaleidoscope: A Graduate Journal of Qualitative Communication Research
Liminalities
Management Communication Quarterly
Narrative Inquiry
Organization
Qualitative Communication Research
Qualitative Health Research
Qualitative Inquiry
The Qualitative Report
Qualitative Research
Qualitative Research Journal
Qualitative Research Reports in Communication
Research on Language and Social Interaction
Southern Communication Journal
Symbolic Interaction
Text and Performance Quarterly
Western Journal of Communication
Women and Language
Women's Studies in Communication

Finally, keep in mind that journal article writing is just one option. A number of good qualitative studies are written as chapters in edited books (see for instance Clair, 2003) or as books. For example, in his book-length treatment of democratic systems, Cheney (1999) weaves together rich qualitative data to illustrate the successes and challenges of the famous Mondragón worker-owned cooperatives in Basque Spain.

Submitting, revising, and resubmitting for journal publication

Some people write qualitative data for themselves, or for small audiences consisting of instructors, friends, or family. However, for those hoping to publish, the following section provides some advice, organized around Goodall's (2008) "five commandments of the academic publication process without elaboration" (p. 114).

1   Thou shalt know the submission guidelines.
2   Thou shalt face rejection.
3   Thou shalt revise and resubmit.
4   With persistence, though shalt eventually succeed.
5   Thou shalt not rest on the laurels of success.

First, let us consider "Thou shalt know the submission guidelines." Most journals and conference venues provide specific instructions to authors regarding the submission process, including guidelines on style, formatting, deadlines, references, and page length. Paying attention to these instructions is crucial. Most editors believe that, "[i]f a writer cannot properly follow directions for form, how can I trust him or her with the content?" (Saldaña, 2011, p. 145).

Second, "Thou shalt face rejection." The publication process should perhaps more aptly be termed the rejection process. People who publish the most face criticism and rejection the most. Prolific writers have thick skin and a resilient spirit. Even when I have poured my heart and soul into a piece, I try not to take criticism personally. I think back to the times when I have provided feedback to other people, and I remember that those critiques and suggestions took time and effort to give. I try to appreciate the reviewer's time and effort in creating the feedback. Rejection and critique are part of the process. It may not feel good, but, if you want to publish, there's no way around it.

Third, "Thou shalt revise and resubmit." About 80 percent of scholarly research is rejected (Silvia, 2007), so if you receive an invitation to revise and resubmit (R & R), I encourage you to celebrate! Every once in a while you might receive an R & R that only asks for minor revisions. Most of the time the revisions requested are substantial, and reading the R & R feedback is painful. So, take a day or two to cuss out the reviewers. Roll your eyes. Bitch about them to your co-authors or anyone else who will listen. Refuse to re-read the reviews. Stick them in a drawer. Lock the drawer. Fling the key across the room in frustration.

Then, on day three, carefully fish out the key from under the sofa, unlock the drawer, take out the crumpled tear-dappled reviews, and re-read them. Open a new document on your computer and across the top write: "They think I can do this. They want me to resubmit this. They want to see my work in print." Then, create an action "to-do" list, breaking down long amorphous critiques into smaller digestible chunks. Make your list efficient, cheery, and organized. Be nice to yourself. Then, begin tackling each action item, one at a time, keeping close notes about how you attended to the various issues (or, in some cases, why you did not). These notes will be invaluable for your "response to the reviewers." This letter, which accompanies your resubmission, is often as important as, or even more than, the actual revisions (and may take just as long to write).

In most cases, a revise and resubmit is more likely to result in publication than an entirely new submission to another journal. However, this is not always the case. Take time to carefully review the requested changes – if they are asking you to fundamentally change the paper in ways that you are not interested or willing to spend time on, you may decide that you would rather search out a better home for the piece.

Fourth, "With persistence, thou shalt eventually succeed." Another way to say this is that you will *only* succeed if you have persistence. The best way to understand the persistence needed for publication is to ask others about the trajectory of their published articles (although many of us block this out, as a method of pain management). The centerpiece article from my dissertation took five years to get published (Tracy, 2005). This was its trajectory:

Table 13.1 A revise and resubmit trajectory of pain, resilience, and eventual triumph.

Version	Timeline	Activity
1	Spring 2000	Defend dissertation – the raw material for the article
	Fall 2000	Rewrite dissertation material into conference paper submission
2	Spring 2001	Present as a "top" paper at the annual conference of the International Communication Association (ICA)
	Summer 2001	Rewrite based on comments at ICA
3	Fall 2001	Submit to *Administrative Science Quarterly* (ASQ)
	Fall 2001	ASQ rejects at editor's desk without sending it out for review
	Winter 2002	Rewrite based on ASQ editor's comments
4	Spring 2002	Submit first time to *Organization*
	Fall 2002	*Organization* invites a major revise and resubmit
	Win-Sp 2003	Rewrite based on *Organization* comments
5	Summer 2003	Resubmit revised version to *Organization*
	Winter 2004	*Organization* invites a 2nd revise and resubmit
	Win-Sp 2004	Rewrite based on *Organization*'s 2nd set of comments
6	Spring 2004	Submit 2nd revised version to *Organization*
	Summer 2004	*Organization* rejects
	Summer 2004	Lots of cussing, hand-wrenching, and chocolate eating
	Fall 2004	Slight revise based on rejection letter from *Organization*
7	Fall 2004	Submit to *Communication Monographs*
	Winter 2004	*Communication Monographs* invites a revise and resubmit
	Early Sp 2005	Rewrite based on *Communication Monographs* comments
8	Late Sp 2005	Resubmit to *Communication Monographs*
	Early Sum 2005	*Communication Monographs* accepts with minor revisions
9	Late Sum 2005	Rewrite based on minor revisions and resubmit to *Communication Monographs*
	Fall 2005	Published – Yahoo!!!!

This process resulted in nine "formal" versions of the article. Within each step were multiple drafts. I have at least 100 versions of this paper, saved in my various computer files. Although the writing and rewriting process was long and sometimes agonizing, the process served to sharpen my thinking and to focus the paper's contribution. Certainly, in some cases, the process of writing and rewriting can lead to a tangled, overwritten mess. However, revisions are usually better than the preceding version. I should note, too, that not all publication stories are long and painful. Some of my research articles moved from first drafts to published form in less than a year.

Finally, let us consider Goodall's fifth commandment: "Thou shalt not rest on the laurels of success." Sure, take some time to celebrate a publication. However, if you wish to be a prolific qualitative researcher, I encourage you to keep multiple projects going at any one time. Therefore, when you are tired of dealing with a difficult revision of one piece, you can turn to creating a file of "motivating ideas" for the next piece, or work on the mindless reference questions for a final page proof revision that is now "in press."

As you consider all these publication commandments, let me add a word of warning. Writing only to publish, like training in sport just to receive a medal, is unwise. When you only have your eye on the prize, it becomes all too easy to ignore the beauty, learning, and play that come through the research and writing process. Yes, it feels great to see something in print. However, the glee of publication is just an exclamation point. Publication is not a panacea for feeling good as a scholar or as a person. "If you're not enough before the gold medal, you won't be enough with it" (Lamott, 1994, p. 218).

Git R done: overcoming common writing and submission challenges

As I discussed in the opening of this chapter, I am a fan of what Lamott (1994) calls the "shitty first draft." We throw up clay in the form of notes, bullet points, and clumsily constructed sentences. And then we shape, nuance, reword, reshape, break it down, and move things around. We write too long, and then have to edit. In the movie *A River Runs Through It*, the young son Norman presents a finished essay to his father, who reads it and says: "Now make it half as long." Norman rewrites and comes back with draft two, which his Dad reads and says: "Again, half as long" (Eberts, Redford, & Markey, 1992). We are all little Normans.

Writing well means writing a lot, rewriting, and editing. In the process, you may alternately feel isolated, bored, or overwhelmed. You may feel like Rumplestiltskin trying to spin straw into gold (Bishop, 1999). Nonetheless, sometimes you just need to lower your standards and, in the words of comedian Larry the Cable Guy, "git r done." Tips and Tools 13.2 provides Spradley's (1980) suggestions for the requisite steps for writing ethnography.

In the following section I add to Spradley's suggestions, providing specific recommendations for qualitative writing. I open with some advice on the writing life, provide frank talk about the publication process, and close with suggestions for addressing common qualitative essay challenges.

How to write a lot

If writing well means writing a lot, then a primary goal for qualitative scholars should be to create habits, rituals, and practices in their lives that promote frequent writing. Here I present tips synthesized from a number of sources (Becker, 2007; Bishop, 1999; Boice, 1990; Goodall, 2008; Kellogg, 1999; Lamott, 1994; Silvia, 2007; Wolcott, 2009).

TIPS AND TOOLS 13.2

Steps for writing an ethnography

Select an audience
Select a thesis
Make a list of topics and create an outline
Write a rough draft of each section
Revise the outline and create subheads
Edit the rough draft
Write the intro and conclusion
Reread manuscript and insert more examples
Write the final draft

Source: J. P. Spradley, 1980. © 1980 Wadsworth, a part of Cengage Learning, Inc.; reproduced by permission, www.cengage.com/permissions

- *Give yourself permission to write a mess* Don't be a perfectionist. "Clutter is wonderfully fertile ground" (Lamott, 1994, p. 28). Just get it all down. You usually have to write a bunch of garbage before you find the gems within it.
- *Write first, edit later* Give yourself time to digest before editing. "Revising while you generate text is like drinking decaffeinated coffee in the early morning: noble idea, wrong time" (Silvia, 2007, kindle location 710). The first drafts are often twice as long as they should be. Keep the good stuff and scratch the rest. Keep in mind that most writing is "the rest."
- *Create a schedule and stick to it* If writing and other research activities are a priority, schedule them, just as you would with other "non-negotiable" activity such as eating lunch, teaching, or attending a required meeting. Other people will try to break into your writing time. However, you must ruthlessly defend it (and, secretly, they'll wish they did the same). Any activities associated with your writing and research can fill this time: reading, analyzing, outlining, creating graphics, editing.
- *Write almost every day, preferably at the same time of day* If you plan on becoming a regular writer rather than just finishing a certain assignment, you should work on your research and writing almost every day. Writing approximately at the same time each day will train your brain for creativity. The ideal schedule for me is writing for two hours early in the day, four to six days a week.
- *Make writing a habitual priority, not a ponderous decision* The activities people do most often are those they *do not* have to ponder and make decisions about. If writing is a priority, then create a structure where you need not brood over, on a daily basis, "if" or "when" you will write. Tell yourself when you will write and then just do it. No excuses.
- *Write in small chunks of time* A common myth is that you need huge expanses of time to write, such as summers, semester breaks, sabbaticals, writing retreats, or full days off. This is simply untrue. The most productive scholars write about 1.5 hours a day

(Goodall, 2008). "Binge" writing (Kellogg, 1999) leads to feeling overwhelmed and exhausted. Writing in small chunks provides a rhythm and helps you approach writing without associating it with late nights, neglect of leisure and family, and carpal tunnel syndrome.

- *Don't reward binge writing with no writing* If you do happen to have a windfall writing day, don't ditch your regular writing schedule. Just as an alcoholic wouldn't reward a long period of sobriety with a drink, it doesn't make sense to reward lots of good writing by skipping the scheduled small goal (Silvia, 2007).
- *Find a friend, or two, or three, or five* A writing partner or writing support group (Grant, 2008) is invaluable if you want to swap drafts, advice, and editing. Writing partners should be supportive and kind enough that you feel comfortable sharing your first drafts, but direct enough to identify the junk and keep you accountable.
- *Create a writing haven* A "good place to write" differs from person to person. Pay attention to what works for you. For some it's a coffee shop without distractions from pets, family members, roommates, or the television set. Indeed many require a space that does not allow Internet or phone access. Most writers like to have a big desk or a table with lots of space. Stephen King (2000) said that the only thing a writer's room needs is "a door which you are willing to shut" (p. 155).
- *Don't buy into the idea of "writer's block"* Prolific writers write whether or not they feel inspired or motivated. Their good ideas come precisely through the activity of writing. Research shows that those who wait for inspiration or just write when they feel like it write less than those who sit their butt down and write on a schedule (Boice, 1990).
- *Set goals* Set goals for what you plan to accomplish in your scheduled writing time. This could be a word count goal (Steven King aims for 2,000 words a day but most mere mortals can only handle 500–1,000), or a goal of accomplishing a certain topic or section. If your goals are big, break them down. However, don't be scared of big goals. They are not overwhelming when you have a scheduled time to accomplish them (e.g. "When am I going to write this essay/conference paper/article/book? Oh yes, of course. I'll write it tomorrow morning from 7 to 9 a.m., and thereafter until I'm finished").
- *Monitor and tie consequences to progress* Monitoring progress is a wonderfully motivating tool and can be accomplished through check-off boxes, by touching base with a writing partner, by creating task logs, or just by keeping tabs in a journal. Provide yourself with consequences on the basis of your progress. Some people will write more if they reward themselves for achieving goals, while others will benefit from the threat of loss (Ayers, 2010). A number of goal-setting websites and computer applications are available – some provide simple motivation by monitoring your progress, others contract you to give away money if you do not reach your goals (e.g. www.StikK.com). Think what you will, but for some people it works!

Hopefully these tips provide inspiration for writing more frequently. As noted, one of the primary parts of writing is editing and revising. With that, the next section discusses some common writing challenges.

Addressing common challenges in qualitative writing

The first time I ever taught qualitative methods and read the first drafts of students' semester paper submissions, I created a document called "overall first draft feedback." Ever since that time, I have modified and added to this document, trying to pinpoint the most common challenges encountered in qualitative writing and how to address them. Now I offer this document to students *before* they submit their first draft, with the hope that understanding and addressing common pitfalls early on may help in creating a stronger first draft to begin with. I also regularly review this list myself. Here I offer these recommendations in outline form.

- Front matter
  - Identify your audience and potential journal or conference submission spot (and share this information with those providing feedback).
  - Write an abstract that will be both informational and invitational.
- Introduction
  - Provide a rationale that shows how and why your study is strong rather than simply pointing out deficiencies in the literature or in other methodological approaches.
  - If you are going to use a writing style or a representational format unfamiliar to your target audience, introduce it and explain it.
  - Goals and purpose of manuscript should be clear. Identifying your goals tells your reader how to judge the value of the paper. Your reader will ask:
    - Are the goals meaningful?
    - Did the manuscript accomplish the goals?
- Literature review and conceptual framework
  - Only include information in the literature review that draws the reader forward.
    - Think of your literature as nails and mortar – use just enough to hold up the structure of the findings. Edit out the rest, and save it for future projects.
  - Don't include long lists of citations without briefly explaining what each piece adds to the paper. Only reference sources you know and understand.
  - Make sure to define/operationalize/explain theoretical terms or concepts.
    - Provide quick "for example" explanations.
    - If there is not enough time or room to explain the concept, then use a lay term that need not be explained. Just because you know a technical or scholarly term, you don't need to use it.
  - Link all concepts and terms to the specific purpose of the paper (e.g. if I introduce the phrase "total institution," I need to remind the reader why this concept is so salient to my study).
  - Sometimes the best theoretical lens is one with which you are already familiar.
    - Theories and concepts are tools to help launch and build your case.
    - It's better to use a common tool, like scissors, properly, than to experiment with an unknown tool, like electric clippers, and make a mess.
    - At the same time, those with the best knowledge of a variety of tools (theories) will be able to create the most vibrant, interesting, and strong projects.
  - Research questions or key purposes should be previewed/anticipated by the literature.
    - It's fine to review research questions or goals at the end of the literature review, but their main ideas need to work their way into the earlier discussion.
  - The reader should be able to easily differentiate past research from this study's contributions.

- Scholarly papers are kind of like puzzles – it's imperative to draw the existing puzzle pieces (past research and concepts) clearly, so that this study's contribution is clear.
- Consider whether you want to give away the punch line of the primary contribution in the first part of the paper or wait until the findings section.

- Methods section
  - Check out models of methods sections in your potential publication venues.
  - In the methods section, overview your total number of research hours and data before getting into specifics.
  - Usually this section includes: background/participants, data collection procedures and sources (with pages of single-spaced data and hours in the field), data analysis methods.
  - Consider including sample interview questions and codes in the methods section, or including an interview guide or codebook in the appendix.
- Findings and interpretation
  - Be careful of over-claiming (better to under-claim and support your ideas generously). Overstatement is a red flag for reviewers and makes the argument less credible overall.
  - Clean up and improve the writing style of fieldnote excerpts.
  - Use participants' names when possible. Or, rather than using "participants," consider a descriptor such as employees, students, volunteers, family members.
  - Let the reader know the context and source of your data (e.g. "In response to an interview question about the best part of the job, Maria said…").
  - Don't become over-reliant on interview data. Be sure to include participant observation data, too.
  - It's more credible to SHOW your argument, and only then TELL it. Showing = "Sweat began to collect on the man's brow, and he darted his eyes around the room." Telling = "The man seemed nervous and paranoid."
  - An elegant rendering of the findings combines vividness with simplicity. As Johnny Saldaña tells his students, "I'd rather read something short and good, rather than long and lousy" (Saldaña, 2011, p. 141).
- Conclusions
  - Do not skimp on this section!
  - Be specific in implications, limitations, and directions for future research.
  - End the piece on something that will inspire the audience to read more of your work, investigate this topic, or conduct a related study.

Writing style

- Incorporate descriptive headings and sub-headings. They are kind gifts to your readers, helping them to pause, track, and return to key arguments.
  - Consider the value of "contentful" rather than generic headers (e.g. "Identity in Organizations" rather than "Background Literature").
- Spend time and care writing transitions between paragraphs and sections.
  - Transitions are not just rhetorical dress-ups, but serve as the logical glue holding together the paper.
  - Headings and asterisks do not stand in for transitions.
- Use a consistent style (APA? MLA?). Some readers will assume that sloppy style equates with sloppy research.

- Overuse of endnotes is distracting and effortful. Usually only two to four are appropriate.
- Pay attention to verb use and tense.
  - When citing scholars, put them in the present tense (Smith argues…," "Corey explains…"). When explicating research methods, use past tense ("I collected data via participant observation," "I used an iterative approach").
  - Consider e-prime (replacing "to be" and "there is/are" with more vivid active verbs).
  - Adverbs are unnecessary if you use good verbs (e.g. she "turtled up the stairs" rather than "crawled slowly.").
  - Avoid passive tense as much as possible. Rather than "the vase got broken," "the puppy's wagging tale smashed the vase to the floor."
- Avoid pronouns with an unclear referent.
  - Pronouns without a (clear) referent occur when there is no clear noun in the immediate context to which the pronoun can refer (or sometimes when there is no noun at all!).
  - For example, in the second sentence, "him" and "they" are both confusing: "The gang members suddenly became aware of the police officers. John told Dave that they were going to attack him." The reader has no idea who "they" are (gang members or police officers?) or whether "him" refers to John or Dave. A better construction would be: "John told Dave, 'The cops are about to attack me'" or John told Dave, 'The gang members are about to attack you.'"
- In most cases, the subject of a sentence should be a topic rather than an author. Rather than "S. Tracy & Tracy (1998) found that emotion labor can have a double-face," use something like: "When employees must simultaneously manage their own strong emotions with those of a client, emotion labor has a double-face (S. Tracy & Tracy, 1998)."
- Mix up words, avoiding overused ones like "look" (instead consider "examine," "investigate," "analyze"); at the same time, simple formulations can be preferable. Rather than "extant literature" or "existing literature," just "literature" is ideal.
- Abbreviations and acronyms may be convenient for the writer, but they are often tedious for the reader.
- Semicolons (;) are used to connect independent clauses; each part of the sentence must be able to stand alone. They are similar to a period, but they indicate a closer connection between the clauses.
- Distinguish dashes from hyphens, and use them correctly.
  - En dashes – they are the width of a capital N – with spaces around them, or, depending on style, closed-up em dashes (these are slightly longer, the width of an M) can enclose a parenthetical expression (as in the first line of this very sentence).
  - Closed-up en dashes are used in compounds like "critical–cultural studies" or "mother–daughter relationship," where the two parts are equal – that is, neither is syntactically subordinate to the other. Closed-up en dashes are also used between figures, in ranges (years 1848–1917, pages 21–32, 3–5 age-group).
  - Hyphens are shorter than en and em dashes. They are used when one of the words is syntactically subordinate to the other (as in "father-figure motif," meaning: "figure of the father"), truncated (as in "socio-economic studies"), or form a semantic unit or the name of a single entity (as in "Bosnia-Herzegovina" or "philosopher-king").

FOLLOWING, FORGETTING, AND IMPROVISING

My hope is that the tips and suggestions provided in this chapter are helpful to a range of students and readers. Nonetheless, I should note that writing, like any interpretive art, is individual, and you must learn what works best for you. Many of the practices described in this chapter are synthesized from professional "writing advice givers" and may not fit your style, values, or goals. Indeed writing occurs differently, depending on one's social position, history, and political context.

For example, after sharing an early excerpt from this chapter with some colleagues and friends, visual ethnographer Eric Margolis responded to me with a beautifully written essay he titled "Anarchist Writing." Among other things, he said: "Many literary and scholarly authors are known for not following routines and sometimes draw their inspiration from altered states of consciousness, sexual encounters, wars, fist fights, political actions, and other peak experiences that do not conform to prescriptive advice about 'how to write.'" Eric referenced famous writers who wrote for various causes, explaining how they were "motivated by a range of feelings including passion, fear, depression," and that they were "quite productive even though we may view some of them as drunks and drug addicts today. When it comes to writing, the best examples of the craft emerge as often from the gut as from the head, or from emotions or social bonds that transcend 'ordinary' academic experiences" (personal communication, October, 2011).

Indeed, simply following the rules does not guarantee high-quality work. That is why, if you conduct an Internet search for "writing quotations" or "writing advice," you will quickly see the great range of suggestions for writing. Regardless of your approach, in the process of writing more, you will invariably become a better writer.

In summary

This chapter opened with a discussion of how writing and representing qualitative data is not a simple task of "writing up" but is fundamentally a method of inquiry. Through the very process of writing, we learn and know. The chapter also discussed the importance of essay structure, formatting, and grammar for presenting qualitative evidence. Interviews, focus groups, and fieldnotes have the potential to provide rich data; but, to do this, qualitative writers should take care to *show* the data before interpreting it, write in rich ways, use vivid and active language, and help the reader distinguish the value and the source of the data through contextualization, editing, and formatting.

One way to set yourself up for publication success is to consider the potential publication home for your essay early in the writing process.

In that regard, I provided suggestions for crafting the piece for a certain audience and a list of journals that have published qualitative research. I also provided a back story about the persistence needed to journey through the revise and resubmit process.

The chapter also synthesized tips about writing prolifically and overviewed how to address some of the most common writing challenges. Even with all these tips, writing may still feel effortful. Silvia (2007), who wrote *How to Write a Lot: A Practical Guide to Productive Academic Writing*, says that "[w]riting a lot won't make you want to write any more [...] Writing is hard and will always be hard; writing is unpleasant and will always be unpleasant" (p. 130). That said, hopefully all these best practices may be helpful as you craft the data in a form that is interesting, invitational, and understandable to your key audiences.

I would add that writing is a bit like running – it is only unpleasant when you attach the activity to a specific, predetermined goal. If you let go and see what happens – like a child running for the sheer joy of it – you can find beauty in the journey. As the late Gordon MacKenzie, creative business revolutionary, said: "The biggest obstacle to creativity is attachment to outcome. As soon as you become attached to a specific outcome, you feel compelled to control and manipulate what you're doing. And in the process you shut yourself off to other possibilities" (quoted in Muoio, 1997). Lamott eloquently expressed what I am trying to say here:

Writing has so much to give, so much to teach, so many surprises. The thing you had to force yourself to do – the actual act of writing – turns out to be the best part. It's like discovering that while you thought you needed the tea ceremony for the caffeine, what you really needed was the tea ceremony (Lamott, 1994, p. xxvi).

Over time, writing does become easier. It becomes a habit, a ceremony, and a journey. And, on the strength of your past experiences, you can sit down to a new project already understanding the advantages, good feelings, and progress you'll feel along the way. As such, you'll be more motivated to do it.

If nothing else, I suggest you need to banish away any mean-spirited perfectionist demons whispering critiques into your ear. Writing is a skill and an art, and one that gets better as you do it, and do it again, and again. Gladwell (2008) said that achieving mastery in a task requires at least 10,000 hours of practice – so becoming excellent requires writing a lot. As you enter the lonely "winter" of writing (González, 2000), I encourage you to find a co-author, a mentor, or a writing partner who can show you tricks of the trade and give you advice and support. Along the way, there will be many "uncool" sentences. That's okay. In fact, that's good! Being compassionate with yourself is integral to getting those sentences to a point where you can re-read them, share them, and smile.

KEY TERMS

→ **e-prime**   a technique for rich writing that forecloses use of any form of the verb "to be"

→ **impact factor**   a measure commonly used to indicate the significance and prestige of a journal this statistic refers to the average number of citations of articles published in the journal in question

→ **luminous data**   data that are poignant, revealing, and often characterized by enigma, paradox, and absurdity

→ **rich data**   bountiful, generous data, which emerge from a variety of sources and contexts

→ **show, don't tell**   the core to qualitative writing – a principle stating that the data described should be more prominent than the claim they support

CHAPTER 14

Qualitative methodology matters
Exiting and communicating impact

Qualitative Research Methods: Collecting Evidence, Crafting Analysis, Communicating Impact, First Edition. Sarah J. Tracy.
© 2013 Sarah J. Tracy. Published 2013 by Blackwell Publishing Ltd.

I entered academia for two reasons. First, I wanted to escape working long hours. Second, I wanted to do research that matters. I still hold out hope for one of these goals. I believe qualitative methods provide myriad opportunities for doing research that matters. In this chapter I come full circle, discussing how researchers can best frame and deliver their qualitative work so that it impacts the world. Before I do that, though, I overview logistical issues about leaving the scene. Then I discuss a variety of types of research reports and representations available and make the case that we must think carefully about the way we deliver our work. I close the chapter with a final note about following, forgetting, and improvising.

Navigating exit from the scene

If you are like many qualitative researchers and students, you may be reading this chapter before you are actually ready to exit the research scene. Indeed, you may only have recently negotiated access *into* the scene, or maybe you are an autoethnographer who consistently lives the scene. Nonetheless, at some point, researchers face the logistics of moving from field and topic immersion to a more separate space of writing and reflection, so it is important to consider how best to do so.

How do you know when it is time to leave? According to Lindlof and Taylor (2011), researchers should continue doing qualitative research until the pieces of the puzzle come together, data become repetitive, and fieldnote writing becomes boring. Then researchers should attempt to see what might be missing from their analyses and, just in case, stay a little longer.

There are all kinds of ways to exit. Similarly to the advice in the rest of this book, there is no "perfect way." It will depend on your relationship with participants, the extent of immersion in the field, and resources (in terms of time, power or money) to travel, present wrap-up reports and conduct member reflections. Gallmeier (1991) discusses several key issues to consider when leaving. These include making sure participants are no worse off for having let us study them. Also, there are times when the most moral thing to do is to leave, especially if watching serves to condone activities that are unethical or immoral. Additionally, we may owe something back in the form of helping participants solve problems or sustain best practices. At the very least, we should create opportunities for them to stay in touch by exchanging contact information.

Although leaving the field is not exactly the same as any other relationship, it is nevertheless worthwhile to bear in mind what you already know about disengaging from other contexts or people: how best to leave a job, a hometown, a party, a hotel room, or a romantic relationship. Consider, for instance, the following:

- In order to best move from one job to the next, employees provide enough notice for their employer to adjust to their absence. It's a small world, and we may run into these people again (whether at work, in our research, or at play).
- People leaving their hometown for college or to find a new job usually hold several rituals signaling their transition to another geographical region. Rituals such as graduation ceremonies and farewell parties allow for the celebration of past experiences and anticipation of what is to come.
- Decent people leave hotel rooms without a huge mess – or, if they do leave a mess, they also leave a generous tip that compensates those who must clean it up.
- To gracefully exit a party, guests can offer to help the host tidy up (even if it was someone else who made the mess), or they can say goodbye and send a thank you note afterwards.

- Leaving a romantic relationship can be emotionally traumatic, even heart-wrenching. Relationally smart people know that this pain is normal and natural, and not something that can or should be "solved."
- When a restaurant, a movie theater, a hotel, or a vacation spot provides good service, then we should be mindful of the ways we publicly "review" any of their faults – so that others, unfamiliar with that scene, do not solely consider the negative.

We can draw some lessons about leaving the scene from what we know about these more common lifetime "exits." As discussed in more detail below, these consist of giving notice, saying goodbye, making room for emotions, not spoiling the scene, and giving back.

Give notice and say goodbye

I recommend that researchers begin thinking about their exit early on and provide participants with information about the time frame of the research. This is especially important for those who are immersed in the field and fulfill a role upon which participants rely. If you have become a full participant (say, a major player, a volunteer, or an employee), your absence will certainly impact others, and it is important to help participants ease into living without you. Researchers should "give notice" and emphasize their exit with an informal ritual – such as bringing in "thank you" snacks, or going out for happy hour. This provides space for final questions, well-wishes, and goodbyes.

Exits can be emotional

Just like leaving friends, family, or romantic partners, leaving the field or holding the last interview with a key informant can be an emotional process. When I left my cruise ship field research to return to graduate school, I experienced a huge sense of relief, but I also felt lost and discombobulated. As I took off in the airplane to go home, I remember peering out of the airplane window at the massive *Radiant Spirit* cruise ship docked just several miles away. With my nose pressed against the glass, I watched as my entire world for eight months grew smaller and smaller until, finally, it was just a little white dot and disappeared. Tears streamed down my face. Even though I had grown to detest certain parts of my cruise ship life, I appreciated its safe routine, and I did not know where my next paycheck would come from. Even if I kept in touch with my cruise ship friends, I was leaving a vibrant and unique chapter of my life forever.

My cruise ship experience was somewhat extreme, due to my complete enmeshment in a field that was effectively cut off from the rest of the world. However, in all research experiences, just as González (2000) described in her "four seasons" epistemology, the "summer" season of fieldwork is hot and intense, and the researcher's exit from the scene in "fall" is marked by ambivalence. Winter – the time of retreat from the scene and writing – often feels cold and solitary. This is something to be expected. If you feel grief, elation, sadness, joy, or even self-righteousness upon exit, you should know that you are not the only one to feel that way. Strong feelings are common when leaving the field.

Don't spoil the scene

My graduate school buddies Greg Larson and his wife, Melissa, are avid hikers and campers. When they leave a campsite, they not only carefully extinguish the campfire and pack up their trash; they also pick up the garbage left by others. During my first camping trip with them in

Colorado, I remember dropping a miniature pickle on the ground. I shrugged my shoulders, disappointed that the pickle was too dirty to eat, and proceeded to go on my way. Out of the corner of my eye, I watched in amazement and chagrin as Melissa picked up the pickle and placed it in her backpack. When she caught me looking, she said something like this: "I know it's just a pickle, but we were carrying it to begin with, and so it's not that hard to pack it out." As an experienced camper and hiker, Melissa was much more attuned to the importance of not spoiling the scene. Lessons I learned: (a) try not to make a mess to begin with; (b) if I do, clean it up; and (c) help ensure a future in which I or others can return to the scene.

Indeed, qualitative researchers should ask themselves this question: If a future researcher approached one of my past research participants for an interview, or approached my past gatekeeper for the opportunity to do research, would the way I conducted myself help or hurt access opportunities for him/her? Just like guests at a hotel who want to be welcomed back (or to make sure their friends and family will be welcomed), researchers should "pick up their pickles" and not spoil the scene.

Give back

Of course, just like in camping, it is impossible to completely "leave without a trace." Our research has an impact even if we try to ameliorate mistakes – only some of which we are ever aware. Given this, it makes sense to consider how we might try to make a positive impact. How can researchers give back to participants? Sometimes, just providing a slice of the data can serve as a thank you gesture. For instance, in our interview study with male executives (Tracy & Rivera, 2010), research assistant Jason Zingsheim sent interviewees a thank you follow-up with an accompanying transcript of the interview. In the letter he thanked them, indicated the trajectory of the project, created space for future interaction, and provided his own contact information (see Researcher's Notepad 14.1). Especially in interviews where participants tell stories that are dear or close to them, the transcript may hold great value.

When engaged in a long-term field study, researchers also commonly meet with key informants before they leave. Some research participants may only have a general and fleeting curiosity about the research, while others may want a detailed report or may even desire to receive suggestions, based upon the research, about what they or their group could do differently. You may interact with some participants only once or twice, while in other cases you may build a stronger relationship over hours, months, or even years – like Rebecca Skloot, who developed a close and complicated relationship with Herietta Lacks' daughter, Deborah, over more than a decade of research (Skloot 2010). In such situations, you may feel an increased obligation to share preliminary findings and provide opportunities for participants to comment on interpretations.

Indeed, no matter how long you have known the participants, another way to give back is by giving presentations or otherwise dialoguing with participants about the results. As my correctional officer research came to a close, I organized six different meeting and presentation times – some designed for the administrators and some for the correctional officers. I have this vivid memory of practicing my presentation (on the basis of my critical poststructuralist analysis) for a good friend. After I finished, my friend looked down and picked at the couch upholstery. Finally he said: "Well, it kinda sounds like you think that they do everything wrong." Needless to say, this was *not* the effect I was hoping for. I stayed up very late that night, tempering my critical tone and crafting better (shorter) take-away documents for participants.

A key part of reporting back to the field means adapting to the audience. We should think about participants' time constraints and create user-friendly research materials.

RESEARCHER'S NOTEPAD 14.1

Thank you note

1 August 2006

Dear [Participant]

I want to thank you again for participating in our study and sharing your experiences and opinions with me during the interview.

While we are not yet ready to conduct focus groups or more interviews, I also want to express my gratitude for your willingness to participate in a future focus group and your indication that your partner might also be willing to participate in such an interview.

We are currently analyzing the transcripts from our first round of interviews. As promised, I have included a copy of your transcript. This draft reflects your answers as they were recorded. Please feel free to contact us if you have any suggestions or corrections, but also please be assured that we will be changing all business and personal names to pseudonyms in all published reports.

As the analysis progresses, we may develop a couple of follow-up questions to assist in clarifying some of the themes we see emerging from the interviews. You indicated during the interview that you would be willing to answer more questions. I understand how valuable your time is, so any further questioning would be limited. Once we solidify these questions, I'll send them to you via email. Thank you in advance for taking time to answer them.

Again, if you have any questions about the study or your participation, please feel free to contact me. You may also direct your questions to Dr. S. J. Tracy, Principal Investigator, Hugh Downs School of Human Com., Arizona State University, P. O. Box 871205, Tempe, AZ 85287 – phone number 480-965-7709.

Sincerely,

Jason Zingsheim, M.A.
Graduate Associate
Hugh Downs School of Human Communication
Arizona State University

Three-page outlines are preferable to 50-page academic reports. Researchers who want their participants to actually read and appreciate their analysis will also consider how they and others might respond to critique or bad news – a topic I turn to next.

Ethically delivering the findings

Ethical researchers carefully consider the way their research will be read, understood, and used by outside audiences. Certainly, as soon as something is published, researchers never have full control over how their work will be taken up. However, they should consider how best to present the research so as to avoid negative or unintended consequences.

From a purely practical point of view, such considerations will affect the extent to which people interpret or believe the research report. "If people feel betrayed by you when they read a report, it becomes almost impossible for them to accept it as a reasonable interpretation of what happened" (Miles & Huberman, 1994, p. 293). In other words, feelings of anger at being misled or tricked almost always trump "accuracy" or "truth."

Researchers should also ensure that they do not confuse voyeuristic or scandalous tales with great research stories. Fine, Weis, Weseen, & Wong (2000) explain how, as researchers, they themselves "continue to struggle with how best to represent the stories that may do more damage than good, depending on who consumes/exploits them" (p. 116). For instance, stories about people who are poor, stigmatized, abused, or otherwise marginalized can serve to portray such people negatively still further – even if that is not the intent of the author.

Hence, qualitative researchers have an obligation to "come clean 'at the hyphen,' meaning that we are reflexive about who we are as we coproduce the narratives we presume to 'collect,' and we anticipate how the public and policy-makers will receive, distort, and misread our data" (Fine et al., 2000, p. 127). Especially if the information is negative, surprising, depressing, or could be used to punish certain participants, authors might consider publishing a "Legend of Cautions" (ibid.), which warns readers about the ways in which the research analyses may be misread, misappropriated, or misused. Although it is rare to see such a formal legend, being ethical includes considering how results might be presented so as to ward off victim blaming and the appropriation of findings that have unjust consequences.

Oftentimes researchers are so concerned with their own academic goals that they give little forethought to how they can best deliver and present their findings to participants. Providing participants with unedited raw data (such as their own interview transcript) is one thing, but providing them with other people's data, or an analysis/interpretation is another – especially if it is critical or revealing. Just as therapy can reveal things to an individual that are painful, qualitative analyses can expose information that is not easy for participants to take (Schein, 1992). Therefore qualitative researchers must go beyond dropping their analyses in participants' "in-boxes" (Deetz, Tracy, & Simpson, 2000). They should also consider offering recommendations about how the information may be fruitfully understood and applied.

FOLLOWING, FORGETTING, AND IMPROVISING

Sometimes, despite one's best efforts, it is difficult or impossible to engage in all the "best practices" discussed above in terms of leaving the field. For instance, although it may be ideal to stay in the scene until the analyses are theoretically saturated, most people must exit due to external factors. For example, they leave because the semester is done, the paper is due, grant funding has run out, or the tenure clock is ticking. All research is partial, and it is impossible to ever get the "full story." Furthermore, time constraints never go away (even if the agent of constraint changes form). Researchers should try at least to get enough data to secure good answers for their research questions. And, if this is not possible, sometimes the researcher must narrow the claims or the research questions. Another option when time is short is to frame the research as a "pilot study" and make note of the many areas available for future research (so that you or someone else can do this work some day).

Additionally, exit and possibilities to return and say goodbye are sometimes decided for us. The researcher's exit may be conjoined with her exit as an employee, team member, or volunteer. Geographical issues or financial constraints could make it impossible to return and present findings. Some researchers feel nervous and as though they do not have enough answers, expertise, or credibility to present their research to the group. In such cases, another option is to provide resulting research papers or executive summaries. Of course, the participant research report is only one way you can make your research matter.

Moving toward research representations with public impact

Research representations can take a variety of forms – and no one form is inherently better than another. Every paper, performance, or presentation is partial and can never hold the whole truth. In this section I discuss a variety of ways in which you can represent your data – and their potential impact.

When considering the hours I have spent over my career writing, most of my energies have been focused on academic essays like book chapters, conference papers, and journal articles – which in many disciplines are considered the "golden ticket" for earning tenure and promotion. However, in addition to scholarly work, presenting for a variety of audiences in non-traditional formats provides further avenues for making qualitative research matter. To achieve such presentations, researchers must often "un-learn" academic writing.

In the process of training and practicing scholarly writing for a narrow disciplinary group, students and researchers can inadvertently learn to write and talk in ways that are indecipherable to many populations. This is problematic, not only because it diminishes the impact of research, but also because indecipherable language reflects poorly on the writer. I like the following quotation from William Schutz from his now out-of-date book *Profound Simplicity*:

> When I look over the books I have written, I know exactly which parts I understood and which parts I did not understand when I wrote them. The poorly understood parts sound scientific. When I barely understood something, I kept it in scientific jargon. When I really comprehended it, I was able to explain it to anyone in language they understood. [...] Understanding evolves in three phases: simplistic, complex, and profoundly simple. (Schutz, 1979, pp. 68–69, as quoted in Weick, 2001, p. 5)

To become persuasive in the public sphere, we must become "profoundly simple" – which is, ironically, the most advanced phase of writing. By doing so we transcend the complexity that is accepted and celebrated in academic forums and move toward public scholarship.

Public scholarship

Public scholarship aims to develop scholarly work that is distributed to, discussed among, and debated by a variety of public and non-academic audiences. Decision-makers, students, and everyday problem solvers are increasingly turning to websites, blogs, social networking sites, and white papers in order to progress in their work, family, and community lives. And translating academic work into these forums offers opportunity for increased impact. Here is a description of public scholarship, developed by the Department of Communication at University of Washington, which was posted on that department's website in 2009:

> Public scholarship may take many forms, such as popularization of research-based ideas in a variety of media and formats, facilitation of deliberation about such social values as equality, justice and freedom, and explanation or appreciation of texts, concepts, values or events. Such efforts can promote constructive dialogue with and among students, citizens, diverse communities, and political and cultural leaders. (Faculty Statement on Public Scholarship)

As noted, public scholarship can take a range of forms. The good news is that qualitative researchers have the theoretical background, methodological skills, and scholarly creativity to engage societal problems and issues in these new and transformative ways. Additionally, some of us have expertise in new media technologies, website development, and journalistic writing, and most of us at least have friends or colleagues with such skills – skills that help ensure that our work reaches a variety of audiences. Finally, qualitative researchers understand the importance of rhetorical presentation and of adapting the message to the audience. Given all these reasons, we should consider representational options such as working with the media, writing short position papers and trade-journal articles, turning research into staged performances, and finding space and opportunities to converse with those who are affected by the research.

Staged performances

Performance offers an excellent way to engage audience members who might otherwise be unlikely to hear a message. Performance can be a theoretical approach and a way of knowing just as much as it is a representation. Through script, dramatic staging, and character production, research can come alive. A wealth of resources are available for those interested in a performance approach to qualitative methods (see Denzin, 2010, for a review of sources and a helpful discussion on how to teach qualitative methods using a performance).

Collaborative partnering can result in innovative representational outcomes even if you are not personally an expert in performance. I have served as a consultant on a couple of different performances that include productions titled *Navigating the Cruise* and *Bullied*. The stage directors of these productions, Linda Park-Fuller and Sara MicKinnon, respectively, created performances based upon the field data: photos, interviews, and fieldnote texts. I also worked with them to develop interactive discussions of analyses and potential trigger questions for the audience. A collaborating researcher may also assist with casting, costuming, discussion leading, or acting.

In order to do such work, the researcher must tackle several challenges that may be unfamiliar, such as memorizing lines and facing immediate audience feedback (which can be simultaneously gratifying and mortifying). Furthermore, as in any collaboration, in partnering with a performance director the researcher must be comfortable about not being in charge. Although I espouse the philosophy of "multiple realities" and of the researcher as "non-expert," it was only through performance that I most viscerally felt and embodied these philosophies. In each of my experiences, the director took a reality that I thought I knew ("my" research), and presented it in a way that (re)presented my data and, at times, their performance differed from the way I would have (re)presented it myself. The performance provided an alternative message and an opportunity to make the research accessible and, arguably, more memorable to people who would not have heard it otherwise.

In Researcher's Notepad 14.2, scholar and performance artist Linda Park-Fuller describes in her own words how she developed a staged performance that had an impact.

RESEARCHER'S NOTEPAD 14.2

Staged performance with impact
A clean breast of it

By Linda Park-Fuller, in her own words

When I was diagnosed with breast cancer in 1989, I became aware of three communication-related problems pertinent to my experience of the disease.

- Although impersonal information about the disease was available, I hadn't heard women talk about their experiences with this illness. I also needed to share, in casual settings, some of the enormity of what was happening to me, but outside of official support groups no one wanted to talk. It was as if no one knew how to talk about it.
- When occasionally people spoke to me about the cancer, they asked me what the doctor said but not what I had learned about this cancer or what I was going through. I was no longer the expert on my life.
- I felt restricted by the unrealistic, limited roles society offered me in relation to cancer: I could be either the pitiful victim or the heroic conqueror. I didn't want my life to be defined by a disease with only two outcomes.

Scripting and performing my story in the presence of live audiences offered a unique opportunity to address these communication issues directly. In performance I could share my experience, and in following talk-back discussion other survivors shared their encounters. These forums gave us a chance to learn what it was like to have cancer and also helped erase the stigma of talking about it. Second, taking ownership of our stories helped us to take back ownership of our bodies from medical sites, procedures, and officials, giving us a sense of re-empowerment. Third, in doing so, we forged and demonstrated more complex roles than those of simple victims or heroes – anyone could see that we had up-days and down-days, good times and bad, which we handled sometimes poorly or well.

In addition to publishing the script, I presented the performance nationally and internationally over fifty times at universities, hospitals, women's centers, conferences, middle and high schools, corporate settings, and video conferences. I've also led workshops and talks in conjunction with the performances that bring me in touch with more people. The opportunity to involve others in this research is very fulfilling and my life continues to be enriched by the stories of the wonderful people I meet in the process (see also Park-Fuller, 1995, 2000, 2003).

White papers

Another avenue for doing research with impact is the writing of white papers. The **white paper** concept has traditionally referred to government-issued papers that identify a key problem and then lay out policy that solves the problem. In the 1990s, businesses employed the short problem-solution format of white papers to market particular products or technologies. Although their form varies, the main point of white papers is to show how a problem can be solved – and to show it in an efficient, short, easy-to-read manner. Increasingly, scholars are turning to white papers to address specific dilemmas and problems. Research, which may otherwise remain isolated within scholarly articles, is drawn upon to tell a story or to make suggestions and help readers educate themselves on how best to make pressing professional, societal, and personal decisions.

For instance, the Center for Strategic Communication, led by Dr. Steven Corman at Arizona State University-Tempe, has developed numerous white papers on communication problems associated with military action in Iraq and the war on terror. The white papers have led to significant media attention – for instance to an op-ed piece in the *Washington Post* – and have been read by high-ranking military and governmental leaders in the state department and the department of defense, and by think tanks like the Brookings Institution and the Heritage Foundation. As such, the research overviewed in the white papers has directly impacted strategic communication policies and practices. The white papers have been published on the consortium's website (http://csc.asu.edu/) as well as in hard copy, in a multi-contributor volume (Corman, Trethewey, & Goodall, 2008).

In addition, I along with colleagues Jess K. Alberts and Kendra Rivera developed a white paper that was based upon research with targets of workplace bullying (Tracy, Alberts, & Rivera, 2007). The piece, entitled "How to Bust the Office Bully," is written as a how-to guide for such targets, giving tips to help them explain workplace abuse to decision-makers. The white paper was distributed and linked to workplace bullying websites and is available, free of charge, at http://humancommunication.clas.asu.edu/files/HowtoBusttheOfficeBully.pdf. If the amount of email response is any signifier, this paper has generated as much practical impact on targets of workplace bullying as any of my scholarly journal articles on the topic, if not more. Some tips on writing white papers can be found in Tips and Tools 14.1.

Grant applications and reports

Like many qualitative researchers, I have funded most of my research through my own pocketbook and a handful of internal university grants to cover small projects (with awards ranging from $5,000 to $20,000). But recently, I have served as qualitative consultant on a variety of larger grants (e.g., Malvini Redden, Tracy, & Shafer, 2012). On the one hand, grant-getting is not required for conducting excellent qualitative research. On the other, a grant can help support larger and more diverse sample sizes, a research team of participant observers, data analysis software, travel, and research assistants. Furthermore, universities are changing every day and professors face increased expectations that they bring in external grant monies. For these reasons I briefly discuss some aspects of grant-getting.

First, many large grants funded through governmental agencies and foundations require preliminary findings in the form of pilot studies. These findings provide an overview of the research and of the feasibility of the larger study, and they point to areas that need further research. So, if you are interested in landing a big grant, do not wait to begin collecting data. First engage in some smaller studies and some smaller grants; then you can work your way up.

In order to succeed, researchers need to write grant proposals so that their studies are understandable to a review board – people familiar with scholarly research, but who may

TIPS AND TOOLS 14.1

White papers

1 Define your audience (e.g. governmental leaders; targets of workplace bullying). Your audience will determine the best venue and distribution channels of the white paper, as well as the writing style and the level.

2 Lay out a specific problem experienced by that audience (e.g. how to encourage peace in a war-torn nation; how to bust an office bully). The paper should avoid a laundry list of problems that is overwhelming. The problem should be something that the research can help solve.

3 Be succinct and use references sparingly. Length should depend on the complexity of the problem. A good rule of thumb is that white papers should be 10–20 pages, with 10–20 references at maximum. If it's longer, consider breaking it into two papers.

4 Provide a 1–2-page summary at the beginning of the document for those who will only devote five minutes to the piece. This part should state the problem and the key aspects of the solution.

5 Make the document attractive and readable. Good white papers break up what might otherwise be pages and pages of text with white spaces, tables, pull-out quotations, lists, text-boxes, and diagrams. The white paper's charm lies in its visual appeal as much as in its content. At the same time, authors should avoid overly complex models that can confuse readers or cheapen the document, especially if they are not of high quality.

6 Use a compelling and readable writing style. Authors should use short sentences, avoid jargon or academic lingo, and infuse the piece with imagery, contractions, humor, and everyday metaphors.

7 Solve the problem. The findings of the research should be laid out in a way that tells a tightly crafted and compelling story about how the readers can address the problem identified early in the paper. In doing so, adduce supporting evidence from the data collected as well as from past research.

8 Provide a summary that repeats the problem and highlights the solution.

have methodological or topical foci that are very different from those of the applicant. Furthermore, qualitative researchers face particular challenges in terms of proposing grants, as many governmental agencies assume that the only sound research is one that is objective, scientific, and quantitative (Denzin & Giardina, 2008). For better or worse, a scan of proposal requests suggests that the federal government does indeed influence research methods, especially when it comes to policy research.

Researchers using qualitative methods can help meet these challenges by being aware of the granting agency's preferences and politics and of whether the agency has supported qualitative projects in the past or has included qualitative researchers on the review board (Cheek, 2005). Given the enduring preference for quantitative research, grant proposals should lay out the value of the qualitative approach as well as pinpoint preliminary promising findings and questions left to be answered. Engaging a mixed methods project and collaborating with researchers already known to the granting agency is also well advised. Applicants should provide a clear timeline and framework for accomplishing the research, complete with step-by-step discussions of how the data will be gathered and analyzed. This is definitely not the time for casual references to a "grounded approach," the "constant comparative method," or the even less specific "significant themes will emerge." Rather, researchers need to delineate their methods with precision, in a language understandable to those who are not intimately familiar with qualitative methods.

Writing up a research report *after* the project is completed is also important. If the research was conducted for a funded project, researchers are commonly required to write a follow-up report. This report provides an executive summary of the research activities and highlights tangible research outcomes or "deliverables" such as instructional materials, governmental briefing papers, conference presentations, articles, or additional grant proposals. Audience members of such reports want to ensure a "return on investment," and, if the project's value is not properly demonstrated, the grant recipient may be ineligible for future funding.

Consulting

Consulting is another key way for qualitative research to have impact. Some qualitative researchers engage in regular consulting and training. For instance, Scott Dickmeyer – a professor of organizational communication and public relations and former chair of the National Communication Association's Training and Development Division – focuses his research on helping build leadership and communication skills in universities, non-profits, and fortune 500 companies.

Other researchers provide consulting as just one slice of their research activities. For example, interpersonal communication scholar Jess Alberts has been contracted to serve as an expert witness, organize conferences, lead training sessions, and even teach an international certification program based upon her research in conflict and communication. During such sessions she has worked alongside participants, as they themselves have discussed ways they might better engage in conflict issues in their personal and work relationships. She has also spoken with various groups – from universities to non-profits and community groups – on issues of conflict, negotiation, communication, bullying, well-being, and gender relations. Such opportunities not only allow for immediate feedback and impact, but also may provide material benefits in the form of consulting fees. The process of designing research so as to meet typical organizational or social issues, of interacting with members of the community, and of hearing a variety of responses to the research helps build the *reach* of the scholarship. Furthermore, consulting serves to sharpen original analyses and provides trajectories for future research.

Media relations

In order to conduct qualitative research that matters, scholars should consider the media venues most commonly accessed by members of their key audience and forge relationships that will encourage their research to be covered by such outlets. Good media options include local newspapers, major nationals like *The New York Times*, websites such as MSN or Yahoo, magazines, web-based media distributors such as *Live Science*, blogs, and radio and television shows.

Many universities sponsor a "speaker's bureau" in which students and faculty members may list their topics of expertise. When journalists need an expert source for their story, or when local groups need a speaker or a consultant, the speaker's bureau constitutes a first point of contact. It can also be useful to work with professionals or publicists in media relations (either through the university or independently hired). These individuals are well trained in writing and distributing press releases. Such work can lead to spotlight articles on the research or to interviews on news shows. However, because university publicists are usually spread thin and overworked, your research must be truly unique, timely, and significant in order to get their attention (and for them to get the media's attention). A more direct route to media consumers is that of sending letters to the editor and/or responding to a forum or blog. These forums need to be brief, but they can include references to longer resources (an academic article or white paper) that readers could turn to for more information.

In addition, many trade-specific journals can target a specific professional audience. Trade journals allow space for more in-depth articles than is possible on most websites or in most newspapers. However, compared to scholarly journals, trade journals focus on practical concerns rather than on building theoretical knowledge. How might one become involved in trade-journal writing? You can contact the trade journal's editors yourself and offer to write an article. Or you can put yourself in places where you might be approached and asked to write a piece. For instance, one of the attendees at a correctional workshop I led passed along my name to the editors of *Corrections Today* – a leading trade journal for correctional administrators. This opened to me the opportunity to write an article for this magazine with a circulation of 21,000 and an estimated pass-along readership of 65,000 (Tracy, 2003). The trade-journal essay provided a direct way to reach thousands of prison guards and their bosses.

Of course, one of the challenges to media relations is transforming complex and theoretical material into catchy headlines and short sound-bites. Despite my undergraduate training in public relations, I still have trouble boiling down my research or figuring out how to talk simply about theoretical ideas. Colleagues and I have had amusingly frustrating conversations about how best to "translate" certain concepts from theory into practice. For instance, one might ask whether an academic phrase such as "the muting effects of discourses of power" could effectively be translated as "certain contexts and messages make it difficult to hear certain messages," or even condensed into the pithy question "Does work make us deaf?" These secondary phrasings are certainly simpler, but they lose the complexities carried by "discourses of power." Grappling with such issues is part and parcel of doing research that makes a public impact.

Websites and web relations

The Internet is one of the most common sources of information. Researchers can make their findings readily available online by posting web-based white papers and by creating hyperlinks to scholarly resources for already developed web pages. For instance, after the researchers of The Project for Wellness and Work-Life developed the "How to Bust a Bully" white paper, we sent the link to several workplace bullying organizations, which added the piece, under "resources," to their own web pages.

Another option for increasing a web presence is to contribute to web-based encyclopedias such as Wikipedia. Wikipedia (www.wikipedia.org) is one of the most popular Internet websites, drawing millions of viewers each day. Anyone is allowed to post and edit on Wikipedia, and this publicly and freely accessible encyclopedia serves to directly assist employees, community members, journalists, students, and scholars. Although many scholars have been ambivalent and even derogatory about Wikipedia as a credible source, phrases like "wiki-it" suggest that open sources of its kind are here to stay (Rush & Tracy, 2010). To increase the impact and reach of their work, I encourage students and colleagues to add their own summaries, commentaries, and references to existing Wikipedia pages, or even to build their own. A scan of the topics associated with qualitative research (ethnography, fieldwork, interview, critical ethnography) suggests that qualitative researchers still have much to offer to this online resource.

Scholars developing their own line of research may find it worthwhile to create their own personal web presence. This can be accomplished through public resources such as Wikipedia and/or through one's university or company. Furthermore, many people are turning to social networking sites such as Facebook and Twitter to share ideas and build a community. Sharing first-draft excerpts of research on such websites has the potential (a) to provide immediate feedback and constructive critique; (b) to connect you with others doing similar work; and (c) to alert others of your current projects. Perhaps most importantly, though, sharing first-draft excerpts yields support and motivation during what could otherwise be a lonely time of writing.

Increasing numbers of scholars are also creating their own personal web pages, separate from their university persona. For instance, qualitative researcher Bud Goodall (2008), pictured in the screen shot (Figure 14.1), offers a number of tips on how best to create a web presence at http://hlgoodall.com/index.html.

Stanford management scholar Robert Sutton also maintains an excellent website entitled "Work Matters" (http://bobsutton.typepad.com/), which boasts a regularly updated blog and a variety of web-based trinkets such as the *Asshole Rating Self-Exam (ARSE) – Are you a certified asshole?* Indeed, Bob might serve as an exemplar of public scholarship. He knows how to simplify ideas so that managers and organizations actually listen; this is exemplified in his books, *The No Asshole Rule* (2007) and *Good Boss, Bad Boss* (2010). These books include many scholarly hot topics – such as conflict, interaction, and work. However, Sutton came up with the irresistible titles and wrote them in a humorous manner, easy to read. As a result, he has been featured in countless news stories about jerks in the workplace.

Figure 14.1 Bud Goodall's website offers an attractive template and a range of resources, including a blog, book reviews, press reports, and summaries of his research. Screen shot from http://www.hlgoodall.com/ (March, 2012).

Warning: doing research that matters can be terrifying

Public scholarship and doing qualitative research that matters are not for the faint of heart. They can be both exciting and nerve-wracking when people with an interest in the results may act on or critique your work. When I receive emails from employees who are suffering from workplace bullying, they often ask me to help them make decisions that will hugely impact their life. Subject lines often read "please help," or "should I quit?" In such cases, when I know with clarity only one small part of the story, I usually craft a careful email, give condolences for the situation, point them in the direction of research articles and other web-based resources, and offer several suggestions. Then, right when I'm about to hit "send," my stomach jumps. This is where the rubber hits the road. Although I feel confident in my research, traditional scholarly training does little to prepare us for working with those who make decisions based directly upon our research.

Discussing one's research with journalists can also be intimidating – especially on a live radio show or in regard to something contentious or political. For instance, I got little sleep the night before I was scheduled to do a live radio spot about workplace bullying for the shock jock, nationally syndicated "Mancow Show." I presumed that the host, Mancow, had heard of our work from the coverage of conservative radio show host Rush Limbaugh earlier that week. Rush had reacted to the research by saying:

> Study reveals widespread office bullying! I know exactly what this is. I know exactly. It's a bunch of liberals behind this, a bunch of pantywaist, limp-wristed, linguini-spined liberals who are out there trying to work their magic and reorder the basic tenets of human nature. (http://www.workplacebullying.org/res/limbaugh.html)/

In order to prepare my panty-waisted self for the show, I pored over the latest research, got all my figures straight, planned 2–3 short key points, and decided I needed to have a sense of humor to survive. I figured I would just do my best – even if that was not so good – living again by the notion that "anything worth doing well is worth doing badly in the beginning" (Canfield, 2005, p. 137, citing business consultant Marshall Thurber).

So, how did I fare? It turned out that too many celebrities were scheduled on the morning of my appearance; my "spot" lasted less than two minutes and consisted mostly of the host making jokes about bad bosses. So it's hard to know how I would have managed in a longer discussion. Regardless, my research and my understanding of workplace bullying became significantly stronger as a result of prepping for the show. As Flyvbjerg (2001) states: "Your senses are definitely sharpened when you carry out your research with the knowledge that people with an interest in the results might do what they can to find errors in your work" (p. 158).

Overcoming lingering obstacles to public scholarship

In order to engage in alternative representations, we must first tackle a couple of obstacles. For instance, we need to be motivated and, given the infrastructure in our universities and associations, to practice and learn communication technologies to their poten-tial. A case in point is the National Communication Association's online magazine *Communication Currents*, available at http://www.communicationcurrents.com/. Although this website hosts a variety of important research reports, its readability and navigational capabilities are still somewhat cumbersome by comparison to those of other readily available web resources (e.g. http://www.psychologytoday.com/). The website is a step in the right direction, but it could have more impact with more reliable server capabilities and greater professional web design support.

We must also consider how to best frame our research so that it may be complex and theoretical, yet understandable to a wide range of audiences. As illustrated in this book, a critical postmodern approach is certainly helpful for teasing out power relations and for situating social problems. Many excellent studies begin with a problem in the field and critique current practices that encourage and maintain the problem (ostensibly, so that these practices might be transformed). At the same time, critical research can come off as haughty – in terms of the language used, portraying research participants as dupes, and tearing open huge holes of critique to gratuitously toss in a few "practical application" pebbles near the end of the article.

Although the focus of much research can be on negative states or problems, I have become increasingly convinced that it is at least as important to understand why it is that people flourish and thrive. Qualitative scholars may have much to learn from researchers at Compassion Lab (www.compassionlab.com), Positive Deviance Initiative (http://www.positivedeviance.org/), and Appreciative Inquiry Commons (http://appreciativeinquiry.case.edu/intro/whatisai.cfm). By focusing on positive deviance as much as, or more than, on the problems and destructive parts of social life, our scholarship may be increasingly well received in the public sphere.

Finally, the success of public scholarship is dependent on a context in which researchers are rewarded for doing research that matters beyond the academy. I would like to see a change in our graduate curriculums, institutional compositions, and research evaluations, toward emphasis on and reward for writing and presenting our research to a variety of audiences. My lay experience suggests that web-based white papers available free of charge through a variety of websites have just as much (if not more) impact as scholarly journal articles that are not publicly accessible. However, it is difficult to be motivated to write white papers when such non-juried articles – and the hundreds of email interactions they generate – count little in terms of institutional reward. If we are to become significant public voices in today's most pressing organizational and societal discussions, we need to find ways to encourage and reward such important qualitative work.

EXERCISE 14.1

Making an impact via public scholarship

Working in pairs or research teams, discuss how your research might make a public impact.

1   What obligations do you have to the community studied? How could you give back?
2   Identify other key stakeholders who may be interested in your research or findings.
3   How might you communicate main findings to these stakeholders? Consider alternative representations such as performances, websites or social media, white papers, news stories, public presentations, or something else.
4   How could you translate your research in a feasible way, given the time and resources available to you?

FOLLOWING, FORGETTING, AND IMPROVISING

In the process of instructing others about the practices of qualitative methods, this book has made implicit judgments on what counts as good research practice. Indeed I have learned that some students and researchers only feel comfortable, ethical, and rigorous when they closely follow established and proven guidelines. By contrast, other researchers feel constrained by rules and formulas, preferring to approach their scholarship in a playful, improvisational manner. Generally I take a middle ground, as I believe that methodological guidelines and best practices should be viewed as paradoxical: simultaneously necessary and constraining.

Most qualitative researchers appreciate that research is more than just following rules. Artistic and narrative form illustrates the world in ways that rule-based or analytic methods do not. Yet many researchers, including myself, find themselves quite attracted to rules and "how-to" tips. Certainly this book has represented a whole range of qualitative "best practices," including immersing oneself in the field for an extended amount of time, developing research questions, designing detailed fieldnotes, systematic interview guides, accurate transcripts, coded data texts, and giving tips on how to create analytic data displays such as matrices and networks. I believe that learning the basic tenets of good ethnography and best practices is worthwhile. Committing this knowledge to memory is also very helpful for encouraging rigor and ethical approaches even when websites and sourcebooks are not nearby.

Although best practices can provide some excellent structure, they can also be constraining. One downside to clear guidelines is that many methodological rules are remnants of positivist thinking that do not fit the epistemological bases (interpretive, critical, postmodern) of much qualitative research. Qualitative researchers are often asked to discuss concepts such as "reliability" and "generalizability," when the original meanings of these concepts took shape in quantitative approaches that do not easily translate into qualitative research.

Further, many qualitative researchers can become discouraged when they are asked to shape research narratives into traditional, deductively written, journal formats – with a linear literature review, research questions, and findings (Tracy, 2012). This transformation preserves the myth that the research questions and problems do not change in the course of a project, when in fact the literature and research questions that accompany a qualitative study are usually determined in tandem with, rather than strictly before, the analysis of the data.

Following established practices can also reinscribe norms and ideologies regarding what types of research are most accepted, moral, and appropriate. The word "rules" implies authority and a single way of doing things. In the spirit of Amira De La Garza's "four seasons" epistemology (González, 2000), we should critically ask questions about *who* created and validated certain rules and consider carefully what qualitative methodological rules might look like if the ways of knowing of traditionally marginalized people had been (or were currently) validated.

Indeed, when researchers continually situate themselves within dominant ideologies, they limit creative possibilities. For instance, most researchers are expected to include established types of information in an article's methods section (number of hours in the field, demographics of interviewees, details about the coding scheme). However, it may be just as worthwhile for the methods section to discuss why the topic was chosen, what the researcher really hoped to gain in doing the study, and what might be done differently in a future study.

In addition, it's simply not true that all people need rules to do good work. Although some musicians appreciate first learning chord structure and scales in order to read music, others learn by ear and feel. Some people never follow a food recipe, but rather rely on memories and family traditions for their inspiration. Sometimes the food turns out, sometimes it's awful, but it reflects the mood, context, and the ingredients at hand.

Finally, and perhaps most importantly, rules only get us so far. Rule-based approaches can succeed at explaining the *competent* practice of research methodology, but they are not sufficient to explain this practice at an *expert* level. Research on learning (Dreyfus, Athanasiou, & Dreyfus, 1986) indicates that a qualitative jump occurs between competent and expert levels of performance (Flyvbjerg, 2001). The same is true in qualitative methods. The interpretative skills needed to do qualitative research may begin with rules, but, if qualitative researchers wish to develop their own skills to an expert level (or encourage their students to do the same), they need concrete, context-dependent experience, and often they must improvise. Indeed the really important interpretive work that moves scholars from competent to expert research is intuitive and holistic. Often enough, the best qualitative research happens when we "forget" the rules, improvise, and go with our gut.

So let's go back to the question: Are best practices necessary, or are they constraining? The answer, I believe, is a resounding "yes." Yes, clear guidelines are necessary. And, yes, they can also be constraining. Like in any form of dialectics, this paradox is not something that can be resolved. But in discussing the tension we can manage it rather than being trapped by it. There's no easy way out. But there are better ways of navigating than others. Qualitative researchers are creative, resilient, and resourceful; and, as creative bricoleurs, all of us will find our own way of attending to it. My hope is that this book has provided guidelines, inspiration, and motivation so that you might engage at your best in the systematic and step-by-step – yet intuitive and holistic – practices that mark high-quality qualitative methods.

In summary

In this chapter I have tried to link multiple representational practices with the goal of this book – in terms of conducting phronetic, problem-based, contextual research. As such, I discussed the issues of practical ethics that researchers should consider when leaving the scene. The heart of the chapter reviewed how researchers can best frame and deliver their qualitative work in multiple representational forms, so that it impacts the world. Such representations suggest that qualitative researchers should not only write papers for their professors and academic colleagues, but also consider transforming their research for a variety of audiences and delivering it through performances, white papers, media representations, and websites. Then I discussed a variety of the types of research reports and representations available and made the case that we must think carefully about the way we deliver our work if we want our research to have impact.

After learning and following these rules – and all the rules of thumb presented in this book – sometimes you just have to forget them, improvise, and go with your gut. In the closing section I share my philosophical approach toward methodological best practices – something that hopefully helps make sense of how rules and "best practices" intersect with the art and dance of qualitative research.

KEY TERMS

 public scholarship   scholarship that aims to develop work that is distributed to, discussed among, and debated by a variety of public and non-academic audiences

 white papers   concept papers aimed at policy-makers or lay people; they identify a key problem and then provide information – in an efficient, easy-to-read manner – that helps solve the problem

Appendix A

The following fieldnote, unpublished, written by Dr. Deborah Way, explores one of her first visits to a hospital inpatient unit (and one of her first ever fieldnotes). All names are pseudonyms. The fieldnote admittedly has strengths (thick description, a drawing, and use of multiple senses) and weaknesses (lack of dialogue). Using the information you have learned, evaluate this fieldnote. What does it accomplish well? How might it be improved?

RESEARCHER'S NOTEPAD

Fieldnote
October 2, St. Matthews Inpatient Unit

St. Matthew's inpatient unit is in an older area of town. The hospice unit occupies a far wing of the hospital. It looks more like an old run-down nursing home from the outside. There are iron bars on the windows and the front doors that face the street are kept locked at all times (because of the neighborhood, they tell me). Entry is gained by going through a side, iron gate (which is open during the day and locked at night – in which case you need to ring the buzzer to gain entry), walking through a cement patio with two umbrella-ed tables, and in through two large glass doors. It is quiet everywhere. Even the "bad" neighborhood gives no indication of distress right now.

I've come today specifically to attend the weekly IDT [Interdisciplinary Team] meeting at the unit. Each inpatient unit has a weekly meeting with the staff doctor, volunteer coordinator, office administrator, spiritual advisor, (head) nurse, social worker, and PCC. Pat, the PCC at St. Matthews, was not in attendance this week, as she was "called in to work the night shift." I don't know what this means, because I thought she was strictly administration, so I don't know what she would be doing at night. Oh I know, maybe doing intake.

We meet in the patient lounge. The lounge contains a table (country style, like I used to have in my old house on Plummers Dr.), credenza with coffee maker and microwave, a couch and a TV, and a couple of plants. Pleasant enough. It would actually provide a visitor a nice respite from the patient rooms. It has a big ass TV!

The meeting   When I walk in, I start to take a seat at the table. Mitzi quickly grabs my arm and ushers me a chair off to the side at the other end of the table, next to her. I realize there is an order at this table that NEVER changes, week after week {Debbie then inserted a drawing, below,

Qualitative Research Methods: Collecting Evidence, Crafting Analysis, Communicating Impact, First Edition. Sarah J. Tracy.
© 2013 Sarah J. Tracy. Published 2013 by Blackwell Publishing Ltd.

of the table, including where the nurse, office manager, volunteer coordinator, doctor, social worker, spiritual advisor and she herself sat}.

Everyone takes his or her seat at the table. The bagels remain untouched in the middle of the table. They are talking about somebody who "bled out" last night. They are all in agreement: it was "a nice family."

NOTE TO SELF   Quit mentioning that I am a communication major. If I hear one more person say, "let's start communicating for the communications major," I'm gonna scream!

The purpose of the meeting is to go over the patient files from the previous week. A carbon copy form detailing each patient's status makes its rounds around the table as they talk about that patient. Each person has a line on which to sign. I sign the first few on the line that either says "volunteer" or is otherwise blank. They indicate this is necessary. But then, when it is pointed out that I am using a blue pen instead of black (the required pen color), they let the forms pass me. And that's actually fine with me.

Karla starts each form and it moves clockwise, making one pass around the table, then past her again, where Sharon retrieves it and puts it in a file. Karla's soft voice details the patients' medical status: medications, inpatient or gone home, dead or alive. It's soooo interesting. Everyone is talking to everyone else, sometimes about the patient, sometimes not. But they all seem to know what the other is saying and what Karla is saying about the patient. It's like they have a heightened sense of hearing, or multiple sets of ears. OR, they just do this so much they can do it with their ears tied behind their back.

Between forms there are lots of personal conversations. I think this is partly a social gathering for them.

The bagels are still in the center of the table. Despite being hungry, I don't dare make a move.

<u>Lots of joking and death humor:</u>

Dr. R says that he had to explain to one of the patients' daughter that her mother was dying: "I told her, look, you're dying. Leave all your valuables and get out." Although I didn't completely get the joke, believe me, I laughed with everyone else.

Another story Dr. R thought was humorous: A patient died several days earlier. Barbara asks Dr. R if he saw the patient alive (Dr. R makes his rounds at the unit in the mornings). He says yes, "The night shift didn't do a good enough job." (Inferring: if they had, the patient would have died prior to his arrival in the morning, thus minimizing his workload.)

This gets tedious. I see why they mix business talk with personal talk. The Spiritual Advisor and the Volunteer Coordinator do this 3 days a week at different locations.

The meeting ends and the bagels are broken into – finally. Dr. R opens the bag and passes it to his left and it begins around the table. I am the third person to pick from the bag. I look in and there is one of several interesting bagel varieties. I can tell from the looks I am getting that there are bagels in here that I should NOT take. I carefully rummage through the bag and discover a plain bagel residing at the bottom of the bag. I retrieve it. It seems as if I have made the right choice. The bag moves on and everyone else takes his or her "special" bagel.

Appendix B

The following focus group guide, unpublished, was designed by Dr. Armando Piña (2010), a psychologist who studies anxiety disorders. The focus groups were part of a larger funded project in which the research team was attempting to learn from school officials how to institute a school program aimed at building anxiety resilience.

RESEARCHER'S NOTEPAD

Focus group guide
Anxiety resilience building project
Moderator sheet for school staff focus groups
INTRODUCTION – 10 minutes

I want to thank you for your willingness to participate in this focus group. My name is Armando and...

> We are conducting this research to learn about: Students' anxiety in the schools, the needs of the schools when it comes to counseling anxious students, your thoughts and feelings about our plans to help anxious students

A There are no right or wrong answers to any questions. We are interested in your honest opinions.
B Please speak one at a time and regard the recording and my note-taking as simply an extension of my memory.

The research team and I will keep your comments confidential and your names will not be associated with any reports.

A We want to take this as an opportunity to share your thoughts and opinions freely.
B We'll spend the next few hours asking questions designed to get a full picture of your thoughts and feelings.

Qualitative Research Methods: Collecting Evidence, Crafting Analysis, Communicating Impact, First Edition. Sarah J. Tracy.
© 2013 Sarah J. Tracy. Published 2013 by Blackwell Publishing Ltd.

Ground rules

In order for this to be a productive discussion it also needs to be a safe place for you to be able to say what you feel. Here are a few ground rules that can achieve this:

A I ask you to agree with me that what is said in this room should stay in this room. How do you feel about that? [get verbal agreement from all]

B It's important to let us know if you see things differently from others. The goal of this focus group is not to get consensus, but to find out about a variety of opinions.

C It is important not to be critical of anyone in this room. If you don't agree with someone, that is fine, but be sure to address the issue, not the person.

D Are there any other rules we should follow? Any questions?

Review process for focus group discussions

A I have a series of questions. I'll ask a question to prompt a discussion of the topic, and then let you take off with it.

B Feel free to talk with each other, not just to me.

C Sometimes I may jump back into the conversation and direct it to go another way.

D Today we have scheduled ~3.5 hours for discussion, 30 minutes for lunch, and a 10 minute break.

QUESTIONING ROUTE: OPENING QUESTION – 30 minutes

Let's start with you introducing yourselves to each other. Tell us a little bit about your typical interactions with the students. It will be most useful if you talk about the anxious students you have worked with.

PROBES   Can you talk (more) about... (e.g. what anxiety looks like in your students, what students are typically anxious about, how you have helped anxious students?)

SEGMENT 1–40 minutes

We want to develop a school-based intervention program for anxiety. The program will be for 4th and 5th graders showing signs of anxiety, and it will be delivered by trained school staff (social workers, counselors, or school psychologists).

1 Do you have intervention programs for anxious students in your school? If yes, what are they like?

2 How important is it to have in the school an intervention program for anxious students?

3 How would you feel about having a new intervention program for anxious students in your school?

Activity 1: Mini-survey   I have a mini-survey meant to help us design a program for students with anxiety. Please write legibly because we will be collecting your responses. We also will be discussing the group's responses in a few minutes.

How long could each session be? (circle one)   30 min   40 min   60 min   other_____

How many sessions should there be? (circle one) 5   7   9   other_____

How many times a week should they be? (circle one) 1× / week   2× / week   other_____

What kind of support materials or help would you need in order to deliver this program (for example, student handouts)?

What do you think would best motivate the school's staff to do the training to deliver the program?

What are some of the reasons why the school's staff may resist or not want to do the training?

What else do you feel is essential for your ideal program?

Aids will prepare a summary of the mini-survey findings for discussion in a few minutes. During the break, aids will write the main findings on the board for discussion (key topics will not be ranked.)

BREAK POINT 1–10 minutes
Bathroom break. Check in with observers. Return and continue session.

Welcome back! Okay, let's begin by talking a little bit about your ideal program. Direct them to the board. In the mini-surveys you reported [provide an overview of the responses on the basis of the summary, as listed on the board].

SEGMENT 2 – 40 to 60 minutes

1 Can you talk about what you feel are the three most important aspects of your ideal program?

PROBES   Can you talk about…

☑   Why you feel these are essential for your program?
☑   The materials you would want to use to deliver the program: Why are those important?
☑   Some suggestions to motivate people to participate in the training?

2 How much do you think anxious students will want to participate in an anxiety intervention program? Tell us more about that.

PROBES

☑   What type of program do kids want to participate in?
☑   What are some of the reasons why students do not want to be part of school programs? What can be done to overcome or avoid these barriers?
☑   To what extent might kids be embarrassed to participate in the program? What can be done to prevent this?
☑   To what extent might kids be picked on or teased for being part of the program? What can be done to prevent this?
☑   To what extent might kids be criticized or hassled at home for being part of the program? What can be done to prevent this?

BREAK POINT 2=LUNCH – 30 minutes
Okay, we are now going to break for lunch and after lunch we want to talk about the anxiety program and your schools.

SEGMENT 3 – 60 to 75 minutes

During the previous hour, you also shared several important issues about your students. Now, we want to talk about the program and your schools.

1 To what extent (or in what ways) do you think school staff will support the anxiety program?
2 What would motivate them to support the anxiety program?

PROBES

☑ To what extent (in what ways) do you think the following stakeholders will support the anxiety program? What would motivate them to support the anxiety program?

☑ Administrators, teachers, school psychologists, parents?

Activity 2: Top reasons   Suppose you had to advocate to a group of parents, teachers, school staff, and administrators for the anxiety program. What would you say? Make a list on the <u>blue sheet</u> and share your thoughts.

CONCLUSION – 10 minutes

Wrap up a conversation thread and close the session. Aids provide a summary.

Is this an adequate summary? Why or why not? What would you add?

This concludes the focus group session. Are there any other thoughts or comments that you would like to share? Do you have any advice for someone developing a school program for anxiety? Do you have questions? [Respond to any]

Before we go there are a couple of final thoughts.

First, as a reminder, we ask each individual focus group member (you) to refrain from disclosing information revealed in today's meeting to other people who are not in today's meeting. This serves to protect other participants in the group. Can we all agree on that? [look for head nods/affirmations]

Second, thank you very much for your participation. We appreciate your time, consideration, and input into this research. If you have any questions or concerns afterward, you are welcome to contact me. If you are interested in a final copy of the report from this research, please contact me.

On your way out, please collect your stipends.

The following data excerpts show various levels of transcription detail.

RESEARCHER'S NOTEPAD

Interview/focus group excerpts with different levels of transcription detail

VERY HIGH LEVEL OF TRANSCRIPTION DETAIL: excerpt of an emergency 911 call

Goal   To show how question-asking can cause interactional sensitivities in the emergency 911 call sequence (Tracy, 2002b).

Notation   CT=911 call-taker; C=citizen calling 911.

CT   OK, umm, where are you at?
C   I'm at 4819 Suarez.
CT   Is that *her residence*?
C   Yeah, that's, she's staying with her mom, yes, (.) and uh, y'know=
CT   =Are you using a cell phone?
C   Yes.
CT   OK, what's your name?
C   Uhh, m-, my name?
CT   Uh huh.
C   Jim Dennis.
CT   ((sound of typing)) (2) And Jim, what's the cell phone number?
C   Uhh, eight seven four, two nine oh eight.
CT   Are you like out in front of that location?
C   Yes I am.
CT   OK, what kind of car are you in?
C   I'm in, uhh, in a Nova.
CT   What color ((flat))
C   Uhh, green? Uhh, four door.
CT   [what year? What year?

Qualitative Research Methods: Collecting Evidence, Crafting Analysis, Communicating Impact, First Edition. Sarah J. Tracy.
© 2013 Sarah J. Tracy. Published 2013 by Blackwell Publishing Ltd.

C   Uhh, jees, hhh ((CHUCKLING)), I'm not sure…Sixty
CT   [Is it older?
C   Yeah, it's an older, an older car.
CT   And what are you (wearing).
C   (3) .hhh
CT   Sir?
C   I'm we:aring a shirt, with uh=
CT   =Like what color shirt?
C   hhh hhh why, why are you asking?
CT   BECAUSE IF I'M SENDING OFFICERS OUT THEY NEED TO BE ABLE TO IDENTIFY THAT IT's YOU. YOU WANT THEM TO COME OUT AND ASSIST YOU.
C   [OK.
CT   You need to say, they're goin' to see you.
C   [ohh
CT   There could be a mi:llion cars in that area.

HIGH LEVEL OF TRANSCRIPTION DETAIL: interview excerpt with male executive

Goal To show the number of verbal disfluencies when a male executive was asked whether his best male employee would be good marriage material for his daughter compared to when he was asked whether his best female employee would be good marriage material for his son (Tracy & Rivera, 2010).

Interviewer Considering for a moment the male employee that you talked about earlier, within your position and the work there, how does that employee compare to the man you would envision for your daughter? Ways in which they might be similar or ways in which you might see a difference?

Respondent I think similar, um, you know, he's very supportive of his wife, his wife is a professional who works. He is very supportive of her, uh very proud of her, speaks very highly of her uh, uh, uh openly supports what she's doing um from you know from what I see I mean (inaudible).

Interviewer [Right

Paricipant [and so I think that certainly would be something that would be qualities that, that I hope if my daughter marries would be present in her husband.

Interviewer Then, uh, thinking about the female employee you talked about earlier that you respected some of her qualities, how does she compare to that perfect partner or perfect wife for your son? Ways in which they might be similar and ways in which they might be different?

Participant I, I, I think that, um, that it would be difficult for my son with kids to have someone who is also a professional. In terms of, just, just it would be difficult, you know, you know because (.) I think in a sense of, you know it, it, it would need to be someone, I think, who would be willing, at some point, I mean with the kids to, if she decided to say, "Okay I'm going to put my career on hold," for example, um, where the [female employee] who I described here is very much into her career.

MID-LEVEL TRANSCRIPTION DETAIL: focus group excerpt with workplace bullying targets

Goal   To ascertain how credible and articulate different targets of workplace bullying were when explaining their workplace abuse (Tracy, Alberts, & Rivera, 2007).

Lynn   My name is Lynn and I'm an accountant at [ABC Engineering]. That's where the harassment, bullying, took place. I didn't know the problem was so widespread until I saw this notice and I have a real problem with the trust factor because the only one I could tell was my husband. So, this is a little difficult but I'm excited about learning about this whole issue.

Moderator   Thanks. We'll try to make it as safe as we can.

Tom   My name is Tom. I worked in the airline industry for a little over twenty years. The first job that I had was working in Southern California and the company got bought out by a larger company and I had to move to another state in order to keep my job. And when I moved, I got to move my seniority with me and many of the people who felt that they were displaced by somebody that came out of nowhere, I believe are the people who were more likely than others to cause problems. It went on the whole time I was at the company and I stayed there six years and it led to my involuntary departure with the company.

LOW LEVEL OF TRANSCRIPTION DETAIL: focus group excerpt about arizona refugee resettlement

Goal   To record the major topics of discussion in a focus group about Arizona refugee resettlement. The specific participant providing the information was not important to researchers.

Focus group leader   In your opinion, what are the responsibilities and goals of Arizona's refugee resettlement efforts?

Information that the focus group leader wrote on the white board included:

- to get refugees to be self-sufficient (several people mentioned)
- jobs
- knowing English
- social and emotional development
- education (and getting parents involved)
- making sure refugees feel safe
- refugee contact with American society (not feeling isolated)
- learn transportation system
- health (learning how to navigate services)

Participant comments touched upon:

- self-sufficiency
- jobs and language
- familiarity with the laws (criminal and civil)

Here are some points of note in the participant's answers:

- Good definition of self-sufficiency <u>beyond</u> employment – social and emotional progress of clients, self-management in the culture.
- "Independence" should go beyond financial – refugees should be able to independently navigate public transportation, education, healthcare, and be comfortable maneuvering in-between systems.
- State needs to continually assess and reassess needs, particularly with different groups (each has different needs, and these change over time).
- Measurable goals appropriate to where client's at – employment isn't always the first step for every client, or attainable. Keep goals case-appropriate (agencies feel they are punished for taking hard cases).

References

Abbott, A. (1999). *Department and discipline: Chicago sociology at one hundred*. Chicago, IL: University of Chicago Press.

Abbott, A. (2004). *Methods of discovery: Heuristics for the social sciences*. New York, NY: W.W. Norton & Company.

Adams, W. J. (2000). How people watch television as investigated using focus group techniques. *Journal of Broadcasting and Electronic Media, 44*, 78–93. doi:10.1207/s15506878jobem4401_6

Adelman, M. B., & Frey, L. R. (1997). *The fragile community: Living together with AIDS*. Mahwah, NJ: Lawrence Erlbaum.

Adler, P. A., & Adler, P. (1987). *Membership roles in field research*. Thousand Oaks, CA: Sage.

Afifi, T. D., Hutchinson, S., & Krouse, S. (2006). Toward a theoretical model of communal coping in post-divorce families and other naturally occurring groups. *Communication Theory, 16*, 378–409. doi: 10.1111/j.1468-2885.2006.00275.x

Agar, M. (1994). *Language shock: Understanding the culture of conversation*. New York, NY: William Morrow & Company.

Akram, A. (2006, June). Muslim gays seek lesbians for wives: Social pressures push some into sexless marriage. *The Washington Post*. Retrieved from LEXISNEXIS Academic database.

Alberts, J. K., & Trethewey, A. (2007). Love, honor and thank. *Greater Good, 4*, 20–22.

Alberts, J. K., Tracy, S. J., & Trethewey, A. (2011). An integrative theory of the division of domestic labor: Threshold level, social organizing and sensemaking. *Journal of Family Communication, 11*, 21–38. doi: 10.1080/15267431.2011.534334

Albrecht, T. L., & Adelman, M. B. (1987). *Communicating social support*. Newbury Park, CA: Sage.

Allen, B. J. (1998). Black womanhood and feminist standpoints. *Management Communication Quarterly, 11*, 575–586. doi: 10.1177/0893318998114004

Altheide, D. L., & Johnson, J. M. (1994). Criteria for assessing interpretive validity in qualitative research. In N. K. Denzin & Y. S. Lincoln (eds.), *Handbook of qualitative research* (2nd ed., pp. 485–499). Newbury Park, CA: Sage.

Alvesson, M., & Deetz, S. (1996). Critical theory and postmodernism: Approaches to organizational studies. In S. R. Clegg, C. Hardy, & W. R. Nord (eds.), *Handbook of organization studies* (pp. 191–216). Thousand Oaks, CA: Sage.

American Psychological Association (2010). *Publication manual of the American Psychological Association*. (6th ed., second printing). Washington, DC: American Psychological Association.

Anderson, L. (2006). Analytic ethnography. *Journal of Contemporary Ethnography, 35*, 373–395. doi: 10.1177/0891241605280449

Angrosino, M. V. (2005). Recontextualizing observation: Ethnography, pedagogy, and the prospects for a progressive political agenda. In N. K. Denzin & Y. S. Lincoln (eds.), *Handbook of qualitative research* (3rd ed., pp. 729–746). Thousand Oaks, CA: Sage.

Argyris, C. (1953). *Executive leadership: An appraisal of a manager in action*. New York, NY: Harper.

Aristotle (2004). *The Nicomachean ethics* (rev. ed.), ed. J. A. K. Thomson, trans. H. Tredennick, introd. J. Barnes. London: Penguin Books.

Ashcraft, K. L. (2001). Organized dissonance: Feminist bureaucracy as hybrid form. *Academy of Management Journal, 44*, 1301–1322.

Ashcraft, K. L. (2005). Resistance through consent? Occupational identity, organizational form, and maintenance of masculinity among commercial airline pilots. *Management Communication Quarterly, 19*, 67–90. doi: 10.1177/0893318905276560

Ashcraft, K. L. (2007). Appreciating the "work" of discourse: Occupational identity and difference as organizing mechanisms in the case of commercial airline pilots. *Discourse and Communication, 1*, 9–36. doi: 10.1177/1750481307071982

Qualitative Research Methods: Collecting Evidence, Crafting Analysis, Communicating Impact, First Edition. Sarah J. Tracy.
© 2013 Sarah J. Tracy. Published 2013 by Blackwell Publishing Ltd.

Ashcraft, K. L. (2011). Knowing work through the communication of difference: A revised agenda for difference studies. In D. K. Mumby (ed.), *Reframing difference in organizational communication studies: Research, pedagogy, practice* (pp. 3–30). Thousand Oaks, CA: Sage.

Ashcroft, B., Griffiths, G., & Tiffins, H. (1998). *Post-colonial studies: The key concepts*. London: Routledge.

Ashforth, B. E., & Kreiner, G. (1999). How can you do it? Dirty work and the challenge of constructing a positive identity. *Academy of Management Review, 24,* 413–434.

Athens, L. (2010). Naturalistic inquiry in theory and practice. *Journal of Contemporary Ethnography, 39,* 87–125. doi: 10.1177/0891241609343663

Atkinson, J. M., & Heritage, J. (1984). Transcript notation. In J. M. Atkinson & J. Heritage (eds.), *Structures of social action* (pp. ix–xvi). Cambridge: Cambridge University Press.

Atkinson, P. (1990). *The ethnographic imagination: Textual constructions of reality*. London: Routledge.

Atkinson, R. (1998). *The life story interview*. London: Sage.

Avnet, J. (director) (1991). *Fried green tomatoes* [motion picture]. United States: Universal Studios.

Ayling, R., & Mewse, J. (2009). Evaluating Internet interviews with gay men. *Qualitative Health Research, 19,* 566–576. doi: 10.1177/1049732309332121

Ayres, I. (2010). *Carrots and sticks: Unlock the power of incentives to get things done*. New York: Bantam Books.

Bailey, C. (1996). *A guide to field research*. Thousand Oaks, CA: Pine Forge Press.

Barry, C. A. (1998). Choosing qualitative data analysis software: Atlas/ti and Nudist compared. *Sociological Research Online, 3.* Retrieved from http://www.socresonline.org.uk/socresonline/3/3/4.html>

Baudrillard, J. (2001). The precession of simulacra. In G. Durham & D. Kellner (eds.), *Media and cultural studies keyworks* (pp. 521–549). Oxford: Blackwell.

Baxter, L. L. A. (1990). Dialectical contradictions in relationship development. *Journal of Social and Personal Relationships, 7,* 69–88. doi: 10.1177/0265407590071004

Bazeley, P. (2007). *Qualitative data analysis with NVivo*. Thousand Oaks, CA: Sage.

Becker, H. S. (2007). *Writing for social scientists: How to start and finish your thesis, book, or article* (2nd ed.). Chicago, IL: University of Chicago Press.

Bernard, H. Russell, & Ryan, G. W. (2010). *Analyzing qualitative data: Systematic approaches*. Thousand Oaks, CA: Sage.

Berry, K. (2011). The ethnographic choice: Why ethnographers do ethnography. *Cultural Studies<=>Critical Methodologies, 11,* 165–177. doi: 10.1177/1532708611401335

Bird, C. M. (2005). How I stopped dreading and learned to love transcription. *Qualitative Inquiry, 11,* 226–248. doi: 10.1177/1077800404273413

Bishop, W. (1999). *Ethnographic writing research: Writing it down, writing it up, and reading it*. Portsmouth, NH: Boynton/Cook Publishers.

Bloor, M. (2001). Techniques of validation in qualitative research: A critical commentary. In R. M. Emerson (ed.), *Contemporary field research* (pp. 383–396). Prospect Heights, IL: Waveland Press.

Blumer, H. (1969). *Symbolic interactionism: Perspective and method*. Berkeley: University of California Press.

Bochner, A. (2000). Criteria against ourselves. *Qualitative Inquiry, 6,* 266–272. doi: 10.1177/107780040000600209

Boice, R. (1990). *Professors as writers: A self-help guide to productive writing*. Stillwater, OK: New Forums Press.

Boje, D. M. (1995). Stories of the storytelling organization: A postmodern analysis of Disney as "Tamara-land." *Academy of Management Journal, 38,* 997–1035.

Bortree, D. S. (2005). Presentation of self on the web: An ethnographic study of teenage girls' weblogs. *Education, Communication, and Information, 5,* 25–39. doi: 10.1080/14636310500061102

Bourland, D. D., & Johnston, P. D. (eds.) (1991). *To be or not: An e-prime anthology*. San Francisco, CA: International Society for General Semantics.

Bowen, G. A. (2006). Grounded theory and sensitizing concepts. *International Journal of Qualitative Methods, 5,* 1–9.

Briggs, C. (1986). *Learning how to ask: A sociolinguistic appraisal of the role of the interview in social science research*. Cambridge: Cambridge University Press.

Brons, L. L. (2009). Concepts in theoretical thought: An Introductory Essay. *CARLS Series of Advanced Study of Logic and Sensibility, 3,* 293–298.

Brouwer, D. C., & Hess, A. (2007). Making sense of "God Hates Fags" and "Thank God for 9/11": A thematic analysis of milbloggers' responses to Reverend Fred Phelps and the Westboro Baptist Church. *Western Journal of Communication, 71,* 69–90. doi: 10.1080/10570310701215388

Bryant, E. M. (2010). A tale of two Orbits: Passenger and community interaction on public transit. Paper presented at annual meeting of the Western States Communication Association, Anchorage, Alaska.

Burke, K. (1945). *A grammar of motives*. Berkeley, CA: University of California Press.

Butera, K. J. (2006). Manhunt: The challenge of enticing men to participate in a study of friendship. *Qualitative Inquiry, 12,* 1262–1282. doi: 10.1177/1077800406288634

Butler, J. (1999). *Gender trouble: Feminism and the subversion of identity*. New York, NY: Routledge.

Buzzanell, P. M., & Liu, M. (2005). Struggling with maternity leave policies and practices: A poststructuralist feminist analysis of gendered organizing. *Journal of Applied Communication Research, 33,* 1–25. doi: 10.1080/0090988042000318495

Cairns, G., & Śliwa, M. (2008). The implications of Aristotle's phronēsis for organizational inquiry. In D. Barry & H. Hansen (eds.), *Handbook of new approaches in management and organization* (pp. 318–328). London: Sage.

Cameron, K. S., Dutton, J. E., & Quinn, R. E. (2003). *Positive organizational scholarship: Foundations of a new discipline.* San Francisco, CA: Berrett-Koehler.

Canfield, J. (2005). *The success principles: How to get from where you are to where you want to be.* New York, NY: Harper Collins Publishers.

Cannella, G. S., & Lincoln, Y. S. (2004). Epilogue: Claiming a critical public social science – Reconceptualizing and redeploying research. *Qualitative Inquiry, 10,* 298–309. doi: 10.1177/1077800404263418

Carbaugh, D. (2005). *Cultures in conversation.* Mahwah, NJ: Lawrence Erlbaum.

Carbaugh, D. (2007). Ethnography of communication. In D. Wolfgang (ed.), *The Blackwell international encyclopedia of communication.* Blackwell Reference Online. Available at http://www.blackwellreference.com/subscriber/tocnode?id=g9781405131995_chunk_g9781405131995397

Carey, J. W. (1975). Communication and culture. *Communication Research, 2,* 173–191. doi: 10.1177/009365027500200204

Carey, J. W. (1994). The group effect in focus groups: Planning, implementing, and interpreting focus group research. In J. Morse (ed.), *Critical issues in qualitative research methods* (pp. 225–241). Thousand Oaks, CA: Sage.

Charmaz, K. (2003). Grounded theory: Objectivist and constructivist methods. In N. K. Denzin & Y. S. Lincoln (eds.), *Strategies of qualitative inquiry* (2nd ed., pp. 249–291). Thousand Oaks, CA: Sage.

Charmaz, K. (2006). *Constructing grounded theory: A practical guide through qualitative analysis.* Thousand Oaks, CA: Sage.

Charmaz, K. (2011). Grounded theory methods in social justice research. In N. K. Denzin & Y. S. Lincoln (eds.), *Handbook of qualitative research* (4th ed., pp. 359–380). Thousand Oaks, CA: Sage.

Chatham-Carpenter, A. (2006). Internal self-esteem: God as symbolic interactionism's "significant other"? *Journal of Communication and Religion, 29,* 103–126.

Cheek, J. (2005). The practice and politics of funded qualitative research. In N. K. Denzin & Y. S. Lincoln (eds.), *Handbook of qualitative research* (3rd ed., pp. 387–409). Thousand Oaks, CA: Sage.

Cheek, J. (2007). Qualitative inquiry, ethics, and politics of evidence working within these spaces rather than being worked over by them. *Qualitative Inquiry, 13,* 1051–1059. doi: 10.1177/1077800407308227

Cheney, G. (1999). *Values at work: Employee participation meets market pressure at Mondragón.* Ithaca, NY: Cornell University Press.

Christians, C. G. (2005). Ethics and politics in qualitative research. In N. K. Denzin & Y. S. Lincoln (eds.), *Handbook of qualitative research* (3rd ed., pp. 139–164). Thousand Oaks, CA: Sage.

Clair, R. P. (2003). *Expressions of ethnography: Novel approaches to qualitative methods.* Albany, NY: State University of New York Press.

Clandinin, D. J. (2007). *Handbook of narrative inquiry: Mapping a methodology.* Thousand Oaks, CA: Sage.

Clarke, A. E. (2005). *Situational analysis: Grounded theory after the postmodern turn.* Thousand Oaks, CA: Sage.

Clifford, J., & Marcus, G. E. (1986). *Writing culture: The poetics and politics of ethnography.* Berkeley, CA: University of California Press.

Coffey, A. B., Holbrook P., & Atkinson (1996). Qualitative data analysis: Technologies and representations. *Sociological Research Online, 1.* Retrieved from http://www.socresonline.org.uk/1/1/4.html

Collinson, D. L. (1992). *Managing the shopfloor: Subjectivity, masculinity and workplace culture.* Berlin: DeGruyter.

Conquergood, D. (1991). Rethinking ethnography: Towards a critical cultural politics. *Communication Monographs, 38,* 179–194. doi: 10.1080/03637759109376222

Conquergood, D. (1992a). Ethnography, rhetoric and performance. *Quarterly Journal of Speech, 78,* 80–97. doi: 10.1080/00335639209383982

Conquergood, D. (1992b). Life in big red: Struggles and accommodations in a Chicago polyethnic tenement. In L. Lamphere (Ed.), *Structuring diversity: Ethnographic perspectives on the new immigration* (pp. 95–144). Chicago, IL: University of Chicago Press.

Corman, S. R., & Poole, M. S. (eds.) (2000). *Perspectives on organizational communication: Finding common ground.* New York, NY: Guilford.

Corman, S., Trethewey, A., & Goodall, H. L., Jr. (eds.) (2008). *Weapons of mass persuasion: Strategic communication to combat violent extremism.* New York, NY: Peter Lang.

Covarrubias, P. O. (2002). *Culture, communication, and cooperation: Interpersonal relations and pronominal address in a Mexican organization.* Lanham, MD: Rowman & Littlefield.

Creswell, J. W. (2007). *Qualitative inquiry and research design: Choosing among five traditions* (2nd ed.). Thousand Oaks, CA: Sage.

Cripe, E. T. (2011). Women helping other women: Communal coping in a breastfeeding support group. Presented at the annual meeting of the Western States Communication Association, Monterey, CA.

Cropanzano, R., & Mitchell, M. S. (2005). Social exchange theory: An interdisciplinary review. *Journal of Management, 31,* 874–900. doi: 10.1177/0149206305279602

Davis, O. (2007). Locating Tulsa in the souls of black women folk: Performing memory as survival. *Performance Research: A Journal of the Performing Arts, 12,* 124–136.

de Marrais, K. (2004). Elegant communications: Sharing qualitative research with communities, colleagues, and critics. *Qualitative Inquiry, 10,* 281–297. doi: 10.1177/1077800403262359

Deetz, S. (2001). Alternative perspectives in organizational communication studies. In L. Putnam & F. Jablin (eds.), *Handbook of organizational communication* (pp. 3–46). Thousand Oaks, CA: Sage.

Deetz, S. (2003). Reclaiming the legacy of the linguistic turn. *Organization, 10,* 421–429. doi: 10.1177/13505084030103002

Deetz, S. (2009). Politically attentive relational constructionism (PARC) and making a difference in a pluralistic, interdependent world. In D. Carbaugh & P. Buzzanell (eds.), *Reflections on the distinctive qualities of communication research in the social sciences* (pp. 32–52). New York, NY: Taylor Francis.

Deetz, S. A., Tracy, S. J., & Simpson, J. L. (2000). *Leading organizations through transition.* Thousand Oaks, CA: Sage.

DeGooyer, D. H., Jr. (2003). Poignant organizing as metaphor. *American Communication Journal, 6.* Retrieved from http://www1.appstate.edu/orgs/ acjournal/holdings/vol6/iss2/articles/degooyer.htm

Delamont, S. (2004). Ethnography and participant observation. In C. Delamont, G. Giampietro, J. F. Gubrium, & D. Silverman (eds.), *Qualitative research practice* (pp. 217–229). London: Sage.

Deleuze, G., & Guattari, F. (1987). *A thousand plateaus: Capitalism and schizophrenia,* trans. B. Massumi. Minneapolis, MN: University of Minnesota Press.

Denzin, N. K. (1976). *Interpretive biography.* Thousand Oaks, CA: Sage.

Denzin, N. K. (1978). *Sociological methods: A sourcebook* (2nd ed.). New York, NY: McGraw Hill.

Denzin, N. K. (1997). *Interpretive ethnography: Ethnographic practices for the 21st century.* Thousand Oaks, CA: Sage.

Denzin, N. K. (2010). *The qualitative manifesto: A call to arms.* Walnut Creek, CA: Left Coast Press.

Denzin, N. K., & Giardina, M. D. (eds.) (2008). *Qualitative inquiry and the politics of evidence.* Walnut Creek, CA: Left Coast Press.

Denzin, N. K., & Lincoln, Y. S. (eds.) (2003). *The landscape of qualitative research: Theories and issues* (2nd ed.). Thousand Oaks, CA: Sage.

Denzin, N. K., & Lincoln, Y. S. (2005). Introduction: The discipline and practice of qualitative research. In N. K. Denzin & Y. S. Lincoln (eds.), *Handbook of qualitative research* (3rd ed., pp. 1–44). Thousand Oaks, CA: Sage.

Derrida, J. (1978). *Writing and difference.* Chicago, IL: University of Chicago Press.

Derrida, J. (1982). *Différance.* Margins of philosophy, trans. Alan Bass. Chicago, IL: University of Chicago Press.

Douglas, J. D. (1985). *Creative interviewing.* Beverly Hills, CA: Sage.

Drew, R. (2001). *Karaoke nights: An ethnographic rhapsody.* Walnut Creek, CA: Altamira Press.

Dreyfus, H. L., Athanasiou, T., & Dreyfus, S. E. (1986). *Mind over machine: The power of human intuition and expertise in the era of the computer.* New York, NY: Free Press.

Du Gay, P. (2007). *Organizing identity: Persons and organizations "after theory."* Los Angeles, CA: Sage.

Dunaway, D. K., & Baum, W. K. (eds.) (1996). *Oral history: An interdisciplinary anthology* (2nd ed.). Walnut Creek, CA: Altamira Press.

Eastland, L. S. (1993). The dialectical nature of ethnography: Liminality, reflexivity, and understanding. In S. L. Herndon & G. L. Kreps (eds.), *Qualitative research: Applications in organizational communication* (pp. 121–138). Cresskill, NJ: Hampton.

Eberts, J., Redford, R., & Markey, P. (producers), & Redford, R. (director) (1992). *A river runs through it* [motion picture]. United States: Columbia Pictures.

Edmunds, H. (1999). *The focus group research handbook.* Lincolnwood, IL: NTC Contemporary.

Eisenberg, E. M. (2007). *Strategic ambiguities: Essays on communication, organization, and identity.* Thousand Oaks, CA: Sage.

Eisenberg, E. M., Baglia, J., & Pynes, J. E. (2006). Transforming emergency medicine through narrative: Qualitative action research at a community hospital. *Health Communication, 19,* 197–208. doi: 10.1207/s15327027hc1903_2

Ellet, W. (2007). *The case study handbook: How to read, discuss, and write persuasively about cases.* Boston, MA: Harvard Business School Press.

Ellingson, L. L. (2008). *Engaging crystallization in qualitative research.* Thousand Oaks, CA: Sage.

Ellingson, L. L. (2011). Analysis and representation across the continuum. In N. K. Denzin & Y. S. Lincoln (eds.), *Handbook of qualitative research* (4th ed., pp. 595–610). Thousand Oaks, CA: Sage.

Ellis, C. (1991). Sociological introspection and emotional experience. *Symbolic Interaction, 14*, 23–50. doi: 10.1525/si.1991.14.1.23

Ellis, C. (1995). *Final negotiations: A story of love, loss, and chronic illness*. Philadelphia, PA: Temple University Press.

Ellis, C. (2007). Telling secrets, revealing lives: Relational ethics in research with intimate others. *Qualitative Inquiry, 13*, 3–29. doi: 10.1177/1077800406294947

Ellis, C. (2008). *Revision: Autoethnographic reflections on life and work*. Walnut Creek, CA: Left Coast Press.

Ellis, C. (2010, August). Interactive testimonies: Survivors of the Holocaust interpret their lives, Society for the Study of Symbolic Interaction (SSSI), Atlanta, GA.

Ellis, C., & Berger, L. (2003). Their story/my story/our story: Including the researcher's experience in interview research. In J. A. Holstein & J. F. Gubrium (eds.), *Inside interviewing: New lenses, new concerns* (pp. 467–493). Thousand Oaks, CA: Sage.

Ellis, C., & Bochner, A. (1992). Telling and performing personal stories: The constraints of choice in abortion. In C. Ellis & M. Flaherty (eds.), *Investigating subjectivity: Research on lived experience* (pp. 79–101). Newbury Park, CA: Sage.

Ellis, C., & Bochner, A. (Eds.) (1996). *Composing ethnography: Alternative forms of qualitative writing*. Walnut Creek, CA: Altamira Press.

Ellis, C., & Bochner, A. (2000). Autoethnography, personal narrative, reflexivity: Researcher as subject. In N. K. Denzin & Y. S. Lincoln (eds.), *Handbook of qualitative research* (2nd ed., pp. 733–768). Thousand Oaks, CA: Sage.

Ellis, C., Kiesinger, C. E., & Tillmann-Healy, L. M. (1997). Interactive interviewing: Talking about emotional experience. In R. Hertz (ed.), *Reflexivity and voice* (pp. 119–149). Thousand Oaks, CA: Sage.

Emerson, R. M., Fretz, R. I., & Shaw, L. (1995). *Writing ethnographic fieldnotes*. Chicago, IL: University of Chicago Press.

Erard, M. (2007). *Um- slips, stumbles, and verbal blunders and what they mean*. New York, NY: Pantheon Books.

Erbert, L. A., & Alemán, M. W. (2008). Taking the grand out of grandparent: Dialectical tensions in grandparent perceptions of surrogate parenting. *Journal of Social and Personal Relationships, 25*, 671–695. doi: 10.1177/0265407508093785

Erickson, F. (2011). A history of qualitative inquiry in social and educational research. In N. K. Denzin & Y. S. Lincoln (eds.), *Handbook of qualitative research* (4th ed., pp. 43–60). Thousand Oaks, CA: Sage.

Faculty Statement on Public Scholarship, Department of Communication, University of Washington. (2009). Retrieved from http://www.com.washington.edu/program/publicscholarship/index.html

Fairhurst, G. T., & Putnam, L. (2004). Organizations as discursive constructions. *Communication Theory, 14*, 5–26. doi: 10.1111/j.1468-2885.2004.tb00301.x

Figley, C. R. (1995). *Compassion fatigue: Coping with secondary traumatic stress disorder in those who treat the traumatized*. New York, NY: Brunner/Mazel.

Fine, G. A. (1993). Ten lies of ethnography. *Journal of Contemporary Ethnography, 22*, 267–294. doi: 10.1177/089124193022003001

Fine, M., Weis, L., Weseen, S., & Wong, L. (2000). For whom? Qualitative research, representations, and social responsibilities. In N. K. Denzin & Y. S. Lincoln (eds.), *Handbook of qualitative research* (2nd ed., pp. 107–131). Thousand Oaks, CA: Sage.

Fisher, W. (1987). *Human communication as narration*. Columbia, SC: University of South Carolina Press.

Fitch, K. L. (1991). The interplay of linguistic universals and cultural knowledge in personal address: Columbian "madre" terms. *Communication Monographs, 58*, 254–272.

Fitch, K. L. (2005). Difficult interactions between IRBs and investigators: Applications and solutions. *Journal of Applied Communication Research, 33*, 269–276. doi: 10.1080/00909880500149486

Fletcher, J. (1966). *Situation ethics: The new morality*. Louisville, KY: Westminster John Knox Press.

Floyd, K., Pauley, P. M., & Hesse, C. (2010). State and trait affectionate communication buffer adults' stress reactions. *Communication Monographs, 77*, 618–636. doi: 10.1080/03637751.2010.498792

Flyvbjerg, B. (2001). *Making social science matter: Why social inquiry fails and how it can succeed again*, trans. S. Sampson. Cambridge: Cambridge University Press.

Flyvbjerg, B. (2011). Case study. In N. K. Denzin & Y. S. Lincoln (eds.), *Handbook of qualitative research* (4th ed., pp. 301–316). Thousand Oaks, CA: Sage.

Fontana, A., & Frey, J. H. (2005). The interview: From neutral stance to political involvement. In N. K. Denzin & Y. S. Lincoln (eds.), *Handbook of qualitative research* (3rd ed., pp. 695–727). Thousand Oaks, CA: Sage.

Foss, K. A., & Edson, B. A. (1989). What's in a name? Accounts of married women's name choices. *Western Journal of Speech Communication, 53*, 356–373. doi: 10.1080/10570318909374315

Foucault, M. (1980). *Power/knowledge*, ed. Colin Gordon. New York, NY: Pantheon Books. (Also at http://www.amazon.com/Power-Knowledge-Selected-Interviews-1972-1977/dp/039473954X).

Fox, R. (2007). Skinny bones #126-774-835-29: Thin gay bodies signifying a modern plague. *Text and Performance Quarterly, 27*, 3–19. doi:10.1080/10462930601045956

Fox, R. C. (2010). Re-membering daddy: Autoethnographic reflections of my father and Alzheimer's disease. *Text and Performance Quarterly, 30*, 3–20. doi: 10.1080/10462930903366969

Fraser, B. (1993). The interpretation of novel metaphors. In A. Ortony (ed.), *Metaphor and thought* (2nd ed., pp. 329–341). Chicago, IL: University of Chicago Press.

Gallmeier, C. P. (1991). Leaving, revisiting, and staying in touch: Neglected issues in field research. In W. B. Shaffir & R. A. Stebbins (eds.), *Experiencing fieldwork: An inside view of qualitative research* (pp. 224–231). Newbury Park, CA: Sage.

Gans, H. J. (1999). Participant observation in the era of "ethnography." *Journal of Contemporary Ethnography, 28*, 540–548. doi: 10.1177/089124199129023532

Geertz, C. (1973). *The interpretation of cultures: Selected essays.* New York, NY: Basic Books.

Gibbs, G. (2007). *Analyzing qualitative data.* London: Sage.

Giddens, A. (1979). *Central problems in social theory: Action, structure, and contradiction in social analysis.* Berkeley, CA: University of California Press.

Giddens, A. (1984). *The constitution of society: Outline of the theory of structuration.* Berkeley, CA: University of California Press.

Gill, R. (2011). The shadow in organizational ethnography: Moving beyond shadowing to spect-acting. *Qualitative Research in Organizations and Management, 6*, 115–133. doi: 10.1108/17465641111159116

Gladwell, M. (2008). *Outliers: The story of success.* New York, NY: Little, Brown and Company.

Glaser, B. G. (1992). *Basics of grounded theory analysis.* Mill Valley, CA: Sociology Press.

Glaser, B. G., & Strauss, A. L. (1967). *The discovery of grounded theory.* New York, NY: Aldine de Gruyter.

Goffman, E. (1959). *The presentation of self in everyday life.* Garden City, NJ: Anchor Books.

Goffman, E. (1961a). *Asylums.* Garden City, NJ: Anchor Books.

Goffman, E. (1961b). *Encounters: Two studies in the sociology of interaction.* Indianapolis, IN: Bobbs-Merrill.

Goffman, E. (1989). On fieldwork. *Journal of Contemporary Ethnography, 18*, 123–132. doi: 10.1177/089124189018002001

Gold, R. L. (1958). Roles in sociological field observation. *Social Forces, 36*, 217–223.

Golden, A. G., Kirby, E. L., & Jorgenson, J. (2006). Work–life research from both sides now: An integrative perspective for organizational and family communication. In C. Beck (ed.), *Communication Yearbook, 30* (pp. 143–195). Mahwah, NJ: Lawrence Erlbaum.

González, M. C. (2000). The four seasons of ethnography: A creation-centered ontology for ethnography. *International Journal of Intercultural Relations, 24*, 623–650.

Goodall, H. L., Jr. (1989). *Casing a promised land: The autobiography of an organizational detective as cultural ethnographer.* Carbondale, IL: Southern Illinois University Press.

Goodall, H. L., Jr. (1991). *Living in the rock n roll mystery: Reading context, self, and others as clues.* Carbondale, IL: Southern Illinois University Press.

Goodall, H. L., Jr. (2000). *Writing the new ethnography.* Lanham, MD: AltaMira Press/Rowman & Littlefield.

Goodall, H. L., Jr. (2004). Deep play in a poker rally: A Sunday among the Ferraristi of Long Island. *Qualitative Inquiry, 10*, 731–766. doi: 10.1177/1077800403257676

Goodall, H. L., Jr. (2006). *A need to know: The clandestine history of a CIA family.* Walnut Creek, CA: Left Coast Press.

Goodall, H. L., Jr. (2008). *Writing qualitative inquiry: Self, stories, and academic life.* Walnut Creek, CA: Left Coast Press.

Goodall, H. L., Goodall, S., & Schiefelbein, J. (2010). *Business and professional communication in the global workplace* (3rd ed.). Boston, MA: Wadsworth.

Gordon, D. F. (1987). Getting close by staying distant: Fieldwork with proselytizing groups. *Qualitative Sociology, 10*, 267–287. doi: 10.1007/BF00988990

Gossett, L. M. (2006). Falling between the cracks: Control and communication challenges of a temporary workforce. *Management Communication Quarterly, 19*, 376–415. doi: 10.1177/0893318905280327

Grant, B. (2008). *Academic writing retreats: A facilitator's guide.* Adelaide, Australia: HERDSA.

Grant, D., & Oswick, C. (1996). The organization of metaphors and the metaphors of organization: Where are we and where do we go from here? In D. Grant & C. Oswick (eds.), *Metaphor and organizations* (pp. 213–226). London: Sage.

Greenbaum, T. L. (1994). Focus group research: A useful tool. *HR Focus, 71*, 3.

Guba, E. G., & Lincoln, Y. S. (2005). Paradigmatic controversies, contradictions, and emerging confluences. In N. K. Denzin & Y. S. Lincoln (eds.), *Handbook of qualitative research* (3rd ed., pp. 191–216). Thousand Oaks, CA: Sage.

Guest, G., Bunce, A., & Johnson, L. (2006). How many interviews are enough? *Field Methods, 18*(1), 59–82.

Habermas, J. (1979). *Communication and the evolution of society*, trans. Thomas McCarthy. Boston, MA: Beacon Press.

Hallier, J., & Foirbes, T. (2004). In search of theory development in grounded investigations: Doctors' experiences of managing as an example of fitted and prospective theorizing. *Journal of Management Studies, 41*, 1379–1410. doi: 10.1111/j.1467-6486.2004.00479.x

Hamilton, A. (2005). The development and operation of IRBs: Medical regulations and social science. *Journal of Applied Communication Research, 33*, 189–203. doi: 10.1080/00909880500149353

Harper, D. (2002). Talking about pictures: A case for photo elicitation. *Visual Studies, 17*, 13–26. doi: 10.1080/14725860220137345

Haskins, E. (2007). Between archive and participation: Public memory in a digital age. *Rhetoric Society Quarterly, 37*, 401–422. doi: 10.1080/02773940601086794

Hawkes, T. (1977). *Structuralism and semiotics*. London: Routledge.

Hesse-Biber, S. N., & Leavy, P. (2006). *The practice of qualitative research*. Thousand Oaks, CA: Sage.

Hickey, J. V., Thompson, W. E., & Foster, D. L. (1988). Becoming the Easter bunny: Socialization into a fantasy role. *Journal of Contemporary Ethnography, 17*, 67–95. doi: 10.1177/0891241688171003

Hochschild, A. (1983). *The managed heart: The commercialization of human feelings*. Berkeley, CA: University of California Press.

Holman Jones, S. (2005). Autoethnography: Making the personal political. In N. K. Denzin & Y. S. Lincoln (eds.), *Handbook of qualitative research* (3rd ed., pp. 763–791). Thousand Oaks, CA: Sage.

Holstein, J. A., & Gubrium, J. F. (1995). *The active interview*. Thousand Oaks, CA: Sage.

Holub, M. (1977, February 4). Brief thoughts on maps. *Times Literary Supplement*, 118.

Howard, J., III, & Prividera, L. (2008). "Freedom isn't free": A critical analysis of nationalism, militarism, and U.S. identity. *International and Intercultural Communication Annual, 31*, 151–174.

Huffman, T. (2012, May). Altruism, selfishness, and volunteer ecologies of social exchange. Paper presented at the annual convention of the International Communication Association, Phoenix, Arizona.

Hymes, D. (1962). The ethnography of speaking. In T. Gladwin and W. Sturtevant (eds.), *Anthropology and human behavior* (pp. 13–53). Washington, DC: Anthropological Society of Washington.

Illingworth, N. (2001). The Internet matters: Exploring the use of the Internet as a research tool. *Sociological Research Online, 6*. Retrieved from http://www.socresonline.org.uk/6/2/illingworth.html

Isaksen, J. (2011). Obama's rhetorical shift: Insights for communication studies. *Communication Studies, 62*, 456–471. doi: 10.1080/10510974.2011.588082

Jackson, S., & Gilbertson, T. (2009). "Hot lesbians": Young people's accounts of off- and on-screen lesbianism. *Sexualities, 12*, 199–224. doi: 10.1177/1363460708100919

Jago, B. J. (2002). Chronicling an academic depression. *Journal of Contemporary Ethnography, 31*, 729–757. doi: 10.1177/089124102237823

Jefferson, G. (Ed.) (1992). *Lectures on conversation*, Vol. 1. Oxford: Basil Blackwell.

Jewison, N. (director) (1999). *The hurricane* [motion picture]. United States: Beacon Communications.

Joinson, N. J., & Paine, C. (2007). Self-disclosure, privacy and the Internet. In A. Joinson, K. McKenna, T. Postmes, & U. Reips (eds.), *The Oxford handbook of Internet psychology* (pp. 237–252). Oxford: Oxford University Press.

Joralemon, D. (1990). The selling of the shaman and the problem of informant legitimacy. *Journal of Anthropological Research, 46*, 105–118.

Kanov, J. M., Maitlis, S., Worline, M. C., Dutton, J. E., Frost, P. J., & Lilius, J. M. (2004). Compassion in organizational life. *American Behavioral Scientist, 47*, 808–827. doi: 10.1177/0002764203260211

Katriel, T. (1986). *Talking straight: "Dugri" speech in Israeil Sabra culture*. New York, NY: Cambridge University Press.

Katriel, T. (2004). *Dialogic moments: From soul talks to talk radio in Israeli culture*. Detroit, MI: Wayne State University Press.

Katz, J. (2001). From how to why: On luminous description and causal inference in ethnography (Part 1). *Ethnography, 2*, 443–473.

Katz, J. (2002). From how to why: On luminous description and causal inference in ethnography (Part 2). *Ethnography, 3*, 63–90.

Kazmer, M. M., & Xie, B. (2008). Qualitative interviewing in Internet studies: Playing with the media, playing with the method. *Information, Communication, and Society, 11*, 257–278. doi: 10.1080/13691180801946333

Kelle, U. (2005). "Emergence" vs. "forcing" of empirical data? A crucial problem of "grounded theory" reconsidered. *Forum qualitative sozialforschung/forum: Qualitative social research* [on-line journal], *6(2)*, Art. 27, paragraphs 49–50. At http://www.qualitative-research.net/index.php/fqs/article/view/467/1000%20%20(27

Kellogg, E. W. (1987). Speaking in e-prime: An experimental method for integrating general semantics into daily life. *Etc., 44*, 118–128.

Kellogg, R. T. (1999). *The psychology of writing*. Oxford: Oxford University Press.

Kemmis, S., & McTaggart, R. (2000). Participatory action research. In N. K. Denzin & Y. S. Lincoln (eds.),

Handbook of qualitative research (2nd ed., pp. 567–605). Thousand Oaks, CA: Sage.

Kemmis, S., & McTaggart, R. (2005). Participatory action research: Communicative action and the public sphere. In N. K. Denzin & Y. S. Lincoln (eds.), *Handbook of qualitative research* (3rd ed., pp. 559–603). Thousand Oaks, CA: Sage.

Keyton, J., & Shockley-Zalabak, P. (2009). *Case studies for organizational communication: Understanding communication processes* (3rd ed.). New York, NY: Oxford University Press.

Keyton, J., Bisel, R., & Ozley, R. (2009). Recasting the link between applied and theory research: Using applied findings to advance communication theory development. *Communication Theory, 19*, 146–160. doi: 10.1111/j.1468-2885.2009.01339.x

Khurana, G. (2010, November). Leading a MOC(k) life: Western South Asians' use of performance and engagement in authenticity within marriages of convenience. Paper presented at the annual meeting of the National Communication Association, San Francisco, California.

Kinchloe, J. L., & McLaren, P. (2000). Rethinking critical theory and qualitative research. In N. K. Denzin & Y. S. Lincoln (eds.), *Handbook of qualitative research* (2nd ed., pp. 279–314). Thousand Oaks, CA: Sage.

King, S. (2000). *On writing: A memoir of the craft.* New York, NY: Pocket Books.

Kirby, E. L., & Krone, K. J. (2002). "The policy exists but you can't really use it": Communication and the structuration of work–family policies. *Journal of Applied Communication Research, 20*, 50–77.

Kramer, M. W. (2004). Toward a communication theory of group dialectics: An ethnographic study of a community theater group. *Communication Monographs, 71*, 311–332. doi: 10.1080/0363452042000288292

Krieger, S. (1983). *The mirror dance: Identity in a women's community.* Philadelphia, PA: Temple University Press.

Krizek, R. L. (2003). Ethnography as the excavation of personal narrative. In R. P. Clair (ed.), *Expressions of ethnography: Novel approaches to qualitative methods* (pp. 141–151). Albany, NY: State University of New York.

Krizek, R. L. (2008, May). Making a case for the worth of our work: New strategies for qualitative researchers and writers seeking tenure and promotion. Paper presented at the Congress of Qualitative Inquiry, Urbana-Champaign, Illinois.

Krueger, R. A., & Casey. M. A. (2000). *Focus groups: A practical guide for applied research* (3rd ed.). London: LSE Research Online. Retrieved from http://eprints.lse.ac.uk/2633

Kuhn, T. (2005). The institutionalization of Alta in organizational communication studies. *Management Communication Quarterly, 18*, 618–627. doi: 10.1177/0893318904273851

Kvale, S. (1996). *InterViews: An introduction to qualitative research interviewing.* Thousand Oaks, CA: Sage.

Kvale, S., & Brinkmann, S. (2009). *InterViews: An introduction to qualitative research interviewing* (2nd ed.). Thousand Oaks, CA: Sage.

Laclau, E., & Mouffe, C. (1985). *Hegemony and socialist strategy.* New York, NY: Verso.

LaFever, M. (2007, May). Communication for public decision-making in a negative historical context: Building intercultural relationships in the British Columbia treaty process. Paper presented at the annual convention of the International Communication Association, San Francisco, California.

Lakoff, G., & Johnson, M. (1980). *Metaphors to live by.* Chicago, IL: University of Chicago Press.

Lamott, A. (1994). *Bird by bird: Some instructions on writing and life.* New York, NY: Pantheon Books.

Larson, G. S., & Tompkins, P. K. (2005). Ambivalence and resistance: A study of management in a concertive control system. *Communication Monographs, 72*, 1–21. doi: 10.1080/0363775052000342508

Lather, P. (1986). Issues of validity in openly ideological research: Between a rock and a soft place. *Interchange, 17*, 63–84. doi: 10.1007/BF01807017

Lather, P. (2004). This is your father's paradigm: Government intrusion and the case of qualitative research in education. *Qualitative Inquiry, 10*, 15–34. doi: 10.1177/1077800403256154

Lawler, S. (2002). Narrative in social research. In T. May (ed.), *Qualitative research in action* (pp. 242–258). London: Sage.

Lederman, L. C. (1990). Assessing educational effectiveness: The focus group interview as a technique for data collection. *Communication Education, 39*, 117–127. doi: 10.1080/03634529009378794

LeGreco, M. (2012). Filling up the food tank: Implementing a multiple stakeholder think tank to enable food policy change. Paper presented at the Society for Applied Anthropology Conference, Baltimore, Maryland.

LeGreco, M., & Tracy, S. J. (2009). Discourse tracing as qualitative practice. *Qualitative Inquiry, 15*, 1516–1543. doi: 10.1177/1077800409343064

Lewins, A., & Silver, C. (2007). *Using software in qualitative research: A step-by-step guide.* London: Sage.

Light, R. J., Singer, J., & Willett, J. (1990). *By design: Conducting research on higher education.* Cambridge, MA: Harvard University Press.

Lincoln, Y. S., & Cannella, G. S. (2004). Dangerous discourses: Methodological conservatism and governmental regimes of truth. *Qualitative Inquiry, 10,* 5–14. doi: 10.1177/1077800403259717

Lincoln, Y. S., & Guba, E. G. (1985). *Naturalistic inquiry.* Beverly Hills, CA: Sage.

Lincoln, Y. S., Lynham, S. A., & Guba, E. G. (2011). Paradigmatic controversies, contradictions, and emerging confluences, revisited. In N. K. Denzin & Y. S. Lincoln (eds.), *Handbook of qualitative research* (4th ed., pp. 97–128). Thousand Oaks, CA: Sage.

Lindemann, K. (2007). A tough sell: Stigma as souvenir in the contested performances of San Francisco's homeless *Street Sheet* vendors. *Text and Performance Quarterly, 27,* 41–57. doi: 10.1080/10462930601046012

Lindemann, K. (2008). "I can't be standing up out there": Communicative performances of (dis)ability in wheelchair rugby. *Text and Performance Quarterly, 28,* 98–115. doi: 10.1080/10462930701754366

Lindemann, K. (2010). Masculinity, disability, and access-ability: Ethnography as alternative practice in the study of disabled sexualities. *Southern Journal of Communication, 75,* 433–451. doi: 10.1080/1041794x.2010.504454

Lindemann, K., & Cherney, J. L. (2008). Communicating in and through "Murderball": Masculinity and disability in wheelchair rugby. *Western Journal of Communication, 72,* 107–125. doi: 10.1080/10570310802038382

Lindlof, T. R. (1987). *Natural audiences: Qualitative research of media uses and effects.* New York, NY: Alex Publishing Corporation.

Lindlof, T. R. (2001). The challenge of writing the qualitative study. In A. Alexander & W. J. Potter (eds.), *How to publish your communication research: An insider's guide* (pp. 77–96). Thousand Oaks, CA: Sage.

Lindlof, T. R., & Taylor, B. C. (2002). *Qualitative communication research methods* (2nd ed.). Thousand Oaks, CA: Sage.

Lindlof, T. R., & Taylor, B. C. (2011). *Qualitative communication research methods* (3rd ed.). Thousand Oaks, CA: Sage.

Lofland, J., & Lofland, L. H. (1984). *Analyzing social settings: A guide to qualitative observation and analysis.* Belmont, CA: Wadsworth.

Lofland, J., & Lofland, L. H. (1995). *Analyzing social settings: A guide to qualitative observation and analysis* (2nd ed.). Belmont, CA: Wadsworth.

Lombard, M., Snyder-Duch, J., & Bracken, C. C. (2002). Content analysis in mass communication: Assessment and reporting of intercoder reliability. *Human Communication Research, 28,* 587–604. doi: 10.1111/j.1468-2958.2002.tb00826.x

Lutgen-Sandvik, P. (2003). The cycle of employee emotional abuse: Generation and regeneration of workplace mistreatment. *Management Communication Quarterly, 16,* 471–501. doi: 10.1177/0893318903251627

Lutgen-Sandvik, P. (2006). Take this job and…: Quitting and other forms of resistance to workplace bullying. *Communication Monographs, 73,* 406–433. doi: 10.1080/03637750601024156

Lutgen-Sandvik, P., Namie, G., & Namie, R. (2009). Workplace bullying: Contributing factors, consequences, and potential for prevention and intervention. In P. Lutgen-Sandvik & B. D. Sypher (eds.), *Destructive organizational communication: Processes, consequences, and constructive ways of organizing* (pp. 27–52). New York, NY: Routledge.

Lutgen-Sandvik, P., Tracy, S. J., & Alberts, J. K. (2007). Burned by bullying in the American workplace: Prevalence, perception, degree, and impact. *Journal of Management Studies, 44,* 837–862. doi: 10.1111/j.1467-6486.2007.00715.x

Lynch, O. H. (2002). Humorous communication: Finding a place for humor in communication research. *Communication Theory, 12,* 423–445. doi: 10.1111/j.1468-2885.2002.tb00277.x

Lyon, A., & Mirivel, J. C. (2011). Reconstructing Merck's practical theory of communication: The ethics of pharmaceutical sales representative–physician encounters. *Communication Monographs, 78,* 53–72. doi:10.1080/03637751.2010.542578

Lyons, R. F., Mickelson, K. D., Sullivan, M. J. L., & Coyne, J. C. (1998). Coping as a communal process. *Journal of Social and Personal Relationships, 15,* 579–605. doi: 10.1177/0265407598155001

Lyubomirsky, S. (2008). *The how of happiness: A scientific approach to getting the life you want.* New York, NY: Penguin.

Malinowski, B. (1922). *Argonauts of the Western Pacific: An account of native enterprise and adventure in the Archipelagos of Melanesian New Guinea.* London: Routledge & Kegan Paul.

Malinowski, B. (1967). *A diary in the strict sense of the term,* trans. N. Guterman. New York, NY: Harcourt, Brace & World.

Malvini Redden, S. (in press). How lines organize compulsory interaction, emotion management, and "emotional taxes": The implications of passenger emotion and expression in airport security lines. *Management Communication Quarterly.*

Malvini Redden, S., Tracy, S. J., & Shafer, M. (2012). Are "liquid handcuffs" worth "money in my pocket"? A metaphor analysis of recovering substance abusers' sensemaking of medication assisted treatment. Presented at the annual meeting of the National Communication Association.

Marcus, G. E. (1994). What comes (just) after "post"? The case of ethnography. In N. K. Denzin & Y. S. Lincoln (eds.), *Handbook of qualitative research* (pp. 563–574). Thousand Oaks, CA: Sage.

Margolis. E., & Pauwels, L. (Eds.) (2011). *Handbook of visual research methods*. Thousand Oaks, CA: Sage.

Martin, J. (1990). Deconstructing organizational taboos: The suppression of gender conflict in organizations. *Organization Science, 1*, 339–359. doi: 10.1287/orsc.1.4.339

Maslach, C. (1976). Burned-out. *Human Behavior, 5*, 16–22.

Maxwell, J. A. (2004). Using qualitative methods for causal explanation. *Field Methods, 16*, 243–264. doi: 10.1177/1525822X04266831

McKeown, B., & Thomas, D. (1988). *Qualitative methodology*. Newbury Park, CA: Sage.

Mead, G. H. (1967). *Mind, self, & society*. Chicago, IL: University of Chicago Press.

Mecho, I. I. (2006). E-mail interviewing in qualitative research: A methodological discussion. *Journal of the American Society for Information, Science, and Technology, 57*, 1284–1295.

Meisenbach, R. J., Remke, R. V., Buzzanell, P. & Liu, M. (2008). "They allowed": Pentadic mapping of women's maternity leave discourse as organizational rhetoric. *Communication Monographs, 75*, 1–24. doi: 10.1080/03637750801952727

Merton, K., Fiske, M., & Kendall, P. (1956). *The focused interview: A manual of problems and procedures*. Glencoe, IL: Free Press.

Meyer, D. Z., & Avery, L. M. (2009). Excel as a qualitative data analysis tool. *Field Methods, 21*, 92–112. doi: 10.1177/1525822X08323985

Miles, M. B., & Huberman, A. M. (1994). *Qualitative data analysis*. Thousand Oaks, CA: Sage.

Mileti, D. S., & O'Brien, P. W. (1992). Warnings during disaster: Normalizing communicated risk. *Social Problems, 39*, 40–57.

Milgram, S. (1974). *Obedience to authority; an experimental view* (1st ed.). New York, NY: Harper & Row.

Miller, K. I. (2007). Compassionate communication in the workplace: Exploring processes of noticing, connecting, and responding. *Journal of Applied Communication Research, 35*, 223–245. doi: 10.1080/00909880701434208

Mills, G. E. (2000). *Action research: A guide for the teacher researcher*. Upper Saddle River, NJ: Prentice Hall.

Minge, J. M. (2006). Painting a landscape of abortion. The fusion of embodied art. *Qualitative Inquiry, 12*, 118–145. doi: 10.1177/1077800405278778

Mitchell, R. G., Jr., & Charmaz, K. (1996). Telling tales, writing stories: Postmodernist visions and realist images in ethnographic writing. *Journal of Contemporary Ethnography, 25*, 144–166. doi: 10.1177/089124196025001008

Modern Language Association (2009a). *MLA handbook for writers of research papers* (7th ed.). New York, NY: Modern Language Association.

Modern Language Association (2009b). *MLA style manual and guide to scholarly publishing* (3rd ed.). New York, NY: Modern Language Association.

Montoya, Y. J. (2012, June 14). Bring your child to work day is any day I choose: Achieving work–life balance through entrepreneurialism. Paper presented at the Work and Family Researchers Network Inaugural Convention, New York.

Morse, J. M., Stern, P. N., Corbin, J., Bowers, B., Charmaz, K., & Clarke, A. E. (2009). *Developing grounded theory: The second generation*. Walnut Creek, CA: Left Coast Press.

Mumby, D. K. (1997). Modernism, postmodernism, and communication studies: A rereading of an ongoing debate. *Communication Theory, 7*, 1–28. doi: 10.1111/j.1468-2885.1997.tb00140.x

Mumby, D. K. (1998). Organizing men: Power, discourse, and the social construction of masculinity(s) in the workplace. *Communication Theory, 8*, 164–183. doi: 10.1111/j.1468-2885.1998.tb00216.x

Muoio, A. (1997, December). How your company is like a hairball. *Fast Company*. Retrieved from Fast Company magazine website at http://www.fastcompany.com/magazine/12/hairball.html

Murguía, E., Tackett-Gibson, M., & Lessem, A. (2007). *Real drugs in a virtual world: Drug discourse and community online*. Lanham, MD: Lexington Books.

Murphy, A. G. (1998). Hidden transcripts of flight attendant resistance. *Management Communication Quarterly, 11*, 499–535. doi: 10.1177/0893318998114001

Murray, C., & Sixsmith, J. (1998). E-mail: A qualitative research medium for interviewing? *International Journal of Social Research Methodology, 1*, 103–121.

Murray, S. D. (1971). That's interesting! Towards a phenomenology of sociology and a sociology of phenomenology. *Philosophy of the Social Sciences, 1*, 309–344.

Nelson, C. (2004). The brave new world of research surveillance. *Qualitative Inquiry, 10*, 207–218. doi: 10.1177/1077800403259701

Nguyen, D. T., & Alexander, J. (1996). The coming of cyberspacetime and the end of polity. In R. Shields (ed.), *Cultures of Internet: Virtual spaces, real histories, living bodies* (pp. 99–124). London: Sage.

Noy, C. (2007) Sampling knowledge: The hermeneutics of snowball sampling in qualitative research. *International Journal of Social Research Methodology, 11*(4), 1–18

Oakley, A. (1981). Interviewing women: A contradiction in terms. In H. Roberts (ed.), *Doing feminist research* (pp. 30–61). London: Routledge & Kegan Paul.

O'Connor, H. (2006). Online interviews. Retrieved from http://www.geog.le.ac.uk/orm/interviews/intcontents.htm

O'Connor, H., & Madge, C. (2001). Cyber-mothers: Online synchronous interviewing using conferencing software. *Sociological Research Online, 5.* Retrieved from http://www.socresonline.org.uk/9/2/hine.html

O'Connor, H., Madge, C., Shaw, R., & Wellens, J. (2008). Internet-based interviewing. In N. Fielding, R. M. Lee, & G. Blank (eds.), *Handbook of online research methods* (pp. 271–289). London: Routledge.

Oleson, J. C. (2004). Sipping coffee with a serial killer: On conducting life history interviews with a criminal genius. *The Qualitative Report, 9,* 129–215.

Olson, L. N. (2004). The role of voice in the (re) construction of a battered woman's identity: An autoethnography of one woman's experience of abuse. *Women's Studies in Communication, 27,* 1–33. doi: 10.1080/07491409.2004.10162464

Olson, L. N., Daggs, J. L., Ellevold, B. L., & Rogers, T. K. K. (2007). Entrapping the innocent: Toward a theory of child sexual predators' luring communication. *Communication Theory, 17,* 231–251. doi: 10.1111/j.1468-2885.2007.00294.x

Orbe, M., & Allen, B. (2008). "Race matters" in the *Journal of Applied Communication Research. Howard Journal of Communications, 19,* 201–220. doi: 10.1080/10646170802218115

Pacanowsky, M. E., & O'Donnell-Trujillo, N. (1982). Communication and organizational cultures. *Western Journal of Speech Communication, 46,* 115–130. doi: 10.1080/10570318209374072

Pacanowsky, M. E., & O'Donnell-Trujillo, N. (1983). Organizational communication as cultural performance. *Communication Monographs, 50,* 126–147. doi: 10.1080/03637758309390158

Park-Fuller, L. M. (1995). Narration and narratization of a cancer story: Composing and performing "A clean breast of it." *Text and Performance Quarterly, 15,* 60–67. doi: 10.1080/10462939509366105

Park-Fuller, L. M. (2000). Performing absence: The staged personal narrative as testimony. *Text and Performance Quarterly, 20,* 20–42. doi: 10.1080/10462930009366281

Park-Fuller, L. M. (2003). A clean breast of it. In L. C. Miller, J. Taylor, & M. H. Carver (eds.), *Voices made flesh: Performing women's autobiography* (pp. 215–236). Madison, WI: University of Wisconsin Press.

Patton, M. Q. (2002). *Qualitative research and evaluation methods* (3rd ed.). Thousand Oaks, CA: Sage.

Paugh, A., & Izquierdo, C. (2009). Why is this a battle every night? Negotiating food and eating in American dinnertime interaction. *Journal of Linguistic Anthropology, 19,* 185–204. doi: 10.1111/j.1548-1395.2009.01030.x.

Paulus, T. (2007). CMC modes for learning tasks at a distance. *Journal of Computer-Mediated Communication, 12,* 1322–1345. doi: 10.1111/j.1083-6101.2007.00375.x

Pearson, A. R. (2012, February). *Shifting ontologies and opening space(s): Structuring gender in the National Park Service.* Paper presented at the annual meeting of the Western States Communication Association, Albuquerque, New Mexico.

Pelias, R. J. (2007). Jarheads, girly men, and the pleasures of violence. *Qualitative Inquiry, 13,* 945–959. doi: 10.1177/1077800407304413

Philipsen, G. (1975). Speaking "like a man" in Teamsterville: Culture patterns of role enactment in an urban neighborhood. *Quarterly Journal of Speech, 61,* 13–22. doi: 10.1080/00335637509383264

Piña, A. A. (2010). School-based prevention for childhood anxiety (principal investigator), National Institute of Mental Health, 1K01 MH086687-01A1.

Pines, A. M., Aronson, E., & Kafry, D. (1981). *Burnout: From tedium to personal growth.* New York, NY: Free Press.

Pini, B. (2005). Interviewing men: Gender and the collection and interpretation of qualitative data. *Journal of Sociology, 4,* 201–216. doi: 10.1177/1440783305053238

Pink, S. (2001). *Doing visual ethnography.* London: Sage.

Podolefsky, A. (1987). New tools for old jobs: Computers in the analysis of field notes author(s). *Anthropology Today, 3,* 14–16.

Pompper, D., Lee, S., & Lerner, S. (2009). Gauging outcomes of 1960s social equality movements: Nearly four decades of gender and ethnicity on the cover of rolling stone magazine. *The Journal of Popular Culture, 42,* 273–290. doi: 10.1111/j.1540-5931.2009.00679.x

Prendergast, M. (2009). "Poem is what?" Poetic inquiry in qualitative social science research. *International Review of Qualitative Research, 1,* 541–568.

Prosser, J. (2011). Visual methodology: Toward a more seeing research. In N. K. Denzin & Y. S. Lincoln (eds.), *Handbook of qualitative research* (4th ed., pp. 479–495). Thousand Oaks, CA: Sage.

Punch, M. (1986). *The politics and ethics of fieldwork.* Beverly Hills, CA: Sage.

Rambo, C. (2007). Handing IRB an unloaded gun. *Qualitative Inquiry, 13,* 353–367. doi: 10.1177/1077800406297652

Real, K., Bramson, R., & Poole, M. S. (2009). The symbolic and material nature of physician identity: Implications for physician–patient communication. *Health*

Communication, 7, 575–587. doi: 10.1080/ 10410230903242184

Reason, P. (1994). Three approaches to participative inquiry. In N. K. Denzin & Y. S. Lincoln (eds.), *Handbook of qualitative research* (pp. 324–339). Thousand Oaks, CA: Sage.

Reinharz, S., & Chase, S. E. (2002). Interviewing women. In J. F. Gubrium & J. A. Holstein (eds.), *Handbook of qualitative research* (pp. 324–349). Thousand Oaks, CA: Sage.

Renzetti, C., & Lee, R. M. (1993). The problem of researching sensitive topics: An overview and introduction. In C. M. Renzetti & R. M. Lee (eds.), *Researching sensitive topics* (pp. 3–13). Newbury Park, CA: Sage.

Richardson, L. (2000a). Evaluating ethnography. *Qualitative Inquiry, 6*, 253–256. doi: 10.1177/ 107780040000600207

Richardson, L. (2000b). Writing: A method of inquiry. In N. K. Denzin & Y. S. Lincoln (eds.), *Handbook of qualitative research* (2nd ed., pp. 923–948). Thousand Oaks, CA: Sage.

Riessman, C. K. (1993). *Narrative analysis.* Newbury Park, CA: Sage.

Riessman, C. K. (2008). *Narrative methods for the human sciences.* Thousand Oaks, CA: Sage.

Riforgiate, S. E. (2008, November). Creating work/life space: Independent home party consultants piecing together the puzzle of work and life. Paper presented at the annual meeting of the National Communication Association, San Diego, California.

Right, K. B. W. (1997). Shared ideology in alcoholics anonymous: A grounded theory approach. *Journal of Health Communication, 2*, 83–99. doi: 10.1080/ 108107397127806

Rivera, K. D., & Tracy, S. J. (2012). Arresting the American dream: Patrolling the borders of compassion and enforcement. In S. May (ed.), *Case studies in organizational communication: Ethical perspectives and practices* (2nd ed., pp. 271–284). Thousand Oaks, CA: Sage.

Robinson, L. (2007). The cyberself: the self-ing project goes online, symbolic interaction in the digital age. *New Media and Society, 9*, 93–110. doi: 10.1177/ 1461444807072216

Rollins, J. (1985). *Between women: Domestics and their employers.* Philadelphia, PA: Temple University Press.

Ronai, C. (1992). The reflexive self through narrative: A night in the life of an erotic dancer/researcher. In C. Ellis & M. G. Flaherty (eds.), *Investigating subjectivity: Research on lived experience* (pp. 102–123). Newbury Park, CA: Sage.

Roulston, K., de Marrais, K., & Lewis, J. B. (2003). Learning to interview in the social sciences. *Qualitative Inquiry, 9*, 643–668. doi: 10.1177/1077800403252736

Roy, D. (1959). "Banana time": Job satisfaction and informal interaction. *Human Organization, 18*, 158–168.

Rubin, H. J., & Rubin, I. S. (2005). *Qualitative interviewing: The art of hearing data* (2nd ed.). Thousand Oaks, CA: Sage.

Rumens, N. (2008). The complexities of friendship: Exploring how gay men make sense of their workplace friendships with straight women. *Culture and Organization, 14*, 79–95. doi: 10.1080/14759550701864918

Rush, E. K. (2010). The conceptual construction of innovation: Performance labor to manufacture mood, chase goals, and assemble success in incubator organizations. Unpublished MA thesis, Arizona State University, Tempe, Arizona.

Rush, E. K. (2012, May). Innovation incubation as mood manufacture: Investigating the communicative construction and consequences of work to organize and perform an innovation organization. Paper presented at the annual meeting of the International Communication Association, Phoenix, Arizona.

Rush, E. K., & Tracy, S. J. (2010). Wikipedia as public scholarship: Communicating our impact online. *Journal of Applied Communication Research, 38*, 309–315. doi: 10.1080/00909882.2010.490846

Saldaña, J. (2009). *The coding manual for qualitative researchers.* Thousand Oaks, CA: Sage.

Saldaña, J. (2011). *Fundamentals of qualitative research.* New York, NY: Oxford University Press.

Sales, B. D., & Folkman, S. (2000). *Ethics in research with human participants.* Washington, DC: American Psychological Association.

Sanger, P. C. (2003). Living and writing feminist ethnographies: Threads in a quilt stitched from the heart. In R. P. Clair (ed.), *Expressions of ethnography* (pp. 29–44). Albany, NY: State University of New York Press.

Sanjek, R. (1990). A vocabulary for fieldnotes. In R. Sanjek (ed.), *Fieldnotes: The makings of anthropology* (pp. 92–121). Ithaca, NY: Cornell University Press.

Sarri, R. C., & Sarri, C. M. (1992). Organizational and community change through participatory action research. *Administration in Social Work, 16*, 99–122.

Sayer, A. (1992). *Method in social science: A realist approach* (2nd ed.). London: Routledge.

Scarduzio, J. A. (2011). Maintaining order through deviance? The emotional deviance, power, and professional work of municipal court judges.

Management Communication Quarterly, 25, 283–310. doi: 10.1177/0893318910386446

Scarduzio, J. A., & Geist-Martin, P. (2008). Making sense of fractured identities: Male professors' narratives of sexual harassment. *Communication Monographs, 75*, 369–395. doi: 10.1080/03637750802512363

Scarduzio, J. A., Giannini, G. A., & Geist-Martin, P. (2011). Crafting an architectural blueprint: Principles of design for ethnographic research. *Symbolic Interaction, 34*, 447–470. doi: 10.1525/si.2011.34.4.447

Scheibel, D. (1992). Faking identity in Clubland: The communicative performance of "fake ID." *Text and Performance Quarterly, 12*, 160–175. doi: 10.1080/10462939209359644

Schein, E. H. (1992). *Organizational culture and leadership* (2nd ed.). San Francisco, CA: Jossey-Bass.

Schein, E. H. (2004). *Organizational culture and leadership* (3rd ed.). San Francisco, CA: Jossey-Bass.

Schneider-Bean, S. (2008). *Beyond tips and sunscreen: Exploring tourist–host encounters through communication, culture and identity*. Saarbrücken: VDM Verlag.

Schutz, W. (1979). *Profound simplicity*. New York, NY: Bantam.

Schwandt, T. A. (1996). Farewell to criteriology. *Qualitative Inquiry, 2*, 58–72. doi: 10.1177/107780049600200109

Schwandt, T. A. (2000). Three epistemological stances for qualitative inquiry: Interpretivism, hermeneutics, and social constructionism. In N. K. Denzin & Y. S. Lincoln (eds.), *Handbook of qualitative research* (2nd ed., pp. 189–214). Thousand Oaks, CA: Sage.

Scott, C. W. (2005). The discursive organization of risk and safety: How firefighters manage occupational hazards. Unpublished PhD dissertation, Arizona State University, Tempe, Arizona.

Scott, C., & Myers, K. K. (2005). The socialization of emotion: Learning emotion management at the fire station. *Journal of Applied Communication Research, 33*, 67–92. doi: 10.1080/0090988042000318521

Seale, C. (1999). Quality in qualitative research. *Qualitative Inquiry, 5*, 465–478. doi: 10.1177/107780049900500402

Seidman, I. E. (1991). *Interviewing as qualitative research*. New York, NY: Teachers College Press.

Shaffir, W. B. (1991). Managing a convincing self-presentation: Some personal reflections on entering the field. In W. B. Shaffir & R. A. Stebbins (eds.), *Experiencing fieldwork: An inside view of qualitative research* (pp. 72–81). Newbury Park, CA: Sage.

Sharf, B. F. (1999). Beyond netiquette: The ethics of doing naturalistic discourse research on the Internet. In S. Jones (Ed.), *Doing Internet research* (pp. 243–256). Thousand Oaks, CA: Sage.

Shavelson, R. J., & Towne, L. (eds.) (2002). *Scientific research in education: Committee on scientific principles for education research*. Washington, DC: National Academy Press.

Sheenan, K. H., Barker, M., & McCarthy, P. (2004). Analysing metaphors used by victims of workplace bullying. *International Journal of Management and Decision Making, 5*, 21–31.

Silverman, D. (2001). *Interpreting qualitative data: Methods for analyzing talk, text and interaction* (2nd ed.). London: Sage.

Silvia, P. J. (2007). *How to write a lot: A practical guide to productive academic writing*. Washington, DC: APA.

Simon, H. A. (1997). *Administrative behavior: A study of decision-making processes in administrative organizations* (4th ed.). New York, NY: Free Press.

Sobré-Denton, M. (2011). The emergence of cosmopolitan group cultures and its implications for cultural transition: A case study of an international student support group. *International Journal of Intercultural Relations, 35*, 79–91.

Skloot, R. (2010). *The immortal life of Henrietta Lacks*. New York, NY: Crown Publishers.

Snow, D. A., Benford, R. D., & Anderson, L (1986). Fieldwork roles and informational yield. *Journal of Contemporary Ethnography, 14*, 377–408. doi: 10.1177/0098303986014004002

Spradley, J. (1979). *The ethnographic interview*. Fort Worth, TX: Harcourt Brace.

Spradley, J. P. (1980). *Participant observation*. Fort Worth, TX: Harcourt Brace.

Srivastava, P., & Hopwood, N. (2009). A practical iterative framework for qualitative data analysis. *International Journal of Qualitative Methods, 8*, 76–84.

Stake, R. E., & Trumbull, D. J. (1982). Naturalistic generalizations. *Review Journal of Philosophy and Social Science, 7*, 1–12.

Stenbacka, C. (2001). Qualitative research requires quality concepts of its own. *Management Decision, 39*, 551–555.

Stewart, K. A. (2010). In dust we trust: A narrative journey in the communal heart of public art at the Burning Man Festival. Unpublished PhD dissertation, Arizona State University, Tempe, Arizona.

Stokes, D. E. (1997). *Pasteur's quadrant: Basic science and technological innovation*. Washington, DC: Brookings Institution Press.

Strauss, A. L. (1987). *Qualitative analysis for social scientists*. Cambridge: Cambridge University Press.

Strauss, A. L., & Corbin, J. M. (1990). *Basics of qualitative research: Grounded theory procedures and techniques*. Newbury Park, CA: Sage.

Strauss, A. L., & Corbin, J. M. (1998). *Basics of qualitative research: Techniques and procedures for developing grounded theory* (2nd ed.). Thousand Oaks, CA: Sage.

Sutton, R. I. (1991). Maintaining norms about expressed emotions: The case of bill collectors. *Administrative Science Quarterly, 36*, 245–268.

Sutton, R. (2007). *The no asshole rule: Building a civilized workplace and surviving one that isn't.* New York, NY: Warner Business Books.

Sutton, R. (2010). *Good boss, bad boss.* New York, NY: Hachette Digital.

Tanaka, G., & Cruz, C. (1998). The locker room: Eroticism and exoticism in a polyphonic text. *International Journal of Qualitative Studies in Education, 11*, 137–153. doi: 10.1080/095183998236935

Terkel, S. (1974).*Working: People talk about what they do all day and how they feel about what they do.* New York, NY: Pantheon/Random House.

Thomas, J. (1993). *Doing critical ethnography.* Beverly Hills, CA: Sage.

Thomas, J. (2003). Musings on critical ethnography, meanings, and symbolic violence. In R. P. Clair (ed.), *Expressions of Ethnography* (pp. 45–54). Albany, NY: State University of New York Press.

Tillmann, L. M. (2009). Body and bulimia revisited: Reflections on "A secret life." *Journal of Applied Communication Research, 37*, 98–112. doi: 10.1080/00909880802592615

Tillmann-Healy, L. M. (1996). A secret life in a culture of thinness. In C. Ellis & A. P. Bochner (eds.), *Composing ethnography: Alternative forms of qualitative writing* (pp. 76–108). Walnut Creek, CA: Altamira Press.

Tracy, K. (1995). Action-implicative discourse analysis. *Journal of Language and Social Psychology, 14*, 195–215. doi: 10.1177/0261927X95141011

Tracy, K., & Tracy, S. J. (1998). Rudeness at 911: Reconceptualizing face and face attack. *Human Communication Research, 25*, 225–251. doi: 10.1111/j.1468-2958.1998.tb00444.x

Tracy, S. J. (2000). Becoming a character for commerce: Emotion labor, self subordination and discursive construction of identity in a total institution. *Management Communication Quarterly, 14*, 90–128. doi: 10.1177/0893318900141004

Tracy, S. J. (2001). Emotion labor and correctional officers: A study of emotion norms, performances and unintended consequences in a total institution. Unpublished doctoral dissertation, University of Colorado at Boulder, Boulder, Colorado.

Tracy, S. J. (2002a). Altered practice→altered stories→altered lives: Three considerations for translating organizational communication scholarship into practice. *Management Communication Quarterly, 16*, 85–91. doi: 10.1177/0893318902161005

Tracy, S. J. (2002b). When questioning turns to face threat: An interactional sensitivity in 911 call-taking. *Western Journal of Communication, 66*, 129–157. doi: 10.1080/10570310209374730

Tracy, S. J. (2003, April). Correctional contradictions: A structural approach to addressing officer burnout. *Corrections Today*, pp. 90–95. Selected and reviewed by editor.

Tracy, S. J. (2004). The construction of correctional officers: Layers of emotionality behind bars. *Qualitative Inquiry, 10*, 509–533. doi: 10.1177/1077800403259716

Tracy, S. J. (2005). Locking up emotion: Moving beyond dissonance for understanding emotion labor discomfort. *Communication Monographs, 72*, 261–283. doi: 10.1080/03637750500206474

Tracy, S. J. (2007). Taking the plunge: A contextual approach to problem-based research. *Communication Monographs, 74*, 106–111. doi: 10.1080/03637750701196862

Tracy, S. J. (2010). Qualitative quality: Eight "big-tent" criteria for excellent qualitative research. *Qualitative Inquiry, 16*, 837–851. doi: 10.1177/1077800410383121

Tracy, S. J. (2012). The toxic and mythical combination of a deductive writing logic for inductive qualitative research. *Qualitative Communication Research, 1*, 109–141.

Tracy, S. J., & Geist-Martin, P. (in press). Organizing ethnography and qualitative approaches. *Handbook of organizational communication* (3rd ed.). Thousand Oaks, CA: Sage.

Tracy, S. J., & Rivera K. D. (2010). Endorsing equity and applauding stay-at-home moms: How male voices on work–life reveal aversive sexism and flickers of transformation. *Management Communication Quarterly, 24*, 3–43. doi: 10.1177/0893318909352248

Tracy, S. J., & Scott, C. (2006). Sexuality, masculinity and taint management among firefighters and correctional officers: Getting down and dirty with "America's heroes" and the "scum of law enforcement." *Management Communication Quarterly, 20*, 6–38. doi: 10.1177/0893318906287898

Tracy, S. J., & Tracy, K. (1998). Emotion labor at 911: A case study and theoretical critique. *Journal of Applied Communication Research, 26*, 390–411. doi:10.1080/00909889809365516

Tracy, S. J., & Trethewey, A. (2005). Fracturing the real-self fake-self dichotomy: Moving toward crystallized organizational identities. *Communication Theory, 15*, 168–195. doi: 10.1111/j.1468-2885.2005.tb00331.x

Tracy, S. J., Alberts, J. K., Rivera, K. D. (2007). How to bust the office bully: Eight tactics for explaining workplace abuse to decision-makers. Available at http://humancommunication.clas.asu.edu/files/HowtoBusttheOfficeBully.pdf

Tracy, S. J., Lutgen-Sandvik, P., & Alberts, J. K. (2006). Nightmares, demons and slaves: Exploring the painful metaphors of workplace bullying. *Management Communication Quarterly, 20*, 148–185. doi: 10.1177/0893318906291980

Tracy, S. J., Myers, K. K., & Scott, C. (2006). Cracking jokes and crafting selves: Sensemaking and identity management among human service workers. *Communication Monographs, 73*, 283–308.doi: 10.1080/03637750600889500

Trethewey, A. (1997). Resistance, identity, and empowerment: A postmodern feminist analysis of clients in a human service organization. *Communication Monographs, 64*, 281–299. doi: 10.1080/03637759709376425

Trethewey, A. (2001). Reproducing and resisting the master narrative of decline: Midlife professional women's experiences of aging. *Management Communication Quarterly, 15*, 183–226. doi: 10.1177/0893318901152002

Tripp, D. H. (1983). Co-authorship and negotiation: The interview as an act of creation. *Interchange, 14*, 32–45.

Trujillo, N. (1992). Interpreting (the work and talk) of baseball: Perspectives on ballpark culture. *Western Journal of Communication, 56*, 350–371. doi: 10.1080/10570319209374423

Trujillo, N. (1993). Interpreting November 22: A critical ethnography of an assassination site. *Quarterly Journal of Speech, 79*, 447–466. doi: 10.1080/00335639309384046

Turner, V. (1969). *The ritual process: Structure and anti-structure.* Edison, NJ: Aldine Transaction.

Undheim, T. A. (2003). Getting connected: How sociologists can access the high tech elite. *Qualitative Report, 8*, 104–128.

United States Department of Health and Human Service's Office of Human Research Protections (2009). Definition of research. Retrieved from http://www.hhs.gov/ohrp/policy/ohrpregulations.pdf

Van Maanen, J. (1988). *Tales of the field: On writing ethnography.* Chicago, IL: University of Chicago Press.

Vande Berg, L., & Trujillo, N. (2008). *Cancer and death: A love story in two voices.* Cresskill, NJ: Hampton Press.

Walsh, S. (2006). An Irigarayan framework and resymbolization in an arts-informed research process. *Qualitative Inquiry, 12*, 976–993. doi: 10.1177/1077800406288626

Way, A. K. (2012). Apprentices & worker bees: Discursive constructions of youth's work identity. Unpublished PhD dissertation, Arizona State University, Tempe, Arizona.

Way, A. K. (in press). There's no "I" in team: Adolescent emotions as a space for organizing feminine identity. *Emotion, Space and Society.* doi:10.1016/j.emospa.2012.01.001

Way, D., & Tracy, S. J. (2012). Conceptualizing compassion as recognizing, relating and (re)acting: An ethnographic study of compassionate communication at hospice. *Communication Monographs, 79*, 292–315. doi: 10.1080/03637751.2012.697630

Weick, K. E. (1979). *The social psychology of organizing* (2nd ed.). Reading, MA: Addison-Wesley.

Weick, K. E. (1985). Systematic observation methods. In G. Lindzey & E. Aronson (eds.), *Handbook of social psychology*, Vol 1: *Theory and method* (3rd ed., pp. 567–634). New York, NY: Random House.

Weick, K. E. (1993). The collapse of sensemaking in organizations: The Mann Gulch disaster. *Administrative Science Quarterly, 38*, 628–652.

Weick, K. E. (1995). *Sensemaking in organizations.* Thousand Oaks, CA: Sage.

Weick, K. E. (2001). *Making sense of the organization.* Malden, MA: Blackwell Business.

Weick, K. E. (2007). The generative properties of richness. *Academy of Management Journal, 50*, 14–19.

Wengraf, T. (2001). *Qualitative research interviewing.* Thousand Oaks, CA: Sage.

Wheatley, E. E. (1994). How can we engender ethnography with a feminist imagination? A rejoinder to Judith Stacey. *Women's Studies International Forum, 17*, 403–416.

Whitaker, B. (2006). *Unspeakable love: Gay and lesbian life in the Middle East.* Berkeley, CA: University of California Press.

Williams, K., Kemper, S., & Hummert, M. L. (2003). Improving nursing home communication: An intervention to reduce elderspeak. *Gerontologist, 43*, 242–247. doi: 10.1093/geront/43.2.242

Wolcott, H. F. (2005). The Art of Fieldwork (2nd ed.). Walnut Creek, CA: Altamira Press.

Wolcott, H. F. (2009). *Writing up qualitative research* (3rd ed.). Thousand Oaks, CA: Sage.

Wolf, M. (1992). *A thrice-told tale: Feminism, postmodernism, and ethnographic responsibility.* Palo Alto, CA: Stanford University Press.

Woods, P. (1985). New songs played skillfully: Creativity and technique in writing up qualitative research. In R. G. Burgess (ed.), *Issues in educational research: Qualitative Methods* (pp. 86–106). Philadelphia, PA: Falmer Press.

World Medical Association (1975). *Declaration of Helsinki: Recommendations guiding medical doctors in biomedical research involving human subjects.* Ferney-Voltaire, France: World Medical Association.

Zimbardo, P., Maslach, C., & Stanford University California Department of Psychology (1973). *Dehumanization in institutional settings* (ONR-TR-Z-10 ed.). Ft. Belvoir Defense Technical Information Center.

Zinn, B. (2001). Insider field research in minority communities. In R. M. Emerson (ed.), *Contemporary field research: Perspectives and formulations* (2nd ed., pp. 159–166). Prospect Heights, IL: Waveland Press.

Index

Qualitative Research Methods: Collecting Evidence, Crafting Analysis, Communicating Impact, First Edition. Sarah J. Tracy.
© 2013 Sarah J. Tracy. Published 2013 by Blackwell Publishing Ltd.